THE PEOPLE'S SCHOOL

The People's School

A History of Oregon State University

WILLIAM G. ROBBINS

Emeritus Distinguished Professor of History

Oregon State University Press   Corvallis

Library of Congress Cataloging-in-Publication Data

Names: Robbins, William G., 1935–author.
Title: The people's school : a history of Oregon State Sniversity / William G. Robbins,
    emeritus distinguished professor of history.
Description: Corvallis : Oregon State University Press, 2017. | Includes bibliographical
    references and index.
Identifiers: LCCN 2017017672 | ISBN 9780870718984 (paperback)
Subjects: LCSH: Oregon State University—History. | BISAC: EDUCATION / Organizations
    & Institutions. | EDUCATION / Students & Student Life. | HISTORY / United States /
    State & Local / Pacific Northwest (OR, WA). | EDUCATION / History.
Classification: LCC LD4346.O433 R63 2017 | DDC 378.009795/34—dc23
LC record available at https://lccn.loc.gov/2017017672

♾ This paper meets the requirements of ANSI/NISO Z39.48-1992
(Permanence of Paper).

First published in 2017 by Oregon State University Press
Printed in the United States of America

Oregon State University Press
121 The Valley Library
Corvallis OR 97331-4501
541-737-3166 • fax 541-737-3170
www.osupress.oregonstate.edu

*This book is dedicated to the hundreds of students who
matriculated through my classes from 1969 through 2005
and to two outstanding administrators—Paul Farber,
former chair of the Department of History, and
Kay Schaffer, former dean of the College of Liberal Arts.
And always, to my partner and best friend, Karla Brewer.*

Contents

Acknowledgments

Writing proper and ethical history should enrich society through the careful examination of sources and thoughtful analysis. To achieve that objective, historians thrive best in environments of academic freedom. Those core principles of intellectual life have been true of my more than forty years' association with Oregon State University and have persisted through the research and writing of *The People's School*. University archivists—Larry Landis, Elizabeth Nielson, Karl McCreary, Tiah Edmunson-Morton, Chris Petersen, Ruth Vondracek, Trevor Sandgathe, and lead reference student assistant, Mike Dicianna—have provided expertise, patience, and always helpful suggestions for tracking down sometimes arcane bits of information. Larry, especially, provided guidance to important documents, valuable counsel on controversial issues, and offered his expertise in the selection of photos. The archival staff and student assistants made my many months in the Special Collections and Archives Research Center on Valley Library's fifth floor a pleasant experience. The ambient light through the room's large north-facing windows creates a comforting place to work, even during the ashen, drizzly days of winter.

Researching and writing this book has been one of the more engaging enterprises of my life. I was retired for a decade and in the finishing stages of a biography when Ben Mutschler, chair of the Department of History, approached me in late 2012 about writing the history of Oregon State University—as the institution prepared to celebrate its sesquicentennial as a land-grant school. For one interested in historical inquiries with a critical edge, doing administrative history always seemed dull, colorless, lacking in feisty intellectual questions. After scrolling through the Special Collections and Archives website, however, I discovered a multitude of diverse themes that would sustain my curiosity. A few months into scanning documents and printing and filing them at home into appropriate categories, I began describing the project as "endlessly fascinating."

I am a Duck (MA and PhD degrees in history from the University of Oregon) who migrated forty miles downriver to happily spend my professional career at OSU. My debts of gratitude for this book are many, but especially to Ben Mutschler for inviting me to research and write the institution's sesquicentennial story. Larry Rogers, dean of the College of Liberal Arts, provided support for my work, and longtime friends Karyle Butcher and Kay Schaffer offered wise council at critical junctures of the writing. President Emeritus John Byrne generously shared drafts of his memoir, *Undercurrents: From Oceanography to University President*, a project that the OSU Press will publish in 2018. John also provided insights into key transitions during his tenure as president. Mary Gallagher, of the Benton County Historical Museum and a former graduate student, provided assistance with the selection of photos of downtown Corvallis. Roy Arnold, provost emeritus, offered details about muddled intracollege issues during his service as provost, and he always asked about progress on the book when we occasionally visited at the Circle Boulevard Beanery coffee shop.

Among those who read specific chapters, I have appreciated the insights of Paul Doescher (emeritus, College of Forestry), Joe Hendricks (dean emeritus of the Honors College), and Larry Roper, vice president for Student Affairs (1995–2014) and professor in the School of Language, Culture, and Society. Marianne Keddington Lang, with extensive experience in the editorial world, provided valuable advice in the early stages of the project. After several drafts of the manuscript—with concerns about the quality of my writing—I contacted Julidta Tarver, my longtime editor and dear friend with the University of Washington Press, who graciously agreed to read the prologue and two chapters and offer her "brutally honest" assessment. With Lita's positive response, I turned the manuscript in to the OSU Press. From there, I was privileged to work with Susan Campbell, copy editor extraordinaire, who saved me from numerous faux pas. Members of the press have also been more than generous in responding to my questions and concerns.

Finally, it has been my privilege to teach, research, and write in a supportive atmosphere encouraging innovation, fresh thinking, and the ability to offer new courses through the years. Teaching has been one of the great joys of my life, urging students from the early 1970s through my last graduate seminar in 2006 to think critically about historical questions and to be skeptical of claims that "history teaches us." Some of the graduate students, a few of them now retired, have become lifelong friends—Laurie Arnold, Katrine Barber, Karyle Butcher, Carmel Finley, Ron Gregory, Lindon Hylton, Tina Schweickert, Nancy Swain, Craig Wilkinson, and Don Wolf. One of the undergraduate students from the early 1970s, my partner and best friend for forty-two years, deserves more than words can express: my appreciation for reading every page of my writing (more than once) and tolerating a sometimes-impatient author. Thank you, Karla.

Prologue
Strategies for an Institutional History

Born of the martyred president amid the violence of America's great Civil War, the Morrill Act granted states thirty thousand acres of federal land for every senator and congressman to support a college "to promote the liberal and practical education of the industrial classes in the several pursuits and professions in life." When Abraham Lincoln signed the bill into law on July 2, 1862, he welcomed the legislation for creating institutions of higher education "being built on behalf of the people, who have invested in these public universities their hopes, their support, and their confidence." With its roots embedded in the land-grant tradition, Oregon State University (OSU) is part of a proud and distinctively American institution whose seminal mission was to offer instruction in science and classical studies, military tactics, and "agriculture and the mechanic arts." That grand educational enterprise was especially suited to an industrializing nation interested in advancing education and offering college instruction to the working classes. As a significant constituent of the land-grant tradition, Oregon State University exemplifies the importance of federal initiatives in fostering agricultural experiment stations, extension programs, and oceanic and space-related research.[1]

Absent the seceded states, the Congress of the United States passed three related pieces of legislation in 1862—the Homestead Act, the Pacific Railroad Act, and the Morrill Act—whose collective purpose was to promote the development of the American West. Enacted amid the exigencies of the Civil War, the Morrill Act prohibited disloyal states from participating and required land-grant schools to offer training in "military tactics" to enable them to supply trained officers for the Union Army. Although the Oregon legislature filed notice to accept the provisions of the Morrill Act in 1863, lawmakers deferred selecting the location for the land-grant school until 1868, when the legislature "designated and adopted" Corvallis College "as the Agricultural College of the State of Oregon." Under the control of the Southern-sympathizing Columbia Conference of the Methodist Episcopal Church, South, the small sectarian academy would be home to the agricultural school until 1885. From

1

those inauspicious beginnings, Oregon State University emerged as one of seventy-six land-grant colleges and universities, sixteen of them historically black institutions in the American South, designated as land-grants through the Second Morrill Act (1890). Congress later awarded land-grant status to thirty-three American Indian colleges through the American Indian Higher Education Consortium in 1994.[2]

There were earlier colonial, state, and federal precedents for granting land to support schools and colleges. American colonies offered land for educational purposes, and the Northwest Ordinance of 1787 awarded two townships of land for "seminaries of learning" when states were admitted to the Union. By the time the Morrill bill was making its way through Congress, the existing states had already received some four million acres of land to support education, including state universities. Jonathan Baldwin Turner of Illinois College preceded Justin Morrill in the 1850s, pressing the federal government to establish agricultural colleges. Turner's ideas may have found purchase in the State of Michigan's constitution of 1850, urging the establishment of an "agricultural school." Michigan's governor, Kinsley S. Bingham, signed a legislative measure in 1855 establishing the Agricultural College of the State of Michigan, the predecessor to today's Michigan State University, the nation's first agricultural college.[3]

Similar to Corvallis College, most of the early land-grant schools were modest institutions of humble origins. Their struggles for survival were epic—enormously heavy teaching loads, marginal students, and unsympathetic legislatures—an effort historian Roger Geiger described as "a long and arduous process." In his workmanlike history of Iowa State University, Earle Ross captures the dilemma of the early land-grants—teachers arriving in Ames in 1868 witnessed "an unkempt campus and unfinished buildings. The students who came to start their college careers . . . were as unprepared as the surroundings."[4]

In East Lansing, Michigan, where the first college building was hurriedly put up in 1856, the agricultural college's opening was delayed several months because roofs were porous, doors would not close, shrunken floorboards did not reach walls, and basement cisterns leaked. The early colleges had other problems as well, some of them systemic. Despite the proud claims of proponents, Eldon Johnson writes, there was no great student demand for land-grant colleges. Early enrollments were anemic. The schools "were ahead of their times, not the slaves of popular demand." Countering another misconception, he argues that land-grant schools paralleled western development and provided little impetus for the agricultural and industrial revolutions.

The original building housing Corvallis College was located on Fifth Street in downtown Corvallis in the center of the block where City Hall is now located. The building housed all Corvallis College classes, including those of its land-grant Agricultural Department, the forerunner of today's Oregon State University. Courtesy of the OSU Special Collections and Archives Research Center.

Johnson concludes, "The college's *own* development had to precede their impact on national development."[5]

The federal relation has always loomed large in the land-grant calculus, an influence that has often been ignored or underestimated. Proceeds from the land-grants themselves—interest, sales, and land rentals—provided the lifeblood for Corvallis College and the early days of Oregon Agricultural College. Federal support also provided an excuse for penny-pinching state legislators to zero out their budgets when it came to funding land-grant institutions. When Oregon took control of its agricultural college in 1885, it did so with the promise that Benton County citizens would pay for a building on the college grounds. Subsequent federal assistance included funding for agricultural experiment stations (Hatch Act, 1887), creating additional agricultural colleges (Second Morrill Act, 1890), federal grants for teacher preparation, and congressional passage of the Smith-Lever Act (1914), a measure establishing cooperative extension programs in agriculture and home economics in places far distant from college campuses.[6]

Those federal measures provided vital support for struggling and financially strapped institutions. The federal endowments expanded with the passing years, including support for military training, a component of the original

Morrill Act of 1862. For Oregon Agricultural College the federal connection was critical, enabling it to survive until additional federal largesse, the Hatch Act, provided support for establishing agricultural experiment stations. There was more to the emerging national land-grant system—institutions were required to make annual reports to the secretary of the interior and to exchange research information with other land-grant schools. Eventually, the colleges formed the Association of American Agricultural Colleges and Experiment Stations in 1887, an organization that would live into the future under different titles. The land-grants also shared common curricula, especially in military training, a core requirement of the enabling legislation. Finally, the land-grants differed from private classical institutions on the Eastern Seaboard, with their emphasis on applied science, research, problem solving, and attracting students from all social classes.[7]

The history of Oregon State University tells us much about the fabric of Oregon's politics, its economy, and its conflicted world of race, ethnicity, and religious persuasion. For most of the last 150 years, Oregon's population has been largely homogeneous, with the state's ethnic makeup beginning to shift during the Second World War, when sizeable numbers of African Americans moved west to work in Portland-area shipyards. Since the 1980s, Oregon's Hispanic and Asian populations have grown apace, with the 2013 federal census estimating that Hispanic/Latino people constitute more than 12 percent of the state's enumeration of 3,970,239 people. Although Oregon's white population of approximately 88 percent was still higher than the national average (77 percent) in 2013, the state and the greater Pacific Northwest were rapidly increasing in ethnic diversity, a trend reflected in college and university enrollments.[8] Since the Second World War, Oregon's population makeover has been part of the larger transformation taking place in the American West.

The narrative strategy for this book is contextual, placing the history of Oregon State University and its predecessors in relation to state, national, and global events. The approach studiously avoids being insular, mindful that national and international crises, wars, and economic depressions affected life on the Corvallis campus during every decade of its existence. Agrarian revolts in the last quarter of the nineteenth century—Grangers, Farmers Alliances, Populists—affected every western state, including Oregon. The Spanish-American War, the First World War, the Great Depression of the 1930s, and the Second World War disrupted institutional life and influenced enrollment, curricular strategies, and the number of faculty and staff. Even peacetime events circumscribed course offerings, hiring and firing, and the allocation of funds to departments, schools, and colleges. Support for land-grant programs—agricultural experiment stations, the extension service, and later the Sea Grant mission—entailed political jockeying and confronting tightfisted federal and state administrations.

The People's School tempers the practice of organizing the narrative around institutional presidencies. The trap in pursuing such an approach allows the story to plod through an exclusively chronological sequence of administrative proceedings and events. This inquiry gives agency to state, national, and international events to provide a broader and more contextual story. That is not to argue that university presidents are unimportant. Benjamin Arnold (1872–1892), appointed president of Corvallis College by the Methodist Episcopal Church, South, served well beyond the date (1885) when the State of Oregon assumed control of the agricultural college. This study uses central administration records and a great variety of grassroots sources—articles and letters published in local and state newspapers, student publications (the *Barometer*, the *Beaver*), and multiple and wide-ranging materials published in the university's digitized ScholarsArchive@OSU, a source for the scholarly work of faculty, students, and materials beyond the university related to the institution's missions and research activities. Other voices—extracurricular developments, local and state politics, campus reactions to national crises—provide intriguing and striking addendums to the university's history.

This book reflects selective accounts gleaned from Oregon State University's archival holdings to profile significant events and circumstances—this is not a definitive accounting of the institution's past. The sheer complexity of the enormous and growing volume of archival material necessitates bypassing important aspects of university history to limit the account to a single volume. A brief look at OSU's online archival inventories provides evidence of what is missing. The subjects woven into the chronicle feature themes that intersect with significant regional, national, and international events. The narrative explores Oregon State's achievements and successes, its struggles and shortcomings, its praiseworthy labors, and those that were misdirected. Archival documents provide the guideposts, accounting for less-pleasant episodes and other moments when the Corvallis institution enjoyed the bright sun of day.

The vast assemblage of materials in Oregon State University's Special Collections and Archives poses problems of selection and focus—how to best use the records to explain the historical evolution of the institution. Because the President's Office and Administrative Council records reveal the most critical issues confronting OSU and its predecessor institutions, those materials provide the centerpiece for guiding the narrative through the fluctuating contours of the school's history. Featuring issues at the epicenter of administrative deliberations and decision-making offers insights to how local, regional, national, and global events played out on the Corvallis campus. The archival documents, and the circumstances and problems they address, reveal dramatically changing cultural, economic, and political environments through the decades and an increasingly complex and expansive administrative structure. While such history can be tedious, the deliberations of the Administrative Council reveal important details about the institution's evolution from a struggling nineteenth-century college to today's modern comprehensive university.

Corvallis College struggled from its inception in 1858 with financial problems until the state legislature designated the institution as its agricultural college in 1868. That early arrangement was a conflicted public-private partnership with church-appointed trustees managing the college and state legislators providing less than minimal oversight of its agricultural component. That curious mix of religious and nonreligious in the institution's development lasted until 1885, when the state legislature mandated that the college's operations would shift permanently to a governor-appointed, nine-member board of regents. The Methodist Episcopal Church, South, challenged the move with a lawsuit that was eventually resolved in the state's favor. Because the agricultural college's beginnings were vested in a religious institution, it is important to follow the increasing secularization of the college after 1885. In our present age of suspicions about mixing church and state in public education, it is interesting to note that Oregon State University's evolution follows a pattern similar to that of other land-grant schools.

In virtually all land-grant universities and colleges, the humanities and social sciences (the liberal arts) functioned as service courses to support degree programs in the mechanical, household economy, and natural-resource fields. The humanities and social sciences followed a similar trajectory at Oregon State, developing slowly, first as the Division of Service Departments, the Lower Division of Basic Arts and Sciences, the School of Humanities and Social Sciences, and finally, the College of Liberal Arts. When the state legislature passed the Oregon Unification Act in 1929, creating a single oversight board to manage its public institutions of higher education, the legislation confirmed the "service" function of humanities and social sciences at the Corvallis school.

The new organizational arrangement placed the renamed Oregon State College under the jurisdiction of the Oregon State Board of Higher Education, which established policies that would avoid the duplication of courses and degrees at Oregon State College and the University of Oregon. The university would be home to the humanities and social sciences, and Oregon State the sciences and professional schools in engineering, forestry, home economics, and pharmacy. That division of labor assured that humanities and social sciences at OSC would have lower-division status for the next half century, with curricular programs consistent with other land-grant institutions. *The People's School* tracks that arrangement through the 1980s and 1990s, when the liberal arts began to achieve a semblance of parity with the older degree-granting disciplines.

The authors of Montana State University's centennial history quote former student Robert Pirsig's best seller, *Zen and the Art of Motorcycle Maintenance*, to underscore the historic role of teaching in the liberal arts at the Bozeman institution:

> The school was what could euphemistically be called a "teaching college." At a teaching college you teach and you teach and you teach with no time for research, no time for contemplation, no time for participation in outside affairs. . . . The reason you teach and you teach and you teach is that this is a clever way of running a college on the cheap while giving the false impression of genuine education.[9]

That tradition persisted on the Corvallis campus at least through the mid-1980s, when College of Liberal Arts faculty achieved a degree of equality with other units in terms of teaching loads.

Oregon State University's development into a comprehensive university was not inevitable, but evolved through protracted and heated internal debates, acrimonious exchanges with University of Oregon administrators, and politicking with legislators and the Oregon State Board of Higher Education. The real institutional civil war involved intense arguments between University of Oregon and Oregon State over responsibility for curricular degrees and programs. The Eugene school argued that it must offer graduate courses in the sciences because they were critically important to a fully integrated university, while at the same time denying degrees in the humanities and social sciences to Oregon State because such a move would duplicate its own programs.

Those disputes, first aired with the formation of the Oregon State Board of Higher Curricula in 1909, persisted through the 1980s.

Surprises abound in telling the Oregon State University story. OSU's designation in 1968 as one of the nation's three Sea Grant universities began with salmon studies dating to the late nineteenth century. Roland Dimick expanded those investigations when he created the Yaquina Bay Fisheries Laboratory in 1939. Those fledgling studies eventually led to hiring oceanographer Wayne Burt and the establishment of the Department of Oceanography in 1959. The department acquired its first research vessel (*Acona*) in 1961 and a second (*Yaquina*) in 1964. Cold War politics and funding from the new Office of Naval Research supported much of the early research. OSU's School of Oceanography, established in 1972, became a college in 1983, and when atmospheric sciences was transferred to oceanography in 1993, the merged unit became the College of Oceanic and Atmospheric Sciences (the name was changed to the College of Earth, Ocean, and Atmospheric Sciences in 2011). OSU thus emerged as a preeminent research institution for sea-oriented investigations. With the emergence of the Hatfield Marine Science Center in Newport serving as the core for much of the research, OSU has been a leader in oceanic and atmospheric studies, with two of its faculty, John Byrne and Jane Lubchenco, serving as directors of the US National Oceanic and Atmospheric Administration (NOAA). The research at the Newport facility today is global, its vessels literally plying the far corners of the earth's oceans.

Readers interested in a more detailed account of university athletic programs should consult Larry Landis's *A School for the People: A Photographic History of Oregon State University* (2015). That said, this volume does recount the early development of men's and women's competitive athletics. Like other colleges of its time, OSU developed men's sports well in advance of women's activities, both in funding and facilities. Athletics, however, did not become an important consideration for OSU administrators until the tumultuous civil rights decade of the 1960s. When Congress passed Title IX in 1972, requiring gender equity in sports programs, change came slowly to women's programs at OSU and other universities and colleges. The racial integration of athletes advanced more quickly on some campuses than others. OSU gained headline news in 1969 when forty-seven members of its Black Student Union marched off campus to protest the treatment of a black football player. Football coach Dee Andros had threatened Fred Milton with suspension from the team unless he shaved his goatee and mustache. The central administration's archives provide copious material related to the Milton case and Title IX issues.

This account addresses a host of student-life issues—the organization of bands, adoption of mascots, yearbooks (*Orange* and *Beaver*), theatrical performing groups and drama clubs, fraternities and sororities, the development of radio stations, the organization of the Memorial Union, faculty and student governing bodies, the formation of student ethnic clubs, and the establishment of recreation centers (buildings), and campus literary societies and magazines, newspapers, and debating societies. As with other matters in the university's long history and its treasure trove of archival documents, the central issue is the question of importance and the selection of topics to pursue. The strategy pursued in these pages follows, in part, administrative discussions that were time-consuming—and therefore important to the institution. Beginning in the late 1960s, antiwar activities, charges of discrimination, Title IX, and athletics budgets appear regularly in university deliberations.

William Jasper Kerr's twenty-five-year presidency receives considerable attention, because his tenure witnessed the most dramatic transformation in the institution's history. Student enrollments and the number of faculty grew, academic programs and research agendas expanded, and the campus underwent a great building boom. During Kerr's first year in office, there were forty faculty and a student population of more than 1,500; before the full effects of the Depression were apparent in 1930, enrollment had increased to 3,347. Kerr, who served through two significant events, the First World War and the onset of the Great Depression, oversaw the establishment of the first campus radio station, summer school programs for teachers, the first correspondence courses, the organization of the Division of College Extension, higher admission standards, new departments and schools, and the accreditation of the college.

The social and economic ravages of the Great Depression and the horrific violence of the two-ocean war that followed were tumultuous experiences for colleges and universities across the land. The collapse of Oregon's already troubled natural-resource economy in the early 1930s forced schools of higher education to reduce instructional staff, with Oregon Agricultural College releasing sixty-six faculty in 1931 alone. The importance of the Great Depression and Second World War, a fifteen-year period of wrenching change and challenges everywhere in America, fits the approach for this investigation—using significant external events to frame the narrative. The campus entered the Depression with an enrollment of just over 3,000 students, a number that reached 4,759 ten years later. The institution's financial struggles during the 1930s were striking, its budget reduced approximately 40 percent between 1933 and 1934. Although dramatic building construction took place during Kerr's presidency, the college saw only two new buildings—Gilbert Hall and the Health Center (Plageman Hall)—dedicated during the 1930s. In their study of the University of Wisconsin between 1925 and 1945, E. David Cronon and John W. Jenkins indicate the obvious—a public university "cannot escape the buffeting of the political and economic currents swirling around its ivory tower."[10]

The Second World War witnessed different challenges, with large numbers of students inducted into the armed forces. OSC was one of a few campuses nationwide participating in the US Army's Specialized Training Program, an instructional tour de force to train military personnel in engineering and foreign languages, including Russian. During the war, OSC's extension service trained agricultural workers for the depleted farm labor supply, including urban women and teenagers, white-collar professionals, displaced Japanese Americans, and Mexicans brought to the United States through the federal government's Bracero Program.

Following the war, college and university enrollments soared across the nation as veterans entered higher education in unprecedented numbers with the support of the GI Bill. OSC's student population increased to more than seven thousand at the end of the 1950s. With A. L. Strand serving as president during the postwar boom, the Corvallis campus witnessed the opening of new institutes, centers, experiment stations, and the completion of Gill Coliseum (1950) and Parker Stadium (1953). Strand's presidency also coincided with the height of the Cold War, the period when Wisconsin senator Joseph McCarthy led the crusade to purge faculties of communists and communist sympathizers. This inquiry looks closely at events on campus, especially the firing of two faculty members, to better understand how the "Red Scare" played out in the Corvallis community.

As Strand was leaving the presidency in 1961, the Oregon legislature elevated the college to university status. With the Oregon State System of Higher Education's approval, OSU's program in oceanography expanded, and under new president James Jensen, a beginning was made in laying the groundwork for the Marine Science Center in Newport. Most important for the lower-division component of the university's curricular programs, the state system granted OSU permission to offer baccalaureate degrees in English, art, economics, history, political science, Russian studies, and speech. As one move toward highlighting the humanities, Jensen approved the hiring in 1968 of renowned historian William Appleman Williams, who had established himself as a prominent scholar and critic of American foreign relations at the University of Wisconsin. Because of the heated antiwar movement in the United States, it was not an easy hire.[11] OSU was also part of the larger environment of 1960s civil rights protests when Jensen confronted a public relations issue in the aforementioned Black Student Union/Fred Milton case.

OSU's growth between 1970 and 2000—both in student enrollment and infrastructure—fell short of similar developments at most state universities. Registrations at OSU numbered 15,509 in 1970; 17,689 in 1980; 16,048 in 1990; and 16,788 in 2000 (an increase of 1,279 students over thirty years). Oregon's volatile resource economy explains the booming enrollments of the 1960s and 1970s, when lively lumber and agricultural markets spurred the state's reasonably healthy economy. President Robert MacVicar (1970–1984) presided over a decade of growth before troubles set in. Beginning in 1980, the lumber economy nose-dived when national construction slowed, triggering a recession that brought widespread sawmill closures from the Douglas-fir region in western Oregon to the pine country of central and eastern Oregon. A rising high-tech sector mitigated some of the layoffs, but primarily in metropolitan Portland. Those disruptions set in motion revenue difficulties affecting all levels of education, including Oregon's institutions of higher learning.

Ballot Measure 5, a property tax limitation initiative, narrowly passed in 1990, reducing state general funds available for public institutions of higher education and prompting OSU to eliminate several departments. For OSU president John Byrne (1984–1995), those were difficult years. Byrne, who came to the presidency via the Department of Oceanography, was the first dean of the School of Oceanography (1972–1976) and then vice president for research and graduate studies (1976–1981). After three years as administrator of the National Oceanic and Atmospheric Administration, he was appointed the institution's twelfth president, serving from 1984 to 1995. Despite the challenges of a strapped economy, Byrne worked with the OSU Foundation in major fund-raising programs, including the expansion of the library. During his tenure, the State Board of Higher Education approved the first disciplinary graduate-degree offerings in the College of Liberal Arts, the university established the OSU Distinguished Professor Award, and the federal government designated OSU a Space Grant University.

Byrne's successor, Paul Risser, left the presidency in 2002, after which the central administration's archival records are understandably spare. The epilogue traces the university's explosive growth during the twenty-first century; however, because those events and proceedings are *very* recent, they offer little perspective beyond fund-raising achievements, new and expanding programs, and the impressive buildings going up around campus. The institution's twenty-first-century story offers a dizzying pace of change, as OSU and universities across the land became fully vested in the digital worlds of record-keeping, web-based and online curriculum, and the ongoing restructuring of administrations. A proper accounting of those developments awaits the availability of digitized documents and the reflective advantages of greater perspective.

The university's relations with the Corvallis community became increasingly strained as student rentals in neighborhoods adjacent to campus created parking problems and more, especially loud parties deep into the night, circumstances that brought university and citizens together in a collaborative effort to resolve those issues. In that sense, *The People's School* attempts to highlight the external and internal forces, the critical and pressing issues, and the individuals who shaped and directed the institution during the last 150 years. Acknowledging that this assessment of the university's long history misses much that will be important to readers, the selected themes in this volume account for most of the dynamic forces that have shaped and driven the development of the institution.

1
Beginnings

Oregon's political origins were deeply embedded in the slavery controversy and the Civil War. Oregon was granted statehood on the eve of the conflict, and voters were divided when they went to the polls in the presidential election of 1860. Pro-slavery states' rights candidate John Breckenridge (with Oregon's pro-slavery senator Joseph Lane as his running mate) received 5,074 votes; popular-sovereignty Democrat Stephen A. Douglas garnered 4,131; and Abraham Lincoln at the head of the new Republican Party tallied 5,344 votes. Similar divisions prevailed across the nation, but Lincoln won the presidency with a solid majority in the electoral college. With the secession of slaveholding states (also opposed to land grants for education), Congress passed the Morrill bill, and President Lincoln signed it into law on July 2, 1862.[1]

The contentious slavery issue had already been at play in the small town of Corvallis when Orceneth Fisher, a member of the Methodist Episcopal Church, South, arrived in the community in 1858, purchased financially troubled Corvallis College in 1860, and transferred the property to the church for use as a meetinghouse for its followers and college classes. Photos show a sizable two-story structure, located between Madison and Monroe on Fifth Street, with a large front entrance and second-story windows overlooking the street below. Six years after the transfer to the church, the Corvallis College Board of Trustees appointed William A. Finley to dual responsibilities as pastor and president of the college.[2]

The Corvallis church and its college serve as a reminder that the great schism in America's Methodist Episcopal Church took place well before the Civil War, when the northern delegation to the general conference demanded that a Georgia bishop give up the vestments of his office when he married a woman who owned large numbers of enslaved people. The conference meeting in 1844 led to a "Plan of Separation" and the establishment of two Methodist Episcopal churches, North and South, with the southern churches eventually erecting a separate ecclesiastical organization, the Methodist Episcopal Church, South (M.E. Church, South). That geographical division lasted until 1939, when they merged to form the Methodist Church. The existence of the M.E. Church, South, in the American West (and Oregon) reflected white immigrants from slaveholding and border states who followed the trails westward during the 1840s and 1850s to establish new settlements west of the Rocky Mountains.[3]

Few people today are aware of Oregon State's link to the Methodist Episcopal Church, South, and its oversight body, the Columbia Conference. The sectarian to nonsectarian evolution of Corvallis College to Oregon Agricultural College paralleled the beginnings of land-grant institutions in a few other states. Although land-grant schools have been associated with major state universities in the Midwest and West, such designations in the East were often bestowed—for a time—on private institutions (many of them with sectarian roots), Yale in Connecticut, and most notably, Cornell in New York. A private school from its inception, Cornell had no religious affiliation, but like most of its peers, it provided religious instruction to students. Cornell has remained the permanent home to New York's land-grant school. Yale was founded in 1701 to prepare students for "Publick employment both in Church and Civil State." In the case of its Sheffield Scientific School, Connecticut's land-grant designee, the state legislature subsequently established Storrs Agricultural School in 1881 and transferred its land-grant unit to the Storrs campus in 1893 (later the University of Connecticut). Corvallis College, however, was unique in its link to the M.E. Church, South.[4]

Grants of land to support public education date to the colonial period, and the practice transferred seamlessly after the American Revolution to the new United States. Long before Congress passed the Morrill Act, the nation had a well-established tradition of using federal lands to support education. Such generosity, however, came at a terrible cost to Native American peoples who were coerced through forced treaties to cede their vast homelands to the federal government. Reviewing federal support for higher education in Oregon, Governor Lafayette Grover observed that during its territorial years, Congress had granted two townships of land to the territory to support a university. The legislation admitting Oregon as the thirty-third state in 1859 provided "seventy-two sections of [federal] land shall be set apart and reserved for the use and support of a State University." The 1859 grant represented the initial public support for higher education in Oregon and one of the founding documents for the state university in Eugene.[5]

There was still more to the statehood act. The enabling legislation provided for the selection of lands from the public domain to support common schools. When Congress created Oregon Territory in 1848, the statute made available the sixteenth and thirty-sixth sections of every township for common schools. The statehood act of 1859 included the same measures, providing a total of 3,399,360 acres of federal land to support schools and a provision of ten sections of land for public buildings. For state support for higher education, however, the Morrill Act offered a different approach, providing grants of land to promote the education of the industrial classes. Legislation for supporting agricultural colleges had been circulating in Congress for several years, with an earlier version of Morrill's land-grant bill passing both houses of Congress in 1857, only to have President James Buchanan veto the bill because it interfered with states' rights. Southerners, who opposed the measure, ignored the government's long tradition of providing federal lands for education. The successful passage of the Morrill Act in 1862, therefore, simply accelerated well-established federal policies—in this instance—for higher education.[6]

Oregon's leading newspaper, the Portland *Oregonian*, kept a watchful eye on developments in the nation's capital, regularly reporting on legislation beneficial to western territories. When Congress passed the Morrill Act, the *Oregonian* characterized the measure as a promise fulfilled, "donations of public lands, the avails of which should be applied to the endowment of an Agricultural College." The newspaper reported that Oregon's federal grant meant the state would receive thirty thousand acres for each senator and representative in Congress, a formula that would total ninety thousand acres. Its purpose was to establish a permanent fund to support colleges whose "leading objective shall be to teach such tactics as are related to agriculture and the mechanic arts . . . to promote the liberal and practical education of the industrial classes in the several pursuits and professions of life."

One year after passage of the Morrill Act, the *Oregonian* asked the vexing question: "Where shall this institution be located?" What place possessed a healthy location, inexpensive living, easy access to transportation, and a willingness to make a "liberal offer for furnishing a site for the college and college buildings?" The newspaper urged the legislature to act quickly, because "the Farmers and Mechanics of Oregon must not let this great endowment . . . be lost to themselves and their children." The legal stipulations of the Morrill Act required states to accept the grant within two years and to establish a college within five years. The Oregon legislature filed acceptance within a year, and when it dallied in locating a college, the *Oregonian* complained that Congress had provided a rich endowment for common schools and higher education, "yet legislative and popular action seems to indicate that the gift is not worth receiving."[7]

Fifteen states had acted on their land grants when the Oregon legislature appointed a committee in 1868 "with power to locate all the lands to which the State is entitled by act of Congress." States were to select their lands from the public domain and either lease or sell the land to fund their agricultural schools. Those making the selections had to avoid earlier grants for homesteaders, railroads, or, in Oregon's case, for military roads. And then, amid considerable opposition and controversy, lawmakers designated Corvallis College as its temporary institution to meet the federal requirement "until other provisions are made." Under the terms of the law, each state senator was to select one student age sixteen or over from each county to attend the college for two years. To meet the terms of the 1862 Morrill Act, the legislature directed that the "act shall take effect from the date of its passage," October 27, 1868.[8]

Endorsing the small Corvallis academy as its interim "agricultural college" was no simple matter, because well-established Willamette University had lobbied for the institutional privilege, agreeing to offer federally required classes "until such time as the state was able to provide an institution." State Representative C. B. Bellinger of Benton County played a major role in landing the agricultural college in Corvallis, his efforts involving empathy for the South and a bit of legislative chicanery. Early in his career Bellinger edited and published newspapers in southern Oregon, an area heavy with pro-Southern sentiment. Corvallis, without a newspaper until Joseph C. Avery published the short-lived *Occidental Messenger*, proved an ideal landing place for the M.E. Church, South. Bellinger, who won a contested election in 1868 to sit in the legislature, contributed to a chaotic session when he led a brilliant move—the *Oregonian* called it a coup d'etat—to deprive Willamette University of being the state's designated land-grant college. The bill was ready for a third reading (to become law) when Bellinger moved to strike Willamette University and insert Corvallis College in the bill. The measure carried, and Corvallis College became the state's agricultural college designee.[9] Among the dissenters was prominent farmer John Minto, later to become a major critic of Corvallis College as the state's agricultural institution.

Designating the M.E. Church, South's, Corvallis College as the state's land-grant school reflected post–Civil War politics in Oregon. With Democrats out of power in 1866, legislators had ratified the Fourteenth Amendment to the US Constitution, granting citizenship to all persons born in the United States (including those formerly enslaved) and guaranteeing equal protection under the law. Two years later, with Democrats dominating the legislature, lawmakers assigned the state's agricultural school to Corvallis College and then voted to repeal the Fourteenth Amendment. The amendment was opposed vociferously in the Southern states, and movements to reject it gained currency in the American West with large numbers of people who had emigrated from Southern and border states.[10] The 1868 legislature's two measures—rescinding its approval of the Fourteenth Amendment and designating a Southern-oriented sectarian school home to its land-grant institution—reflect a distinctive political tone.

While the Oregon legislature was moving to designate its land-grant school, the M.E. Church, South, and the Columbia Conference had been struggling financially to support Corvallis College. Meeting in Rickreall in 1867, the conference discussed an appropriate endowment for the college, recommending immediate action "to raise a fund of not less than $5,000" for new buildings. The conference later appointed a board of trustees to oversee the operation. The trustees, most from Corvallis, incorporated the school in August 1868, declaring its name to be "Corvallis College," whose objective would be "to acquire and hold property in trust for the Methodist Episcopal Church, South."[11]

The Columbia Conference devoted increasing attention to Corvallis College in the late 1860s. President William Finley and professor of mathematics Joseph Emery, both ordained ministers and pastors with the M.E. Church, South, regularly attended conference meetings and tendered assessments of the college's financial health. Conference reports varied between enthusiasm for the college's "prosperous condition" and decreasing indebtedness, and acknowledgment at the same moment that "our friends at large have not been as fully informed [of the debt] and as a consequence [are] not as fully interested as necessary for future prosperity." The conference's report for September 1869 expressed fear that the college would never be secure until it had "an endowment fund of at least $25,000." The Corvallis College Board of Trustees took charge of the fiscal and academic activities of the institution in the fall of 1868, with the trustees' president informing members about the condition of the college and its financial health. The board established annual salaries for Finley ($1,000) and Emery ($900), and set the college calendar at three sessions of fourteen weeks' duration. The board voted on October 31, 1868, to accept the Oregon legislature's temporary designation of Corvallis College as home to the agricultural institution, promising "to faithfully carry out the provisions of said act."[12]

The trustees directed faculty to create a course of study for students in the "Agricultural Department," acknowledging that the institution's agricultural component would be part of, yet separate from, other activities at the college.[13]

Early trustees' meetings reveal Columbia Conference requests regarding information about the college's "apparatus fund"—that is, the institution's need for specialized equipment. As further indication of its more important responsibilities, the board authorized hiring staff for its Primary Department (elementary grades) and Preparatory Department (high school), units of the college consistent with those of many land-grant schools. Despite the college's expressed interest in agricultural education, the catalogue for 1868–1869 treated the subject as an afterthought, mentioning only the legislature's designation of the Corvallis school as the "Agricultural College of the State."[14]

The Columbia Conference appointed a commission with power to transact business between sessions to assist the college's agent to secure funds to pay debts. Because of growing interest in the college and "to give it rank among the first Institutions of the land," the conference recommended the need to properly endow the college and raise funds for additional buildings. Its 1870 session observed that the college and its agricultural unit had been successfully operating for three years, evidence "that the Institution is permanent."[15] Conference meetings still made no mention of the school's agricultural department.

Despite that oversight, state lawmakers voted "to permanently locate the Agricultural College of Oregon" with Corvallis College in 1870, and the board of trustees accepted the legislature's provisions. Legislators also appointed a committee to locate the ninety thousand acres the state was entitled to under the Morrill Act. At their meetings, trustees discussed the legislature's powers and the board's responsibilities in "relation to the Agricultural College" and resolved to canvas Benton County citizens to raise money to purchase land for a farm.[16]

Fronting criticism that it offered little in the way of practical agriculture, trustees moved in 1873 to establish an "Agricultural College Farm," to hire "a Practical Farmer," and to furnish the enterprise with proper equipment. In truth, establishing the farm was no simple matter. Although lawmakers designated Corvallis as the location for the agricultural college, they provided no financial support. Benton County legislators and friends, however, pledged to purchase suitable land for a farm, meeting with some success when supporters purchased thirty-five acres for $4,500 in 1871 and deeded it to the college. The buyers paid $2,500 and expected to pay off another $500 through subscriptions. The remaining $1,500, however, was a problem, placing the property in danger of foreclosure and threatening the viability of the agricultural college. In an advertisement in the Corvallis *Gazette*, trustees asked citizens "to contribute of your means, not only to liquidate the debt on the land already purchased, but to enable the Regents to increase the Farm to at least One Hundred Acres."[17]

The prevailing sentiment during Oregon's early statehood years was to support "common" (public) schools but to avoid taxing citizens to fund institutions of higher education. According to Frederick G. Young, an early-twentieth-century University of Oregon social scientist, Oregon would have written into its constitution that the university's grant be used to support common schools if Congress would have approved such a change. Young indicated that the location for the state university went to "the community that showed the highest appreciation." Over time, he observed, Oregon legislators grudgingly loosened their purse strings for higher education. According to historian John Thelin, governors and legislators wanted "to reduce their responsibility for oversight and support for higher education."[18]

Among the college's chief critics were the State Agricultural Society and its founding member John Minto, a Salem-area sheep farmer, orchardist, and advocate for progressive farming. Minto edited *Willamette Farmer*, a weekly newspaper devoted to technological advances in farming that frequently criticized Corvallis College for failing to offer instruction in agriculture. When the Corvallis College Board of Trustees sought the Agricultural Society's support after the college gained permanent status, the society refused, citing the legislature's decision as "premature," ill-advised, and beneath the standards of agricultural colleges in other states.[19]

Corvallis and Benton County's population grew apace during the 1860s, with the county's population increasing to 4,584 in 1870. Although the town lacked a rail connection to Portland, it had enjoyed steamship service between Portland, Corvallis, and points upriver since 1867. Until investors completed the lock and canal at Willamette Falls in 1873, upriver and downriver travelers (and goods) were forced to portage around the falls and board another steamship. Although the Oregon and California Railroad linked Portland and Roseburg by 1873 (via Albany), farmers welcomed the canal and locks at Willamette Falls for overcoming the major obstacle to river navigation, making "competition possible" and lowering prices for shipping goods. During the rainy season, steamers made regular departures upriver from Portland to Oregon City, Salem, Albany, Corvallis, and intermediate points.[20]

Although Corvallis was incorporated in 1857, the *Gazette* worried that elected officials were lax in enforcing city ordinances. While the act of incorporation empowered the city to "license, tax, regulate, or prohibit bar-rooms, tippling houses, billiard tables . . . and to prohibit bawdy-houses, gaming and gambling houses," many citizens thought local statutes were meaningless, because offenders were never punished and local officials were oblivious to "flagrant violations of law." On occasion the newspaper referred to transgressors as "our enemies," people who cared little about "peace, quiet, and sound morality." They were "moral vultures" who benefitted from the "misfortunes of others." The *Gazette* was certain that it had taken a stand "boldly and defiantly on the side of Temperance, Morality, and Virtue."[21]

In the midst of improved transportation links to the outside world, the Columbia Conference of the M.E. Church, South, appointed Benjamin Arnold as the new president of Corvallis College in 1872 when William Finley left for Santa Rosa, California, later serving as president of Pacific Methodist College. Arnold, a Virginian educated at Randolph Macon College who had served in the Confederate Army under General Robert E. Lee, assumed the presidency after a brief interlude with Joseph Emery as acting president. Arnold, who was not an ordained minister, surfaced as president through the auspices of the M.E. Church, South, and served until his death in 1892. In board of trustees records, he is described as a person of integrity and an honest broker for the needs of Corvallis College and its agricultural department. While he lacked expertise, Arnold was willing to venture into the world of agricultural experimentation, with some of his efforts ridiculed in the *Willamette Farmer*.[22]

Acting president Emery submitted the college's first "Biennial Report of the Trustees of the State Agricultural College" to the governor in August 1872, reporting that students were being "instructed, as far as practicable" to comply with federal legislation. He cited the purchase of "an experimental farm" with a house, barn, and orchard and applauded the institution's emphasis on "practical agriculture." The college employed two professors to teach its classes and to "meet its imperative demands," expenses far exceeding the state's contribution. Emery requested and was awarded a legislative appropriation of $5,000 for the biennium to meet instructional demands and to stock the farm with animals and agricultural implements.[23]

Corvallis College graduated its first three students in 1870 with bachelor of science degrees, two men and one woman. Taught in the Department of Chemistry, the agricultural curriculum enrolled twenty-five students from eleven Oregon counties, all appointed by state senators (as mandated by federal law). Because many students were ill-prepared for academic work, they soon left campus in sizable numbers. The board of trustees, however, focused on other matters, engaging in a rueful repetitiveness during the early 1870s—with members wondering what "amount would be necessary to secure a good practical farmer" and what was "to be done on the Farm to meet the requirements of the law." Trustees worried whether the "Course of Studies and the Degrees now Conferred by the College" fully complied with congressional legislation and state laws.[24]

The board of trustees appointed Captain Benjamin D. Boswell the college's first professor of military science in 1873, and in keeping with Southern cultural preferences, cadets wore Confederate gray uniforms and matching caps until the presidency of John Bloss (1892–1896), who had served in the Union Army. The trustees' minutes for September 1874 continued to reflect questions about religion, quoting from a letter in the school's "Daily Bulletin" that Corvallis College was "offensively partisan and Sectarian" and that one faculty member "fraudulently" claimed to have a master of arts degree. The trustees responded that the professor, Joseph Emery, held a master of arts degree from Pacific Methodist College and was competent to teach his assigned courses. The charge, therefore, was "an *unmitigated misstatement of facts* and could *have been prompted only by malice.*" Although the trustees muted most doctrinal commentary about the college, the Columbia Conference was more assertive, citing in its 1874 session the need for "moral instruction, moral science and philosophy."[25]

In his first biennial report to the governor, Arnold described the institution's poverty—indebtedness and "no money and scarcely any resources." Although the college could do little with the state contribution of $5,000, it organized literary and scientific departments and enrolled forty-four students during the biennium. There were serious problems with enrollees, however, because state law allowed admission to "any youth sixteen years of age, no other requirements." As a consequence, many students in the agricultural department were illiterate and therefore unable to complete their courses. The faculty responsible for the departments were Emery (mathematics), B. J. Hawthorne (languages), Captain Benjamin Boswell (military), and Arnold (physical science and moral science). With no formal training, the president had undertaken soil analysis and experiments with wheat, "the great staple of Oregon."[26]

In the midst of testy conference and trustee meetings, life at the college continued apace. Arnold arranged for Reverend E. J. Dawme of Salem to deliver a series of scientific lectures, and the college building committee finalized plans for more classroom space. Although still without the railroad-inspired growth of Albany and Eugene in the mid-1870s, Corvallis boasted good warehouses along the Willamette River, excellent mercantile establishments, and "a prosperous college of 150 students," according to the *Oregonian*. With prospects for a railroad from Corvallis to Yaquina Bay, development seemed imminent. The completion of that line would save Corvallis merchants as much as one hundred miles in shipments to and from California. The pending completion of the westside railroad from Portland through Corvallis would provide another alternative to river travel.[27]

Oregon's fledgling agricultural school gained a competitor when the legislature took advantage of the statehood act, which provided seventy-two sections of public land to support a university. Lawmakers coordinated their effort with Eugene's Union University Association to secure a site and provide a building "of not less than $50,000." The association achieved its objective in 1876, when the university opened with a president, two college-level faculty, and teachers to oversee a preparatory department. The legislature vested governance to a governor-appointed "Regents of the University." Like the agricultural college, the legislature extended student scholarships to attend the university to each county in the state. In a significant departure from legislative oversight of the agricultural college, however, Section 11 of the 1876 act establishing the university stipulated, "No political or sectarian test shall ever be allowed or applied in the appointment of regents, professors, teachers or employees of the University."[28]

The legislature's decision to site the state university in Eugene placed Corvallis College and its agricultural department in the crosshairs of more than a century of contentious relations with the state's new collegiate institution. Jealous that Portland lacked a comparable school, the *Oregonian* complained it would have been better to "have one state educational institution that could support itself instead of two, each struggling for existence." Legislators erred, the newspaper reported, when they used the general fund to sustain the agricultural college, because the land grant would never provide sufficient income to support the school. The problem rested with the legislature's grand bargain designating Eugene home to the state university, Salem the state capital, and Corvallis the location for the agricultural college.[29] Neither the *Oregonian* nor the legislature was enthusiastic about supporting higher education.

Critics of the state agricultural school directed most of their barbs at its religious affiliation. A letter to the *Oregonian* took issue with a member of the Corvallis College Board of Trustees for arguing that the M.E. Church, South, did not control the college, because everyone knew that the church and its bishops had appointed the reverends Finley and Emery. The same was true for Arnold. "Why," the writer asked, "is it that all the actions of the board of regents, their selection of teachers, etc., must be voted upon by the conference?" Moreover, the college farm was "at best only a good sized vegetable garden." Citizens wanted the state, not a church, to run the school.[30]

The state agricultural college had its defenders when a letter to the *Oregonian* took issue with a March editorial in 1878 calling for state control of the institution. There was nothing unusual about sectarian control of agricultural colleges, the writer argued, citing Yale and Dartmouth as eminent denominational schools charged with such instruction. States attempting to support agricultural colleges were "finding it impracticable and are gradually abandoning it." Oregon's state university was an example of the burden institutions place on public funds. The agricultural college, in contrast, was being operated with "the utmost economy," the "salaries of the professors as low as they can be put consistently with the employment of none but men of high character." Experience has shown, the writer concluded, that "higher education should be left to religious schools. Godless education has never been in favor with the people."[31]

In truth, Corvallis College struggled mightily to survive, with the majority of its students in the Primary and Preparatory Departments. Of the 169 students enrolled in 1870, only twenty-eight were at the college level. Although qualified students increased over the years, the number graduating was low, reflecting Arnold's report about students ill-prepared for college work. Through the 1870s, graduating classes averaged 4.5 students per year. During the 1880s, the numbers increased to an average of 6.6 students per year; however, in 1890, there were only four students in the graduating class.[32]

Arnold's biennial reports candidly described the condition of Corvallis College and its agricultural department. The president's blunt assessments referred to the Morrill Act requirements as a great model for educating students in the agricultural sciences and mechanical arts. His accounts summarize instructional programs and his research with "white soil" and wheat culture. The agricultural college was in crisis in 1880, because lawmakers eliminated the institution's annual appropriation of $5,000, placing the college's support on interest from the unpredictable land fund. Arnold worried about the college's limited means and the uncertainty about the funds it might expect. Regular funding over several years, he noted, was necessary to undertake significant agriculture experiments.[33] Financially strapped Corvallis College and its agricultural unit mirrored the struggles of other land-grant institutions for funding.

Governor W. W. Thayer's biennial message to the legislature in 1882 offers a troublesome profile of the respective land grants to the state university and the agricultural college. Of the Eugene university's seventy-two reserved sections, twenty-nine thousand acres had been sold, leaving forty-three thousand remaining. The agricultural college had sold twenty-six thousand of its ninety-thousand acres, with sixty-four thousand remaining. The university received $62,000 for its sales, and the agricultural college, $65,000. The governor reported that property incomes for the two institutions differed, because earnings on interest sometimes reflected lower rates. The university's land-grant fund earned $12,061 for the biennium, and the agricultural college, $10,792—the figures representing both low market prices for land and buyers with questionable credit.[34] There would be little stability in support for the agricultural unit until the legislature assumed full control in the late 1880s.

Reflecting exchanges of information with the commissioner of agriculture in Washington, DC, Arnold's biennial reports take on a broader perspective about the function of the agricultural unit at the onset of the 1880s. The Corvallis institution hosted John Minto, one of its chief critics, who addressed students on behalf of the Oregon State Grange and the State Agricultural Society. The best-informed agriculturalist in the state, Minto commended the faculty for their hard work but thought they deserved more support. The college's problem, he believed, could be attributed to "a lack of . . . interest in it as a school of Agriculture and Mechanical Arts." The legislature renewed its $5,000 biennial appropriation for the agricultural college in 1881 and added another $2,500 to the institution's support because its revenue had "become seriously impaired."[35] Arnold left unsaid the M.E. Church, South's, meager support—its reliance on voluntary "subscriptions" from members to fund the college.

Beyond observations about the college, Arnold reported experiments with grasses, "the only one allowed by our means." On campus, faculty members were unable to enforce the requirement for manual labor, because there were no funds "for this purpose." Although the college had met its financial obligations, it could use additional funds to hire another teacher. The president emphasized a new land-grant pedagogical strategy in his 1884 report, "A Practical Education Based on Science." To implement the model would require three distinct faculties: scientific and literary, technical studies, and general education. Arnold reminded Oregon legislators that federal requirements obligated him to organize the agricultural college on the basis of those three faculties. The president added news from the nation's capital important to the future of the Corvallis school—Congress was considering a bill (the Hatch Act) to establish agricultural experiment stations that would provide $15,000 to each state for conducting agricultural investigations.[36]

Although the Columbia Conference worried about funding new buildings, its minutes through the 1870s and into the 1880s reflect great attention to both education and religion, pledging its "liveliest interest in Corvallis College," while complaining about the moral harm "wrought by simply educating the mind to the neglect of training the soul." Although the conference denied that strict Methodist doctrines should be taught in the college, it believed "that we should have a zealous eye to the teachings of the morals of our Holy Christianity." And despite its dismal financial situation, the conference continued to praise the college's healthy finances and the legislation conferring on the school "the Rights, amenities and benefits accruing from the Sale of Lands thus munificently endowing the Department of Agriculture."[37]

The catalogue for 1879–1880 listed schools of physics, mathematics, moral science, languages, history and literature, English, and agriculture. At the same time, the conference worried about its jurisdiction over the agricultural department, with a note of desperation evident in the minutes of an 1882 session when it received a Benton County citizen's petition asking "to segregate the Agricultural Department from the College." The conference disagreed that segregating the agricultural department from the college would benefit the county and the interests of education. If the college released the agricultural department to the state, the county would be left with Corvallis College and no agricultural department. Submitting to the petitioners' request would be "educational suicide," because the petitioner's central issue resolved "itself into one word, the *church*."[38] A note of desperation is evident in both the conference and trustees' deliberations at this point, anxieties that would soon lead to dramatic changes in control over the agricultural unit.

The Columbia Conference compared Oregon's situation with states where agricultural institutions were under the control of the church or had some comparable relation with the state. Those schools were flourishing and educating their full share of students. "Why is this?" the conference minutes ask. "We answer that religion and morals are so connected that you cannot separate them, and thoughtful and intelligent men generally concede this." In a bit of defensive posturing, the conference indicated that Corvallis College compared well with any institution in the state, enrolling more students than the university in Eugene (154), and that it spent less money on instructional staff. The conference voted "in favor of sustaining the school as now constituted," its obligations prohibiting it from complying with the petitioners' demands.[39]

In the midst of growing concerns about the agricultural department, the trustees asked the legislature in August 1882 to fund a mechanical department, an important component of the Morrill Act. The trustees offered a startling quid pro quo—if the legislature provided a mechanical department, they would convey the farm to the state, and the legislature would be asked to accept the property:

It [the farm] is for educational purposes and such trusts are
seldom allowed to fail or die—and therefore it would be [illegible
word] for the College to vest its title in the State if thought best.
The State would simply hold the title in trust, subject to the same
conditions and limitations, and for the same purposes that it is
now held by the College.[40]

The trustees' move was the opening round in a series of decisions that
would eventually vest control of the agricultural department fully with the
state.

Corvallis College faculty and its board of trustees were increasingly sensitive to critics who questioned their management of the agricultural department. Wallis Nash, a British immigrant and soon to be an important figure
in guiding the college when it reverted to state control, offended the faculty
when he charged in his 1882 book, *Two Years in Oregon*, that the college did
"not teach agricultural subjects." The faculty, according to board of trustees
minutes, was indignant, pronouncing the statement "palpably untrue" and
"calculated to do harm to the best interests of our college." At its February
1882 meeting, the faculty termed "the statements false in every particular"
and instructed Arnold to publicly correct the misrepresentations.[41]

With the Oregon legislature circling ever closer to seizing control of the
agricultural college, the Columbia Conference and the trustees were divided
over what to do with the college farm. Meeting in Dayton, Washington Territory, in September 1884, the conference endorsed the board of trustees'
decision to transfer the agricultural farm to the state, declaring, "We have
never claimed this property." If the conference was unable to raise $25,000 to
erect a college building, it directed trustees to ask the legislature to dissolve
the compact between "Corvallis College and the State of Oregon to take effect
at the close of the present Scholastic year, June 1885."[42]

The Dayton meeting would prove the coup de grace in ending ties
between Corvallis College and the state's agricultural unit. When the conference failed to raise the money, the legislature approved an "Act to confirm
the Location of the State Agricultural College at Corvallis, and to provide for
the Maintenance and Government thereof" (approved February 11, 1885).
The legislation required Benton County citizens to fund and erect a building
to cost no less than $25,000. The law established a thirteen-member board
of regents to oversee the college, with responsibility for supervising the curriculum in accord with the federal mandate. Section 13 of the act directed
Corvallis College "to relinquish to the State the control and management of

the State agricultural college to take effect at the time and in the manner provided in this act."[43] In effect, the state would assume control of what Corvallis College trustees referred to as the "agricultural department."

When the Columbia Conference met in Albany in September 1885, it reversed course, declaring the 1884 proceedings "null and void" and rescinding all resolutions to dissolve its jurisdiction over the agricultural department. The conference asked the legislature in September 1886 to restore the relationship between Corvallis College and the "State Agricultural College," indicating that only a bare quorum of conference members was present at the Dayton meeting. Because the vote was four to three to transfer the agricultural department to the state, the conference asked lawmakers to reconsider their decision to take control of the agricultural department.[44]

The board of trustees added its voice in March 1887 in an effort to reclaim the endowment and property of the agricultural department. They argued, evidence to the contrary, that the Dayton meeting transferring the agricultural college to the state was "unauthorized," as was the decision to deed the college farm to the state. Trustees argued that they had never consented to end the contract between the state and the college. That accord, agreed to at "an illegal special meeting of this Board . . . was now void, and is hereby withdrawn." The board approved the motion eleven to five, with A. Cauthorn, Jas. A. Cauthorn, M. Jacobs, J. M. Applewhite, and Arnold opposed. The trustees then appointed a committee "to assert, maintain, protect, or defend in the courts" its rights to Corvallis College.[45]

Four days removed from the meeting, a Corvallis resident published a letter in the Oregonian documenting the relationship between the M.E. Church, South, and the agricultural college. After retelling the conflicting resolutions of the Columbia Conference and its board of trustees, the writer cited widespread disgust in Corvallis over the board of trustees' decision to void its agreement with the state. "The indignation here is great. The majority of the board was burnt in effigy last night." While citizens had labored hard for the college, they viewed the trustees' latest decision as an attempt to delay the obvious: "Nobody doubts much the ultimate defeat of the church." If the trustees' move had any legal standing, the writer concluded, "it is by virtue of irregularities in the proceedings of its own authors." The greater question was the legislature's power to "convey a state institution in perpetuity to any church."[46]

Critics abounded, with one Corvallis citizen accusing Arnold of misleading the legislature in his biennial reports. In a letter to the Oregonian, the anonymous writer described the college's curriculum as unpretentious—"schools of physics, mathematics, moral science, ancient languages, modern

language, history and literature, engineering and agriculture." This was a cha-
rade, the notion that three teachers were responsible for "this voluminous and
extensive work." The writer mocked "Reverend Emery," a preacher for twenty
years, who was teaching stock-breeding to students. Oregon "needed an agricultural school, but it should be like the State university—nonsectarian."[47]

Because the new board of regents did not take full control of the agricultural college until the summer of 1888, opponents of Corvallis College
continued to belabor the M.E. Church, South, for attempting to rescind its
1884 resolution. The college was "a classical and literary institution," an anonymous letter to the *Oregonian* charged. The school had a competent scholar
as president, but one who knew nothing about agriculture. With construction
of a building on the farm nearly completed, the future of a true agricultural
college seemed bright. Corvallis citizens resented the Columbia Conference's
rearguard action to reclaim management of the college: "The people will
never consent to pay their money to a college that is run by a religious sect."
The Hatch bill, working its way through Congress, with an annual appropriation of $15,000 for agricultural experiment stations, made it incumbent to
"rescind sectarian control."[48]

The murky legal fight between the M.E. Church, South, and the State of
Oregon continued long after the legislature took control of the college farm.
Disgruntled Columbia Conference members brought suit against the state,
charging that the transfer of property was illegal. Circuit court judge R. S.
Bean determined in January 1888 that the agricultural college had always
been vested with the state, and that the M.E. Church, South, had relinquished
control over its holdings in 1885. Bean dismissed the case as without merit.
The Columbia Conference appealed Bean's decision to the Oregon Supreme
Court, which determined that the deed transferring the farm to the state was
illegal, because the decision belonged to its oversight body, the Columbia
Conference, not the board of trustees. The plaintiffs, who had put up money
to purchase the farm, therefore deserved recompense.[49]

Despite the legal setback, Governor Sylvester Pennoyer's message to the
Oregon legislature in 1889 was optimistic—the agricultural college was doing
well and deserved the state's support to purchase land for a larger farm. With
its $15,000 annual endowment for an agricultural experiment station and fru-
gal management, the Corvallis school, like the university in Eugene, should be
prosperous, "without being a perpetual pensioner upon the taxpayers of the
state." The lawsuit against the state's possession of the agricultural college, the
governor insisted, was "entirely without foundation." Since he had accepted
the buildings and grounds on behalf of the state, Pennoyer reasoned that the

property belonged to the state. Aggrieved parties would have to appeal to the legislature, and if there were justice in their demands, "the legislature should grant it; if there be none, it should deny it."[50]

A joint legislative committee visited the college in early 1889 and returned to Salem convinced that the agricultural college deserved support once the legal claims were cleared. Since the state had ceased funding Corvallis College because it no longer controlled the agricultural department, the *Oregonian* reported that the college had "dwindled to a mere handful of students and is on the downward road to certain decay." The college had been plundering "the State treasury for sectarian purposes in direct violation of the State constitution," and so little had been accomplished that farmers regarded "the institution as little more than a farce."[51] The newspaper charged that the behavior of the church was "so dishonest and perverse" that two of its members, Reverend J. R. N. Bell and Senator Thomas E. Cauthorn, had abandoned it in disgust. The *Oregonian* was confident that the legislature would settle the small claims for the farm. "The state is not to be speculated on in that way."[52]

The litigated world of the agricultural college extended into the 1890s, long after the Oregon Supreme Court remanded the case back to Benton County. Remnant members of the Columbia Conference again brought suit in the county against the agricultural college's board of regents to recover the original farm. When church representatives won in the circuit court in 1892, the regents appealed to the Oregon Supreme Court, which reversed the circuit court's decision. Oregon's highest court found that Corvallis College had the legal right to convey the land to the state, and that the agricultural college's board of regents was legally empowered to accept the title.

> Neither the Methodist Church South, or its members, or any of them, or Corvallis College have any title to said land or right to the possession thereof.
>   It is therefore considered, ordered and decreed that the complaint herein be and the same hereby is dismissed.

In a brief report on the litigation, the Corvallis *Gazette* brought finality to the issue: "This is the celebrated Corvallis and M.E. church south case and involved the title to the state agricultural college grounds in this city."[53]

With governance shifting from sectarian to nonsectarian control, the mid-1880s marked a crossroads for Oregon's agricultural college. From this point forward, legislative mandates guided hiring and firing, curricular guidelines, and counsel for college administrators. For Arnold and the faculty, the new regime would mean more watchful oversight of college affairs, including its top administrator. In the following decades, the board of regents would keep a careful eye on spending. In addition to the president, other personnel made the transition to the new institutional oversight, some of them faculty who had sided with the state during the difficult days after the legislature assumed control of the college.

The Corvallis school would continue to grow and mature into the next century, its faculty gradually assuming the hues of a legitimate agricultural college. Federal government largesse, however, not state support, spurred most of the college's development during the next two decades. The Hatch Act was critical, providing the college with regular financial support and accelerating exchanges of information with other land-grant institutions. The increasing contacts with the outside world broadened the cultural and political worlds of the isolated Corvallis campus. With the completion of a transcontinental railroad to Portland in 1883 and the state's rapidly growing population, the state legislature slowly increased support for the University of Oregon, Oregon Agricultural College, and the normal schools in Monmouth and Ashland.

Sectarian matters aside, the Columbia Conference and its board of trustees were ill-suited to sustain and manage a state agricultural college. The conference and the land-grant college harbored different missions—Corvallis College and its oversight bodies served religious purposes while the objectives of its agricultural department were clearly secular, "to promote the liberal and practical education of the industrial classes." Corvallis College faculty, dominated by members of the M.E. Church, South, strived to provide a comprehensive curriculum, but their courses veered toward classical education. With the state-appointed board of regents guiding the Agricultural College of the State of Oregon in 1888, its faculty more than doubled, its curriculum differing dramatically from that of Corvallis College. The Agricultural College of Oregon had moved through two very difficult decades and achieved a semblance of stability. John Bloss, who became president in 1892, commented that 1888 marked a milestone in the college's history, a point in time when it began "to come into harmony with the purpose of its existence.[54] The Morrill Act, the Hatch Act, and other congressional legislation, Michael Cohen observes, contributed to the nationalization of American life, with land-grant schools providing common educational experiences through federally mandated curriculum and admissions reforms.[55]

2
Coming of Age

External developments, especially the great railroad-building spree in the Pacific Northwest between 1880 and the outbreak of the First World War, affected urban and rural communities and significantly influenced the region's social, economic, cultural, and political life. Improvements in rail and water transportation triggered a demographic explosion in Oregon and the Northwest, boosting Portland's population from 17,500 in 1880 to 46,385 in 1890 and to 90,426 at the onset of the twentieth century. Railroads were cathartic, bringing new people, new ideas, and new ethnic groups to the region. Corvallis's connection to the outside world via rail routes begins with the Oregon and Pacific Railroad (later the Corvallis and Eastern Railroad) completed in 1887, linking Yaquina Bay on the coast (through Corvallis) to the Southern Pacific line in Albany. An enterprising and engaging Southern investor, T. Edgenton Hogg, had ambitions to turn tide-bound Yaquina Bay into a seaport and build a transcontinental line across the Cascades to the east. His aspirations foundered on the inability to raise capital, and the line eventually terminated high in the North Santiam Canyon.[1]

In Corvallis, the agricultural college was finding its way through a new regulatory environment under very different administrative procedures. President Benjamin Arnold was a transitional administrator, whose tenure bridged the shift from the Methodist Episcopal Church, South, and its board of trustees to the jurisdiction of the governor-appointed board of regents. Arnold provides insights to the three-year period between the legislative act of February 1885 and July 1888, when the board of regents assumed control of the college. In his biennial report for 1889, he reviewed the regents' activities in accepting custody of the college farm and the M.E. Church, South's, legal efforts to reverse the decision to convey the farm to the state. In the midst of those distractions, Benton County citizens funded and erected the college building and handed the keys to the board of regents. Because the church voluntarily conveyed the farm and agricultural college to the state, Arnold reported, the legislature had codified the exchange through legal enactments. The regents, therefore, had acted properly in accepting control of the school.[2]

Citing institutional models to follow in the United States, Canada, and European nations, Arnold's report for 1889 outlined a proposed "plan of study" for the faculty, suggesting a balance between practical and theoretical education. "Agriculture is a science, and not an art," Arnold argued; "scientific thinking" was the foundation to achieving practical results. To improve its stature, the college should hire new faculty. Although it was unreasonable to expect an immediate, smoothly functioning academic environment after such dramatic changes, the college had made progress. In its first full calendar year as a public institution, it hired Grant Covell as its first engineering professor to head a new department and appointed Margaret Comstock Snell, its first female professor, to lead the new Department of Household Economy and Hygiene.[3] With her appointment, the college was following the examples of other land-grant institutions—Iowa State College, Kansas State, and the University of Illinois.

Although Oregon State University celebrates its sesquicentennial in 2018, a persuasive argument can be made for dating its origins to July 1888 when the state-appointed board of regents assumed governance of the agricultural department from Corvallis College. In a biennial report shortly before his death in 1892, Arnold underscored the college's sharp departure from the past—"only two years, from July 1888 to June 30, 1890, cover the whole history of the college under state control." John Bloss, his permanent successor, extended that argument in his biennial report for 1893, citing the college's reorganization in 1888 as "a milestone in its history. It then began to assume its proper sphere and to come into harmony with the purpose of its existence." The college's transition "from a literary and classical school to an agricultural, mechanical, and industrial school," Bloss explained, was almost complete. The first students in the mechanical department would graduate in June 1893, reflecting the new curriculum in industrial instruction. Through this period, Bloss observed, the college had changed "from an institution of one character to another." And, important to the institution's future, the faculty meeting on May 2, 1893, voted to adopt "Orange" as the school's color.[4]

William S. Ladd, prominent Portland banker and president of the board of regents, also noted that the college had lost "whatever was local and restricted in its roll of students." Responding to criticisms that Corvallis College drew most of its students from Benton County and the mid-valley, Ladd indicated that young people from all parts of the state were now applying

Funded by Benton County citizens and turned over to the Agricultural College of Oregon in the summer of 1888, Administration Hall (Benton Hall) served as an all-purpose building for campus activities. Built on the original thirty-five acre college farm, this photo shows some of the horticultural representations, with the college building to the left. Courtesy of the OSU Special Collections and Archives Research Center.

for admission. The first class of graduates trained in the "State Agricultural College" would pass into the wide world in the spring of 1894. President Bloss cited the need for new buildings, laboratories, cabinets, machinery, greenhouses, silos, and all varieties of plants, grasses, and trees for experimental work. Although the federal government provided generous support for the school's internal work, the state legislature was responsible for college buildings and the campus infrastructure.[5]

The *Oregonian* praised the college's focus on "farmers' education for the farm" and learning about scientific agriculture, but argued that the state needed well-trained and skilled teachers to educate students. Wallis Nash, secretary to the board, informed readers about new faculty hires and positions yet to be filled. He praised the college for opening its new building in September 1888 with student numbers approaching one hundred. Although the college farm of thirty-five acres was adequate, the school's new agricultural experiment station required a much larger acreage. The British-born and sometimes pretentious Nash would serve the regents well.[6]

The officially designated State Agricultural College of the State of Oregon changed its name in 1890 to Oregon Agricultural College (OAC). Under the last year of church control, the college listed four faculty members, a

Born in England and trained as a lawyer, Wallis Nash (1837–1926) moved to Oregon in 1879. He was an original member of the board of regents and served as its secretary. During his time with the regents, Nash was instrumental in hiring Margaret Snell, the founder of what became the home economics program, and he promoted the development of farmers' institutes, the predecessors to the extension service. Courtesy of the OSU Special Collections and Archives Research Center.

number that doubled in the fall of 1888 under the board of regents. The board elected Benjamin Arnold college president at an annual salary of $2,000 and commissioned him to travel the state and beyond "in the interest of this State Agricultural College." At home in Corvallis, Arnold confronted adjustments to new administrative decrees, especially the directives of board secretary Wallis Nash, who demanded that all communication between the faculty and regents be channeled through the president. When those directives were breached, as they often were, Nash reprimanded Arnold. One case involved Edgar Grimm, in charge of the experiment station, who submitted a letter directly to the board. Nash forwarded the letter to Arnold, with a reminder that "all such matters must, under the new Regulations, come through you to the Board."[7]

Nash moved from one issue to the next with the same unapologetic tone. When the faculty informed the regents that students wanted different uniforms, Nash expressed "regret," because the board "had considered it settled." He asked Arnold about the "dissatisfaction"—who were the students complaining, and in what manner? On another matter, Nash directed the president to exercise closer watch over the college and agricultural station, urging him to delegate some of his teaching responsibilities "to allow yourself ample time for this still more important duty." On another occasion Nash asked for the return of his "Minute book without delay—I ought not to have allowed it to be out of my possession."[8]

Wallis Nash's criticisms of Arnold's administrative shortcomings continued into 1890, and he lectured him again about proper protocol for communicating with the board. When Professor P. H. Irish left a memorandum in Nash's office, Nash fired off a letter to the president: "It is a matter of great regret to me that I fail to make it plain that what is desired by the Executive Committee [of the board] is, from Professor Irish to yourself, plain answers to the plain questions put in my letter to you, and from yourself to me." Arnold should also add his own "opinion as President of the College." In another directive two months later, Nash wanted detailed annual reports from the faculty, their plan of work for the next year, and the estimated costs. The reports were due "as soon as possible, certainly not later than Monday next."[9]

In preparing the board's first annual report to the legislature, Nash asked Arnold to provide a description of the teaching staff and curriculum, the students' names, class standing, and place of residence, a list of future farmers institutes, and indicate deficiencies in the courses offered. Nash's directives were unceasing, with the most petulant a memo to Arnold in late October 1889:[10]

> My dear Sir
> I am excessively vexed at this
> mistake of [last] evening or morning, which I
> feel confident is not my mistake—
> Please come down at once *to this office*
>   Leave your class to someone else, and
> come—It will not take you over an
> hour's absence from the College
> Very truly
> Wallis Nash

It was serendipitous that the board of regents would assume governance of Oregon's agricultural college just as the initial appropriation of $15,000 under the Hatch Act became available.[11] Enacted in 1887, the Hatch Act was long in gestation. First introduced in the House and Senate in 1882, the bills fell victim to congressional wrangling. Finally, the chair of the House Agricultural Committee, Missouri's William H. Hatch, took control of an old bill in 1886 and moved the measure forward in both houses of Congress. To avoid state legislative raids on federal appropriations, the Hatch bill required federal funds to "go directly to [agricultural experiment] stations without the intervention of the State legislatures." For Oregon's reconstituted and financially strapped college of agriculture, the Hatch Act's $15,000 annual appropriation would prove liberating to the institution's financial health. Its agricultural experiment station dates its official founding to February 25, 1889, when Governor Sylvester Pennoyer signed legislation accepting the provisions of the Hatch Act.[12]

To obtain its initial Hatch Act funds, the regents had to apply to the United States Treasury Department for payment of the $15,000. After receiving the first installment, the regents organized the Oregon Agricultural Experiment Station and appointed its faculty. The college president served as director. Administrators had to exercise due diligence in spending the Hatch funds, because the law limited expenditures on experiment station buildings to one-fifth of the appropriation. The regents subsequently spent the one fifth fraction to outfit the college building with rooms for chemistry and botanical research. Although the first year at the station was organizational, the college would eventually establish branch stations in different parts of the state to accommodate diverse climate and soil conditions. Most important to the success of the agricultural experiment station would be enlarging the college farm to at least two hundred acres, a precedent that colleges had pursued in Illinois, Kansas, Iowa, and Michigan. "Oregon," the president reported, "has not hitherto followed the good example of her older sisters."[13]

When the experiment station published its first bulletin in the fall of 1888, the *Oregonian* praised the institution for being "more of a farmer's college than it was a year ago." The station immediately assumed significance in college deliberations, more than doubling its operating budget. With executive responsibility for the experiment station, the board of regents drafted regulations for the unit—creating a station council comprising the college president, station director, and an agriculturist and chemist. As ex officio, the president represented the station to the regents. The council's primary function was to prepare "plans of work" for the regent's approval, with director Edgar Grimm, a graduate of the college, in charge of everyday affairs.[14]

The station's botanist, E. R. Lake, posed problems for the staff from the beginning. The board of regents intervened in late 1889, ordering Lake to "work in harmony and courtesy with all members of the faculty and staff" or resign. When Lake resigned two years later, the board asked the president for an explanation. Arnold was blunt: Lake was frequently absent from the station and had missed several classes. The college would be better off without his services.[15]

The college hired Moses Craig as the new botanist and George Coote as horticulturist, both men to serve in the classroom and the station. The president had already hired P. H. Irish as chemistry professor and chemist to the station. After a few months, Arnold cautioned Irish that he was devoting too much time to his classes and giving insufficient attention to the station. Irish should also avoid dismissing students from class who had failed only one examination, because refusing seats to students who failed "tends to disorganization, to demoralize the student and to lead to his ultimate failure." When those cautionary words failed, Arnold brusquely told Irish to restore the dismissed students and to drop one of his classes so that he could devote more time to work at the station: "This is all I have to say about the matter."[16]

Expanding the acreage of the farm was critical to the station's success, an issue the regents acknowledged from the beginning. In his biennial report for 1889, Arnold observed that the thirty-five-acre farm was adequate for student instruction, but had limited utility for "the practical work of the farmer, the dairyman, the stock raiser, and the horticulturalist." When the legislature provided funds for land and buildings, the regents took steps to expand farming operations. The board examined a local map showing distances, land ownerships, and boundaries in proximity to the college. When President Arnold offered to sell five acres of land west of the college, the regents purchased the site as a location for additional buildings and used the legislature's appropriation to buy 155 acres adjacent to the college farm. With state support, the college erected an octagonal barn equipped with feeding stalls, a silo, and storage for hay and grains. The president reported in 1891 that the new facility was already "inadequate for the increased production of the farm."[17]

Under the leadership of Professor Edgar Grimm, agricultural experiment work moved ahead, the station publishing its first bulletin in 1888 (providing information on a variety of agricultural issues). Wallis Nash, still secretary to the board, criticized the quality of subsequent bulletins, telling Arnold there was a need for clear prose, because "careless writing causes both delay and extra expense." Horticulturist George Coote issued an ambitious work plan for his department in 1891—testing varieties of vegetables and fruits to determine their suitability to climate and the best means to control insects and mildews. His most ambitious project was planting thirty-three varieties of apples to determine their adaptability to the area.[18]

To augment the station's research, farmers and ranchers donated beef and dairy cattle to establish herds for study. Station publications offered advice on raising hogs, strategies to irrigate pastures and control weeds, and appropriate crops for certain soil types. Station publications were descriptive and provided information about ongoing experiments. During its first decade, the station published fifty-eight bulletins and circulars. Station council meetings focused on day-to-day operations, building a library, allocating funds to departments, and ordering publications from other experiment stations. Council meetings determined topics for research and reported on farmers' institutes, an important aspect of station and college activities.[19]

Farmers' institutes offered across the state were one of the college's most significant innovations. Although the institutes were closely affiliated with the experiment station, they predated the Hatch Act. Iowa State College began sponsoring farmers' institutes in 1870, and the State Agricultural College of Michigan in 1875. In the Midwest, the institutes were designed to counter criticisms from the Grange that agricultural colleges in the 1860s and 1870s were not meeting the needs of farmers. The institutes provided good public relations and promoted the work of agricultural colleges. Differing from previous agricultural convocations, the college-sponsored institutes provided the personnel who traveled throughout their respective states.[20]

Oregon Agricultural College sponsored its first farmers' institutes in 1889, with the events drawing only modest attention. A committee of five, two from the board of regents and three from the college, planned the institutes and the topics to be presented. The college provided financial support and speakers for the events, which numbered about five per year. Lasting approximately two days, institutes were held in Gearhart on the Oregon Coast and in the Willamette Valley towns of McMinnville, Dallas, and Lebanon in 1894. The college sponsored a six-week institute on campus in January and February 1895. Although they varied, institutes addressed issues important to farmers, from treating diseases to "agricultural and horticultural production." By the mid-1890s, attendance at the institutes had increased dramatically, with as many as five hundred people at some evening events. The master of the Oregon State Grange enthusiastically supported the farmers' institutes, hoping that farmers would host such events across the state.[21]

Oregon's land-grant college benefitted from the federal government's generosity again when Vermont representative (now senator) Justin Morrill, principal sponsor of the 1862 act, authored a bill to expand the endowment for existing land-grant colleges and to fund new agricultural and mechanical schools. Signed into law August 30, 1890, the Second Morrill Act's key provision appropriated federal funds from public land sales "for the more complete endowment and maintenance of colleges for the benefit of agricultural or mechanical arts now established or which may be hereafter established."[22] An additional provision in the act played directly to land-grant universities and colleges in the Old South, none of which admitted students of color.

Six years before the United States Supreme Court declared its infamous separate but equal doctrine in the *Plessy v. Ferguson* decision (1896), the Second Morrill Act stated,

> No money shall be paid out under this act to any State or
> Territory for the support and maintenance of a college where
> a distinction of race or color is made in the admission of
> students, but the establishment and maintenance of such colleges
> separately for white and colored students shall be held to be in
> compliance with the provisions of this act if the funds received in
> such State or Territory be equitably divided.

Additional provisions for addressing the "just and equitable" division of funds for "white" and "colored" students were left to state and territorial legislatures to determine, with mandatory reports to Congress. A product of the post–Civil War accommodation between the North and the South, this peculiar legislation led to the creation of seventeen perpetually underfunded black land-grant colleges in the former Confederacy. When Oregon governor Sylvester Pennoyer accepted the provisions of the act, he wrote, "No discrimination is made in the admission of students at the State Agricultural College of Oregon, by reason of race or color."[23] With the state's infinitesimally small African American population, there were no blacks enrolled at Oregon's agricultural college until the twentieth century.

The Hatch and Second Morrill Acts provided a great boost to the fiscal stability of Oregon's agricultural college. With the regents revising the curriculum and the experiment station expanding its activities, the institution joined the ranks of other land-grant colleges teaching agriculture and mechanical arts to underserved constituencies. The standards and procedures shaping the school in the early twentieth century were established in the half-dozen years after the state assumed full control of the college in 1888. President Arnold acknowledged those changes in his 1891 report, citing increased enrollments, the broader geographic areas represented in the student population, and the fact that students were older, more mature, and better prepared for college. The college was doing well in "practical, technical matters," its principal areas of responsibility, and requiring a "thorough training in English grammar and literature, and in mathematics and its allied sciences."[24]

At the regents urging, the faculty adopted formal procedures for the library, issuing hours for checking out books: students, noon to 1:30, and faculty, 2:30 to 3:00. Books, newspapers, magazines, and bulletins could be checked out for two weeks, with late returns subject to fines. The librarian was responsible for record-keeping and posting new books, newspapers, and bulletins in its collections. Students could use the library for reading during the noon hour, subject to such regulations as the faculty chose. Finally, the librarian was charged with post office mail and keeping the library neat. If the librarian failed to carry out those responsibilities, the faculty could request the person's resignation.[25]

President Arnold, who died suddenly in January 1892, served as head of the college through a turbulent twenty years. After a few months under John Letcher as interim president, the board of regents selected John Bloss, a career educational administrator and superintendent of schools in Topeka, Kansas (1886–1892), as the institution's third president. Bloss symbolized a changing of the guard. Unlike Arnold, who fought with the Confederacy, Bloss served in the Union Army during the Civil War, winning distinction at the critical battle of Antietam. As the regents' first presidential appointment, Bloss would enjoy striking successes—rising enrollments, a growing faculty, and lively construction activity on campus. He successfully appealed to the regents and the legislature in 1893 for an appropriation of $26,100 for additional campus buildings. To elevate the standing of the college, Bloss curtailed enrollment in the Preparatory Department and then eliminated it altogether in 1896. From that point forward, enrollment figures reflected students functioning under college educational standards.[26]

The college's rapid growth increased pressure on the institution's president, requiring Bloss to expand his administrative staff. His letter to the regents in 1895 suggests a workload that may have hastened Arnold's death and likely contributed to Bloss's early retirement when he became ill in 1896. During the 1894–1895 academic year, Bloss taught two courses fall term and one each winter and spring term. Beyond the classroom he advised teachers and students "involving so many phases that it would be difficult to describe." He regularly spoke to public schools and teachers' institutes, and carried on a voluminous correspondence. With the board's agreement, he hired a clerk to assist with letter-writing and preparing reports, tasks that his wife had been doing for $40 a month. The clerk's duties were so complex and varying that Bloss had no idea of the time involved.[27]

Tenure for the president and faculty in the first years under state jurisdiction was arbitrary, based on annual "elections," practices dating to the M.E. Church, South, and the Corvallis College Board of Trustees. When the board of regents adopted similar procedures, the faculty was unhappy. The board required college instructors and experiment station staff to sign letters agreeing to salary and to approve—as horticulturist George Coote did when his contract was renewed in June 1892—that they could "be removed at a moment's notice if the Regents see fit to do so." If the "Honorable" regents thought this system was just, Coote requested that his college-owned residence be repaired "before winter sets in." Mechanical arts professor Grant Covell signed his reappointment with a brief note—"the condition as very unjust and arbitrary." Moses Craig of the experiment station replied to the regents: "In compliance with your requirement, I now say that I accept the condition."[28]

A troubling case with the annual election of faculty involved station chemist G. W. Shaw, the object of a regents directive to revise his responsibilities to devote more time to experimental activities. Shaw wanted to know the reasons for the change—was the board "satisfied with his management of the department as it formerly existed?" Because his teaching responsibilities had curtailed his work at the station, he wanted to know if the adjustment was "permanent or temporary." Three months later Shaw requested, for reasons "*vital to myself and family*," an early decision about his election to the faculty. He asked for the board's support before their June meeting. Although the documents reveal nothing about the issue, Shaw continued as a member of the faculty and chemist at the station. When the board elected H. B. Miller (one of its own) to succeed Bloss as president in August 1896, his appointment was "subject to removal at any time during the year, at the pleasure of the Board."[29]

If a case can be made that today's Oregon State University's male and female faculty still carry pay differentials, that disparity has a long history, dating from the appointment of Margaret Snell, the institution's first woman professor. Elected in 1889 as professor of household economy and hygiene, Snell soon concluded that her department did not meet with the regent's approval, because they had never elevated her unit "to the same rank with other professions, with the same salary of sixteen hundred [dollars]." Snell, who took great pride in her department, protested that her salary and the funds for her department's work were "rated at $200.00 or less than the salaries of beardless youths." Snell hoped the board would share her "indignation that the State holds her daughters (one third of the school) in such

Hired in 1889, Margaret Snell (1843–1923) was Oregon Agricultural College's first woman professor. She established the Department of Household Economy and Hygiene, a major that became a four-year program as Oregon Agricultural College expanded its curricular offerings. Snell also forcefully addressed inequities in salaries between men and women. Courtesy of the OSU Special Collections and Archives Research Center.

light esteem." Writing at length about the virtues of educated women, she asked the board to judge "her fitness to carry on work similar to what she had been doing in other schools."[30]

Morrill Act colleges and universities formed professional organizations to represent their interests to Congress and the US Department of Agriculture. With the approach of Chicago's great Columbian Exposition in the summer of 1893, George W. Atherton—founder of the Association of American Agricultural Colleges and Experiment Stations (and president of Pennsylvania State College)—coordinated an effort to organize exhibits to celebrate the work of land-grant institutions. Oregon's part in the undertaking was complicated when President Arnold died and Atherton's correspondence went unanswered. H. T. French, acting director of the experiment station, picked up the lapsed communication thread and asked the organizers about the nature of the exhibit, space limitations, and expenses. The matter lingered into early 1893, when another exhibit organizer urged the Corvallis school to participate.[31]

The Columbian Exposition's Cooperative College Exhibit invited "objects attractive to the eye"—photographs, maps, charts, apparatus, models, drawings, specimens, and books—which would be on loan for the duration of the exhibition. Institutions were to limit expenses for preparing exhibits to $200. True to its mission, Oregon Agricultural College chose an experiment station project in which students had been gathering insects indigenous to the state, including codling moths, injurious to fields and orchards. The college shipped three boxes of two thousand insects to Chicago in May. The Oregon Department of Agriculture also sent exhibits to Chicago—jars of grain, sacks of wheat, and twenty-five thousand pamphlets of its publication, *Resources of Oregon*, with the objective of attracting more settlers. The *Chicago Tribune* praised Oregon's displays of fruit, "monster pears, quinces, plums, peaches, apricots, cherries and grapes."[32]

As part of their responsibilities, federal law required land-grant schools to offer military instruction to students, although it was not clear if this was legally mandatory.[33] Until the state took control of the agricultural college, its participation with the military requirement appears to have been episodic, limited to army officers assigned to the Corvallis campus who conducted drills for students. Captain Benjamin Boswell taught military science from 1873 to 1876, with President Arnold assuming the duties until 1884. Because Arnold taught other courses in addition to his administrative responsibilities, military drill was probably not a priority. Beginning in 1888, the War Department asked if the college wished to host a detail of campus troops, the responsibilities of which required room and board for an officer. The college would be responsible for selecting a lieutenant and arranging for rifles and other equipment. If the college applied for a detail, it was to list several officers, ranking them in preference. An important change occurred during the presidency of John Bloss—cadets were outfitted with blue uniforms in lieu of the old Confederate gray.[34]

The college's regular faculty continued to handle military instruction until the institution obtained the services of Lieutenant C. E. Dentler in the fall of 1894. During his first year heading the military department, Dentler led a class of forty-three students through infantry exercises and a series of lectures on military-related subjects—duties of guards and sentinels, army regulations, the use of troops in enforcing public laws,[35] defending against infantry fire, and recitations on military discipline. Bloss praised Dentler's accomplishments but worried that he had to hold military drills in hallways and unoccupied rooms during western Oregon's long rainy season. Aware of the need for a larger building, the president initiated the process of constructing an armory on campus.[36]

The control regents exercised over Oregon Agricultural College would surprise faculty and administrators in later years. The board "selected" the faculty, set their salaries and workload, and oversaw minute purchases, including books for the college library. Wallis Nash, the most active member of the regents, wrote President H. B. Miller in August 1896—in the midst of the climactic presidential race between William McKinley and William Jennings Bryan—that it would be advisable to purchase good books on "the money and social questions." Because the president and board were responsible for the library, Nash urged Miller to seek bids from a Boston bookseller for bulk purchases. The faculty should make suggestions for book purchases, with the president and regents' library committee making the final decisions.[37]

In their annual reports to the US Department of Agriculture, OAC presidents always credited the board of regents for campus improvements. Thomas Gatch, who assumed the presidency in 1897, reported to the secretaries of agriculture and interior that "the Regents furnished new well-lighted quarters for the physical laboratory." A new dairy building was outfitted in similar fashion, including a modern butter-making machine. In its deliberations, the board frequently referred to "ownership" of the college and its grounds, a point of reference dating to the transfer of the college farm to the state in 1888. The regents' report for 1889 mentions "the conveyance of the farm to the State board of regents," placing the board in possession of the property.[38]

The decade of the 1890s witnessed the nation's first significant industrial depression (1893–1896), the important presidential election of 1896 over the money question, and the Spanish-American War (1898) that took the lives of 3,289 US servicemen—2,957 of them from disease. The depression began in the banking sector in the spring of 1893—with international ramifications related to the price of silver—and spread quickly across the United States. When a Multnomah County financial institution closed that summer, the *Oregonian* blamed "Eastern money interests" for the failure. With credit tightening and loans being called in, the conservative *Oregonian* feared that "fools and demagogues" backing the silver standard would sap the financial foundations of the country.[39] The nation's troubled agricultural economy in the early 1890s also fostered the emergence of a powerful reform movement, the People's Party, or Populists.

Although Oregon was distant from eastern banking houses, the effects of the economic crisis were palpable. Falling wages in the industrial East found its counterpart in Oregon's agricultural, lumber, and mining districts, where prices for food, lumber, and metal products plummeted. Portland's Oregon National Bank and the Northwest Loan and Trust Company closed in July 1893, tying up Multnomah County funds. The shuttering of the banks created a run on other houses, causing them to close. In Corvallis, the banking house of Hamilton, Job, and Company suspended business in mid-June and went into receivership. The Corvallis *Gazette* reported that the bank's closure was the "first failure in the state since the panic began." Attempting to put a positive spin on Oregon's banking difficulties, the newspaper reported that similar bank closures in Washington state had been of short duration.[40]

The depression's most telling effects on the agricultural college are reflected in the institution's report to the legislature in 1897. Although lawmakers had been appropriating $5,000 annually to the college, "during the three years past," regents' president J. T. Apperson reported, "no part of this last named sum has been received from the State." Apperson compared the state's agricultural college with legislative appropriations in California and Washington and found Oregon wanting. Comparing Oregon with eastern states indicated an even greater disparity, what Apperson referred to as the "undeveloped State of Oregon." He acknowledged, however, the difficulty in placing additional tax burdens on citizens to bring the college into parity with wealthier states. At the same time, college and station buildings needed repairs to maintain the integrity of the properties. Apperson pointed out that Oregon's experiment station ranked twenty-seventh among its peers in the number of station staff and faculty.[41]

There were other indicators of the depression's effects on the college. The institution had been in the midst of a growth spurt in the early 1890s, with steady increases in enrollment, from ninety students in 1888–1889 to 283 in 1892–1893. Those numbers reversed in the next two academic years: 240 students in 1893–1894 and 261 students in 1894–1895. Registrations for 1895–1896, however, increased sharply, to 397. Other residual effects of the depression were associated with the failure of Hamilton, Job, and Company, where the college kept its accounts. When the bank closed, the institution lost $10,510, funds representing legislative appropriations for the college. Federal monies designated for the college and station were accounted for, despite the bank's suspension.[42]

An exhausted John Bloss left Corvallis in the summer of 1896 for his Iowa farm, where he lived until his death in 1905. During his presidency, campus buildings doubled from two to four, and by the time he left office, the nation's economy had righted itself. Agricultural and wood-products prices were up, and resource-dependent states like Oregon had returned to a modicum of prosperity. The improved economic environment benefitted the agricultural college, with student enrollments increasing and building plans once again assuming priority. The institution welcomed its fifth president, Ohio-born Thomas Gatch, in 1897. The new executive was experienced, having held several academic appointments in California, Washington, and Oregon and served as president of Willamette University (1859–1865 and 1870–1880) and the University of Washington (1887–1895) before accepting the Corvallis position. His tenure as president spanned nearly ten years of relatively stable support for the college.[43]

Regents' president J. T. Apperson set the tone for returning prosperity, calling 1898 "one of the most prosperous in the history of this institution." Student enrollment had recovered from the depression to reach an all-time high of 440 men and women. President Gatch, however, pointed to problems with the closure of the college's Preparatory Department, citing graduates from "country schools" who were ill-prepared to succeed at the next level. Because students from rural schools were often deficient in English, he proposed a "sub-freshman class," where English grammar would be required. Looking to the future, he thought Oregon Agricultural College would become "the great industrial school of the Pacific coast." Although classics and cultural inquiries belonged to the state university, "industrial studies belong particularly to us."[44]

Following practices at other schools, Gatch asked the faculty in 1897 to draft rules "to govern the athletic interests of the college" and to coordinate with other schools in the state. The Alumni Association had already expressed interest in requiring students to pay incidental fees to participate in athletics (one dollar for male students and fifty cents for females). The association required that "athletes bearing the colors and name of the Oregon Agricultural College shall be of good moral character," have passing grades, and be enrolled as students. Participants should meet all expenses and could not participate if they had been excused from military drill or campus work.[45]

In correspondence with the Department of Interior's Bureau of Education, Gatch learned that the Second Morrill Act (1890) funds could be used to hire faculty to teach pharmacy courses. The bureau's commissioner, W. T. Harris, reported that pharmacy could be considered a natural science and, therefore, a special branch of chemistry and botany. Federal support for pharmacy was fortuitous, because the college had just created a pharmacy department and, responding to requests from Oregon druggists, now enrolled twenty students. The college established a four-year pharmacy degree in 1898, an advanced program at the time, because most pharmacy training required only two years.[46]

Because the Morrill Act required land-grant colleges and universities to participate in military drill programs, the land-grants preceded other institutions in offering training for military service. The schools, therefore, were never insular, isolated from regional, national, or international events. The depression of the 1890s and the Spanish-American War exemplified how events in distant places affected life on small rural campuses. The war with Spain was rooted in a decadent empire struggling to suppress a revolt in colonial Cuba, a phenomenon that captivated the American public. When the battleship *Maine* mysteriously blew up in Havana Harbor on February 15, 1898, killing 266 US sailors, President William McKinley demanded action and Congress authorized armed intervention.[47]

Oregon's proximity to Pacific waters meant that troops (including agricultural college cadets) would be called into action to seize the Philippines, the most distant colony in Spain's oceanic empire. Although the number of Oregon servicemen involved in the war would pale beside the great conflicts of the twentieth century, the state's all-volunteer forces still numbered several hundred. At OAC's commencement exercises in June 1898, the audience applauded when it was announced that two members of the graduating class were serving in the Philippines. Although the US Navy quickly dispatched aging Spanish ships in Manila Harbor, US forces soon confronted a very different conflict when Emilio Aguinaldo and Philippine insurgents resisted the incursion of American troops.[48]

Harvey McAlister was among the Oregon Agricultural College enlistees who returned home in September 1899 with an injured buddy who he suspected would be crippled for life. When an *Oregonian* reporter asked him if the Philippines were "worth holding on to," McAlister answered in the affirmative. In a prophetic foretelling of American views of future insurgencies in foreign lands, he portrayed Aguinaldo's forces as treacherous: "When our men take a town, they go on to the next, and the insurgents fall in behind, having hidden their arms in the outskirts."[49] The United States would face similar circumstances following the Second World War, especially in Vietnam, when its forces would be in the midst of populations where it was difficult to distinguish between friend and enemy.

Among the causalities of the Philippine intervention was Captain Woodbridge Geary, a former instructor in military tactics at the agricultural college, who was honored with a memorial service at the Corvallis Opera House. Beyond the celebrations for returning veterans and memorials for those who died, there were occasional stories about officers who paid little attention to the comfort of their troops. To make matters worse, the army's Salem recruiting office reported that members of the Second Oregon Volunteers—just returned from the Philippines—were refusing to reenlist. Less heralded, and receiving scant notice in newspapers, were the atrocious number of enlistees who died far from the battlefield, most of them from food poisoning, yellow fever, or malaria. The agricultural college made provisions for returning veterans who petitioned to earn credit for course work they did not complete. The college gave them credit providing they had passing grades for the time they had attended class. In addition, returning veterans success-fully petitioned to be excused from military duties during their remaining time in college.[50]

The onset of the twentieth century witnessed the continued growth of Oregon Agricultural College. The school dedicated its new Mechanical Hall on June 30, 1900, following a fire that destroyed the old building. The new two-story structure was designed to accommodate a large number of students. Con-struction crews also completed the armory/gymnasium, a building suited for gym classes and to house military drill exercises. In the introduction to his annual report for 1900, board of regents' president J. T. Apperson enthused about "one of the most prosperous years in the history of this institution," with enrollment reaching an all-time high. If the trend continued, the col-lege would need another building equivalent to Mechanical Hall, improved greenhouses, a new heating plant, and new "closets" (toilets) connected to the sewer system. Apperson closed his statement with a tribute to "the People's school," a matter of personal satisfaction to one "having had connection with this Board since its organization."[51]

Apperson's "People's college" had experienced more than a decade of growth and maturity since the state assumed control of the institution. Still heading the board of regents, Apperson pointed to the college's advances since 1888. Under the old regime (1868 to 1888), the institution had graduated ninety students (twenty-nine women and sixty-one men). In thirteen years under the board of regents, the college awarded degrees to 133 women and 173 men, all of whom took a more rigorous curriculum. The 380 surviving gradu-ates were "living monuments [to] the work of this college." Taking his cue from President Gatch's report, Apperson predicted the college would be the foremost "agricultural and industrial school of the State of Oregon." The 436 students enrolled for the academic year ending in 1901 indicated the school's growing popularity.[52]

The college's annual reports reveal interesting data beyond enrollments. For the collegiate year ending in 1902, the school enrolled 488 students (321 men and 167 women). The students' parental backgrounds revealed that 71 percent were farmers, 10 percent were mechanics and day laborers, 8 percent were merchants and capitalists, and 11 percent belonged to the professions and other occupations.

The report estimated that 80 percent of students returned to the farm or workshop after graduation. Except for room and board, their education was free—"free tuition, free library, free magazines, free printing, free diplomas, free commencements—everything is free." The administration, however, sought incidental fees to offset other expenses during the college year. To resolve athletic funding problems, students agreed to tax themselves in the fall of 1901 to support sports programs, although those who skirted the voluntary obligation paid nothing.[53]

Other traditions carried over to the twentieth century, especially farmers' institutes, which continued to thrive. The experiment station sponsored nineteen institutes in 1903, with attendance reaching 3,255. One farmer's institute in Holly (outside Sweet Home) attracted some three hundred people. The audience was appreciative, the *Oregonian* reported, of the great work the college was doing for agriculture. James Withycombe, director of the experiment station, accepted words of welcome in Holly and predicted a prosperous future for the region. Withycombe later joined others in delivering lectures on plants, animals, the influence of railroads in agriculture, milk tests, and crop rotation, cautioning farmers to avoid purchasing seed from eastern sales companies.[54]

The Corvallis experiment station's successes suggested the need for a similar station in a climatic zone with varying diurnal and seasonal temperatures. The college eventually purchased 620 acres near the town of Union in eastern Oregon in 1901. The legislative appropriation included funds for constructing and furnishing buildings. From its inception, the eastern Oregon station focused on draining and irrigating valley bottomlands for grazing livestock. Other programs carried out in the first years involved improving the breeds of cattle, sheep, hogs, and draft horses.[55]

On the Corvallis campus, however, the title "Agricultural College" seemed a misnomer to many people, because the institution was much more than a school of agriculture. Timothy Davenport, the sage of Silverton—medical doctor, teacher, and legislator—observed that critics grumbled because many of the college's students were not studying agriculture. Davenport called the college "a modified polytechnic school," its annual catalogue showing ratios of academic majors that "correspond to the wants of society." If the expected incomes for mechanical and electrical engineering paid better than farming, Davenport concluded, one could expect students to follow that logic in choosing academic majors. From the classical institution of the 1870s, the college was now a school of agriculture and the mechanical arts.[56]

The two-story brick-and-stone Agricultural Hall, completed in 1902, was touted to be the finest building on campus. The regents were pleased with the local experiment station, especially the valuable additions to its Jersey and Shorthorn herds and flocks of Cotswold and Shropshire sheep. The board praised the working relationship between the station and ranchers, dairymen, and sheep owners. The station's bacteriologist assured buyers that milk coming directly from the cow contained no contaminants. The board's one area of concern was strengthening the Department of Household Economy, and its need for more equipment.[57]

Because of its land-grant mandate, OAC operated on a variable revenue stream: state funds from interest on its land grant ($10,943 in 1904) and biennial legislative appropriations, the Morrill Act as amended in 1890 ($25,000), and the Hatch Act of 1887 ($15,000). There were limitations on federal support, however, because Morrill funds were restricted to classroom teaching and Hatch Act appropriations were to maintain buildings and grounds and for investigative work at the experiment station. Since the presidency of John Bloss, administrators had carefully used funds in compliance with the law. The regents reported in 1904 that federal support was "sufficient to pay salaries and the ordinary expenses of the college." The state, on the other hand, was responsible for buildings, equipment, and furnishings necessary to enable the college and station to function smoothly.[58]

Despite lively construction activity, enrollment increases during the remainder of President Gatch's tenure placed continuing pressure on the need for more buildings. Table 1.1 indicates student numbers that nearly tripled between 1902 and 1909. Enrollment of the 1,156 students at the end of the 1908 academic year represented every Oregon county, twenty states, and two foreign countries. That explosive growth had consequences in a student–faculty ratio greater than most other land-grant schools, despite the college's growing faculty (forty in 1906–1907 and seventy-seven in 1908–1909). Although the national association of land-grant schools recommended a student–faculty

Table 1.1. Student Enrollment, 1902–1909

Year Ending	Enrollment	Year Ending	Enrollment
1902	480	1906	735
1903	541	1907	835
1904	530	1908	1,156
1905	680	1909	1,351

Table 1.2. Student–Faculty Ratio for Land-Grant Institutions, 1908–1909

California	11.2
Cornell (NY)	10.3
Illinois	12.0
Indiana	12.1
Iowa	16.9
Kansas	19.0
Massachusetts	9.8
Montana	8.4
Washington	16.6

ratio of about fifteen to one, OAC administrators projected twenty-eight students to every teacher for 1908–1909. Table 1.2 provides comparable figures for other land-grant institutions. The average for all land-grant colleges and universities at the close of 1907 was 11.5 students per faculty.[59]

Athletics began to appear regularly in the regents annual reports in the early twentieth century. The board's president praised the success of the college track and field team when it returned to Corvallis with a trophy from an indoor meet at Columbia University in April 1914. The college prided its academic requirements, demanding more than course work in agriculture, mechanical arts, and household economy. The institution wanted to provide students with "a thorough knowledge of the sciences, literature and art," an educational background that would "make of them truly men and women of solid worth." The board's report for 1906 was emphatic: "To educate the youth of the state to be good citizens, capable of performing all the duties devolving upon them as members of the community." To better serve students, the college added courses in agronomy, poultry husbandry, veterinary science, and industrial pedagogy, the latter directed to prepare students for public school teaching. The college organized its departments into schools at the end of the 1907 academic year: agriculture, domestic science and art, engineering and mechanical arts, and commerce. Retiring president Thomas Gatch passed this organizational structure to his successor in January 1907.[60]

By all accounts, President Gatch was in excellent health when he retired at age seventy-three. With resolutions of commendation from the board of regents, Governor George Chamberlain, and the *Oregonian* for "distinguished service," Gatch taught for a short time and then retired to his home near Seattle.[61] A storm of controversy followed the appointment of his successor,

William Jasper Kerr, criticisms that did not subside until the Kerr family moved to Corvallis in the summer of 1907. The dispute centered around Mormonism and rumors (they were true) that Kerr, the former president of the Agricultural College of Utah in Logan, had been a polygamist. And there was more. When the college announced Kerr's appointment, its news release stated that "Dr. W. J. Kerr" would be the institution's new chief executive. Kerr, a recipient of an honorary doctorate from the Mormon General Church Board of Education in 1898, held a bachelor's degree from the University of Utah and had earned only a handful of graduate credits. Even his Utah critics, however, admitted that Kerr possessed outstanding, if sometimes overweening, administrative talents.[62]

Although Kerr reportedly had disavowed his Mormon faith, the rumor mill abounded with insinuations following the regent's decision. Kerr, indeed, had plural wives for a time: Lenora, his first wife, and, later, Lois Morehead from Smithfield, Utah. Two children, a boy and girl, were born to the latter marriage, a union that ended in a church divorce two years before he became president of the Agricultural College of Utah in 1890. Fearing that rumors would prompt the regents to reverse their decision, Kerr asked Utah friends to intervene on his behalf. L. A. Ostien, who taught at Utah's agricultural college, wrote E. E. Wilson of the regents that Kerr's dual marriage was a system that was "then in vogue here," but was "an incident of youth." Kerr should be praised for breaking with such traditions. Newton Clemenson, a Presbyterian pastor, urged departing president Gatch to ignore Mormon criticisms of Kerr, because a few critics would like to see him dismissed from the Oregon job. There were Oregon detractors as well, most notably Eugene newspapers, who joined in denunciations against Kerr. As two historians suggest, the Eugene papers used Kerr's appointment as a political issue that would discredit the college and benefit the university.[63] Kerr survived those challenges and remained chief executive of the college for twenty-five years.

Kerr inherited a modernizing institution of departments organized into schools, many offering sophisticated degree programs. The college still confronted difficulties, especially rural districts without high schools, whose students were interested in technical training. The board of regents spoke for President Kerr when it cited the need for more land and buildings in its 1908 report. The administration building was inadequate for its purpose, and the Armory, designed to accommodate up to 330 men for drill, was outdated for the current enrollment of some eight hundred cadets. Kerr's path also crossed with Margaret Comstock Snell, who had announced her retirement but agreed to stay on as dean of household science and hygiene until 1908. As the college's first woman professor, Snell had completed twenty years at the institution.[64]

Like President Bloss before him, Kerr assumed the presidency just as Congress passed another land-grant bill, the Nelson Amendment to the Agricultural Appropriations Act of 1907. The measure provided annual increases of $5,000 for five years until the sum reached $50,000 "for the more complete endowment and maintenance of agricultural colleges." The legislation included wording similar to the Morrill Act of 1862, to provide "courses for the special preparation of instructors for teaching . . . agriculture and the mechanic arts." With ambitious building plans pending, the Nelson funds—designated solely for teaching—would maximize legislative appropriations for construction projects. The expanded federal largesse prompted one Corvallis student to write the *Oregonian*: "The Oregon Agricultural College is a Government as well as a State institution."[65]

President Kerr's first biennial report[66] addressed questions about the college's policies and organization and its courses of study. The new president paid homage to the rich federal endowment providing incentives to fund new buildings and to increase operating expenses for the college and experiment station. Kerr reflected that land-grant institutions should "promote the liberal and practical education, primarily of the industrial classes—to apply science in the industries of life." Military training was required, and instruction in classical subjects was not to be excluded. The president emphasized courses important to a liberal education: English, literature, history, political science, and knowledge of modern languages "to keep in touch with the scientific development of at least one foreign country."[67]

In response to Kerr's requests, the Oregon legislature funded an advanced heating plant with concrete tunnels and machinery. The structure's location along the railroad tracks on the south side of campus enabled the easy delivery of fuel. A new four-story, brick agricultural building would be ready to house classes and laboratories in September 1910. The legislature also appropriated $20,000 to purchase additional land for other projects. During Kerr's tenure, legislators regularly supported construction projects, while increasing enrollments suggested an unlimited future for the college. Like other public colleges and universities, obsessions with growth periodically visited the Corvallis institution. College administrators touted with pride that its campus was the State of Oregon, and that its students represented every county in Oregon and many states and territories. Beyond students resident in Corvallis, others enrolled in correspondence courses, did extension work, or took short courses.[68]

Of the institution's 134 faculty in 1912, forty-five had attended OAC. Twenty-six faculty had attended other colleges and universities. Most of those below the master's level worked part time as shop and laboratory assistants and were progressing toward more advanced degrees. Faculty held advanced degrees from other institutions including the University of Chicago (seventeen), Cornell (fifteen), University of Illinois (eleven), University of California (ten), Harvard (ten), and Iowa State (eight). Most faculty took part in the college's three principal activities—teaching, research, and extension—with the extension department responsible for bringing the work of the college to the citizens of the state.[69]

At the end of the first decade of the twentieth century, Oregon Agricultural College had made advances in curriculum, restructured its administration, and raised standards for entering freshmen. In an important initiative for the future, the administration created a four-year forestry degree in 1906 and established a Department of Forestry in 1910. The college established a committee on advanced graduate degrees to accommodate its expanding graduate programs. With schools of agriculture, commerce, engineering, and domestic science, the college was at one with other land-grant colleges and universities. In a move to direct curriculum at OAC and the University of Oregon, the Oregon legislature created the State Board of Higher Curricula in 1909. No legislative measure would have a greater influence in shaping the direction and mission of the college and university for the next two decades. The Board of Higher Curricula set in motion more than a half century of internecine conflict between the Corvallis and Eugene schools over curriculum development and degree programs.

3
In War and Peace

The City of Corvallis joined the modern urban world in 1910 when it began paving local streets to eliminate clouds of dust in summer and the predictable mud when the seasonal rains returned in the fall. Improvements to the city's infrastructure paralleled a population increase, from 1,819 in 1900 to 4,552 in 1910. New building on campus, including the eighty-five-thousand-square-foot Armory, coincided with similar activity in the city, with the business district gravitating westward from Second to Fourth Street. The Corvallis Hotel, the city's hallmark at the corner of Second and Monroe, was extensively remodeled and reopened as the Julian Hotel (under the ownership of Julian McFadden). Other signs of modernity in the community included women gaining access to the ballot in 1912 and Corvallis voters passing a bond measure to build a bridge over the Willamette River (completed in 1913).[1]

The new bridge provided quick passage for horse-drawn carriages and wagons and a noticeable increase in automobile traffic to and from the

The first bridge across the Willamette River in Corvallis, the 249-foot-long Van Buren Street Bridge opened in 1913. Funded with state support and a Corvallis bond measure, the bridge provided two-way vehicular traffic with a sidewalk on its south side. Courtesy of the Benton County Historical Society.

city. The mid-valley's attractions were multiple: grain production on the old prairie lands, hop yards north and south of town, and Corvallis itself, as one brochure advertised, with "more phones per capita than any town its size in the U.S." The community's economic mainstay, Oregon Agricultural College, possessed many of the conveniences of the state's metropolis, Portland, whose population reached 207,214 in 1910. With its efficient heating plant, power house to generate electricity, stone and brick buildings, and paved walkways, the college was in the midst of a growth surge that would continue until the financial collapse and soaring unemployment of the Great Depression.[2]

The college celebrated the opening of academic year 1910 with twenty-one new faculty, four new buildings, and additional equipment for laboratories and classrooms. Among the new hires, Dr. J. F. Morcl, from universities in Belgium and Paris, would oversee the new Department of Veterinary Science, and H. S. Marks, a Cornell graduate, would fill a position in mechanical engineering. The new structures included Agricultural Hall, a brick-and-stone four-story building with over forty classrooms, laboratories, and offices. The impressive thirty-six-thousand-square-foot, steel-reinforced-concrete Armory provided unobstructed space for military drills. A heating plant for buildings on the south side of campus and greenhouses rounded out the new physical structures.[3]

The Morrill Acts (1862 and 1890), the Hatch Act (1887), and the Smith-Lever Act (1914) provide the legislative framework for the major functions of today's land-grant colleges and universities. Although new and innovative, the Smith-Lever Cooperative Extension Act reflected work already being carried out at many land-grant colleges. Like many such institutions, Oregon Agricultural College was doing extension work well before Congress passed the Smith-Lever Act. The institution's original mission—instruction in agriculture and the mechanical arts—and the addition of its agricultural experiment station in 1888, implied public outreach, disseminating scientific knowledge to horticulturalists, dairy and row-crop farmers, growers of wheat and other grains, cattle ranchers, and homes and families.[4]

Salem's *Capital Journal* observed in 1911 that the agricultural college provided service to people across the state "and not for the privileged few who can attend classes on the campus." The newspaper praised President William Jasper Kerr for the college's "instruction in rural districts [and] public demonstrations of the best methods of agriculture for farmers who cannot attend college courses." The college assisted thousands of people through bulletins and circulars addressing various problems. The institution's extension work had grown to the point that it was "necessary to organize a separate department" to carry on the work. The *Journal* applauded farmers' institutes and demonstration trains as "traveling schools of agriculture constantly in the field."[5]

President Kerr was an early and passionate advocate for extension programs, seeking to advance them when he was still in Utah. In his first report to the board of regents, he recommended expanding extension programs to bring farmers "up-to-date information on agricultural subjects." If the college was to carry out its service mission, the extension unit should be equal "in rank with the Experiment Station." Although no formal extension division existed when the college began sponsoring farmers' institutes, those activities were intended to bring scientific expertise to the people. With a passion for statistics, Kerr cited national data to underscore the importance of outreach to farmers. Before Smith-Lever, therefore, Oregon Agricultural College was actively supporting extension functions—institutes, publications, correspondence courses, demonstration farms and orchards, and subjects related to household economy.[6]

The *Oregonian* praised land-grant institutions for being inclusive rather than exclusive, applauding the University of Wisconsin for "carrying education to the people." Wisconsin's faculty were "pilgrims . . . sallying forth to almost every village in the state with their treasures of knowledge." The innovative extension movements were centers of light, creating "new life for a great commonwealth." The *Oregonian* congratulated President Kerr, who "asks the legislature for means to . . . carry his good work to the people everywhere." More than any other class of people, the newspaper concluded, farmers deserved the best the agricultural colleges could deliver.[7]

President Kerr appointed H. D. Hetzel to direct the newly created extension department in September 1911, with responsibilities divided into five units: "(1) Institutes, Itinerate Schools, and Demonstration Trains; (2) Correspondence Courses, (3) Junior and Senior Improvement Organizations; (4) News and Exhibits; and (5) Demonstration Farms."[8] The president's strategy reached beyond agriculture to engineering, industrial, and civic courses. He asked the dean of the School of Agriculture and the directors of the experiment station and extension to coordinate their areas of responsibility. Experiment station director James Withycombe later recommended a modification of extension's responsibilities, suggesting that it have charge of all outreach other than work done on campus or "the Experimental work at the Station."[9]

Because extension programs were already operating in several states, the Smith-Lever Act provided a clearinghouse to publicize "useful and practical information on subjects related to agriculture and home economics."

Kerr praised Smith-Lever as "the most constructive educational measure ever adopted by the United States Government."[10] It was President Theodore Roosevelt's Commission on Country Life that recommended adding "a third coordinating branch" to the divisions of teaching and research in land-grant colleges. The third branch—extension—would be important to land-grant institutions, the commission reported, "without which, no college of agriculture can adequately serve its State." The commission overstated its proposal, because Oregon Agricultural College and many other institutions were already fully engaged in extension work.[11]

Southern congressmen and senators shaped the Smith-Lever bill, like the Second Morrill Act of 1890, to meet the requirements of segregated institutions in the Old South, leaving the distribution of funding to state legislatures. The sponsors of the legislation—Senator Hoke Smith of Georgia and Congressman Asbury Lever of South Carolina—stipulated that funds would be allocated according to each state's farm population, which meant that the bulk of extension funding would go to the rural and agricultural South. Before the bill was sent to the Senate, Congressman Lever attached an amendment that allowed Southern states to direct Smith-Lever funds to white institutions only. The language of Lever's amendment was clearly race-based: "In any state in which two or more such colleges have been . . . established, the appropriation hereinafter made to such State shall be administered by such college or colleges, as the legislature of such State may direct." This seemingly innocuous wording meant that the measure excluded black land-grant colleges in the South. As Mississippi senator James Vardaman argued, agricultural extension programs should be carried out by "the Anglo-Saxon, the man of proven judgment, initiative, wisdom, and experience."[12]

Although Oregon experienced problems in obtaining matching funds for Smith-Lever appropriations when parsimonious state legislators temporarily refused to support extension in 1915, its programs would endure with the passage of time into a major component of land-grant college work. OAC's extension service considered support for agriculture and home economics its most important endeavors. With a full-time staff of sixty-five, extension published bulletins and circulars for farmers and supported county agents in activities such as assisting the Farm Bureau with land reclamation and soil improvement. A popular extension program was supporting county-level boys' and girls' clubs, subsequently known as the 4-H.[13]

Despite the disruptions of the Great War in Europe and America joining the conflict in April 1917, extension activities continued uninterrupted, its staff cooperating with organizations sponsoring one-day "schools" on a variety of topics. Extension personnel spoke at high school commencement exercises, served as judges at county fairs, and instructed at "Farmers Week" gatherings. Because of the influenza epidemic in 1919, extension postponed its annual Farmers' and Homemakers' Week at the college until early 1920, when more than eight hundred people attended. Agents promoted county-level agricultural improvement programs that varied across the state depending on agricultural specialties. Extension assisted in organizing branches of the Farm Bureau to promote agricultural and home economics programs.[14] Later in the century this intermingling of the public and private would invite criticisms from environmental organizations.

Although there were no open declarations of war between the older agricultural experiment station and the upstart extension service, station director James Withycombe strived to clarify lines of responsibility. The problem was overlapping boundaries of teaching, research, and outreach. In a memorandum to Kerr, Withycombe asked that funds be clearly segregated between the college and station. Too many experiment station staff were "consumed in College work" to the detriment of research, he complained; moreover, many station people were doing extension work. Withycombe's concerns were overlapping jurisdictions involving several operations—agronomy, dairy husbandry, and animal husbandry.[15]

After the official launch of extension, college administrators classified the faculty into three groups: resident instructors, experiment station, and extension. At the end of academic year 1914–1915, the college employed six deans, 129 faculty (from instructor to full professor), forty-five experiment station staff (twenty-seven taught part time or worked with extension) and thirty-three full-time extension staffers (with thirteen part-time instructors doing experiment station work). College faculty taught more than 3,200 students that year, a figure that included enrollees in short courses. In the School of Agriculture, enrollments in freshman and sophomore courses necessitated the division of some classes into sections, a development that would affect courses across campus in the coming years.[16] Faculty and students were also adjusting to the dictates of a jarring new reality, the Oregon State Board of Higher Curricula, the legislative oversight body established in 1909 with responsibilities for eliminating duplication of courses and majors in the state's two flagship institutions. That effort would initiate more than seventy years of contentious relations between the University of Oregon and Oregon Agricultural College and its successors.[17]

In an effort to solve higher education's ongoing funding problems, the state legislature passed a millage tax in 1913 with the hope of establishing permanent, reliable fiscal support for Oregon's public colleges and university. The initial House millage bill supporting the University of Oregon would levy a tax of three cents on every $100 of taxable property in the state. A companion measure would provide a levy of four cents of every $100 of taxable property for the agricultural college. The Senate approved both bills, and Governor Oswald West signed them into law. H. J. Parkison, a cost-conscious Portland activist, immediately promised to refer the university millage to voters. His larger objective, however, was to consolidate the two institutions on the Corvallis campus, arguing that there was "strong sentiment to abolish the university and have the college at Corvallis add such studies as conditions and the public demand."[18] The rationale behind his proposal was to deny support to the university and starve it into mediocrity.

Parkison and his allies formed the Oregon Higher Educational Betterment League in April 1913 and began gathering signatures to refer the millage tax to a public vote. The university's friends rallied quickly—forming the Oregon Citizens' Educational League—to fight the referendum. Its supporters included some of the state's leading banking and commercial organizations, and well-known newspaper editor Colonel E. Hofer, of Salem's *Capital Journal*.[19] During the petition drive, the *Medford Sun* accused the agricultural college of engaging in a stealth campaign to defund the university: "The truth about the O. A. C. should have been published, its political activities exposed, its padded statistics deflated and the people informed as to how little agricultural education is so expensively disseminated." Placing itself above the fray, the *Oregonian* observed that "a quarrel between the two institutions" would only help its real enemy, Parkison's Betterment League.[20]

The petition campaign was successful, and the measure to deny millage support to the university appeared on the ballot in November 1913 with another measure, a building repair fund and a new building appropriation for the university. Before voters went to the polls, the *Oregonian* declared the legislative appropriation "comparatively small" ($175,000) and badly needed to reduce the "cramped quarters" on the Eugene campus. Although consolidation was unlikely, the newspaper called the referendum to defund little more than "enmity toward the university." The Eugene institution's supporters easily turned back the effort to defund the university, and voters approved the building repair fund and the new building appropriation. Eugene Brookings, spokesperson for the Oregon Citizens' Educational League, cited the vote as confirmation that "the people of Oregon want our university maintained at Eugene."[21] The struggle over funding and consolidation was merely the opening salvo in events that would become increasingly bitter with the passing years.

The effort to defund the university was a mere sideshow to problems with millage funding. The ink was barely dry on the measure when its inadequacies became apparent. The agricultural college pointed out in 1916 that reduced state support for instruction and increased maintenance costs made it impossible to use millage funds for new buildings. The inadequacies of the millage continued to fester. In his report to the legislature in 1918, President Kerr asked lawmakers to supplement millage receipts, because current revenue was inadequate to meet enrollment increases, maintenance costs, and salaries and wages. By 1920, Kerr was adamant, declaring that millage income had decreased between 1915 and 1920.[22]

Enrollment increases after the First World War worsened matters and created emergency situations at the University of Oregon, Oregon Agricultural College, and the state normal school in Monmouth. Since passage of the millage measure, the college's enrollment had increased from 1,364 to 3,378 full-time students, and the University of Oregon's from 691 to 1,745. Appeals to the legislature finally convinced lawmakers to submit an increase of $1.26 million to voters in the May 1920 election. The voters' pamphlet declared that Oregon's colleges and university had "come to the end of their rope." Shortages of classrooms, abysmally low salaries, and delayed maintenance were critical issues. After a statewide publicity blitz, voters overwhelmingly approved the millage increase. When the results were final, the Corvallis *Daily Gazette-Times* reported a "Great Jolly-Up" on campus to celebrate the "auspicious occasion."[23]

Following the election, President Kerr wrote a lengthy letter to the US Bureau of Education explaining Oregon's campaign strategy. The approach was tactical, urging the governor to call the legislature into special session and then convincing lawmakers to place the levy on the May ballot. Because sentiment among voters "was strong that the burden of taxation had reached the limit," college and university supporters—for strategic reasons—conducted the campaign in the name of the alumni, with alums and friends of higher education footing the bill. Kerr described the publicity campaign—distributing nearly one million pieces of literature, placing advertisements in major newspapers, putting up posters, and sending speakers to commercial and fraternal organizations (including "four-minute speakers" used during the First World War to address theater audiences). The millage increase measure enjoyed the support of "practically the entire press of the state."[24]

The modest millage increase, however, did not resolve the funding issue. Administrators and legislators continued to grapple with strategies for stable financial support, with the Oregon Tax Reduction League the leading complainant about the tax burden on landed property. The league supported the millage tax until a member urged the organization to back a Grange income tax bill. Although league members differed over taxing options, some favored repealing the millage tax for the university and agricultural college. Finally, through a special election in November 1923, and by a bare majority (58,647 to 58,131), voters adopted a state income tax to replace the millage levy to support state services.[25]

President William Jasper Kerr's long tenure left an indelible imprint on Oregon Agricultural College. Most significant was the president's influence in shaping the campus physical environment. During his presidency (1907–1932), the college undertook an impressive construction program, putting up more than twenty buildings, including the Memorial Union. Even more significant to many observers, Kerr hired the famous Olmsted Brothers landscape architecture firm to provide strategic advice on what had been a helter-skelter approach to campus planning. John Charles Olmsted visited campus twice in 1909 and submitted a sixty-page report providing a detailed plan for campus development. The Olmsted proposal recommended an expanded and more sophisticated strategy that would honor the State of Oregon. The institution's growth would require additional land for buildings "to permit a more spacious and a more systematic and dignified disposition of buildings than that which a crowded condition would permit."[26]

Under "nomenclature," Olmsted recommended classifying dormitories as "houses" and classroom, administration, and laboratory structures as "halls." The Powerhouse, for example, might better be called the Power Plant under a more consistent appellation. The report cited the rapid expansion of agricultural colleges in the United States, suggesting they be called "technical colleges" because of their instruction in engineering and related fields. The Olmsted study included a range of technical programs—hydraulic engineering, bacteriology (related to municipal sanitation), applied chemistry, and physics. To improve the attractiveness of the campus, the report recommended a feature that is recognizable today: "For the sake of securing a dignified frontage and to open up the College to view from the city and from trains, the college grounds should be extended eastward the width of half a block to 9th St. and from Monroe southward to Jefferson Street."

Oregon State University's longest-serving president (1907–1932), William Jasper Kerr (1883–1947) oversaw a remarkable building program on campus, the establishment of the Extension Service, vastly expanded academic programs, and most significantly, the hiring of John Charles Olmsted (of the famous Olmsted Brothers' landscape designers) to draft plans that are still visible today in the campus footprint. Kerr became the first chancellor of the Oregon State System of Higher Education in 1932, serving until he retired in 1935. Courtesy of the OSU Special Collections and Archives Research Center.

The landscape on the eastern side of the campus should be "a system of walks, a public square" that would add to "the dignity and agreeableness of this approach to the college." The low wetland to the east should remain as an "imposing park meadow between the principal entrances and the buildings." In a less entertaining observation, the report noted that such a space afforded a means to keep at arm's length "the sordid and more or less ugly details of the city." The Olmsteds paid great attention to architectural agreement, citing "the lack of harmony between the different important buildings" on campus, which future designs should rectify. The remainder of the document addressed fire prevention, altering existing buildings, tree and shrub assemblages, and similar features.[27]

Although no blueprints or drawings accompanied the Olmsteds' document, college landscape architect Arthur Lee Peck used the report to prepare an illustrated drawing showing the location of campus quadrangles and existing and future buildings. The final piece in implementing the Olmsted plan was hiring building designer John V. Bennes to coordinate architectural unity among new and old structures. Bennes subsequently designed every building put up between 1909 and 1925. Bennes and his successor, A. C. Taylor (1926–1944), remained faithful to the Olmsted format. To honor their work, the National Register of Historic Places designated part of the Oregon State University campus a National Historic District in June 2008. University archivist Larry Landis describes President Kerr's decision to contract the Olmsted firm "a stroke of genius."[28]

The president was an attentive, hands-on administrator. Ten years into his presidency, he directed the institution's deans to hold biweekly faculty meetings to facilitate communication about department, school, and college issues: deans should be in touch with students to provide assistance; all administrators should "cultivate among the staff a spirit of institutional unity;" and deans should assure that students were enrolled in appropriate programs.[29]

President Kerr was popular on campus and in the community. When he returned to Corvallis from a visit to Kansas State Agricultural College in November 1917—where he had been offered the president's position—some two thousand people and the cadet band gave him a rousing ovation when his train arrived. The board of regents, alums, and faculty joined students and townspeople to greet the president when he stepped from the train into a downpour. Kerr followed a large escort to the men's gymnasium where master of ceremonies Dean George Peavy oversaw musical renditions and a series of addresses. Student-body president Theodore Cramer praised the president's friendship with students; Dean of Women Mary Fawcett applauded Kerr's "understanding of women's problems"; and board of regents president James Weatherford emphasized the high regard all Oregonians held for the president. Despite the warm reception, the president gave no indication of his decision.[30]

In the midst of those sensitive deliberations, Kerr faced a family crisis, traveling to Portland to meet a train carrying the body of his son, Horace, who had died in Denver. While the president attended to funeral arrangements, the business community, alums, and newspapers urged him to remain at the helm of the agricultural college. The *Oregonian* praised his educational leadership and acknowledged the difficulty of finding "the right man to take his place." Students returning on trains from Thanksgiving—to the accompaniment of ukulele and banjo—sang the refrain:

> Kansas Ag must choose a lesser light
> For we cannot lose you from the fight.
> Hail! hail! hail! hail!
> Chief of old O. A. C.

Because he enjoyed his work in Oregon, Kerr agreed to stay, and the regents raised his salary from $7,000 to $8,400 a year. Regents' president James

Weatherford thanked him for the "decided monetary sacrifice." (Kansas State had offered him $9,000 per annum.)[31]

As Oregon State University celebrates its sesquicentennial as a land-grant institution, the centerpiece to the campus—the Memorial Union building—is a monument to a long-ago conflict, known then as the Great War (1914–1918)[32], in which 113,000 American soldiers lost their lives (51,000 in battle, 62,000 from disease). President Kerr dedicated the Memorial Union in 1929 to those who gave "the fullest measure of their strength in *faithful service, heroic deeds,* and *noble sacrifices.*" The union building is a reminder that events external to college and university campuses have periodically disrupted academic life, whether during struggles with economic downturns or sending students and faculty to fight in foreign wars. America's first brief flight into oceanic conflict involving Spain and then the Filipino insurgency (1898–1900) was little more than a blur compared with the experiences associated with the Great War in Europe.[33]

Until the United States declared war on the Central Powers (Germany, Austria-Hungary, Bulgaria, and the Ottoman Empire) in April 1917, the violence in Europe had little effect on Oregon Agricultural College. When the conflict descended into bloody trench warfare in northern France, and German submarines began attacking American merchant ships bringing munitions and food supplies to beleaguered England, President Woodrow Wilson moved from professed neutrality to intervention. The president, who campaigned for a second term in 1916 under the catchphrase "He Kept Us Out of War," delivered his war message to Congress on April 2, 1917, declaring "the world must be made safe for democracy." Oregon's US senator Harry Lane was one of six members of the Senate to vote against the declaration of war.[34]

"War service" quickly disrupted college life when 204 male students left campus on April 27 for an Officers' Reserve Corps training camp at the Presidio in San Francisco. They were the first of more than two thousand students, alumni, faculty, and staff to join the military. During the biennium 1917–1918, 171 faculty resigned to join the war effort. When it was all over, more than 1,900 OAC-affiliated people had served in the military, with forty-nine students and two faculty paying with their lives. Of the two faculty deaths, Wendell Phillips, the college physician, died from influenza in October 1918 at Camp Lee in Virginia. The other, Mark Middlekauff, an assistant professor of bacteriology who joined the Aviation Service, died when his plane crashed just before the Armistice.[35] The two faculty deaths—one from disease and the other in battle—reflected national statistics indicating a slightly higher percentage of deaths attributed to illness, most from food poisoning.

The war had a significant influence on campus life. Because Germany's submarine campaign had sent thousands of tons of foodstuffs to the bottom of the Atlantic, the US Food Administration urged the public to conserve food and to increase production. Along with other land-grant colleges in the West, President Kerr pushed an accelerated food program in Oregon, urging students to volunteer for military service or to help with food production during the emergency. Students withdrawing from classes for the latter purpose would be treated equal to those entering the military.[36]

Under Herbert Hoover, the Food Administration promoted several voluntary initiatives. One of them, the War Garden Movement—"Every Garden a Munitions Plant"—involved the OAC Extension Service, which issued publications offering advice for gardening as "a source of profit and pleasure." Bulletins urged gardeners to sustain the "Spring enthusiasm for planting" through the growing season. Professor A. G. B. Bouquet, a sixteen-year resident of Oregon, wrote periodic newspaper columns reminding people of the mantra of good gardening—patience! The college quickly exhausted the ten thousand copies of Bouquet's publication, Bulletin 287, and immediately ordered a second printing. Another Bouquet bulletin offered advice on "methods and practices of Spring seeding and plant settings."[37]

Because Oregon Agricultural College was in good measure a technical school, faculty members were heavily involved in war-related activities. Through the Federal Board for Vocational Education, the college organized courses in radio and signal work during the summer of 1917. Oregon's acting director of vocational education, Frank Shepherd, organized classes for some four hundred military conscripts that continued until March 1918. Shepherd assumed a new mission in the spring of 1918 to train men in technical fields (telephone repair, telegraphers, auto mechanics, carpenters, linemen, machinists, blacksmiths, electricians, and switchboard operators). Under the auspices of the War Department's Committee on Education and Special Training, Shepherd invited Northwest schools to participate.[38]

Among its war-related activities, the college hosted a California detachment of 244 recruits, arriving in June 1917. With federal funds, the college put up barracks and made cafeterias available to trainees. The men were given physical exams, vaccinated for typhus, outfitted with uniforms, and assigned to classes of their choice: auto trades, radio, blacksmithing, or carpentry. Commanders organized the vocation-like boot camp into squads and platoons. President Kerr made college facilities available for the technical courses and found instructors and equipment for classes. An internal assessment of the program reported good successes with the apprentice-like instruction.[39] While the men were training, the War Department embarked on an even more ambitious agenda, the Student Army Training Corps (SATC).

The War Department's Committee on Education and Special Training, whose objective was to provide trained officers for the war effort, developed the SATC initiative. The brainchild of C. R. Dooley, educational director for the Standard Oil Company, the SATC would slow the drain of students to the military and provide them with specialized training, especially in engineering. One supporter enthused that the army was building a department of education that would have great significance. The subtext to the SATC plan was to assist colleges and universities in militarizing their institutions. Few faculty, according to historian David Noble, raised questions about the program's approach to seizing colleges and universities for military purposes. Samuel Capen of the War Department noted that schools of higher education were "falling in line and the majority of them are hailing us as the saviors of both education and the trained personnel of the country."[40]

The War Department announced in May 1918 a proposal to use colleges and universities on a more substantial scale, combining training and education to prepare men for military service. In a June circular to college presidents, the department outlined the details, and then in July the secretary of war explained the purpose of the SATC: "To provide for the very important needs of the Army for highly trained men as officers, engineers, doctors, chemists, and administrators of every kind." The SATC would "mobilize and develop the brain power of the young men of the country for those services which demand special training." Enlistment was open to all physically able students at least eighteen years old who were qualified to enter college. The War Department would provide the enlistees with uniforms and equipment, a salary of $30 per month, free tuition, and room and board. A typewritten summary of the Corvallis program was succinct: "No single event in the history of the college is comparable to it in magnitude of material changes, number of people involved, or intensity of effort expended." Although its duration was brief, "the task involved was colossal."[41] Left unsaid in such narratives was the extent to which the federal government had subsumed higher education to its purposes during the war.

The Student Army Training Corps dwarfed what colleges had been doing. Under contracts with the War Department, more than 150 colleges and universities implemented SATC programs to train draftees in trades associated with the war effort. In many cases SATC activities overwhelmed already burdened college campuses, and in small towns such as Corvallis, flooded the community with new recruits.[42] Preparations for the program developed slowly through the summer of 1918, with Oregon Agricultural College forsaking its ROTC units in favor of hosting SATC students. Those matriculating in the program were expected to enlist in the military before reporting to campus. Once accepted into the SATC, students were treated as part of the military services. OAC anticipated enrolling approximately two thousand men for training in military science and tactics, auto mechanics, and other technical fields.[43]

The program accepted two classes of students, a group who could not meet college entrance requirements (Class A), and a second comprising high school graduates eligible for college admission (Class B). The two groups would take different classes under designations A and B. There would be no college vacations, and students were expected to devote 25 percent of their time to military training and the remainder to academic work. Class A students were urged to devote extra hours to preparatory subjects, while their Class B counterparts would take war-related classes in lieu of regular courses. Those interested in becoming commissioned officers would be designated for advanced training if they qualified.[44]

To accommodate the student training corps, the army required institutions to offer courses on three-month terms rather than the semester system. OAC complied, adjusting regular and special war courses in September from a semester to a term calendar to meet SATC requirements. Although documents suggest those last-minute changes were disruptive to students in the regular curriculum, faculty and students accepted the situation in the spirit of cooperation. College administrators also had to deal with minimum standards for entering Class B students, determining in early October "to hew rigorously to the stipulated requirements for entrance." Ultimately, Pacific Northwest institutions enrolled far more students under the SATC program than originally anticipated. To limit their numbers, OAC officials accepted only those at least nineteen years old. As late as October 24, SATC students were still being quartered in the gymnasium, waiting for the completion of a new barracks. Although the exact number of SATC inductees at OAC is a bit muddled, one source lists 1,431 men.[45] In the end the Corvallis program was much ado about nothing, lasting about two months and then disbanding shortly after the Armistice.

The war-related activities of Oregon Agricultural College paralleled the experiences of other land-grant institutions. Iowa State College combined "campus and army camp, scholastic studies and military drill, and military discipline with collegiate administration," according to David Ross. Like OAC, the Iowa institution provided housing and instruction for an Army Training Corps contingent. There were differences in living quarters, however, with Class A students bivouacked "in improvised barracks under the bleachers, with the collegiate group in fraternity houses." Despite the more luxurious quarters, the Iowa school faced problems with disorganization, attributable to dual civilian and military administrators. In the midst of this confusion, however, the Armistice brought an end to the SATC program.[46]

At Cornell University, New York's land-grant institution, SATC students attended military classes and regular courses in mathematics, science, and engineering. Paralleling the experiences at Iowa State, Class B soldiers were housed in fraternities, as many as seventy cots to a house. "Cornell," writes Morris Bishop, "became in 1918 a military school." The university's SATC enlistees, unlike those in Corvallis, suffered grievously from the influenza epidemic—nine hundred cases on campus and 1,300 in the City of Ithaca, with thirty-seven student deaths. Purdue University in West Lafayette, Indiana, contracted with the War Department to house 1,500 SATC enlistees under conditions common at other institutions. The university put up five military barracks to house the troops—buildings that came down shortly after the Armistice. "Proportionately," Robert Topping concludes, "the War to End All Wars crowded the campus with war activities almost as much as did World War II."[47]

During America's participation in the war, OAC officials struggled with collegiate and vocational courses and the scramble to meet housing and cafeteria needs. There was friction, prejudices toward an unnamed department, students requesting to be exempt from economics, and endless discussions about "apportioning" credit for those withdrawing from classes to join the military. The college offered a special course in Spoken French—dubbed "Wartime French"—and a class for tractor operators, "a course of immediate war value." Officers asked the administration for more time for military drill, suggesting that the college sacrifice the "student hour" on alternate Wednesdays as one alternative.[48]

In the midst of the frenzy to accommodate the Army Training Corps, Corvallis and the agricultural college were caught up in the great influenza epidemic of 1918–1919. Purportedly originating in Spain, the "Spanish flu" epidemic took an estimated fifty to one hundred million lives worldwide, including some 675,000 Americans. Its effects in Oregon were less severe, with the Oregon State Board of Health reporting 48,146 cases of flu and 3,675 deaths. Although Oregon identified its first reported case on October 5, newspapers attempted to minimize its severity. Portland's *Oregonian* reported in mid-October that several agricultural college students were housed on the third floor of Waldo Hall with "grippe and colds," but none had influenza. Although many students were ill, the college never suspended classes. Fears of the epidemic, however, prompted Corvallis officials to cancel all public meetings, and the college cancelled an October 18 football game between the Multnomah Club of Portland and OAC.[49]

The *Oregonian* reported additional flu cases in late October, including twenty-two in Corvallis, but the newspaper insisted that influenza was "being stamped out" on campus. A contingent from the United States Medical Corps (with hospital equipment) arrived to assist the city's physician in protecting against the flu, and the college postponed extension programs across the state until December. Because a few cases still existed on the OAC campus, influenza patients were housed in Shepherd Hall, the former YMCA building, and college officials continued to quarantine fraternities and sororities, even if they harbored a single infected student.[50]

And then it was over—abruptly—with the signing of the Armistice on November 11, 1918. "Whole Northwest in Joyous Tumult," headlined the *Oregonian*. Around Coos Bay, workers left the mills and shipyards to celebrate on the streets of Marshfield and North Bend. With bottles of "stimulant waving promiscuously in the patriotic air," the Marshfield police chief politely stood aside in the wake of the revelers. In Corvallis, students and townspeople participated in a downtown parade and then gathered in the Armory to hear President Kerr congratulate the college on the assistance it had rendered and to remark that the end of the war would "go down in history as the greatest day in the civic history of the world." On the eve of Thanksgiving, patriotic songs wafted through Portland's churches and theaters in gratitude for the Armistice and the waning of the influenza epidemic that took a greater toll on human life than the war. Because the flu still kept hospitals busy, the *Oregonian* urged that celebrations be muted for the present.[51]

The ink was barely dry on the Armistice agreement when college officials announced the immediate demobilization of the Student Army Training Corps and the college's return to normal. Although military training would remain a vital part of campus life, it would be "the usual type prevailing in land-grant colleges before the war." College officials determined that Class B students completing the eight-week SATC courses would be eligible to matriculate in regular college work. State officials asked the administration to accept veterans "soldier specials" who could not qualify under standard entrance requirements.[52]

Responding to a request to assess the SATC, Grant Covell, dean of the School of Engineering, indicated that military obligations seriously affected student academic work. Moreover, the overwhelming military presence prompted many students to treat their academic responsibilities as "incidental" to their military duties. On the other hand, Covell thought the faculty favored coupling military and academic training, because the college was "organized on that basis." Faculty and students took the war years in stride, he believed, because the campus had always enjoyed a military presence. Covell indicated the importance of combining vocational and military training—"a potent factor for good in training the youth of the country for usefulness in industry and at the same time developing proper ideal of citizenship."[53]

Grant Covell reflected the attitudes of the Society for the Promotion of Engineering Education, which had been urging changes in higher education to better conform to industrial requirements. Reformers pushing the SATC viewed the program as having lasting significance. David Nobel, a critic, argues that educators across the country began reshaping engineering education to produce "efficient and loyal corporate employees and competent and dedicated 'leaders of industry.'" Covell reported that the effects of war on "engineering education will be to eliminate subjects which do not have immediate commercial value."[54] Such proposals would bedevil curricular initiatives at the institution far into the future.

"O.A.C. ON PRE-WAR BASIS," the *Oregonian* headlined on January 8, 1919, praising the college's enrollment of more than three thousand students. Waldo and Cauthorn halls had reopened to women, and fraternities had returned to normal activities. Academic departments that had given way to SATC instruction resumed regular schedules. Dean of Forestry George Peavy, who chaired the student affairs committee, announced that normal social activities would resume, with precautions for lingering cases of influenza. The administrative council decided to maintain the three-term calendar in lieu of returning to the semester arrangement. After accommodating SATC contingents, administrators thought the three-term system provided flexibility to offer more courses. In an address to the National Education Association during the war, President Kerr indicated a preference for college and university work "to continue over a period of forty-eight weeks, divided into four terms" instead of the semester plan.[55]

Elected governor in 1914, former agricultural experiment station director James Withycombe served in office through the end of the war. A British national, Withycombe oversaw the Oregon State Council of Defense and organized its police force in 1918 with a legislative appropriation of $250,000. Although the force was to protect against enemy agents, the new state police began arresting people for bootlegging and breaking Oregon's prohibition law. Withycombe warned men joining the military about venereal diseases, declaring that contracting such a disease was treasonous, one of Germany's "fiendish devices of war" to weaken its enemies. Although most states moved away from restrictive legislation at war's end, Withycombe asked legislators to enact a penalty for treason: "While the poisonous influences of sedition and sabotage are fresh in our minds it might be well to set down in the statutes" a firm response to disloyalty.[56]

Not everyone harbored the suspicions of Governor Withycombe; indeed, a strong case can be made that the state acted responsibly for those who had served in the war. The legislature advanced programs to aid returning veterans when it provided financial aid to those pursuing higher education. The lawmakers offered a maximum of $200 per year for four years and excluded SATC students. The state sent funds directly to institutions for "lodging, board, and other necessities." Oregon voters twice approved support for the program, and some three thousand Oregon veterans filed applications for support under the act.[57]

With the return to peacetime routines, Corvallis and the agricultural college were crossing into new and different cultural and political waters. Republican presidential candidate Warren G. Harding urged a return to "normalcy" after nearly a decade of progressive reforms, war, and contentious debates over President Woodrow Wilson's League of Nations.[58] In Corvallis, administrators and faculty retooled curriculum and classes, and with veterans graduating, the institution returned to more rigorous entrance requirements. President Kerr and his staff resumed their focus on expanding professional schools in engineering, agriculture, forestry, and home economics. College officials jousted with the State Board of Higher Curricula over the duplication of courses and majors with the University of Oregon.[59] OAC's School of Agriculture had grown from a single department in 1883 to ten in 1922, despite losing four departments to the college's "service" units to conform with the state board's mandate.[60]

Agriculture Dean A. B. Cordley praised the work of Professor C. I. Lewis, chair of the horticulture department, who was taking a position with the Oregon Growers Cooperative Association. Lewis had developed a department of great value, one that ranked with the best in the country. The school's departments had performed well; the only downside was the large number of assistant professors and instructors who had resigned because of low salaries. Cordley hoped that passage of the millage tax measure (May 1921) would reverse the trend. Through the extension service the School of Agriculture had trained students to become high school teachers. Because of the program's success, Cordley proposed establishing a department of extension methodology to train young men and women for extension work and to provide students who planned to farm with knowledge about services available to the public. The school's objectives, however, remained unchanged—"to provide the best possible training for leadership in agriculture."[61]

President Kerr paid close attention to administrative details, telling deans in 1921 to make certain that faculty were "given a full load but not an overload." Classes should not be offered to "unjustifiable small groups of students." The president was concerned with the paucity of graduate students and recommended targeting fellowships to increase enrollment. In his biennial reports he touted the campus building program, praising the completion of Commerce Hall (1922), which provided additional classroom space. The president was proud of the campus's heating facilities, extending underground conduits to Commerce Hall, Home Economics, and other buildings. Although separate oil and wood heating plants served different sections of campus, Kerr recommended that a single plant should provide heat for all buildings in the interests "of efficiency and economy."[62]

At administrative council meetings the president raised questions about entrance requirements, directing deans to impose only those listed in the catalogue, leaving the enforcement of prerequisites to the registrar. When the director of physical education proposed that swimming be required for graduation, the administrative council approved the measure for male students only, effective with the freshman and sophomore classes of 1922–1923.[63]

The narrative styles of academic administrators shifted with the passing decades. President Kerr urged deans and the faculty in October 1923 to address "student mortality," which simply meant students who had dropped out of school. The president hoped faculty would contact students who had not returned and invite them to reenroll. He raised the question again at the beginning of the 1924 academic year, indicating that it was important for the faculty to give "consideration and study to conditions . . . which might have contributed to the apparent heavy mortality in registration." Faculty should look for flagrant absences as one way to prevent students from withdrawing from college.[64] The president's awareness of student attrition would confound all future administrators.

Through the 1920s, Corvallis and Oregon Agricultural College adjusted to the modernizing world of motor vehicles, motion pictures, and the nation's shifting cultural mores. While administrators wrestled with regulations governing automobile traffic and parking on campus, the college continued expanding its agricultural and engineering extension programs. At the invitation of Portland Local 87, Steam and Applied Engineers, extension began offering engineering courses in Portland in 1915. According to a Portland engineer, the extension courses were the first of their kind in the nation, "allowing the operating engineer to work upward into professional engineering." OAC continued its traditional Farmers' Week and winter short courses addressing issues important to farmers and ranchers. Short courses included crop rotation, horticulture, raising livestock, beekeeping, tractor mechanics, and dairying. The Department of Domestic Science sponsored annual homemakers conferences featuring labor-saving devices ("Use your head and save your heels"), sanitation in home and school, and "better babies"—instruction in "rational prenatal care."[65]

Oregon Agricultural College was coming of age by the mid-1920s, earning respect for its standards of scholarship and physical facilities. The Northwest Association of Colleges and Secondary Schools declared the college fully accredited in 1924, an assessment that placed OAC on the National Council of Education's list of accredited institutions. The college's women faculty joined 150 other institutions as members of the American Association of University Women. And following several days of inspection, the Department of Interior's Bureau of Education rated the college equal to other landgrant institutions for its entrance requirements, curriculum, and graduation standards. Finally, the United States Department of War continued to rank the college equal to other distinguished institutions for its thriving military programs.[66]

Equally significant, after an exhaustive investigation, the University of Illinois gave the college a "Class A" rating, enabling its graduate students' admission to the Illinois institution on the same basis as its own students. OAC's admission requirements filed with the University of Illinois listed fifteen units of high school credits required for admission, including English, elementary algebra, plane geometry, foreign languages, laboratory science, history, economics, and additional units to bring the total to fifteen. Although physics was not an entrance requirement, students planning to major in engineering should take a full year of high school physics. The self-assessment included enrollment details from 1920 through 1925, graduate curricula, and requirements for admission to advanced standing for students from other colleges.[67]

In his biennial report for 1924–1926, President Kerr reviewed the dramatic changes to the college, citing its enrollment of 405 students in 1900 against the 3,593 full-time enrollees in 1926. Students hailed from twenty-seven Oregon counties and three other states and the Territory of Alaska in 1900. In 1926 students represented every Oregon county, twenty-three states, and seven foreign countries. When the Oregon legislature required its colleges and university to charge out-of-state students a nonresident tuition fee, the decision triggered a decline in out-of-state enrollment. Because transfers from other institutions remained strong, Kerr believed the institution's reputation was solid.[68] There were other advances on campus: a Student Health Service was established in 1916 with two full-time physicians and two nurses. The college had thirty full-time faculty in 1900 and twelve experiment station personnel, numbers that increased to 216 faculty, thirty-two experiment station investigators, and seventy extension service employees in 1926.[69]

The teaching staff was vastly improved, with a greater percentage of faculty with advanced degrees. The college now expected staff to have a master's degree or to be working toward one. New hires with doctoral degrees were increasing with each passing year. The president enumerated the colleges and universities where faculty had earned their degrees—194 institutions, eleven from Europe and four from Canada. The University of Wisconsin ranked first in degrees awarded to OAC faculty (seventeen), Columbia University second (thirteen), and the University of Illinois third (twelve). Faculty were increasingly publishing books, articles, bulletins, and contributing research papers at countless professional meetings.[70]

The college's imprint was physical as well as academic. Its grounds and farm in 1900 covered 184 acres, the campus and its buildings taking up about forty acres. By the mid-1920s college lands totaled 1,667 acres, with 1,047 located in or near Corvallis and a 620-acre plot, part of the Eastern Oregon Branch Experiment Station, in Union. The 341-acre forest north of Corvallis had been named Peavy Arboretum, after prominent forestry dean George Peavy. The college managed a 160-acre tract on Mary's Peak, a donation from the Spaulding Lumber Company for experimental purposes. The campus, including experimental fields and the farm, covered about 545 acres, with the central grounds of 135 acres embracing buildings, quadrangles, parade ground, and athletic and recreational fields.[71]

The dramatic growth of Oregon Agricultural College paralleled experiences across an increasingly industrialized nation. The City of Corvallis reflected changes elsewhere in the state and nation during the early twentieth century.

The Eighteenth Amendment to the US Constitution prohibiting the sale and distribution of alcoholic beverages was ratified in 1919, and the Nineteenth Amendment enfranchising women was approved the following year. Compounding this period of change, Oregon's lumbering and agricultural economies were increasingly troubled in the decade following the Great War. Amid this social and economic unease, Oregon's largely homogeneous ethnic and religious population became ready recruiting grounds for groups appealing to white, Anglo-Saxon, Protestant values. Guardians of 100 percent Americanism, the Ku Klux Klan, made headway during the early 1920s. Equally interesting are student reactions to changes occurring during the college's first few decades.

4
Student Life, 1868–1940

Student experiences at American college and university campuses in the last half of the nineteenth century varied between metropolitan and rural institutions and among state universities and land-grant colleges. Following the Civil War, land-grant schools were customarily located in small towns, many of them with limited access to the nation's expanding rail networks. Communities such as Ithaca (New York, Cornell), Ames (Iowa Agricultural College), East Lansing (Michigan Agricultural College), Logan (the Agricultural College of Utah), Pullman (Washington Agricultural College), and West Lafayette, Indiana (Purdue) were removed from the nation's great industrial and commercial centers. Young men and women attending those institutions faced limited opportunities for travel, even if they had the means. Students attending Corvallis College were restricted to horse and buggy transportation or stern-wheelers that had been making regular stops in Corvallis since 1858. Although most of the early students were residents of Benton County, the rainy season further limited travel.

Small, isolated campus environments, obligations to work on college grounds, and off-limits drinking establishments and billiards halls characterized student life in places like Corvallis, Pullman, and Ames. Students coming from rural environments to the Corvallis College building on Fifth Street had to reckon with a new reality—punctuality, showing up for classes on time. The college adopted a system of demerits for students who were late for recitations, left without excuses, were disorderly, or for "Ladies and Gentlemen conversing on College premises." The faculty adopted resolutions that students accumulating five demerits would forfeit their place in class. On occasion, administrators showed compassion and remitted demerits for those who breached a rule only once. More often, officials attached stringent requirements to disciplinary cases, as happened with F. Chrisinger, who had been suspended from school. He was reinstated in February 1875 "upon the solemn promise upon his part that he will not again violate any law of this

College, and that in case of violation of 'Remark 5,' Catalogue 1873–74 under 'Regulations,' he shall be *ipso facto* expelled."[1]

Although Christian influences weighed heavily in college and university activities in the late nineteenth century, Corvallis College supervised student life more closely than many. Because of the institution's sectarian roots in the Methodist Episcopal Church, South, rules and regulations for students changed little until the state assumed control of the college in 1888. Following the precepts of the college board of trustees, the faculty established punishment for those failing to hew to its regulatory norms. College president William Finley and Professor Joseph Emery often appeared before the trustees to explain charges against students for misbehaving.[2]

The "Board of Commissioners on Regulations and Course of Study for the Agricultural College" issued specified rules in 1873 requiring students to attend daily religious services, observe study hours, and avoid loitering around town. Students were prohibited from gambling, playing cards and billiards, purchasing intoxicating beverages, and smoking on campus. At its weekly meetings, the faculty reviewed student excuses, requesting on occasion that the president "settle the matter of the present offenders against the College in accordance with his judgment." Toward the end of its jurisdiction over the college, the M.E. Church, South continued to have faculty warn students about loitering around the hall, requesting that they "go as quietly as possible" and commissioning a student "to preserve order in and about the hall."[3]

On their own initiative, students published the institution's first newspaper, *The Gem*, in February 1883. Later that spring, male students played a loosely organized "base-ball" game in Monmouth against Monmouth Christian College. This first documented evidence of the college participating in the "national pastime" would culminate more than a century later in Oregon State University's baseball team winning two College World Series titles in a row. The Corvallis Council also approved an ordinance in 1883 making it unlawful for anyone to play "cricket, football, basketball, townball, the game of cat, or games of like nature within the corporate limits of the City of Corvallis on the first day of the week, commonly called Sunday."[4]

Despite the formal transfer of governance from church to state in 1888, many former regulatory requirements remained. The faculty doubled from four to eight, daily chapel was still required, and students who were not occupied should study—"the ladies in the library, and the gentlemen in the chapel." The faculty added an additional note at its September 1888 meeting, "no loud talking, noise, or disturbance in or about the buildings." There were

With baseball teams dating to the early twentieth century, Oregon State University won the College Baseball World Series in Omaha, Nebraska, for the first time in 2006. The next year, the astounding Beavers repeated as College Baseball World Series champs—a rare feat—winning back-to-back world series titles. Photo credit: Rich Heins, courtesy OSU Athletics.

restrictions on recitations—students were prohibited from attending recitations in a class other than the one they had been assigned.[5]

Corvallis College's Board of Regents paid considerable attention to student labor practices followed at most land grant schools. The faculty determined that students age fifteen and older should work one hour each day for twelve and a half cents per hour. The president and the experiment station regulated the type of labor and hours. The board of regents reaffirmed the faculty requirement in 1890, directing students to work on the farm or "the horticultural grounds for one hour a day gratis unless excused by the resp. heads of these departments." The faculty repeated again in February 1892 the importance of students' obligation to work: "The required labor . . . is as much a compulsory part of the course as are the classroom exercises for all students of the College." Faculty directives assigned student work details during their first three years with the agricultural and horticultural departments.[6]

The state-controlled college introduced other innovations. Although the Alumni Association elected its first officers in February 1873, its alumni did little to involve graduates in campus activities. To promote better relations with former students, the faculty invited alumni in 1889 to hold their annual reunions in conjunction with graduation. Although the faculty attempted to curry favor with graduates, it kept a watchful eye on resident students for violating college rules, passing a sharply worded resolution in January 1890 forbidding students from smoking on campus. In the fall of 1891 the faculty noticed "the increasing popularity among students of the dried leaves of the plant known as *Nicotiana tabacuni culuminate*" and resolved again to prohibit "students from using the noxious weed on the College-premises."[7]

Other demons were threatening to lure students toward the dark side, none more worrisome than the battle with saloons and liquor establishments. A faculty committee overseeing alcohol-related issues praised the regents for "their effort to bring Saloonmen to justice" involving liquor sales to minors. Students were periodically suspended and then reinstated for disorderly behavior related to booze. The problem, campus officials argued, was easy access to liquor at local establishments. In a flare-up of relations between town and gown in 1900, the faculty appointed a committee to confer with city officials about closing "all saloons, gambling places, billiard and pool rooms on the Sabbath day, and to regulate and prevent the attendance of students at the places named."[8]

Student behavior was positive as well, especially when students attempted to form a marching band. They asked permission to create such an ensemble in November 1890, promising to provide their own instructor and instruments, and to schedule practices that would not conflict with other responsibilities. The faculty was not impressed, resolving that students practicing at unreasonable hours would disturb the tranquility of the campus or fall behind in their studies. When students petitioned again in the fall of 1891, the faculty simply referred to its earlier resolution.[9]

To twenty-first-century readers, the social mores and rules and regulations imposed on student conduct seem antiquarian and dated. The agricultural college's conventions, however, did not notably differ from other colleges and universities. The Iowa legislature banned the sale of alcoholic beverages within two miles of its state college in 1868. At Cornell University, another land-grant school, local clergy often interfered with social activities when students engaged in ungodly acts inconsistent with Christian values. Cornell administrators harshly punished students for hazing. Michigan State Agricultural College reprimanded students for smoking, but those accused of major breaches of regulations were hauled before the faculty for discipline. While male students were expected to exercise good behavior on campus, women were subject to more watchful supervision.[10]

There was Christian immediacy in meting out discipline on the Corvallis campus. The faculty refused the request of Marion Chandler, a suspended student, when he applied for reinstatement. When Professor John Letcher offered to reinstate Chandler if he "manifested the proper spirit of repentance and shall have been reprimanded by the President," the faculty agreed. On the other hand, when Gertie Carlisle and Mark Meeker had accumulated more than the monthly limit of demerits, they were suspended for the excessive demerits and "for general neglect of work and utter carelessness."[11]

The years of draconian regulations began to moderate when John Bloss assumed the presidency in 1893. In his inaugural address, he reaffirmed the college's tradition of student labor, telling the faculty "to encourage students to work rather than fill their minds with information simply." His most significant message, however, breached conventions dating to the school's founding: "During study hours boys and girls will hereafter be together for the reason that in such a manner they can best be properly managed." Bloss deprecated scolding and suspicion, advocating "forbearance with the mistakes and indiscretions of the young and the cultivation of self-respect." Avoiding "malicious satisfaction" in punishing students would give students confidence in their teachers.[12]

Despite relaxing gender mixing, restrictions on alcoholic beverages and smoking continued both on and off campus. When the regents asked about an increase in smoking, the faculty confirmed that the "pernicious habit" was on the rise, behavioral habits that would offend visitors. The faculty believed students should be forbidden to use tobacco unless they furnished written consent from their parents or guardians. Wallis Nash, a member of the board, thought faculty should be restricted from smoking except in their private rooms.[13]

Some aspects of today's Oregon State University were beginning to take shape during the 1890s. Baseball, football, "'girls' basketball," the "College Color," the student newspaper, and literary societies were becoming part of everyday life. Students challenged the faculty to "a friendly game of baseball" in the spring of 1893. During that season, the baseball committee attempted to organize a team, the faculty adopted "orange" as the school color, and a faculty committee struggled to come up with "a suitable College cry (yell)." The football team played its first game against Albany College in the fall of 1893. Those initiatives marked the beginning of formalizing structures for student athletes, creating financial support for sports teams, managing the college newspaper, directing student activities, and overseeing the college's membership in collegiate athletic associations.[14]

As the college baseball and football programs advanced, administrators adopted regulations mirroring standards at other institutions. To fund athletics, the Alumni Association agreed to provide "one dollar ($1.00) for each male student and fifty cents (50c) for each female student." The association urged the board of regents to authorize collecting incidental fees from

The development of baseball at Oregon Agricultural College was incremental, with the first report of students playing a loosely organized "base-ball" game against Monmouth Christian College in 1883. Students and faculty played a baseball game in 1893, with notice that a baseball committee was attempting to organize a team. Although the college's first yearbook, The Hayseed, posted photos of football and baseball teams in 1894, baseball did not become an organized sport until 1907. Courtesy of the OSU Special Collections and Archives Research Center.

students when they registered in the fall, a proposal the regents rejected. To participate in athletics, the faculty required students to "be of good moral character" and maintain passing grades. The faculty supervised all athletic clubs and approved intercollegiate contests. Trainers for each sport were to "be of good moral character" and have the approval of the athletic committee. Finally, the student body was required "to meet all expenses, whether for general or specific athletics."[15]

The student newspaper, the *Barometer*, which began publishing in 1896, had no faculty oversight until April 1900, when the administrative council raised the question of supervision "to eliminate errors and objectionable matter" from its columns. The council appointed a committee to oversee the editor and manager, stressing the importance of students electing competent editors who met faculty approval. The newspaper's early issues were marginal productions with few visuals. As commencement approached in the spring of 1900, the *Barometer* staff asked the faculty "to contribute photos and money" to help illustrate an appropriate graduation issue.[16]

By the 1890s, senior students were becoming more venturesome and, with the faculty's permission, scheduled "an excursion to Newport" to celebrate the conclusion of their collegiate studies. Students boarded the train in the morning of May 26, 1894, and headed for the coast. College administrators reading an account in the institution's first yearbook, the *Hayseed*, may have winced at one student's account of the venture as the train emerged from a tunnel en route to Newport: "We heard many sighs of different size as various individuals expressed their regret at the tunnel being no longer." Although students brought their own lunch baskets, they discovered a "free lunch" on the beach in the form of a dead whale, "an enticing sight—from the windward side." The pleasure-seekers then boarded a boat for the trip to Yaquina (today's Toledo) for the rail trip back to Corvallis.[17]

Seniors who were soon to appear in commencement exercises were excused from further recitations. And for future generations of students at the college, the faculty adopted a resolution in the spring of 1900 that would resonate with students into the twenty-first century: "All regular written examinations are hereafter to be written in uniform 'blue books.'" Collegiate athletics achieved a similar milestone when a faculty committee urged the board of regents to secure the services of "a competent physical director—one qualified to oversee all branches of athletics and who can be held responsible by the faculty for the conduct of all students while under his charge." Regents granted the request, and the college hired James Patterson in the fall as the college's first "Physical Director."[18]

Along with Washington and Idaho institutions, Oregon Agricultural College joined the Northwest Collegiate Athletic Association in January 1903. The association required athletes to have passing grades. If they were failing, athletes were prohibited from participating until the work had been completed. The college recognized its first official women's sports team in 1905, when the faculty council agreed to organize "a girls Basket Ball Team to participate with other college teams." The council approved the request with the proviso that a woman faculty be added to the athletics committee. In a stunning turn of events, a February 1906 council session refused to give "unqualified consent to the continuation of basket-ball for girls ... during the present season." There was no discussion preceding the vote.[19]

Prospective students and parents reading newspaper reports about Benton County and the mid-Willamette Valley would find the location inviting and pleasing to the eye. In an illustrated portrait in 1904, the Benton County Citizens' League described "a land unsurpassed in the fertility of its soil," a congenial climate, a wealth of natural resources, and charming scenery. The Willamette River was "an artery of commerce," navigable beyond Corvallis. The area's basaltic soils would "be among the last to require artificial fertilizers." The "mild and equable" climate and modest temperatures would advance the human welfare. The Citizens League publication praised the quality of agricultural productions and stock raising, offering an energetic person a "wide range of productive pursuits."[20]

The college catalogue for 1905–1906 offered an equally idealized description. Situated in the heart of the Willamette Valley not far from the head of navigation on the river, Corvallis occupied a setting free of epidemic diseases. Occupying land above the worst of the seasonal floods and with rail transportation in all directions, the community was home to some two thousand people with "many churches and *no saloons*." The college, at the center of the city's vigorous development, was graced with a landscape devoted to crops, orchards, and pasture, while lawns, athletic fields, and flower gardens make up the remaining land.[21]

Students arriving at the growing college would see a community with saloons and billiards halls, despite the claims of the catalogue. Campus buildings welcoming students in the fall of 1905 included the three-story brick administration building, the first structure erected on the college grounds. Others included Agricultural Hall, a three-story granite and sandstone building; Mechanical Hall, another granite and sandstone building; the Armory, a two-story wooden facility for athletics and cadet drills; and two dormitories— Cauthorn Hall (men) and Alpha Hall (women). Cauthorn Hall had hot and cold running water, bathrooms, steam heat, and electric lights. The bedrooms were furnished with a bed, mattress, chest of drawers, and a table and chairs. Alpha Hall was similarly outfitted with a stove to provide heat, because it was not linked to the campus heating system. The catalogue advertised Corvallis and the campus as "amply supplied with pure water from a mountain stream."[22]

Students were assured of a vibrant social life, with campus YWCA and YMCA meetings to assist in "developing the social and spiritual life of members." The college catalogue encouraged vocal and instrumental musical participation, student involvement in "physical culture"—bowling, fencing, weight lifting—and playing baseball, football, basketball, tennis, and golf. The campus offered ten literary societies, five for women and five for men. The societies sponsored social and literary activities, debates, public speaking, music, and writing essays. Students with writing talents were encouraged to volunteer with the *Barometer*. The catalogue listed college membership in the Northwest Collegiate Athletic Association and the Student Athletic Union's

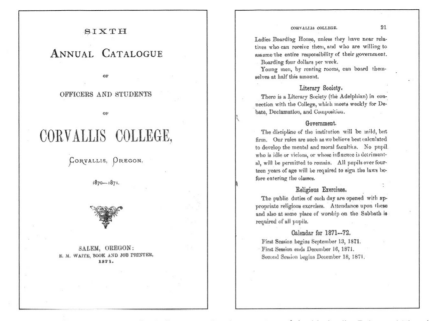

Beginning with sectarian Corvallis College—under the auspices of the Methodist Episcopal Church, South—and continuing after the state took control, students were required to attend chapel and observe other behavioral restrictions or receive demerits for failing to follow college protocols. Courtesy of the OSU Special Collections and Archives Research Center.

responsibility for directing sports. Although students would be treated with respect and without religious discrimination, their spiritual life would not be neglected. The catalogue warned that egregious behavior would lead to expulsion from the college.[23]

Oregon Agricultural College students continued to face conventions dating from the institution's founding—required attendance at chapel and all classes (although students could miss the first day of classes if they secured a temporary leave). While faculty reported absences to the registrar, professors could allow students "to make good the work thus missed by submitting to [a] special examination . . . on that work."[24] Giving the faculty greater autonomy over tardy and absent students would gain momentum with the passing years.

Sunday sporting events were also forbidden, a point made public when a group of students traveled to McMinnville to play a Sunday baseball game in May 1901. They did so without permission and in violation of the orders of the president and board of regents. The administrative council considered suspending the miscreants indefinitely; however, after further investigation, the council determined that two suspects were innocent and only seven students played in the Sunday game. The council limited punishment to minor penalties for the guilty "owing to certain mitigating circumstances."[25]

The great evil, students frequenting billiards halls, continued to annoy college officials into the twentieth century. Worried that young men were wasting time in such places to the neglect of their studies, the faculty council repeated its prohibition that students not enter places "where any game of billiards, pool or any similar game is being played." The council asked the Corvallis City Council in 1902 to enforce its laws regarding billiards halls. President Thomas Gatch subsequently suspended four students for entering a billiards room. With summer term approaching, however, and a host of teachers returning for institutes and postgraduate work, the council suspended the rule relating to billiards and pool rooms.[26]

The faculty council approved the first student-body election in early 1903 and endorsed the election of officers for the student athletic union, with both groups to proceed "as may be satisfactory to the Faculty." President Kerr later suggested strategies for student self-government to assure they were "exemplars of the highest ethical and social standards." OAC formally adopted student self-government in 1910—a thirteen-member council "under the authority of the President of the College . . . to make and enforce regulations and consider other matters pertaining to student discipline." The new student council gradually gained the right to establish and regulate student fees, although decisions were still subject to faculty approval. Student government, however, managed the yearbook and campus newspaper.[27]

Literary, drama, and debating societies flourished on college and university campuses from their inception. Students at Iowa's agricultural college organized literary societies in the 1860s with members participating in writing, debating, and other skills. During the first month of classes at Michigan's agricultural college, students formed the Agricultural College Students' Lyceum to sponsor speakers and debates on issues important to local audiences. Corvallis College students formed the Adelphian Society in November 1868—the institution's inaugural year as the state's agricultural school. Although the society barred females from membership, when liberals became ascendant in 1872, the Adelphians admitted women. That effort ran aground because of declining membership, and a new group revived the Adelphian Society in 1881, with women again admitted as members. When the society disbanded in 1889, its library reverted to the college.[28]

Two surviving copies of the Adelphians literary pamphlet, the *Gem*, offer a snapshot of the publication, first issued in 1883. "The Society is to the school what the bee is to the flower," the editors wrote in the maiden issue. A column in that issue titled "Irregular Attendance" parroted faculty positions on the vital topic of attendance. Another column, "Home," was a classic example of student overwriting in an effort to impress college peers. Another piece, "Locals," included statistics on students attending college and those traveling out of town, and an announcement of the Adelphian's literary contest. The April issue of the *Gem* offered more of the same: a column "Are Practical Writings Injurious to the Mind" and an essay urging readers to seek "solid substantive books" rather than "fiction that neither enriches the heart nor develops the mind." Another column, "Locals," reviewed an upcoming literary drama, "Not So Big A Fool As He Looks."[29]

The college traces its annual yearbooks to the publication of the *Hayseed* in 1894, a journal dedicated "To every 'Hayseed' in the State." With "feelings of doubt and misgiving" the editors launched the project upon an "uncertain sea of public sentiment," hoping that *Hayseed* would provide memories of the college as graduates left "to battle with life's sterner duties." The editors encouraged future classes to continue the tradition. The initial *Hayseed* listed the board of regents, college faculty, and the rolls of undergraduate and graduate students. Because the college still hosted a Preparatory Department, the annual included those students under the rubric, "Preparatory Primer." It recognized two literary societies, the Ciceronians and Websterians. Given the cadet's prominent role in land-grant institutions, *Hayseed* devoted significant attention to the military contingent, posting photographs of cadets and the football and baseball teams.[30]

Today's campus newspaper, the *Barometer*, originated in March 1896 when literary societies "and college classes" published the monthly *College Barometer*, a journal that evolved over time to a semiweekly and then to the *Daily Barometer* in 1923. The first issue adopted the *Gem's* format, and a "locals" column, without the yearbook's inclusion of college classmates and the regents. Early issues published stories, essays, and poems, but were devoid of photographs and sketches. In its second year it began reporting on land-grant functions, including exhibits at the Oregon State Fair.[31] Through the years the *Barometer* assumed the look of a regular newspaper, reporting events important to the college and beyond. When it began publishing dailies, the paper covered legislative policies affecting higher education and related issues.

With the arrival of President Benjamin Arnold, an officer in the Confederate Army, the cadet experience became a seminal part of student life. The practice was rooted in the Morrill Act of 1862, which required land-grant colleges to offer instruction in agriculture, the mechanical arts, and military tactics. Arnold began teaching military science when he arrived in 1872. For much of its early history the military department functioned under the direction of the president or a willing faculty member, with cadets wearing Confederate gray uniforms and Civil War–era caps. Under President John Bloss, Arnold's successor, cadets began wearing blue uniforms. On occasion, the college was able to retain a retired military officer to head the unit. Beginning with Lieutenant C. E. Dentler in 1898, however, regular military personnel commanded the campus cadets. At the turn of the century the military department included a battalion of three companies and an eighteen-piece military band.[32]

Finding appropriate drill hours for cadets was a perennial problem, especially during the rainy season, with limited indoor facilities until completion of the Armory and Gymnasium (now Gladys Valley Gymnastics Center) in 1898. Under the National Defense Act of 1916, the college's Department of Military Science became responsible for all military training. During the closing months of the First World War, the Student Army Training Corps made brief use of the new Armory (McAlexander Fieldhouse).[33] When the secretary of the army authorized the establishment of an Army Reserve Officers Training Corps in 1918, the building became home to the ROTC unit. The college's ROTC added a field artillery battalion and a motor transport corps following the First World War. The new units reflected recently developed technologies of warfare involving greater troop mobility.[34]

The first decade of the twentieth century witnessed several new developments. Greek organizations appeared on campus when Gamma Delta Phi established a chapter in April 1905. Although Alpha Tau Omega made a brief appearance in 1882, it did not establish a permanent chapter until 1916. The college fielded its first intercollegiate baseball team in 1907, finishing with a five and two record. The following year, Forrest Smithson, an OAC graduate, won the high hurdles in a record fifteen seconds at the Olympic Games in London. Students began publishing regular annual yearbooks, with a new title, Orange, in 1908. The first reference to athletics teams as the "Beavers" appeared in the Daily Barometer the same year.[35]

The perennial issue of temperance—banning alcoholic beverages on campus and prohibiting students from frequenting saloons and billiards establishments—hovered over student life at Oregon Agricultural College. The Oregon legislature gave a boost to temperance when it referred a ballot measure to voters in 1904 that would grant local governments the option to prohibit sales of alcoholic beverages. When Oregon citizens approved the Local Option Law, Benton voters, by a majority of 1,975 to 1,750, declared the county "dry." Temperance advocates achieved statewide success in 1914, five years before national prohibition, when voters amended the Oregon Constitution 136,842 to 100,362 prohibiting the manufacture and sale of alcoholic beverages.[36]

Oregon's temperance issue had always been closely contested, with voters turning back a prohibition amendment in 1887. Farmers, brewers, and distillers opposed banning sales of beer, wine, and liquor. Despite the claims of its proponents, prohibition was an abysmal failure. Evidence in Oregon and nationwide indicates widespread violations of prohibition, with imports of liquor and thriving bootleg operations in rural areas. For those willing to test the dark side of the law, it was relatively easy to brew applejack, hard cider, and other homemade beverages. And, true to form, college administrators persisted in punishing students "regarding the use of intoxicating liquor."[37] Given the folk history associated with underground booze, it is likely that Corvallis students and others had ready access to alcoholic beverages.

Football captured newspaper headlines when University of Oregon and agricultural college students clashed after a game in Corvallis on November 12, 1910. The previous evening freshman built a huge bonfire in advance of the much-anticipated contest. The match itself turned into a solid victory for the visitors, with Oregon blanking the "Aggies" 12–0. "Outgeneraled, Outweighed and Outplayed," declared Portland's *Oregonian*, the Eugene team clearly superior in every respect. The events following the game had more lasting effects, when college supporters attempted to wrest hats from departing university fans on their way to the train station. Scuffles broke out, charges and counter-charges followed, and a blow to the head knocked unconscious a university student. In the absence of President Kerr, college administrators immediately ordered an inquiry to place "the blame where it belongs."[38]

The *Oregonian* characterized the event at the depot as "a riot," with skirmishes that lasted an hour before the train departed for Eugene. University president Prince Lucien Campbell, who was present, attempted to calm the crowd and then stayed the night in Corvallis, conferring with faculty about the melee. He left the next day with assurances that the perpetrators would be punished. The college's Ralph Hetzel attributed the fracas to university supporters taunting Corvallis fans. The event that struck the university student unconscious, Hetzel believed, was a blameless accident, because "everyone took part in the general shoving." In the next few days misinformation, fabrication, and charges of fake injuries filled the pages of newspapers, with fingers of censure pointing north or south depending on one's institutional affiliation.[39]

Accusations escalated during the next days, with college students charging that Eugene firebrands were stirring enmity between the schools. The waters were roiled further when the university's student newspaper, the *Daily Emerald* published "Saturday's Outrages," an editorial attributing blame to Corvallis students whose behavior was "more befitting savages or hoodlums than students in the state college." Student leaders in Corvallis then called a mass meeting in the gymnasium demanding that the college terminate relations with the university. After further deliberation, the students limited the resolution to severing athletic ties only. The *Oregonian* described the student's decision as unanimous, calling for "the immediate severance of all athletic relations between this institution and the University of Oregon." The resolution of November 21, 1910, lasted into 1912, when a joint committee from the schools resolved their differences, and football competition resumed in the fall of 1913.[40]

In addition to performances of the cadet band, campus activities multiplied with the passing years, including instrumental and "barbershop" quartets and a glee club. President Kerr and Captain Harry L. Beard, director of the band, attempted to establish a college orchestra in 1913. The administrative council drafted rules for participating in orchestra: students were excused from physical education and could earn one credit in music; the orchestra would serve the college at public functions; and rehearsals would be held twice a week. Other student activities included the selection of "yell" leaders to cheer the home team at sporting events. OAC students regularly supported school teams, requesting on occasion that classes be cancelled for an hour or two on Friday afternoon to accompany the football team to the train station.[41]

Despite occasional sorties away from campus, such as the senior class's annual excursion to Newport, administrators kept a close watch over student life, forbidding political clubs on campus, reasoning that "the College is practically within the limits of the City" where opportunity abounded to join such organizations. The administration's greater concern was maintaining supervision over "student domiciles," undergraduates residing off-campus. Their purpose was to look after "the best interests of the students." Because some coeds lived off-campus, three women faculty were assigned to watch over "girls in boarding houses."[42]

Oregon Agricultural College differed little from other institutions of higher education in establishing policies to protect student virtue and safety. This was evident when officials noticed a new seasonal activity—canoeing on nearby Marys River. Although the stream was a dangerous fast-moving brown torrent during heavy winter rains, administrators likely overreached when they directed young men to pass a canoe-handling test before embarking with a coed on the river. There was still more—young women were to have parental consent before stepping into a canoe. College restrictions further codified Victorian mores for women students, requiring them to have permission to be away from their dormitories: "All picnic parties, parties going for long walks, rides, or canoeing, or parties planning to be out during meal time, shall be properly chaperoned." Such social privileges were not to exceed two per week.[43]

In addition to excusing football players and other athletes from classes and adjusting schedules for cadet drill, no issue vexed administrators more than students repeatedly absent from class. The problem was the subject of countless deliberations, and the administrative council established guidelines in February 1909 to discipline persistent absentees—prohibiting students from taking final examinations if they missed 10 percent of class meetings, "except with the consent of the College Council." The administration required faculty to report absences to the registrar at the close of business on Fridays, to "make a complete and prompt report at the time specified." If faculty reports were late, the registrar was to inform the president. The council modified its rules in 1910, giving the attendance committee power to enforce rules, including suspending students from classes.[44]

The administrative council continued its song and dance with attendance in December 1911, when President Kerr stressed the importance of faculty providing information promptly to the registrar. The council reiterated its support for attendance—adding a new twist—faculty late in reporting absences could be placed on probation. The beleaguered registrar responded with a request that the council appoint a committee to handle attendance cases. The council strengthened its regulations in May 1914: (1) students missing three consecutive classes in one course could have their registration cancelled; (2) students absent more than once a month in two or three credit courses would "Condition themselves," removing the condition required passing an examination; (3) instructors could condition students for failing to maintain a 70 percent grade; (4) students were expected to keep a record of their absences; and (5) students entering a class after roll call would be marked absent unless they presented a satisfactory explanation.[45]

The American declaration of war against the Central Powers in April 1917 significantly affected student life. Within days of President Wilson's message to Congress, young Corvallis men were enlisting in the military, including two Corvallis High School students. At Vancouver Barracks across the Columbia River from Portland, Company K of the Third Oregon Infantry (from Corvallis) mustered on the drill grounds in readiness for transport, with Lieutenant Ulysses Grant McAlexander, head of the OAC cadet corps, temporarily in charge. The mobilization dramatically altered campus life, with so many up-per classmen withdrawing from school to enlist in the military that the 1917 graduating class suffered a precipitous drop in numbers. Registrations for fall semester also declined sharply. The *Oregonian* reported that OAC students were heavily involved in Red Cross drives and war-related work. Responding to the student council's request to curb unnecessary expenses, clubs, fraterni-ties, and sororities eliminated social functions, and many students took jobs off-campus to aid the war effort.[46]

Parroting the Wilson administration's war-related statements, the US district attorney in Portland, Clarence Reames, theatrically declared the ex-pectations for patriotism: "Every person in the United States is either with us or against us." Reames expected "the highest spirit of ungrudging loyalty and service from citizens," cautioning against loose talk and careless criticism of the United States, warning that the federal penal code would punish transgres-sors. A Corvallis correspondent to the *Oregonian* suggested that public school teachers be required to lead daily exercises in the Pledge of Allegiance. Hint-ing that some schoolchildren were not dedicated to their adopted country, the writer thought it the duty of patriotic Americans to insist that all citizens meet standards of loyalty to their country.[47] With little ethnic diversity in Corvallis, few citizens felt threatened from such public harangues.

With the agricultural college taking the lead in assisting the war effort, life in the city settled into routines. Reflecting the federal Food Administration's campaign for citizens to grow war gardens, the extension service accelerated its effort to increase food production. Sororities, fraternities, and other living groups participated in a variety of war-related enterprises. Women carried knitting bags to classes, making squares for bed quilts if they were beginners, advancing to scarves and sweaters as their skills improved. Coeds reserved Tuesday and Thursday evenings for Red Cross knitting projects and gave up sweets and wheat cakes for fruits and vegetables. "Today," one coed told a re-porter, "is my butterless day." Women's dormitories cut back on food portions, serving bread in half rather than full slices. To meet Food Administration recommendations, women served simple refreshments at parties, decorating tables with ferns, wild roses, and seasonal leaves gathered on campus. Home economics instructors presented class materials suited to aid war projects.[48]

As spring approached in 1918, townspeople and students turned their attention again to war gardens. Because commercial wheat and meat produc-ers were selling most of their goods to the military, citizens on the home front were urged to expand their gardens. To increase food production, the college purchased equipment to guide students and townspeople in proper techniques of canning and drying fruits and vegetables. Visitors to campus occasionally praised students and faculty for their patriotism and loyalty. University of Ohio president W. O. Thompson told a large crowd gathered in the gymnasium in March 1918 that college students had been generous in responding to the nation's needs. Colleges were training students "not to hold theoretical interest in industry," but to prepare them "to be world builders." Oregon Governor James Withycombe followed with brief remarks, praising the Corvallis crowd for their work as 100 percent Americans.[49]

After the United States declared war on the Central Powers, many college and university athletic programs suspended intercollegiate competition. On the Pacific Coast, Stanford University, University of California, and University of Washington postponed athletic contests until further notice. Because of their close proximity, the University of Oregon and the college pledged "to carry on their athletic relation." The college celebrated its second annual Homecoming in the fall of 1917, featuring intra-fraternity competition, an interclass cross-country run, and the main event, a football game between OAC and Washington State College. By December, however, Pacific Coast institutions had eliminated all competition between California and Northwest teams except for football. Pacific Coast intercollegiate athletic officials in June 1918 agreed to resume athletic competition with a strict eye on economy. Although a War Department edict in fall of 1918 dampened hopes for competition, Washington and Oregon teams participated in their annual games without violating the order.[50]

The dawn of the 1920s ushered in an adventurist and inquisitive spirit on college campuses, a phenomenon that contemporaries tended to exaggerate. The public's resistance to social and cultural change, especially strong in states with heavily Protestant populations, manifested itself in several ways—opposition to teaching the theory of evolution in public schools and fears about the influence of immigrants, especially Catholics. Those developments contributed to the resurgence of the Ku Klux Klan, an organization that found a ready audience in Oregon, with its largely homogeneous ethnic and religious population. The temperance movement, dominating early issues of the Corvallis *Gazette*, prevailed at the national level with the adoption of the Eighteenth Amendment. The suffrage amendment granting women the voting franchise further disrupted political and cultural norms.

In a study of white, middle-class college students during the 1920s, Paula Fass contends that young people did not reject authority but had "a shrewd eye for the limits of acceptable conduct and belief." They were practical rather than idealistic, condemning anything truly radical—they "were bigoted and nationalistic." Few young people openly challenged prohibition laws, or denied the moral competence of their parents' generation or the legitimacy of the political system. If there was a class overtone to student activism, it was directed at academic standing and not at social class related to wealth, Fass argues. Although student activists in northern institutions discussed race and racism, their protests were gestures rather than overt demands to end discrimination.[51]

Nevertheless, campus high jinks proliferated in the 1920s, reflecting greater automobile travel, a slight increase in resistance to authority, and, in Corvallis, a slow move away from the Victorian rectitude of previous years. One notable incident attracting attention beyond Corvallis was an inter-fraternity smoker at the local Majestic Theater on February 7, 1923. Advertised as a fraternity stag party involving "Smokes, Jazz, and Complete Extras," the event was the first of its kind in the community. When the curtain rose at 7:15 p.m., only fraternity members were to be in the audience and no latecomers would be admitted. The program included seven skits, each involving the collective effort of three fraternity houses. A sampling of the program reveals intriguing titles: "The Tramp Ticklers," "Jazz Wedding," and "Judgment Day." Revelations about the "Smoker Affair" eventually appeared in the *Barometer*, the deliberations of college administrators, and the *Oregonian*'s coverage of disciplinary measures.[52]

A letter to the *Barometer*, signed "Vox Populi," called the affair a vaudeville show and asked if fraternities "wished that next years crop of pledges were present." The sponsors would likely have presented something quite different if their fathers or President Kerr were in the audience. If the "brains" organizing the event had put on something really funny, the occasion might have been fitting for women. Vox Populi cited the "orgies of indecency" that took place as justification "for people calling us the 'cow college.'" Another letter to the *Barometer* remarked that many fraternity men regretted some of the performances put on in their name.[53]

The smoker fit with the merrymaking characteristic of fraternities nationwide during the 1920s. Following the First World War, college and university administrators welcomed fraternities and sororities as a way to alleviate housing pressures caused by the growing numbers of students. Fraternities served to maintain internal discipline and provided a vehicle to enforce institutional rules and regulations. "By playing on the fraternity's sense of self-importance," Paula Fass writes, administrators hoped to "influence the social norms of campus." There was an additional caveat: with the declining significance of the traditions of four-year academic classes, fraternity membership (and to a lesser extent, sororities) offered students a sense of social identity and administrators a means of controlling student conduct. Fass concludes that in the 1920s fraternities "became the watchdog of campus mores and were . . . identified with college life and traditions."[54] When such living groups pushed the bounds of acceptable behavior, college officials had a ready means to counter such actions.

If OAC fraternities were restive over the smoker affair, their reactions were tepid compared with the administrative council's penalties. The council considered the case of three fraternity leaders who testified about the event and then classified those who attended into three groups. Five students in Group I were suspended from their fraternities and excluded from participating in student or institutional activities for one year. Forty students in Group II were required to read J. N. Larned's *A Study of Greatness in Men* and to pass a two-hour examination. The president simply reprimanded the forty students in Group III.[55]

President Kerr met with those implicated in the smoker on February 27 to advise them of the college's displeasure. At a general convocation the next day, the president addressed students on "college standards, ideals and deportment" to make clear the institution's position on such matters. A subsequent administrative council meeting reviewed the requirements imposed on students in Group II before they could register for spring term: purchase the book, *A Study of Greatness in Men*, and a manila folder for holding outlines of the book, and pass a two-hour examination.[56]

The principal organizers of the smoker were charged with allowing the evening to proceed, with each group attempting to outdo the other "in putting on something racy." According to the *Oregonian*, the evening escalated and the skits became "too frank for comfort to serious minded students." The president prohibited future smokers and asked students to eliminate the word from their vocabularies. At the beginning of the next school year, Kerr remitted the penalties against the five men in Group I.[57]

Despite women's advances during the 1920s, most college activities in Corvallis were reserved for males. When the student council drafted seemingly democratic rules for electing yell leaders, the document boldly declared: "Only male members of the Associated Students are entitled to vote for yell leader or assistant yell leader." Charged with oversight of student affairs, the administrative council sanctioned the exclusion of women when it approved amendments to Section 8 of the associated student constitution. The council again asserted itself on the side of established protocol when it "unanimously" denied the *Barometer* the right to accept tobacco advertisements. For rural colleges, such decisions were commonplace, reflecting the need to cling to cultural mores.[58] Although OAC may not have been a social backwater, the homogeneity and conservatism of the larger community prompted administrators to act when students violated conventional norms associated with drinking, smoking, or dancing improperly.

By the onset of the twentieth century, the acronym "agricultural college" no longer reflected the majority of the institution's graduates. President Gatch's annual report ending in June 1900 listed a total of 405 students enrolled in degree programs, among them agriculture, forty-eight; mechanical engineering, ninety-nine; electrical engineering, six; and household economy, ninety-six. Although the figures do not account for all students attending the college, they indicate proportionality between agricultural and other majors, with only 19 percent of students enrolled in agriculture. The figures for the years between 1911 and 1914 indicate a greater disparity than 1900 (table 4.1).

With this information at hand by the mid-1920s, students and alumni began urging President Kerr and the regents to change the name of the college. Engineering students charged that "agriculture" was a handicap to their careers. E. C. Allworth, secretary to the Alumni Association, believed that a majority of graduates, even those with agricultural degrees, would support changing the name to Oregon State College. Writing on behalf of the Oregon Board of Pharmacy, alumnus Frank Ward endorsed Allworth's suggestion, because "agricultural college" did not reflect the true nature of the institution. F. A. Gilfillan, a 1918 graduate in pharmacy, told Allworth that only 11 percent of students were studying agriculture in 1926. The "agricultural" imprint on the achievement of engineers, pharmacists, and other nonagricultural majors diminished the significance of the diploma, especially beyond Oregon.[59]

The Oregon State Agricultural College Alumni Association submitted a request to President Kerr and the board of regents in 1928 to change the name of the institution. The title "Agricultural College" was outdated, the association insisted, because land-grant colleges were now choosing names better suited to their broader purpose. The association contended that OAC was "a

Table 4.1. Agriculture Majors as Percentage of Enrollment, 1911–1914

	1911	1912	1913	1914
Agriculture	237	303	429	496
Total	970	1142	1364	1579
Percent	28%	26.5%	31.45%	31.4%

George W. Peavy (1869–1951) joined the new Department of Forestry at Oregon Agricultural College (OAC) as department chair in 1910. When OAC established the School of Forestry in 1913, Peavy was named its first dean, a position he continued to hold when he became acting president of the college in 1932. The Oregon State System of Higher Education named Peavy the college's seventh president in 1934. A widely respected forester, Peavy served as dean and president until he retired in 1940. Courtesy of the OSU Special Collections and Archives Research Center.

closely articulated group of technical colleges" and pledged its support for a change to Oregon State College. Undergraduate students joined the alumni, petitioning President Kerr and the regents to adopt Oregon State College as the institution's name.[60]

The dance over a proper title for the Corvallis school continued into the 1930s, with William Jasper Kerr now in the chancellor's office. When acting president George Peavy forwarded a senior class petition in January 1934 to the chancellor requesting a name change to Oregon State College, Kerr asked the students to withdraw their request, because the legislature would not favor such a petition in the midst of the Depression. Although the institution had been referred to as Oregon State College since 1932, the old name continued to appear in college catalogues until 1937, when the state system's new chancellor, Frederick M. Hunter, granted permission to change the name to Oregon State College.[61]

A casual reading of the college yearbook, the *1931 Beaver*, suggests that all was well and nothing of major consequence was amiss beyond campus. In the midst of rising state and national unemployment, the yearbook featured the Oregon Trail as its inspirational theme, reporting that graduating seniors— like the hardy pioneers who reached their destination with cooperation as their guiding light—had successfully completed four years of college through organized and purposeful direction. William Jasper Kerr, in his twenty-fourth year as president, wrote a brief column extolling Oregon Trail traditions, as "the most heroic in North America," a people who continue to inspire the present generation to "bring the Oregon country into its magnificent heritage."[62]

Yearbook editors compared achieving a college degree to the heroic story of pioneers—with some dropping by the wayside, the struggle of the crossing too heavy a burden to bear. Some failed because of their inability to get along with others or for financial reasons. "So it is today in this modern college," the editors declared, graduation goes to the successful, and like the pioneers of old, "the launching of a new life." The *Beaver* compared student social life to the immigrants who took time from their busy lives for "square dances and waltzes to the tune of the 'Irish Washerwoman.'" The editors admitted, however, that students had the leisure to participate in activities that their pioneer forebears had little time for.[63]

No yearbook incident provides greater contrast with the past than the 1931 editors' decision to submit the photos of five OSC women to the Ziegfeld Theater in New York City. The editors asked theater officials to choose the photograph of the coed—all of them dressed in 1920s "flapper" attire—most representative of the Jazz Age. Back came a short note, under the letterhead, "A Playhouse like no Other in America," indicating that judging the photos was difficult. The writer explained that the theater's decision was based only on the pictures provided, with the hope that they "meet with the approval of your organization." Although the yearbook did not indicate the results, the photo of Alice Fisher appears first in the annual.[64]

The Oregon State College *General Catalogue* for 1931–1932 reminded students about the duties of the new Oregon State Board of Higher Education and its mission to see that courses "shall not be duplicated in the higher educational institutions of Oregon." The catalogue listed degree-granting schools and departments for the University of Oregon and Oregon Agricultural College and the prerequisites for admission as a freshman and for advanced standing. Registration and student fees for the 1931–1932 year totaled $78. There were fees for taking one course, for late payment, and other incidentals. Board and room (for double occupancy) was about $75. The following are the estimated annual charges per resident student:[65]

Registration	$30
Associated Student	$15
Health Service	$9
Physical Education	$9
Laboratory	$24

| Board | $180–$250 |
| Room | $45–$100 |

The catalogue listed student publications, including the *Barometer*, now a four-page, eight-column daily supported with student fees. The catalogue proudly described the yearbook, the *Beaver*, as "a full-dress carnival of the year's life, representing the dignity, the beauty, the versatility, the gaiety, the traditions, the sentiment, and solidarity of Oregon State." The catalogue featured the English Department's literary magazine, the *Messenger,* with student essays from composition classes. With undergraduate assistance, the Alumni Association published the *Oregon State Monthly*, which included news of schools, faculty, and alumni. Engineering students issued the *Oregon State Technological Record*, a compilation of regional engineering news, student scientific investigations, and other technical information. Forestry students issued the *Annual Cruise*, promoting scientific forestry, providing the latest lumbering news, and reporting faculty and graduate student technical studies.[66]

Beginning with the All-College Formal Dance on October 25, OAC students held five major dances during the 1931–1932 school year. With a sunny south setting, in the palm-decorated Memorial Union ballroom, students at the first event danced to the music of the Romney Pearce orchestra. The Sophomore Cotillion was next up on January 24, with gay streamers and colorful balloons representing a Mardi Gras theme. Romney Pearce's eight-piece ensemble again provided musical accompaniment. One month later, students attended the Junior Prom, where Alice Fisher was chosen queen, according to the *Beaver*, for her "pulchritude, personality and queenly dignity." With president and Mrs. W. J. Kerr attending, the familiar Romney Pearce orchestra provided music. The Memorial Union was the setting on April 11 for the Military Ball, under the sponsorship of Scabbard and Blade, the military science honorary fraternity. For this occasion, Jimmy Whipplo's orchestra served up a variety of popular music. The Senior Ball on May 2, the last formal of the year, offered a modernistic setting, with flowers and greenery to create an impression of a spring night. The *Beaver* provided a lengthy list of students responsible for the preparations, and the honored guests included governor and Mrs. Julius Meier and members of the State Board of Higher Education. No mention was made about musical offerings.[67]

Jayne Walters, who attended Oregon State from 1936 to 1940 and earned a bachelor of science in secretarial science, represents a transitional figure between the closing years of the Depression and the acceleration of German and Japanese aggressions in Europe and Asia. Walters was assistant editor of the *Barometer*'s women's page; associate editor of the *Lamplighter*, a literary magazine; a member of Alpha Chi Omega sorority; and active in campus activities such as modern dance. She helped organize women's weekend events, dance recitals, and wrote occasional pieces for the *Lamplighter*. One contribution, "To Torture with Pleasure," was a short, humorous essay on "rally dances," where coeds stand in groups waiting for "a boy" to ask them to dance. Her *Barometer* columns described coeds "getting smarter and smarter with a strong 3 point average in the fashion line." The Walters materials in the OSU Archives include copies of the "Rook Bible," the "Women's Handbook" for Oregon State, the "CO-ED Code," and "Social Regulations, 1935–1936." Her freshman commitments included all of the above as well as service as publicity chair for the inter-fraternity council, publicity cochair of homecoming, and membership on the *Beaver* editorial staff.[68] The wartime world that Jayne Walters lived through would be far different from her experiences on the Corvallis campus.

5
The "Real" Civil War—Curriculum

College football in the United States is renowned for rivalries among in-state institutions state universities and land-grant colleges—Michigan and Michigan State, Kansas and Kansas State, Oklahoma and Oklahoma State, Iowa and Iowa State, and, in Oregon, one of the oldest of all "civil war" games, the University of Oregon and Oregon State University. The Oregon edition dates from the first official football game between the agricultural college and the state university in 1894. When Oregon State celebrates its sesquicentennial in 2018, the schools will participate in their 122nd civil war match.

Although Oregon's annual gridiron fest has captured news headlines, infinitely more significant turf wars have involved struggles over academic programs, with state legislators keeping a sharp eye on the duplication of courses. Interspersed with the fights between the university and the college have been periodic efforts to consolidate the schools on one campus. Oregon's two flagship institutions have waged those competitions through most of the twentieth century, with rural interests supporting the "Ag School" and urbanites favoring the university. To underscore the significance of their differences, the archival material related to curricular fights in Oregon State University's Valley Library dwarfs most other collections.

William Jasper Kerr—the person at the center of the curricular battles during the most volatile years, spent seven years as president of the Agricultural College of Utah before moving to Corvallis in 1907. Prior to moving to Corvallis, Kerr addressed the annual meeting of the American Association of Agricultural Colleges and Experiment Stations in the nation's capital in 1905. The president posed an unsettled question to his peers about schools of agriculture: What were the respective spheres of land-grant colleges and state universities? In several states, he noted, legislators were discussing questions about the duplication of courses. Despite problems common to many states, Kerr argued that no blueprint would fit all the schools, because their situations were so diverse. Despite those variations, however, it was possible to agree on important issues.[1]

Kerr reviewed the objectives of the Morrill Act of 1862 "to promote the liberal and practical education of the industrial classes," an effort to create new academic institutions that would offer "a liberal as well as a technical education." Focusing on "agriculture and the mechanic arts," land-grant colleges covered a broad array of courses, technical classes, the basic sciences, and "general training in language, literature, history, and civics—the components of a liberal education." In states where land-grant schools were separate from universities, Kerr believed the functions of each "should be clearly defined in such a way as to avoid, as far as practicable, the duplication of expensive courses." It was important, therefore, for schools to avoid "encroaching unnecessarily upon the distinctive field of the other."[2] Therein rests the strategy most Oregon legislators would follow through most of the twentieth century.

Land-grants were schools of technology whose distinctive features were agriculture, mechanical arts, domestic economy, and commerce. In that division of labor, Kerr continued, colleges offered technical courses and universities classical, literary, and professional work. The land-grants would focus on training that "relates most directly to the development of the resources and industries of each state," and should promote training in mathematics and the physical and natural sciences. Kerr argued that state universities should offer sciences, and state colleges would have classes in language, literature, and history, the requisites of a liberal education. States should determine revenue available for higher education and then fund each institution accordingly. Doing so would relieve the state from contentious haggling over funding for land-grant colleges and state universities.[3] Kerr's dispassionate assessment of curricular divisions between state universities and land-grant colleges in 1905 would be sorely tested during his three decades in Oregon.

Two years into his tenure at Oregon Agricultural College, President Kerr confronted the very issues outlined in his 1905 address—the state legislature's creation in 1909 of the Oregon State Board of Higher Curricula. The board's responsibility was to allocate courses and majors between the agricultural college and the University of Oregon. Speaker of the House Clinton McArthur, author of the bill, wanted to end the duplication of courses and majors at Oregon's university and colleges. The measure provided for a governor-appointed five-member board to oversee "studies or departments" that might be duplicated. McArthur's bill was pointed directly at the duplication of courses between the university and the agricultural college.[4]

The measure limited the board's review to the duplication of courses and promised to serve the public's interests and avoid restricting institutional autonomy. After the House and Senate approved the bill, Governor George

Chamberlain signed it into law and appointed the five-member board.[5] It quickly became apparent that the Board of Higher Curricula held limited power. When its secretary, Joseph Hedges, submitted questions about the board's power to Oregon's attorney general, Andrew Crawford, the responses were disappointing. Crawford wrote Hedges: "The power granted to your board takes away no powers . . . exercised by the board of regents, except the power to say what particular branch shall be taught in the school." In a supplemental judgment, Crawford told the board that it was limited in restricting the agricultural college's programs because of its federally mandated guidelines as a land-grant institution. The attorney general advised the board to contact President Kerr about federal requirements.[6]

The Board of Higher Curricula first moved to assign mining and mechanical engineering courses solely to the agricultural college. Both institutions could offer civil and electrical engineering because of the demand for graduates. The university would continue to teach economics and commerce while the college would offer courses of a commercial nature. The board approved several new courses for the University of Oregon in 1911. When a legislative committee proposed to consolidate the schools in 1912, university president Prince Lucien Campbell opposed the move, telling lawmakers the college and university worked well "in isolation" from one another. Moreover, the schools' cooperative spirit indicated there would be little savings in having one institution. Plans for consolidation would never pass muster, Campbell argued, because "there would be a factional difference in arriving at the details of the plan."[7]

The University of Oregon president proved a diplomatic friend of the college, welcoming a commission to study consolidation while telling everyone that merging the institutions was unwise. Campbell told a group of Portland businessmen that he had no objection to Governor Oswald West appointing a commission to look into the matter. Consolidation deserved a "practical discussion," because both institutions had a vested interest in the issue. Both were well organized and each school had a large alumni body and a host of friends across the state. Campbell cautioned that legislation relocating one of the institutions would "involve the repudiation of a contract."[8]

President Kerr made few public statements during the early years under the Board of Higher Curricula, and his biennial reports had few complaints with the state's management of higher education. When legislators directed the curricula board to investigate duplicated courses in 1913, Kerr defended the college's responsibility for engineering courses. "The function and field of the Agricultural College is in strict accord with the provisions of the organic act of Congress passed in 1862," emphasizing academic programs in applied science and technical education. The board acknowledged that the college's courses in physical and natural sciences were essential to a college education.[9] Kerr was clearly pleased that the college would be allowed to pursue its programs efficiently and economically.

The board of regents advanced the departments of forestry and mining engineering to schools in 1913, with each unit offering a wide variety of courses. Establishing the School of Mining Engineering paralleled the legislature's creation of the Oregon Bureau of Mines and Geology. Following legislative directives, the Board of Higher Curricula floated a proposal to concentrate all engineering courses within the agricultural college and to assign the fine arts (including architecture and music), economics, higher commerce, education, and the graduate school to the university. Such changes would leave students in each institution "working along the same general lines." The board delayed a final decision until December, because members disagreed about assigning all engineering courses to the college.[10]

When UO's president Campbell and the Oregon Society of Engineers insisted on keeping professional engineering courses in Eugene, the board again postponed its decision. Those deliberations dragged on for several weeks, the board contending that chemical, electrical, and mechanical engineering should remain with the college, leaving civil engineering to the university. Board of Higher Curricula members continued to debate the transfer of fine arts and humanities to the university. An *Oregonian* editorial urged the board to quit "straddling" and carry out its responsibility of ridding the institutions of duplicated courses.[11] The board's deliberations continued into 1914, with members finally assigning civil engineering to the university and other engineering departments to the college. Its discussions centered on the pure versus the applied sciences, an argument that would be contested for several decades. John McNulty of the Oregon Society of Engineers criticized placing civil engineering with the university. "Where," he asked, "can civil engineering be separated from electrical engineering in this day of electrical railroads and transmission lines?" There should be no division in engineering education in the state, McNulty contended.[12]

The curricula board's next decision regarding engineering surprised everyone—civil engineering would be denied to both the University of Oregon and Oregon Agricultural College. Representatives of both institutions and the Oregon Society of Engineers were stunned. Civil engineering posed a significant problem for the college, because other schools and departments— forestry, agriculture, highway construction, and irrigation systems—required backgrounds in civil engineering. The curricula board cited economy as the basis for its decision—annual savings of about $40,000. Curricula board member C. J. Smith cited the improbability of hosting a top-rate engineering school in a state with such a small population. Students interested in advanced engineering work could enroll in other state institutions with strong programs.[13]

When the Board of Higher Curricula finalized its engineering decisions, it also transferred architecture, music, economics, education, and the graduate school to the university. The *Oregonian* called the move "a conclusive decision," giving the college responsibility for "agriculture, the mechanical arts, and the applied sciences," and the university the "liberal arts and pure sciences and kindred subjects." The object of much criticism, the university now held a defined place, thanks to the Board of Higher Curricula.[14] Although the contentious struggle had subsided, both institutions would have bigger fish to fry in the future.

The controversy over duplication of courses continued to bubble to the surface when a legislative bill or newspaper editorial stirred public emotions. While critics continued to pontificate, the university and college made inroads against some of the curricular board's strictures against duplication. When the university proposed a course in home economics in April 1917, citing the need for a class in domestic arts and sciences, the curricula board approved. The board continued its laissez-faire decision-making a few weeks later when President Kerr announced that the college would resume its courses in civil engineering. In his *Biennial Report* for 1920, Kerr summarized the curricula board's most important directives affecting the agricultural college. Civil engineering topped the list, with "War Emergency Courses" for the calendar year 1917–1918 a close second. The president added that the board approved a course in industrial journalism in May 1920 to meet the needs of graduates in agriculture and those with degrees in industrial subjects.[15]

Kerr's *Biennial Report* for 1922 provided details for two new programs, one for the School of Vocational Education, which would prepare students to teach high school subjects that were offered in the college's technical schools, with education courses required as minors. The president justified the program because of difficulties finding college graduates with technical training in specialized skills to teach high school classes. The second curricular addition was a bachelor's degree in military science, the college's military faculty providing instruction. The president described the new programs as "a curriculum definite in its purposes but liberal in its scope."[16]

Another curricula board revision involved changing the name of OAC's Division of Service Departments to the School of Basic Arts and Sciences. The twelve departments affected were art and rural architecture, bacteriology, botany and plant pathology, chemistry, English language and literature, entomology, history, mathematics, modern languages, physics, public speaking and dramatics, and zoology and physiology. For several years the departments provided lower-division instruction in the basic sciences for the college's technical schools.[17] In the face of the university's strenuous objections, however, there would be few changes to programs in the humanities and social sciences until the 1960s.

The first major clash over course offerings between the university and college took place in the spring of 1925, when the University of Oregon Board of Regents delivered a broadside to the Board of Higher Curricula, charging that Corvallis administrators had organized a college of basic arts with the intention of "becoming a state university." Those who believed "civil war" contests between the two schools took place only on the football field were wrong. Nothing in the rivalry between the university and the college compared with the heated exchanges over the control of curriculum, institutional majors, and degrees. To accusations that including the School of Basic Arts and Sciences was an effort to become a full-fledged university, Kerr responded that the curricula board had approved courses that were "basic to modern work in higher technology."[18]

The university's demand was bold, demanding that the Corvallis school cease duplicating courses and be prohibited from offering majors in "economics, sociology, political science, or any branch thereof, banking and finance and social work." The university insisted that the college be barred from teaching courses in European economic history, "money and banking, public finance, transportation, employment management and business cycle." Sociology courses should also be limited to one term. Eugene administrators demanded that classes in Western civilization and world history be prohibited, and they objected to the college's course in industrial journalism (approved by the curricula board in 1920).[19]

In his eighteen-page response, President Kerr charged the university with "opening a general attack upon the work of the College." The university had been objecting to curricula board policies since its inception, he stated, "every page containing errors of fact, insinuations, and fearsome prophecies." Kerr argued that the college's commerce courses were better suited to a technical school than a liberal university. Since the curricula board had ruled that undergraduate courses in commerce should be offered in Corvallis, the School of Commerce had offered classes to more than seven thousand students who were majoring in other fields. The president suggested that the university's undergraduate degree in commerce duplicated work at the college and should be eliminated.[20]

Kerr's rejoinder continued, rejecting the university's accusation that OAC offered educational courses valuable to teachers and educational administrators. The college had granted vocational education degrees to 275 students who were now teaching in Oregon high schools. Kerr accused the university of suggesting that a person majoring in agriculture could not serve as an administrator in a rural high school. It was important that the college offer courses for educational administrators. The president aggressively defended the college, protesting "the sublime assurance, wisdom and authority of 18th century classical learning." He ended with biting satire: "Give them the marketing of farm products, they tell you, but take away those courses on transportation, concentration and monopoly in business, and the business cycle."[21]

Shortly after the two schools exchanged their curricular missiles, J. K. Weatherford of OAC's Board of Regents played the institution's trump card. Of first importance, the college had to meet Morrill Act requirements and the federal legislation that followed; second, because its economy was underdeveloped, Oregon needed people trained in technological fields. Weatherford reminded the board that its rulings of 1910, 1913, and 1914 had already outlined the respective fields of both institutions.[22] The *Oregonian* summarized the curriculum struggle in midsummer 1925 with a barbed headline: "CURRICULA FIGHT IS ENDED IN DRAW." The board subsequently recommended only the elimination of the university's pre-engineering course and the college's premedical course. Curricula board chair Dr. C. J. Smith assured the public that it had limited liberal arts courses at the college to undergraduate, nondegree programs.[23]

The School of Basic Arts and Sciences at the college represented an effort to organize lower-division departments in one unit rather than scattering them across the technical schools. Arts and sciences dean Elwood Smith argued that his unit would be economical, improve departmental effectiveness, and boost the visibility of nontechnical courses. From the Morrill Act to the present, technical curricula had "attained a defensible footing in science," Smith reported, and most land-grant schools recognized that "arts, letters, and the social sciences" made modern life intelligible. Moreover, studying biology, botany, entomology, and zoology supported professional work in agriculture and home economics. The same could be said for art courses and their relation to commerce ("advertising, window posters and displays") and home economics.[24]

The State of Oregon was not alone among institutions seeking legislative favoritism for academic programs and budgetary allocations. Although other states differed in time and circumstances, the differences among land-grants and state universities share common features. Iowa State College, the standard-bearer among early land-grants, parried with the University of Iowa during the 1920s, the presidents of both institutions openly hostile to one another. According to Earle Ross's history of Iowa State, the two presidents were "rivals for support and popular favor." Iowa State's president, Walter Jessup, was aware of the public's growing impatience with rising costs. When the two Iowa schools commissioned a study seeking to resolve their differences, the results recommended only improving institutional relations. Purdue University president E. C. Elliott, speaking to a group of land-grant administrators in 1926, observed that no state had successfully bridged the differences between the "condescending attitude of the universities and the over-pretentions of the colleges."[25]

Although Montana State College joined the ranks of land-grant institutions relatively late (1893), it confronted issues similar to those in other states. Following statehood in 1890, the Montana legislature debated where to locate the capital and the state university. In the interests of economy and educational quality, several legislators wanted the university and college in one location. Legislative logrolling eventually placed the capital in Helena, the university in Missoula, and the land-grant college in Bozeman. In the following decades the Montana Board of Education investigated the duplication of programs and recommended consolidating the state's far-flung institutions on a single campus. Because of ongoing threats, Montana State College presidents were cautious about expanding liberal arts programs, fearing that tightfisted lawmakers would tighten the institution's purse strings. Those circumstances persisted into the 1970s, with Bozeman and Missoula waging bitter conflicts to secure legislative support. In the midst of such legislative wrangling, there was little coordination and cooperation.[26]

The State of Michigan's record is similar, with some legislators attempting to designate the state university as the agricultural college. A majority of lawmakers thought otherwise, however, arguing against having the college under the university's board of regents because they knew "as much about farming as the man in the moon did about cheese." The passage of the Morrill Act in 1862 posed another problem when a Michigan legislative committee proposed to assign land-grant status to the university and consolidate the two schools. East Lansing prevailed when transportation improvements lessened its isolation and legislative friends came to its defense. The college fought off attacks again in the late 1880s, when legislators worried that East Lansing's environment harbored contagious diseases and that the college's students had a reputation for rowdiness. Michigan State struggled into the next century and then began to prosper amid a rising tide of student enrollments. During the 1920s, the college fought to keep its engineering division and staved off another consolidation effort.[27]

New York's Cornell University, a private institution and one of the earliest land-grants, has largely retained its independence with the passage of time. Cornell is an anomaly among the Morrill Act schools, because its conflicts usually involved the state. With some parallels to Purdue, Ezra Cornell provided an endowment of $500,000 and tuition-free attendance to one student from every assembly district in the state. Legislation to acquire the land-grant designation—including Cornell's financial obligation—passed the New York Assembly and Senate and the governor signed it into law in 1865. In this way, Cornell joined the ranks of private schools (Yale, Rutgers, and Brown) as early land-grants. Shrewd Cornell administrators brokered agreements with the state, committing the school to putting up a building in 1893 if the state would establish a veterinary college on campus and contribute to its support. Despite significant opposition, farmer organizations and Cornell's influential lobby prevailed.[28]

The New York legislature conferred on Cornell the first college of forestry in the United States in 1898, a short-lived venture because lawmakers ended their support in 1903. A more serious threat to Cornell's independence as a private school occurred after the Second World War, when the State of New York established "contract statutory colleges" of agriculture, home economics, veterinary medicine, and a school of industrial and labor relations on the Ithaca campus. Under the agreement, the units were constituents of the new State University of New York system. Cornell continues to exercise significant land-grant responsibilities into the twenty-first century, its extension programs reaching rural and urban constituencies and its experiment stations carrying on traditional work in agriculture. The university is proud of its public-private partnership—"unique in American higher education—between a privately endowed, Ivy League institution and the State of New York."[29]

After Oregon's publicly aired curriculum battles in 1925, the university and agricultural college muted their protests, and the curricula board agreed to new courses for each institution. The board approved courses in agricultural engineering, lumber manufacturing, and real estate for the college, and Governor I. L. Patterson called the respective boards of the college and university to Salem in June 1927 for a peace-making parley. "Competition between the college and the university," the governor told the regents, "should be confined strictly to athletic events." Patterson convinced the regents to strike a truce—on paper at least—with the boards agreeing to work together. Their agreement suggested both boards would ride off into a happy sunset:[30]

> That we pledge ourselves to loyal co-operation in administering
> our trust to the taxpayers of Oregon through promoting
> harmony and good will between the two institutions.
> That we enjoin the officers, faculties and as far as our influence
> may extend, the alumni and students of the two institutions, to
> like harmony and cooperation.
> That to give effect to these resolutions a joint organization of
> the two boards be effected to consider matters of mutual interest.

Other than gridiron and basketball competitions, the scrimmages before the curricula board and news media abated for a while. At the college, faculty and friends celebrated President Kerr's twentieth anniversary as head of the institution. The gala "birthday party" observed that Kerr had served longer than any current president of a land-grant. The college's press release praised the president's leadership in promoting higher education initiatives—avoiding duplication of courses, establishing the Oregon State Board of Higher Curricula, and adopting the millage tax to support higher education.[31]

Governor Patterson's attempt to promote peaceful coexistence had a brief shelf life. Ten months after meeting with the governor, the university unleashed another sweeping attack on the college, threatening "an open and state-wide fight." Its principal charge—delivered to the curricula board in April 1928—was the "*unnecessary* and *costly* duplication in regard to certain specific fields of instruction." Work at the schools would be more efficient and economical if their roles were well defined. President Kerr and the college responded with a twenty-eight-page accounting of errors and misstatements in the university's "renewal of the old onslaught of 1925."[32]

Kerr indicated that the university's attack on the college's curriculum was its third in six years, despite everything being "sanctioned by the Board of Higher Curricula." How often, he asked, did the board have "to reaffirm its decisions regarding the curricula at the College?" Corvallis administrators were upset with persisting accusations that the college's music, industrial journalism, and physical education classes duplicated work in Eugene, subjects that should be taught, even if they were not leading to a degree.[33] It referred to curricula board decisions in 1914 designating the broad fields of inquiry assigned to each institution. Through twenty years of rulings, the college had never challenged the board's decisions, while the "university has repeatedly done so." Because the Eugene school threatened to complain to the legislature, Kerr offered a compromise—the schools should invite the United States Bureau of Education to conduct an impartial survey of curriculum at both institutions.[34] The future would show that such a request would create problems for everyone.

The legislature's biennial session in 1929 ushered in momentous changes for higher education in Oregon when Washington County senator Edward Schulmerich introduced Senate Bill 192 to create a single board to oversee all public institutions of higher education. The measure would abolish the existing boards of regents in lieu of a single nine-member board appointed by the governor (with the consent of the Senate). The board would be responsible for hiring a chancellor to direct day-to-day operations. The *Oregonian* declared Schulmerich's proposal dead on arrival, because university and college lobbyists were well organized and would defeat the measure.[35] The Senate, however, put the lie to that prediction and approved the measure with only five dissenting votes. The bill sent to the House included a provision for commissioning a federal survey of the state's five institutions (the university and agricultural college and normal schools in Monmouth, Ashland, and La Grande) to provide a blueprint for action. Governor I. L. Patterson was optimistic about the bill's prospects in the House, citing Iowa's success in restructuring its higher education system along the lines of the Oregon bill.[36]

Through all the legislative maneuvering, the *Oregonian*'s Salem correspondent, John Kelly, was optimistic, believing Senate Bill 192 offered a way "out of the fog of conflicting rivalries." With Representative Hector Macpherson piloting the bill, the House overwhelmingly approved the proposal. Because SB 192 included an "emergency clause," it went into effect as soon as the governor signed it.[37] As legislators and the governor congratulated themselves over their seemingly breathless accomplishment, university and college administrators prepared to navigate new and difficult currents with a panel of supposedly politically neutral appointees.

The new blueprint proposed a truly revolutionary framework for its five academic units. Because the legislation provided guidelines affecting generations of Oregon college students, Chapter 251 of the *Codes and General Laws of Oregon* deserves close attention:

> To provide for the management, control, support and operation of the state institutions of higher education; to create a state board of higher education; to determine the method of its appointment; to prescribe its powers and duties; and to abolish the board of regents of the University of Oregon, the board of regents of the Oregon State Agricultural College, the board of regents of the Oregon normal schools and the board of higher curricula; providing for a survey and reorganization of the work and . . . [amending and repealing sections], and all acts and parts of the acts in conflict herewith, and declaring an emergency.

The principal sections of the legislation provided a framework for action:

> Section 1: created the department of higher education with a board of nine directors.
> Section 2: the nine directors to be appointed by the governor, with the consent of the Senate.
> Section 3: directors to serve without salary; they could not be affiliated with affected institutions; no more than three alumni of the institutions could serve at one time; directors would serve rotating terms of nine years.
> Section 6: the board to assume "all the powers and duties" of the former boards of regents.
> Section 7: the board to take complete "control of all records, books, papers," and properties of the state's higher education institutions.
> Section 9: the board to commission a "nationally recognized authority" to conduct a survey of Oregon's public higher education institutions.
> Section 11: directors to develop a "standardized system of accounts and records" for all institutions.
> Section 12: "The board shall hire an executive secretary" whose office would be in Salem.
> Section 13: the state system's advertising and publications to be centralized in Salem, with the board empowered to authorize all publications.

Section 14: relations with the legislature should be through the department of higher education; "no subordinate official, representing any of the separate institutions shall appear before the legislature or any committee except upon the written consent of the board."[38]

The governor's signature was barely dry on the document when it became obvious that depoliticizing the relations between the Corvallis and Eugene institutions would be difficult. University alumni frothed at Governor Patterson's list of nominees sent to the Senate, according to *Oregonian* columnist John Kelly, because it heavily favored the agricultural college. When the Senate took a brief recess, university alumni and friends swarmed the chamber complaining of the "loaded" and "stacked" list favoring the college. Kelly called the episode "the warmest lobbying and wire pulling that lawmakers had experienced since the session opened." When senators reconvened in the evening, spectators filled the gallery as legislators heatedly debated the governor's recommendations. At the end of a rancorous evening, the Senate approved all but one of the governor's recommendations.[39]

As the American and international economies plunged downward with the onset of the Great Depression, the newly created Oregon State System of Higher Education fumbled its way toward organizing the state's institutions. First and foremost was the legislature's directive to commission the United States Office of Education and Dr. Arthur J. Klein to conduct a survey of Oregon's institutions of higher education. The investigation was slow to materialize, and after Klein signed his contract, the interviews, research, analysis, and writing consumed nearly a year. The survey was "to determine the economic and social ability of the state . . . to support the existing institutions of education and to provide a basis for field extension." Optimists hoped the inquiry would enable the board to make recommendations free of bias. Oregon Agricultural College President Kerr was proactive, urging administrators to prepare an analysis of their respective schools, with unit costs per student, buildings, and equipment, and to be prepared for a "searching investigation."[40]

Klein visited Oregon in October 1930 and returned east without saying a word about his findings. The months whiled away into April 1931 before board members and institutional presidents received copies of the US Office of Education's *Survey of Oregon State Institutions of Higher Learning*.[41] The document pleased the State Board of Higher Education and upset member institutions. The study addressed legislators' most critical concerns—relations between the University of Oregon and Oregon Agricultural College—and praised lawmakers for unifying and establishing state control over its institutions of higher education, referring to the governing board as "a real arm of state wide responsibility." The *Survey* applauded legislators for prohibiting institutions from appearing before the legislature without board approval and applauded the law's strong centralized control, which promised to restrain institutional autonomy.[42]

The *Survey* commended the new Department of Higher Education for having power over all real estate and property and the authority to allocate funds, and for assuming responsibility for publicity. It noted that the education department should be able to implement its directive "with a minimum of legal restriction and a maximum of necessary information and authorization." The *Survey* provided data on major fields of study, the state's "economic and occupational requirements," and questioned whether state funds were properly apportioned between its member schools. It urged board members to be bold and to avoid having previous decisions direct its strategy. [43]

If the Board of Higher Education adopted the *Survey*'s arrangement, it would be a step "the state should not hesitate" to take. The report recommended choosing educational principles that could be administered efficiently and at the lowest cost. The duplication of courses was unimportant at the lower-division level, but in upper-division courses, especially in the sciences, they were expensive because of smaller class sizes. All upper-division science courses, therefore, should be taught in Corvallis. Where duplication existed in upper-division social science courses, the university should be responsible for such classes.[44]

In the summary chapter, "Findings and Recommendations," the *Survey* judged Oregon below the national average in students majoring in the liberal arts, law, and enrollment in graduate school. The percentages of students in agriculture, commerce, business, engineering, and pharmacy, however, exceeded the national average. The summary emphasized the historic missions of the two institutions: the university, humanities and the social sciences; and the college, "sciences and their technical application in a wide range of occupations." In a statement with striking consequences for the future, the *Survey* declared: "Historical developments that disregard these distinctive characteristics will have to be ruthlessly amputated in order to secure economy and unity in the educational system of the state."[45]

Oregon's contentious curriculum fights were literally suspended on the eve of the greatest depression in American history. The US Office of Education report landed in the laps of the University of Oregon and Oregon Agricultural College in the midst of out-of-work loggers and millworkers and plummeting agricultural prices. Glutted markets for agricultural products and a weak California construction industry in the last half of the 1920s had already put the economies of Oregon and Washington in a tailspin. Plunging state, county, and local taxes sharply curtailed revenue for education and community services, forcing retrenchment everywhere, including Oregon's flagship university and college. Beyond campus, bank failures, bankruptcies, and escalating unemployment fostered desperation and mounting protests.[46]

Oregon's troubled economy prompted Governor Julius Meier in March 1931 to cut $500,000 from the legislature's appropriation of $1,181,176 to support higher education. Although this was only 5 percent of Oregon's operating budget of $11,358,378, the State Board of Higher Education strongly opposed the governor's decision, arguing that it could accomplish the same end through efficient management and eliminating "unnecessary duplication" of courses and programs. Meier explained that he reduced the budget because the state's revenue situation was "so acute that people are unable to pay their taxes."[47] That initial tussle involving the board, the governor, and legislators over collapsing revenue was the first in a near-decade of similar skirmishes.

The federal survey's recommendations disappointed President Kerr, who argued that they were impractical, experimental, and without precedent. "Oregon should not be made a laboratory in which to experiment with the theoretical philosophy of education." University president Arnold Bennett Hall thought some of the proposals were bizarre, especially the suggestion that all upper-division science should be taught at Oregon State College. No self-respecting university in the country, he declared, operated without offering programs in chemistry, physics, mathematics, zoology, and geology. While the higher education board appeared to sympathize with the presidents, its more immediate problem was implementing the governor's retrenchment decision.[48]

A greater threat to the higher education budget emerged when a Salem group initiated a petition to refer the legislature's $1,181,376 appropriation for higher education to voters. If the petitioners gathered enough signatures, the higher education appropriation would be tied up until the measure appeared on the ballot in November 1932. The *Oregonian* thought the effort to refer the budget to voters ill-advised in light of the state board's willingness to follow the recommendations of the federal report. The newspaper agreed with the public's interest in belt-tightening, but urged citizens to be patient.

The signature gatherers prevailed, however, and the higher education budget, already reduced through Governor Meier's mandate, would be held in abeyance until the November election in 1932.[49]

With its budget uncertain, the Board of Higher Education instructed the Eugene and Corvallis schools to revise their expenditures to accord "with the reallocation of functions between the University and College." Because the board had yet to provide curricular guidelines, President Kerr submitted an amended budget based on current course offerings, reminding board members that the college carried an "overload of duties" in its extension and experiment station work. Under the present emergency, the board should understand that "calls for assistance in agriculture and the industries are more numerous, widespread and insistent than ever."[50]

The higher education board ultimately navigated through the budget morass without eliminating departments, schools, or reducing wages, determining that the college needed to save $513,000 and the university $342,000. In examining "unexpended balances" in departments and schools at the two institutions, the board estimated a savings of $226,000. The three normal schools, suffering far worse from the Depression, were exempt from further cuts. To achieve additional savings, the board directed the college and university to increase teaching loads and suspend hiring for vacated positions. The *Oregonian* applauded the strategy, in which "few essentials seem to be slated for discard."[51]

The university and college, which had grown apace for three decades, were now struggling for mere survival and to protect their treasured autonomy from threats of consolidation. As the national and state economies continued their downward spiral, Governor Meier asked state employees to donate one day's pay each month to assist individuals and families in distress. Following the governor's announcement, President Kerr called a staff meeting to place the idea before his colleagues. After extended discussion, the faculty agreed to fully cooperate during the emergency, authorizing Kerr to make arrangements for "a cooperative contribution to the relief fund" for five months.[52]

From its first meeting in 1929 until the federal survey was released in 1931, the Oregon State Board of Higher Education took few initiatives. In the interim, the University of Oregon and Oregon Agricultural College jousted over courses, credits, majors, and degree programs, each submitting documents to the board accusing the other of deception and manipulating data to its advantage. The college fought tooth and nail to retain its School of Commerce and the university did likewise to retain its curriculum in the "pure" and theoretical sciences. Their behavior frustrated the board, a point it acknowledged in its biennial report for 1932. While the college and university believed their policies were high-minded and generous, their responses reflected a desire to continue conventional functions and activities. The board's assessment was blunt: "The deadlock in the attitude of the two major institutions regarding the recommendations of the Survey Commission continued without appreciable modification throughout the period of negotiations, except that the College took a more aggressive attitude, especially in rebuttal, in its succeeding briefs."[53]

The state board did not implement its legislative mandate to unify the state's five public institutions until March 1932. The effusive *Oregonian* applauded the board's proposal for creating "the first 100 per cent unified system of state colleges, universities and normal schools" in the nation. The grand experiment promised to bring about transfers of courses, changes in faculty, and "daring economies." The newspaper praised the board's willingness to "overthrow the old and establish the new system in less than three hours." The proposal would be implemented in September 1932.[54]

The higher education board's strategy hewed closely to the survey commission's recommendations, assigning six schools each to the university and college. The University of Oregon medical school would continue in Portland, and the Eugene campus would be home to schools of law, social science, fine arts, business and commerce, physical education, and literature and language arts. The college would host home economics, agriculture, physics and biological sciences, engineering, pharmacy, and forestry. The reorganization eliminated the School of Journalism in Eugene and the industrial journalism course and School of Mines in Corvallis. The board's initial organizational chart had an executive head overseeing the entire system, with lieutenants heading the university and college campuses. The board hoped to hire its top administrator from out of state. A final item on its agenda—eliminating radio station KOAC on the Corvallis campus—brought a strong rejoinder from President Kerr, who indicated its educational and instructional value to both the university and the Board of Higher Education. Board member B. F. Irvine, a newspaper editor, argued that KOAC was "an instrument that helps people think." KOAC survived.[55]

The State Board of Higher Education's decision to abolish the university's School of Journalism proved the most unpopular component of its reorganization strategy. While praising the overall plan, newspapers across the state unanimously criticized the demise of the university's journalism program. The *Bend Bulletin* observed that the journalism school's "presence in Oregon is a credit which should not be lightly nullified." The *Hillsboro Argus* described the elimination of journalism programs at the university and college as "serious losses to the education system." It was with great regret, the *Dalles Times-Itemizer* wrote, "that we witness the death of the school of journalism at the University of Oregon." Not to be deterred, University of Oregon students appealed the board's elimination of journalism, drafting a petition to be presented at its next meeting.[56]

When President Kerr presented the board's directive to the faculty, he observed that a drastically reduced budget dictated much of its work. Because board members were acting under trying circumstances, the president promised to cooperate with the reorganization effort. Although the proposal was all-encompassing, it would likely not be perfect; therefore, "provision has been made for changes or readjustments that may be necessary." The president applauded the board's honest effort to seek constructive solutions and urged the faculty to work in a spirit of cooperation with the new system.[57]

The State Board of Higher Education had taken a sledgehammer to systematically restructure the curriculum of the University of Oregon and Oregon Agricultural College. To unify programs between the university and college and to honor the unique functions of each, the board mandated the creation of common undergraduate curriculum at both institutions—the Lower Division of Arts and Sciences—where students could enroll in their freshman and sophomore years and then transfer in their junior year to the institution offering their chosen area of specialization. The board explicitly followed the survey commission's recommendation: the university would be home to the "humanities and social sciences and their application to the various professions," and the college "to the sciences and their technical application in a wide range of occupations."[58] Although the board admitted the arrangement needed fine-tuning, its division of spoils left the Eugene campus bereft of natural and physical sciences and the college without social sciences and commerce.

The board's denying the university upper-division science courses, especially what it termed the "pure sciences," would frustrate Eugene administrators for the remainder of the decade. The respected Charles Sprague, publisher and editor of the *Oregon Statesman*, objected to denying sciences to the university. In an August 1932 editorial, he referred to the state board's policy as a "Frankenstein System of Higher Education." Refusing upper-division science courses to the university would cripple its legitimacy as a comprehensive institution of higher education. The scientific enterprise was important, Sprague insisted, to any "well developed college or university of liberal training." Removing advanced science studies from the Eugene school would "strike a serious blow at the very life of the institution."[59] Elected governor in 1938, Sprague would provide vital support for the restoration of science to the university.

During the next months, the higher education board attempted to accommodate the impassioned appeals of the university and college to rectify the shortcomings of lower-division courses that failed to prepare students for technical and professional programs on their campuses. The economic crisis vastly complicated matters, with the dire financial news of late 1932 and 1933 placing both institutions in ever-worsening circumstances. Students, who supposedly would benefit from the restructuring, had no voice in the decisions other than to provide talking heads for their respective institutions. It is ironic that the legislature's decision of 1929 to restructure its public institutions of higher education—made before Wall Street's Black Thursday of October 24, 1929—would be implemented amid the worst depression in American history.

6

The Academy in the Great Depression

When Democratic presidential candidate Franklin D. Roosevelt visited Portland in September 1932, he remarked that only foolish optimists could "deny the dark realities of the moment." The American economy was in freefall that election season, with 30 percent of the nation unemployed and thirty thousand people in greater Portland looking for work. With Hoovervilles dotting urban landscapes and hungry vagrants wandering the countryside, Roosevelt swept to a landslide victory over the beleaguered incumbent President Herbert Hoover. In that epic election, Roosevelt garnered large majorities in Oregon, Washington, and Idaho, sweeping every county in the Northwest except two: Bear County, Idaho, and Benton County, Oregon.[1] Benton County and its principal city, Corvallis, would continue to be a stronghold for conservative politics for several decades.

Roosevelt's electoral success in the West would continue through three successive campaigns for the presidency—1936, 1940, and 1944—during which he attracted the support of impoverished westerners and maintained their allegiance for the rest of his life. In his four successful tries for the presidency, he ran well ahead of other Democrats in the West. Historian Richard White writes that Roosevelt "regularly secured 20 percent more votes than other Democratic candidates on the [same] ticket." When Roosevelt was not on the ballot, Democrats suffered losses, but in presidential election years, "Democratic candidates carried almost 75 percent of the western gubernatorial and Senate elections." The Roosevelt coalition in the region did not survive his presidency, with Republicans becoming the majority party after his death in 1945.[2]

The worsening financial crisis had been hammering Oregon's economy for more than a year before the 1932 election. The State Board of Higher Education had directed the presidents of the university and college in June 1931 to examine their budgets and eliminate expenses to meet the funding emergency. In Corvallis, the president called a college meeting to address the looming budgetary crises and to discuss state-mandated restructuring of its curriculum.[3] In the midst of those crises, state institutions confronted the Zorn-Macpherson legislative bill, a measure referred to voters that would consolidate the university and agricultural college on the Corvallis campus, relocate the three state teachers' colleges to Eugene in one teacher-training school, and convert the Monmouth, LaGrande, and Ashland campuses into junior colleges. The bill stirred fierce passions in Corvallis and Eugene. The *Oregonian* attributed the plan to disgruntled meddlers, "a drastic shifting around, destruction of identity of one of the most important units and the setting up of one completely new independent unit."[4]

With Zorn-Macpherson simmering below the surface, the Board of Higher Education vacillated through the spring and summer of 1932 in selecting a chancellor to oversee the state system. The Oregon State College Alumni Association initiated a letter-writing campaign promoting President William Jasper Kerr for the position. Rumors circulated that University of Oregon alums would be making a similar push. With Kerr's candidacy gathering momentum, the Oregon Alumni Association asked the state board to defer its decision, because university supporters were being forced into competition over the choice of a chancellor. When a board member indicated that Kerr was not a candidate, the OSC president confirmed the point. In the midst of the gala banquet celebrating his twenty-five years as president, Kerr said nothing about leaving his post as president. The *Oregonian* added its voice, urging the board to look out of state for a competent administrative head.[5]

The rumor mill continued to buzz, with anonymous sources again predicting that Kerr would be the next chancellor. In the interim, the state board invited George Frederick Zook, president of Akron University, to interview for the chancellor's position. In the midst of those maneuvers, Oregon's president, Arnold Bennett Hall, resigned on September 4 to take a position with the Brookings Institution; two days later the board selected Kerr as the first chancellor for the state's higher education system. The *Oregonian* learned that the vote for Kerr was larger than the board's earlier decision to reject Akron's president Zook. As part of the political maneuvering, Kerr agreed to locate the chancellor's office on the University of Oregon campus, and he asked the board to appoint acting presidents at the university and college in the interests of economy.[6] At this grim moment in the depths of the Great Depression, William Jasper Kerr became responsible for implementing a revolutionary reorganization plan amid soaring unemployment.

Kerr's selection as chancellor provided an interlude in the divisiveness between the University of Oregon and Oregon State College.[7] The *Oregonian* characterized the moment as a time to restore "harmony and progress" and bury "differences and contentions for the sake of the general good," and urged friends of higher education to support the board and new chancellor. The newspaper praised the higher education board for eliminating duplicated courses and achieving a semblance of economy. The circumstances called for "an end to strife over our higher educational affairs." For alumni and patrons of the flagship institutions—and to the satisfaction of the chancellor—voters rejected the Zorn-Macpherson consolidation measure (47,275 yes to 292,486 no), a resounding victory for continuing the revamped Oregon State System of Higher Education.[8]

In its biennial report published in November 1932, the Oregon State System of Higher Education reported a dismal revenue forecast for the coming biennium—declining income from property valuations, fewer students registering for classes, reduced proceeds from the sale of commodities, and a legislature unable to resolve the funding crisis. All state institutions were directed to eliminate capital expenditures, publications were terminated, faculty positions went vacant, and professors taught larger classes. Many extension and agricultural research services were jettisoned. Finally, college salaries and wages would be reduced beginning with the academic year 1932–1933. The state board's formula for reducing pay deserves notice: "On the first thousand dollars, 5 percent; on the second thousand dollars, 8 percent; on the third thousand, 11 percent; on the fourth thousand, 14 percent; and on all sums above four thousand, 15 percent."[9]

The higher education board appointed forestry dean George W. Peavy acting president of Oregon State College in 1933. At the University of Oregon, where Arnold Bennett Hall had resigned, leading administrators made key decisions in the absence of an interim or permanent president for sixteen months. The state board appointed Clarence Boyer as acting president in January 1934 and full president in April. The confusion over the presidencies of the two institutions was rooted in the uncertainty about whether the university and state college would continue with fully entitled presidents, or whether they would have "lieutenants," as an earlier organization chart indicated. Peavy's designation as acting president in September 1932 remained in limbo for two years, until the board named him the college's seventh president in 1934. As acting president, he struggled mightily with the state board's reorganization plans, while dealing with a revenue stream that plunged 41 percent in one year. Peavy, who kept his position as dean of the School of Forestry, was widely respected in the state as an administrator not to be trifled with.[10]

In his first report to the state board in 1934, Peavy detailed the impositions placed on the state college, stressing the increased responsibilities and workload of the faculty and their "excessive duties, and even hardship and sacrifice." In addition to drastic budget cuts and obligations to assist with federal emergency programs, the state board had mandated "one of the most drastic reorganizations of a state-supported system of higher education ever undertaken." Through those trials and tribulations, the board's audit for 1931–1932 accused the college of financial irregularities, whereas the issue rested with the board's own misinterpretations. As Peavy pointedly stated, "complete and conclusive evidence" proved the suspicions and charges without merit.[11]

As the fully empowered president of Oregon State College, Peavy could point to "significant and highly constructive" improvements in the state system—the board's appointment of a chancellor with administrative and executive powers and the decision to appoint full-fledged presidents for its two major institutions. The board reaffirmed lines of authority and responsibility for deans and directors. A third and important action, effective July 1, 1934, placed "all non-major lower division and service courses at the State College . . . under a single organization, known as the Lower Division and Service Departments," a close relation to the statewide Lower Division of Liberal Arts and Sciences.[12]

The college's Lower Division and Service Departments established a curricular framework that persisted—with minor adjustments—for three decades. As the university restored its science programs through the passing years, the college's Lower Division symbolized a land-grant "aggie" school, absent important components of a comprehensive institution of higher education. With the vantage of hindsight, the long-lived Lower Division raises questions about how vigorously Corvallis administrators fought for curricular parity between the sciences and humanities. As President Peavy reported in 1934, the state board decreed that the Lower Division should provide the "elements of a general college education," a curriculum that "should be widely distributed in the State System."[13] Under that formula, the primary function of the college's Lower Division was to provide service courses to schools offering professional degrees.

Administrators commonly referred to the Lower Division as "non-major departments," confirming their status under the Oregon State Board of Higher Education's mandate. In the division of spoils, the Oregon State College lost its long-standing School of Commerce to the University of Oregon, the School of Mines was closed, and the college and university administered Landscape Architecture and Structural Design as a joint curriculum.

The timeworn struggles between Corvallis and Eugene would continue, even in the face of the state board dictating curricular divisions between the schools. As a freshly minted president, Peavy faced down a series of crises, not all of them related to budget matters. The first incident involved Herman Swartz's 1934 commencement address, "The Superfluous Generation." Swartz, president of the Pacific School of Religion in Berkeley, California, bewailed the nation's high unemployment and the noisome threats of communists and fascists abroad. Swartz's focus was the international "rivalry of armaments," the failure to limit the production of battleships and troop buildups, and nations such as Russia and Japan looking to expand their military might.[14]

Swartz compared armaments manufacturing to "preparing for collective suicide," yet in the midst of such developments, nations were declaring their opposition to wars of conquest. While he opposed profiting in arms production, Swartz believed in defending national boundaries. Claude Ingalls, the conservative editor and publisher of the Corvallis Gazette-Times, censured Swartz's address, calling for heads to roll at the college and urging the state board to demand an end to such gratuitous affronts. Ingalls charged that Swartz gave graduates a poor send-off, insulted the ROTC, and breathed "the kind of poison that ought to deprive him of citizenship."[15]

Colonel W. H. Patterson, commandant of cadets and professor of military science, protested Swartz's selection as a speaker, because he "gratuitously insulted, demeaned and belittled" the military department. In a letter to President Peavy, Patterson demanded reprimands for those responsible for selecting the speaker. He then turned his wrath to Fred R. Murrow, pastor of the local Westminster House, who had circulated an antiwar pamphlet among students, literature "published for subversive purposes and by a subversive organization."[16] Patterson added that the League for Industrial Democracy had formed a chapter at Westminster House following a talk by the league's "visiting agitator," Monroe Sweetland. According to Patterson, Elizabeth Dilling's The Red Network listed the League for Industrial Democracy as a subversive organization under "communist, socialist, IWW, and proletarian party (communist) control." He concluded his accusatory letter with information that the University of Oregon's "Radical Club" was sending "a truck load of food to Portland" to aid striking longshore workers.[17]

President Peavy mailed two letters in response to Colonel Patterson's accusations: one to Patterson, acknowledging receipt of his complaints, and another to General Malin Craig at the Presidio, requesting that he dispatch at his earliest convenience "to this campus an inspector, on a confidential mission to my office." Peavy would provide the person "with certain information now in my possession" and add other pertinent details. While the letters were in the mail, the Corvallis *Gazette-Times* and Albany *Democrat-Herald* asked the State Board of Higher Education to look into the selection of the college's commencement speakers. The Albany paper described the address "an insulting diatribe against the United States army and navy and the ROTC." The Eugene *News* chided both newspapers for suggesting that it was proper to let prophets speak "so long as they let the army and navy alone and keep clear of the sacred subjects of preparedness and armaments."[18]

In preparing to meet the Presidio investigator, Peavy drafted a one-page memorandum for the record, with details about Colonel Patterson. The president was unapologetic, pointing out that Patterson was an employee of the state college with an annual salary of $1,200 and was responsible to the president. Peavy planned to use Patterson's letter against him, citing the colonel's insistence that his department be guaranteed against further embarrassments of this kind. The president noted that Patterson and other employees of the institution had the right to present a case for consideration. "He is not, however, in the position of demanding guarantees for anything." Furthermore, Patterson was insubordinate: when he sent copies of the letter to the president and members of the state board, he embarrassed the president and discredited the college. Peavy's memo mentioned reports that faculty women found Colonel Patterson's behavior "crude, boorish, and offensive" and that he often mingled with faculty and students with liquor on his breath. The military department, Peavy wrote, "would be vastly improved by a change in the position of Commandant of Cadets."[19]

The Presidio inspector visited with Peavy on June 20, and a subsequent memorandum indicates full agreement with the president's decision that Patterson be transferred. Peavy agreed with the inspector that the only documents submitted to the Presidio would be Patterson's letter to the president and acknowledgment that copies were also mailed to the chancellor, members of the state board, and General Craig, and one was published in the *Gazette-Times*. The colonel made a last-ditch effort to keep his position as commandant, appealing to Peavy that his daughter had one year remaining in high school and that his wife was not well. Peavy's notes read: "No good reason for modifying the decision previously arrived at."[20]

Oregon State College and its peer institutions experienced unprecedented fiscal problems through the depression decade, difficulties that worsened when enrollment recovered from the low numbers of the years between

Table 6.1. Fall Term Enrollment at Oregon State College, 1928–1940

Year	Head Count	Year	Head Count
1928–1929	3,490	1935–1936	3,124
1929–1930	3,430	1936–1937	3,785
1930–1931	3,347	1937–1938	4,075
1931–1932	3,060	1938–1939	4,406
1932–1933	2,277	1939–1940	4,619
1933–1934	1,960	1940–1941	4,759
1934–1935	2,577		

1932 and 1934. The figures for the Corvallis school provide stark reminders of the dilemmas administrators faced in the wake of draconian budget cuts and declining enrollments, followed by increasing numbers of students without corresponding financial support. The low enrollment figures for 1932, 1933, and 1934 mirror the financial crisis and the state system's dramatic reorganization that may have discouraged students from enrolling (table 6.1). When enrollment increased in 1934, no reciprocal infusion of funding materialized to meet the increased workload. The consequences were senior faculty leaving for better-paying positions.[21]

President Peavy proved himself a team player, praising the "Survey of Land-Grant Colleges and Universities" for promising that stability was "the surest road to sound development." Surviving the suspense-filled years of the early 1930s, the state college had the security to serve its statewide constituencies.[22] Coming from the college's professional ranks, Peavy was satisfied with the State Board of Higher Education's division of spoils. He fought for the faculty, decrying their drastic reduction in numbers while enrollment was increasing, and railed against the loss of important professors to industry and other institutions. In his numerous reports and memoranda, however, Peavy raised few questions about the state board's curricular allocations.

OSC's small graduating class of 1936 reflected low enrollments in the freshman class four years earlier. In normal times, 18 percent of students graduated in four years and another 18 percent eventually earned degrees, for an aggregate of 35 to 38 percent. The statistics for the class of 1936, however, revealed that, although the number graduating was lower, a higher percentage graduated in four years. The degrees awarded in 1936 reveal the proportional distribution of the disciplines involved:[23]

Doctor of Philosophy	1
Professional Degrees	5
Master of Art	4
Master of Science	46
Bachelor of Arts	12
Science	8
Education	1
Home Economics	3
Bachelor of Science	271
Science	31
Agriculture	38
Education	49
Engineering	71
Forestry	18
Home Economics	38
Pharmacy	22
Commerce	2
Nursing Education	2

Because of Oregon's unified system of higher education, policy decisions in Salem directly affected every member institution. Although Chancellor William Jasper Kerr promised to serve only until the new structure was operating smoothly, the board asked him to stay on until his successor was hired. After a lengthy search, the board hired Frederick Hunter, chancellor of the University of Denver, who took office in September 1935. Hunter's appointment opened new and more contentious relations between the state college, the university, and the chancellor's office, much of it spilling over into timeworn skirmishes over curriculum.[24] In his first biennial report, Hunter praised the unified system, citing Oregon as the first state to dispense with an unworkable governing structure and "commit full responsibility to a wholly new and centralized authority." He applauded the state for providing his office with "authoritative executive" responsibilities for finances and academics, comparing the heads of the university and colleges to "an executive cabinet for the entire system."[25]

The future would put the lie to Hunter's glowing account of stability, permanence, and a smoothly functioning system of academic units. The university and state college carried on internecine warfare under his watch, quieted only with the Japanese bombing of Pearl Harbor in December 1941. The quarrels between the institutions, aired through grievances filed with the chancellor's office, ran the gamut of complaints—equipment divisions related to the board's curricular reorganization of 1932, Corvallis office furnishings that President Kerr hauled to Eugene when he became chancellor, and battles over courses, degree offerings, and budgets. Those were trying times for President Peavy, who had to respond to aggressive requests from the chancellor's office and University of Oregon administrators.

The university initiated the fireworks in November 1933 when a faculty group issued several pages of "whereas," complaining about state board president Roscoe Nelson's "violent partisanship." When Nelson visited both institutions, he defamed his Eugene hosts, according to the faculty complaint, while "effusively complimenting" his Corvallis audience. The UO grievance charged Nelson with erecting an "impassable social barrier between the Chancellor and the University faculty." The state college offered a rejoinder a few days later, scolding the university faculty for refusing to acknowledge its long-standing enmity toward the "cow college." In the midst of the worsening economic crisis, the university's legislative partisans threw fuel on the fire, urging an end to appropriations for agricultural research and similar programs.[26]

The dance of acrimony continued when the university's School of Fine Arts demanded that craft tools in possession of the college be turned over to the Eugene school for use in upper-division courses. (In the curricular reorganization, the college could no longer offer such courses.) J. Leo Fairbanks of the college's Department of Art and Architecture contended that the university could not claim them, because student funds paid for the craft tools. When the university's Ellis Lawrence, dean of the School of Architecture and Allied Arts, reminded Corvallis administrators that the state board had allocated such courses to Eugene, the issue landed on President Peavy's desk. Dean Ellwood Smith of the Lower Division told the president that the items were purchased with student fees and that a lower-division course—Decorative Design, AA 295—would be making use of the equipment. Peavy resolved the issue, writing President C. V. Boyer about student funding for the equipment and its continued use in lower-division courses. Another sticky issue involved former president Kerr, who took his Corvallis office furniture to Eugene to equip his new headquarters. When he retired, his old college furnishings and equipment remained in Eugene, prompting President Peavy to ask Charles Byrne, secretary to the Board of Higher Education, to return a bronze-base library table lamp ("value $35.00") and a "Sheaffer [sic] Desk Set, Base L-14, fitted with two Wahl Pens, value $22.50."[27] The items were returned.

A larger hassle arose when the chancellor's office asked that Kerr's Cadillac be made available for Hunter's use. Peavy reminded Byrne that the vehicle belonged to the college, and that Kerr had returned it to Corvallis when he retired. Although he had no use for the vehicle, Peavy asked Byrne to file the normal property transfer forms so that a proper accounting could be made. "You will note that this is a personal letter," he wrote. Miffed at the tone of Peavy's letter, Byrne responded in kind, noting that he took his orders from Chancellor Hunter. Whether the chancellor had the authority to demand such a transfer "is, of course, beyond me," he told Peavy. "I merely do as he requests." Peavy complimented Byrne on the "effervescence" of his communication, appreciating that his note was above "the humdrum of conventional correspondence":

> It is my lot, in common with yours, to take orders from the Chancellor. Far be it from me to question his authority. On the other hand, I assume he would be the last man to deviate from regular procedure. I had regarded you as his counsellor and friend, and as such I had hoped you would see that his footsteps were directed in the straight and narrow path of administrative rectitude. In other words, I see no reason why the customary procedure of property transfer should be varied from by any one, from janitor to Chancellor.

Peavy's only concern was that a proper accounting of transferring college property be provided.[28] The curricular wars, on the other hand—seemingly resolved with the implementation of the unified system in 1932—would recur with increasing intensity in the late 1930s.

New Deal agencies and programs to alleviate suffering and unemployment reached into the most distant sectors of the American economy, including the nation's land-grant colleges and universities. Oregon State College took advantage of federal programs through the Public Works Administration (PWA), the Civilian Conservation Corps (CCC), and the Works Progress Administration (WPA), especially the WPA's Federal Art Project. In cooperation with the PWA, the college built a new chemistry building (Gilbert Hall), a Student Health Services center (Plageman Hall), and a dairy barn. To create space for the chemistry building, the college purchased and moved three homes adjacent to Monroe Street. Portland architect John V. Bennes drafted plans for the structure, and with financial support from the PWA, the facility was ready for occupation in 1940. Planning for the Student Health Services building followed similar procedures, the finished product opened to students in 1939. The new health center increased infirmary beds from eighteen to thirty and included X-ray equipment to improve diagnostic services. When the Agricultural Engineering Building (now Gilmore Hall) burned in 1938, the PWA provided $27,000 to rebuild and expand the structure.[29]

The PWA funded some of the new dairy barn, and the college made use of WPA money to hire laborers to finish landscaping around the new buildings. The WPA paid unskilled and skilled workers for campus projects ranging from the dairy barn's east wing to installing irrigation systems and other improvements on college-owned farm properties. Those enterprises involved clearing and draining land, planting flower gardens on the central campus, relocating roads, creating parking areas, constructing miniature models of farm buildings, and erecting wrought-iron gates for the Madison Street entrance to campus.[30]

The most impressive and remarkable of the college's New Deal projects were those carried out under the WPA's Federal Art Project. They involved the artistry of Orion B. Dawson, a master blacksmith from Portland, who crafted ornamental wrought-iron edifices for different locations on campus, and Aimee Gorham, whose intricately carved wood inlays would decorate the entrances to the Forestry Building and Commerce Hall. Their combined works on the Corvallis campus, Timberline Lodge on Mount Hood, and numerous locations around the state serve as a magnificent, lasting tribute to some of the finest work carried out under the Federal Art Project. In framing the accomplishments of the federal program, historian William McDonald described the agency's labors "in material size and cultural character . . . unprecedented in the history of this nation or any nation."[31]

W. A. Jensen, President Peavy's executive secretary, deserves most of the credit for the federal arts work on campus. Jensen contacted WPA administrators in Portland in late 1935 about acquiring talented people to create ornamental features for the campus. He wrote R. G. Dieck, state supervisor, and Burt Brown Barker, Federal Art Project director for the western region, and visited Portland to see Dawson's wrought-iron creations and other art productions. He canvassed his colleagues about appropriate decorative work for buildings and the campus grounds. By the summer of 1936, Jensen was enamored with the work of Dawson and Gorham, who were busy preparing ornamental assemblages for Timberline Lodge. Dawson ranked at the top of his list, and with Dieck's urging, Jensen filed application with the WPA for his services.[32]

Jensen followed Dieck's suggestion and considered C. E. Price, the artist commissioned to create a mural for Timberline Lodge. Price, whose subjects

involved humans in natural landscapes, was one of the first modernist paint-
ers in the American West. Although Dieck praised Price's work, Jensen was
less enthused—"His colors are all dark with occasional splashes of high,
bright color." When he learned that Price's paintings were on display at the
university medical school and that staff wanted "to get rid of them," Jensen
concluded that his work was ill-suited for the college. Aimee Gorham's wood
crafting, however, was another matter, impressing Jensen from the beginning.
With Jensen's encouragement, President Peavy traveled to Portland to see her
wood inlays at Jefferson High School and immediately decided the college
should acquire her services to "give representation to the commercial woods
of the State of Oregon." The president chose the lobby of the Forestry Building
as an appropriate location for her work. In a letter to Portland's WPA office,
he itemized Oregon's lumber-producing prowess and wanted an art exhibit
promoting its products.[33]

When the WPA approved Gorham for OSC projects, Jensen and John
Leo Fairbanks, professor of art and architecture, traveled to Portland to meet
Gorham and Marjorie Hoffman Smith, interim head of WPA art productions.
Jensen immediately sensed that Smith and Gorham did not agree with the
college's industrial approach to Gorham's wood-inlay project. Smith, who had
traveled to Corvallis to see the Forestry Building, observed that everything
in the structure's interior was "practical and instructive," a suggestion that
Fairbanks (who was representing the president) vehemently disagreed with.
In a memorandum for the record, Jensen reported that Fairbanks lacked "the
finesse and diplomacy necessary to carry WPA officials with us." The group
then visited Gorham's shop, viewed her drawings, and discussed her design
proposals. Jensen again likened Fairbanks' attitude to "that of the 'big stick'
and sort of domineering—a 'bludgeon' attitude" that upset Smith and Gorham. His overbearing behavior reduced Gorham "to the point of tears" in
defending her design proposal.[34]

In a lengthy concluding note, Jensen was convinced that Gorham's
preferred design would make a "lovely" addition to the Forestry Building.
Continuing to argue otherwise might jeopardize the college's standing
and threaten its cooperation with WPA artists. Jensen planned to inform
Fairbanks that Gorham should proceed with her art design, because the
decorative value of the panels would greatly enhance the appeal of the Forestry Building. He emphatically endorsed Gorham's work: "The College is
getting so much for so little in this art program that we must risk no chance
of antagonizing or discouraging those who are and have been cooperating so
splendidly with us." [35]

During the Great Depression, W. A. Jensen, executive-secretary to President George Peavy, sought the assistance of the Works Progress Administration in Portland to create ornamental features for the Oregon State College campus. Among others, Jensen contracted talented blacksmith Orion Dawson to produce a wrought-iron fence and gates for the Madison Street entrance to campus, a project completed in 1940. Although Dawson also did projects for the library and Memorial Union, the Madison Gates are the best example of his artistry. Courtesy of the OSU Special Collections and Archives Research Center.

Jensen thanked Burt Brown Barker, who had returned as state director of the Federal Art Project, for approving Gorham's approach to the wood inlays, and invited Barker to visit campus to see the already completed artwork. Jensen was especially pleased with Gorham's progress on the marquetry, remarking that the finished product will be "an everlasting credit and monument to the WPA art work in this State." Because the Forestry Building panels made use of "different woods from around the world," he wanted to retain Gorham for similar work in Commerce Hall.[36]

To enlist Orion Dawson's talents to produce the wrought-iron fence and gates at the Madison Street entrance to campus, Jensen had to raise $1,000 to qualify for WPA support. The executive secretary wrote countless letters, consulted with the alumni and business offices, and solicited the support of several college classes to fund the blacksmith's work. The capstone to the effort was the Corvallis Garden Club's sale of "Put-Up-The-Gates" buttons during the 1939–1940 academic year. Jensen completed the fund-raising in June 1940, when college physical plant crews began the summer work of landscaping and putting up the fence and gates. Although the college library and Memorial Union sported examples of Dawson's work, the Madison Street gates were the most significant and lasting of his creations.[37]

Aimee Gorham eventually completed wood mosaic panels for both the Forestry Building and Commerce Hall. She produced two facing panels for the Forestry Building, one descriptive and evocative and the other portraying logging operations, but incorporating several species of wood inlays amid flora and fauna. Installed in the Forestry Building (now Moreland Hall), the panels were moved to the College of Forestry's Richardson Hall when it opened in 1999. The panels in Commerce Hall (now Bexell Hall) are equally compelling, providing allegorical representations of the "pioneers of Oregon" and the founders of Oregon State College. Two panels serve as end pieces to a central panel, the "Tree of Life." Historical figures represented in the pioneer panel include Abigail Scott Duniway, John McLoughlin, J. K. Weatherford, and Clara Waldo, the last important to the history of the state and college. The college panel pictures the old administration building (Benton Hall) and the Memorial Union, along with historic figures James Withycombe, President William Jasper Kerr, deans Grant Covell, Arthur Cordley, John Bexell, and two women important to the institution—home economics professor Margaret Snell and librarian Ida Kidder.[38]

The Civilian Conservation Corps (CCC) has been the most celebrated and popular of all New Deal relief programs. Enshrined in popular literature for its conservation work, CCC crews labored in soil erosion, reforestation, fire protection, flood control, and state and national parks. With its vast federal, state, and private lands, Oregon hosted hundreds of camps between April 1933 and June 1942, when the government disbanded the CCC in the face of the war crisis. During its existence, the CCC placed young men with seven different federal agencies in Oregon as well as state conservation units. The corps' impressive work involved planting trees and controlling diseases; fighting forest fires; building roads, trails, and fire lookouts; installing telephone lines; improving grazing lands; developing water holes for livestock; and significant conservation activities on the Malheur and Hart Mountain National Wildlife Refuges. Through nine years of activity in Oregon, the CCC operated an annual average of fifty camps of one hundred to two hundred men.[39]

Oregon State College was an early participant in hosting the CCC when the agency established "Camp Arboretum, S-220" in June 1933 ("S" camps were assigned to state lands). Like others across the nation, the camp proper was under the jurisdiction of the US Army. Nationwide, the most controversial aspect of CCC administration was the War Department's operation of the camps, while various federal and state agencies supervised fieldwork. A second "veteran's side camp" simultaneously began putting up buildings and other facilities at the arboretum. The US Forest Service Region Six office in Portland supervised the conservation work of the crew until October 1934, when the Oregon State Department of Forestry assumed control.[40]

Four different CCC companies, each with a distinct personality, occupied Camp Arboretum during its nine-year run. The enrollees in Company 697, the first contingent, were mostly late teenagers from urban areas in Illinois. Self-named the "Chicago Alley Rats," the boys were good workers, helping establish the arboretum's expanding nursery stock. When Company 697 moved to Missoula, Montana, in June 1936, Company 1922—veterans of the First World War and a few veterans of the Spanish-American War—arrived. These men were older and more skilled, with an average age of forty-four. The veteran contingent posed different problems, much of it related to alcohol. When that company was transferred in December 1937, Company 3503 moved in, another younger group from the Midwest border states of Ohio, Kentucky, and Indiana. Head nurseryman Vern McDaniel remembered them as "the Southern Boys," who worked well in the nursery and expressed openly their prejudices against blacks.[41]

The last group to occupy Camp Arboretum, Company 6418, arrived in July 1940. This cohort enjoyed an enviable record, in which the company commander jailed six men for refusing to work in the rain. A succeeding commander found continuing discontent, with men dissatisfied with the weather and the surrounding countryside. Another seven enrollees refused to work in the wet weather despite being outfitted with protective gear. A special investigator thought the commandant used poor judgment in jailing men simply for the purpose of intimidating them. Otherwise, the investigator found the camp operating in a "highly satisfactory" way. The following assessment appears in the Camp Arboretum commander's annual report to CCC director Robert Fechner in December 1937: "There is no subversive activities in the camp. The camp is also free from bed-bugs, and all other vermin."[42]

Camp Arboretum's work projects made significant and lasting changes on McDonald Forest landscapes. The one constant in the camp's conservation work was assigning twelve to fifteen men to work with Vern McDaniel in the Oregon Forest Nursery. When the nursery was transferred from the Forest Service to the Oregon State Department of Forestry, it provided growing stock for reforestation projects across the state. A "Work Project Report" for Camp Arboretum submitted to Director Fechner's office in September 1941 included the following: "*Work Completed*: Construction of truck trails, fences, telephone lines, Guard Stations, lookout towers, fire breaks, signs and markers, and one dam. Maintenance of truck trails. Forest Nursery work. Boundary survey. Fire Suppression."[43]

During the summer and early fall, the state forester sent men to join firefighting crews over a wide swath of Oregon. The use of CCC men in fighting forest fires marked the first time that the Forest Service and state agencies used organized crews to build containment lines around fires.[44] In the college forest, CCC crews built the first road from the arboretum westward across the ridge to Lewisburg Saddle and over another ridge to the Oak Creek drainage. In addition to putting in gravel roads in 1941, CCC crews built eight miles of trails through the college forest and constructed a guard station along Oak Creek, including a single-story residence of five rooms and an adjacent barn. Its original function to provide housing for summer fire crews evolved over time to become a research facility for the college's Department of Fisheries and Wildlife. The carefully constructed rock walls at the site reflect traditional CCC work elsewhere.[45]

The curricular wars, latent since the State Board of Higher Education implemented the unified system in 1932, resumed in May 1937, when the board's Interinstitutional Curricular Advisory Committee proposed establishing bachelor's and master's degrees in science at the university and similar degrees in social science and arts and letters at the state college. The advisory committee believed the proposal "would be highly desirable from the standpoint of complete institutions." The college's administrative council thought the plan would create deviltry, launching both institutions into competition for new degree programs. Suspicious that the University of Oregon was behind the proposal, state college officials pointed to economic conditions mandating that the state continue its present degree allocations. The advisory committee was wrong, the college believed, to suggest the plan would "not involve any appreciable increase in budgets on either campus." Following President Peavy's lead, the council reaffirmed the college's commitment to the degree programs established in 1932. The state college, Peavy reminded the council, "suffered losses in the original allocations which were extremely vital"; however, it had kept the faith in the best interests of the state.[46]

Chancellor Hunter, who sought the administrative council's "frank judgment and advice" about the curriculum committee proposal, left Corvallis with the understanding that the college was "unfavorable to any immediate action." When the University of Oregon refused to take no for an answer, its faculty appealed to the State Board of Higher Education in the fall of 1937 to reinstate a full-fledged science program. University president Clarence Boyer sent copies of the faculty's science proposal to members of the board, a move Peavy considered a "serious threat to the unified system." College administrators followed with a statement opposing the university's initiative:

> The State College Administrative Council enters vigorous objection to the procedure whereby a University brief requesting the restoration of science to the University, accompanied by a disparaging letter, was transmitted to the State Board of Higher Education without providing the State College with a copy of the brief or letter, and without even notifying the President of the College. Such action threatens to undermine and destroy the very foundations of the structure on which the Oregon State System of Higher Education rests.[47]

The university's aggressive moves to restore science degrees in the face of struggling regional and national economics disturbed college administrators. In thinly veiled criticism of the state board, the college reaffirmed its opposition to changing present curricular arrangements, reminding board members that their procedures required the university's claim to be matched with similar advances for the college. OSC administrators protested "the irregular and unjust procedure by which this issue reached the Board," accusing the university of violating the board's bylaws—communications should be routed "from the President to the Chancellor and *from the Chancellor* to the Board."[48]

Although the board shelved the university request, friction between the college and the chancellor's office increased on a number of fronts. When Chancellor Hunter suggested in March 1938 that medical school degrees carry the imprimatur of only the University of Oregon, President Peavy viewed the proposal as an affront to the college's science programs. Bachelor's and advanced degrees at the medical school hitherto had been "conferred by the University or the State College according to the 1932 allocation of major work." The initiative would confer on the university the privilege of granting degrees in science, "a field assigned exclusively to the State College." Bachelor's degrees qualifying students to enter the medical school should be offered at both the university and the college.[49]

To quiet the hornet's nest stirring among state college faculty, Chancellor Hunter traveled to Corvallis and explained that the medical school issue would not be implemented until a "full hearing and consideration of the evidence." President Peavy told the chancellor that the college was sensitive to the university's repeated efforts to reinstate science degree programs. The college, in contrast, was not lobbying to seek the return of commerce or landscape architecture, programs it had lost in 1932. He added that the university's "permanent committee for the Restoration of Science" did not inspire confidence among college supporters.[50]

Although the State Board of Higher Education made no changes in degree privileges for the medical school, the University of Oregon floated a major initiative in January 1940 to establish an undergraduate degree in premedical science. The chancellor again traveled to Corvallis, to where M. Ellwood Smith, dean of the Lower Division of Arts and Sciences, presented the college's argument, tracing the history and dangers of breaking with the curriculum allocations of 1932. To the surprise of everyone, Hunter assured administrators that the matter would not be brought before the board. A few days later, new University of Oregon president Donald Erb met with Corvallis administrators, explaining that the university's proposal did not encroach on the college's proprietorship of science. College executive secretary W. A. Jensen, who kept minutes of the meeting, observed that a "free exchange of opinion was accomplished."[51]

Chancellor Hunter's biennial reports ignored the contentious relations between the university and state college, assuring the higher education board and governor that the system was functioning smoothly. Although the board had made some adjustments to the original curricular design, state institutions were operating as "a closely coordinated and cooperating group . . . with special assignments." The unified system, the chancellor believed, had eliminated costly duplication and placed "all institutions under a central authority." Hunter applauded the college as the most important service institution in the region and praised it for applying "science to production."[52] There was a twist to the chancellor's praise for the college's science program, repeatedly emphasizing the association with production. That theme would play into the hands of the university when it declared its intention to establish a program in *pure science*.

When University of Oregon president Daniel Erb forwarded a copy of his biennial report to OSC's new president Frank L. Ballard in the spring of 1941, he made a mockery of Chancellor Hunter's assurances that all was well with the unified system. Erb's message directly challenged the board's policy of allocating degree programs. Chancellor Hunter's appointment, Erb noted, gave hope to the university that its science programs would be restored. "This academic outrage," he wrote, was a matter of "political expediency" guiding the chancellor's decisions rather than reasoned argument. Was the Eugene school to be a legitimate university, Erb argued, or simply "one branch of a State System of Higher Education?" Based on need and self-respect, state authorities should permit the university to grant bachelor's and master's degrees in science.[53]

Although the renewed academic turf wars coincided with worsening violence in Europe and Asia, Oregon newspapers gave voice to the curricular struggles at home. Salem's *Oregon Statesman* reported that university partisans had "been thumping for restoration of science as a degree-granting" privilege for some time. The public would want to know the necessity for such a decision before changes were made. Expressing alarm at this turn of events, F. A. Gilfillan, chair of OAC's administrative council, asked the chancellor's office for copies of official documents to keep the college fully informed.[54]

State College administrators lobbied strenuously through the summer and fall of 1941, opposing significant changes to the 1932 curricular allocation. Gilfillan, who assumed President Ballard's responsibilities when the latter became ill in 1940, was named acting president on September 10, 1941, when Ballard resigned. In his brief tenure heading the institution, Gilfillan aggressively defended the unified system when the University of Oregon moved to restore science. He traveled to Silverton that month to visit state board member Dr. Rudolph Kleinsorge to discuss the "critical" situation in higher education. Kleinsorge was receptive to Gilfillan's defense of the unified system, but thought "more science should be allowed at the University and more liberal arts at the College." When Gilfillan urged the board at its next meeting in Ashland to base its decision on the "real educational needs of the state, rather than political expediency," Kleinsorge asked Gilfillan to send him a typed copy of his remarks. Toward the close of the two-hour conversation, Kleinsorge commented that he admired President Erb, an able man of excellent character, a person one should avoid in public debate.[55] Gilfillan's memorandum of the evening's conversation is mute on whether he had convinced Kleinsorge to oppose the university's proposal.

As the clock wound toward the October 28 state board meeting in Ashland, the college's administrative council restated its long-standing opposition to major changes in the unified system. Newspaper editorials offered advice, and alumni from both schools wrote letters to the chancellor supporting or opposing the university's proposal. The Roseburg *News-Review* declared that it was embarrassing for the University of Oregon to be the only state institution bearing the title "university," yet it was without science degrees. The state board was treating the university's request like a hot potato, the *Review* contended, fearful of "a very small group of dog-in-the-manger people." A state college graduate added an alternative voice, imploring the chancellor to protect the savings generated under the current strategy "over the old 'competitive' plan."[56]

The state board's Ashland meeting was perfunctory and decisive, with board members voting six to two to restore science to the University of Oregon. In the workup to balloting, Chancellor Hunter proposed establishing three undergraduate science majors at the university and three social science majors at the state college. President Erb and acting president Gilfillan opposed such a move, but for different reasons. Gilfillan reasoned that the college had made no such request, and with the state's economy still foundering, the moment was not opportune for change. He questioned the university's claim that it lacked a comprehensive program: "Under the state system the two institutions are not expected to conform to the patterns of traditional state universities and land-grant colleges as these exist in populous and wealthier states." President Erb countered that a true university "must have at its heart a complete college of liberal arts, including the sciences." When the board rejected the chancellor's proposal, Hunter accepted its judgment and promised to implement its decision.[57]

The board's majority believed restoring science to the university would strengthen the state system and take nothing away from other institutions. The university's request was reasonable, members argued, because it had given assurances that its science curriculum would be developed only as the budget allowed. President Erb indicated that the Eugene school was the only university in the nation that did not graduate students in "mathematics, chemistry, physics, zoology, geology and botany." Rudolph Kleinsorge, whom Gilfillan respected and visited in mid-September, voted with the majority. As the board moved to other items on its agenda, Gilfillan congratulated the university for gaining its objective, although he did not believe the change was in "the best interests of higher education in Oregon."[58]

With science restored to the university, board member R. C. Groesbeck poured salt on the college's psyche in an address to the Portland City Club, criticizing the college's sustained opposition to the restoration of science at the university. Offended, Gilfillan fired off a letter to the City Club accusing Groesbeck of being "grossly unfair," because the college was simply defending its assigned curriculum and supporting the board's allocation of majors. The college had never asked for a course in violation of the board's guidelines. Board member E. C. Sammons came to Gilfillan's defense, refuting Groesbeck's charges and suggesting the college could expect the restoration of commerce and business-related courses. As for the university, when it applied for upper-division science courses, it quickly realized that there was no clear distinction between pure and applied science.[59]

With the vantage of hindsight, the state college's strategy of clinging to the 1932 formula was misguided. College and university educational policies are dynamic enterprises, subject to periodic readjustment. President Peavy and acting president Gilfillan clung to the 1932 protocol in the face of the university's increasingly aggressive moves to reestablish its science programs. There is no evidence that state college leaders considered compromises that would have moved its own curricular programs in a more comprehensive direction. After the Ashland meeting, the college sought to restore the commerce and mining engineering degrees it lost in 1932, but it made no move to expand programs in the liberal arts, objectives that it would only belatedly address in the decades following the Second World War.

The restoration of commerce (business courses) to the state college seemed reasonable in the wake of the Ashland meeting. Chancellor Hunter praised the college when it proposed to grant bachelor's and master's degrees in commerce and mining engineering, reminding OSC administrators that the Ashland decision was not his recommendation. The college's Alumni association supported the restoration of commerce as a sign of "fairness to students" attending a land-grant college, and noted that it should also offer degrees in mining engineering and landscape architecture. Acting president Gilfillan thought the restoration of commerce only a matter of time, because the state board had already abandoned the unified program. The *Oregonian* added perspective—the state college and university had "revive[d] an old family row." The capstone for the college was the state board's approval in April 1942 to create "a curriculum leading to appropriate degrees" in business.[60]

The UO/OSC skirmish took place amid darkening war clouds over Europe and Asia. Adolf Hitler and the rise of National Socialism in Germany and the occupation of the Rhineland (a treaty-protected buffer zone between France and Germany) in March 1936 set off alarm bells in Europe and America. Germany's alliances with Japan and Mussolini's fascist Italy in November 1936 marked the beginning of collaboration among the Axis powers that escalated the sense of crisis in the Roosevelt administration, wary of Nazi advances in Europe and public isolationist sentiment at home. Japan's invasion of China in July 1937 and the "Rape of Nanking" prompted Roosevelt's remark that an "epidemic of world lawlessness" was threatening world peace. Comparing the military contagion to a disease, the president called for a quarantine to stay the course of the perpetrators. "There is no escape through mere isolation or neutrality," he told Americans skeptical of foreign wars. The effect of the president's "Quarantine Speech" was to slowly shift public opinion away from isolationism.[61]

Germany's occupation and annexation of Austria in March 1938 and continued Japanese advances in China set the table for Roosevelt's State of the Union address in January 1939, when he asked for stronger measures to stop aggression. "There comes a time in the affairs of men when they must prepare to defend the tenets of faith and humanity on which their churches, their governments and their civilization are founded. . . . To save one we must now make up our minds to save all." Two months after Roosevelt's address, Hitler famously ignored the promises of the Munich Agreement and sent German armies into Czechoslovakia. Then came the surprising Soviet-German nonaggression pact of August 1939, and Hitler sending several German divisions deep into Poland on September 1, 1939.[62] Europe was fully embroiled in war.

Those international events accelerated defense-related activities on the Oregon State College campus long before the Japanese attack on Pearl Harbor. It is important to know that the United States was not a defenseless nation on that ill-fated day. While President Roosevelt patiently engineered the nation's preparedness, the state college provided the federal government with data on Oregon's natural resources and agricultural production. The college ROTC was involved in preparedness as well, activities that changed dramatically after September 1, 1939. In his final biennial report in 1940, President Peavy warned that totalitarian powers were on the march, with Germany's "mass attacks on religion [and] the fomentation of race prejudice." Oregon State College was prepared to offer its service "to the state and the nation," he wrote, urging the faculty and community to put forward leaders who would "stand staunchly against the forces of inflexibility, on the one hand, and the forces of radical change on the other." In words that would resonate during the Cold War, Peavy urged citizens to be on the watch for anyone advocating doctrines "communistic or otherwise . . . hostile to the commonwealth."[63]

Chancellor Hunter delivered an even more ominous message, referring to the violence in Europe and Asia as a "world-wide attack on democracy, an aggressive and fanatical religion of conquest." The United States, which had supported "disarmament and world understanding," had now reversed direction and demanded "the most prodigious armed preparation of all time." Educational institutions had a special responsibility to provide for the "spiritual defense" of democracy, Hunter wrote, although there were weaknesses in the nation's "social issues"—public complacency, citizens whose lives centered on luxury, an aversion to hard work, too many dependent on government, and ten million people still unemployed. The chancellor called for developing psychological and material defenses to provide citizens with "a unified faith in democracy, a confidence that is worth keeping for ourselves and for the world."[64]

The War Department, the federal agency initiating inquiries about natural resources, asked the college about research useful for military purposes, especially studies related to structural materials that would withstand the rigors of modern warfare. Major Howard Starret prefaced his letter with a bit of flattery—"Your patriotic interest has occasioned this communication." William Schoenfeld responded that the agricultural experiment station would provide immediate assistance. The Department of Physics offered research about portable spectrometers, while the School of Forestry's materials research had little to offer for defense purposes.[65]

Major Starret appreciated the response, telling acting president Gilfillan that the War Department would be interested in research "of value to the National Defense Program." He followed with another inquiry involving metals and substitute alloys that would meet the need for critical materials. The college offered a mixed response, one faculty reporting there was little time for such work. Another person responded that research using explosives in drainage ditches indicated that a study of soils would be useful. One of the college's problems, the director of the engineering experiment station observed, was that previous research had focused "on the arts of peace and construction rather than war and destruction," urging the War Department to outline immediate problems and assign them to specific laboratories.[66]

The National Defense Research Committee (NDRC), requested the National Research Council to identify scientists suited for defense research. Three School of Engineering faculty signed on with the NDRC, and Gilfillan was asked to recommend additional personnel in the coming months. As summer 1941 moved into fall, the NDRC asked Gilfillan to list courses and college projects related to national defense. By mid-October that list included virtually every unit in the college, including the Lower Division, where Dean Ellwood Smith reported several departments involved with "problems of defense and national well-being." The School of Forestry reported that it had used congressional appropriations to train crews to fight forest fires. As expected, the schools of science and engineering amassed lengthy lists, including courses in chemical warfare and the chemistry of explosives.[67]

Although unemployment still hovered around 10 percent at the outset of 1940, those conditions quickly changed with the buildup in arms production and military aircraft after German armies overran Denmark, Norway, and the Low Countries of Holland and Belgium in the spring of 1940. The surrender of France in June and Germany's air attacks on British coastal installations in July 1940 launched what has been called the Battle of Britain. In the midst of a European world on the verge of conceding to the vicious enterprises of National Socialism and Fascism, President Roosevelt guided the nation through perilous waters. Using sleight of hand, deception, and expanded executive powers, the president moved public opinion to support preparedness. His decision to run for an unprecedented third term in the summer of 1940 exacerbated politics on the home front. During election season, Congress passed the Selective Service Act on September 16, the first peacetime draft in the nation's history. Within a month, the draft rolls numbered some sixteen million men between the ages of eighteen and thirty-five. Between the president's reelection in November 1940 and the Japanese attack on Pearl Harbor, Roosevelt struggled in word and deed to supply British forces with munitions and other supplies and, ultimately, the Soviet Union as well. Pearl Harbor, however, brought the United States full circle from the isolationism of the mid-1930s into a climactic two-ocean war.[68]

7
Wartime: 1938–1950

The Japanese naval air attack on Pearl Harbor on Sunday morning, December 7, 1941, rent asunder normal routines on the Oregon State College campus and catapulted the institution full bore into the ranks of war research and training student-officer corps for military service. Students were enjoying a tranquil weekend, with the downtown Whiteside Theater showing the comedy film, *The Thin Man*, an adaptation of Dashiell Hammett's novel. Sororities and fraternities were carrying on conventional activities, perhaps laying plans for a train trip to the Rose Bowl in Pasadena, where OSC's football team would play Duke University in the "Granddaddy" of all bowl games. Athletic Director Percy Locey had been in Pasadena on December 4 negotiating ticket purchases for the Beaver faithful, where he learned that OSC alumni living in southern California needed to purchase tickets through the Rose Bowl office rather than through the college. The *Oregonian* reported that the college's fifty-piece band would be accompanying the team.[1]

The editorial in Monday's *Oregonian*, "America Pledges It," promised that a united nation would destroy Japan "through a righteous sense of unspeakable outrage." Comparing Japan to "an alley gunman . . . who shoots from the pocket while he bows and smiles," the editorial declared Pearl Harbor an example of "fundamental dishonesty." The attack was part of Japan's compact with Hitler, extending the European conflict to the rest of the world. "Now no people and no land is so remote as to escape." Ignoring the American nation's rich ethnic mix, the *Oregonian* unfurled a dubious send-off—"The Anglo-Saxon and the Teutonic branches of European civilization are staking their positions for a combat to the death"—assuring readers that Americans were carrying "the banners of God." Meeting the day following the attack, the Oregon State College administrative council praised acting president Gilfillan's statement that the emergency required "All Out" cooperation to meet "the treachery of the Japanese Empire." The college would make available to the state and the nation "its many scientific and technical facilities that are so vital to modern warfare."[2]

Jack Yoshihara (1921–2009), who grew up in Portland, played on the Oregon State College football team scheduled to play in the Rose Bowl against Duke University on New Year's Day 1942. After the bombing of Pearl Harbor on December 7, 1941, the game was shifted to Durham, North Carolina. Because military restrictions prohibited American Japanese from traveling more than thirty-five miles from home, Yoshihara was forbidden to make the trip. When Japanese students were forced to withdraw from OSC in the spring of 1942, most them went to internment camps for the duration of the war. Yoshihira and some forty Japanese who left campus in 1942 were awarded honorary degrees at Oregon State University's commencement in 2008. Courtesy of the OSU Special Collections and Archives Research Center.

Jack Yoshihara, a member of the college's Rose Bowl–bound football team, had taken the train to Portland to visit his parents that ill-fated weekend. When he heard news bulletins of the attack on Sunday afternoon, he returned to Corvallis with a heavy sense of foreboding. "For Jack Yoshihara," writes Rebecca Landis, "Dec. 7 was the day his dream of playing football in the Rose Bowl died." When Pacific Coast Conference officials moved the Rose Bowl contest to Durham, North Carolina, Duke's home field, Yoshihara, a wide receiver on the football team, remained in Corvallis, because military restrictions prohibited Japanese Americans from traveling. College administrators had already been examining the citizenship status of Japanese students. Glenn Bakkum of the Department of Sociology counted thirty-eight students of Japanese ancestry on campus, only two of them born in Japan. One of those, Marjorie Horagama, born just after her mother made a return trip to Japan, returned to the states with her mother shortly afterward. Ms. Horagama learned that she was born in Japan when she was eighteen years old.[3]

Jack Yoshihara and his Japanese student peers were not alone in experiencing the sting of discrimination. The events that followed in the coming months were increasingly perilous for America's 120,000 mainland citizens of Japanese ancestry, nearly two-thirds of them born in the United States (another two hundred thousand lived in the Territory of Hawaii). Oregon State College had more students of Japanese ancestry than the University of

Oregon, and these Japanese American students and their brethren elsewhere persisted through five decades for redress of their treatment, until they succeeded in gaining reparations in 1988, when President Ronald Reagan signed legislation awarding each living Japanese person who had spent time in an internment camp an apology and twenty thousand dollars.

In the midst of the war emergency and helter-skelter defense initiatives at the state college, a sense of routine characterized many activities. After the Beaver football team vanquished Duke's Blue Devils twenty to sixteen, OSC administrators planned to celebrate their return to Corvallis. The original greeting at the railroad station and a celebration in the Memorial Union was delayed a week when coach Lon Stiner and members of the team were delayed in their return. In the interim, loyal alumni and enthusiastic fans initiated a "Bonds for the Beavers" drive to raise money for the war effort. The big occasion, however, was a crowd of some seven hundred people gathered in the Memorial Union's banquet hall to honor the Rose Bowl champions. Guest of honor, Oregon secretary of state Earl Snell, presented the players with gold rings instead of bonds to protect their amateur status. Praising the accomplishments of the football team, acting president Gilfillan compared their achievements to the problems the nation confronted: "We only hope that all of us will do our job as well as you did yours at Durham." Governor Charles Sprague, Chancellor Frederick Hunter, student-body president Andy Landforce, and *Gazette-Times* editor Claude Ingalls closed out the program.[4]

In the midst of this celebratory occasion, the state college was adjusting to wartime conditions, abbreviating the school year to maximize summer work for students and to free the campus for defense-related short courses. The administrative council eliminated the week for final examinations, directing faculty to hold exams on the last day of regular classes. The council jettisoned the weeklong break between winter and spring terms, shortening the academic year by two weeks. There were other war-related changes: large numbers of women leaving for defense-industry jobs and men joining the military services.[5] Student enrollments would continue to hemorrhage throughout the war, recovering with huge increases toward the end of the conflicts in Europe and Asia.

After delaying for more than a year, the State Board of Higher Education initiated a search to replace President Ballard, who became ill shortly after becoming president and then resigned in the spring of 1941. F. A. Gilfillan, head of the administrative council, filled in until the board made him acting president that fall. When the chancellor's office advertised the search in the spring of 1942, its procedures angered OSC administrators and patrons of the institution, because they had no voice in identifying candidates or in selecting finalists. And, lurking in the shadows behind state policymakers, university representatives were ready to dash the hopes of the college when it sought to broaden its degree programs. The state board's curriculum committee continued to delay the college's request to restore commerce courses, with board chairman Willard Marks indicating there was no timeline for a decision. As for the OSC presidential search, Marks reported that the board was "making progress" with interviews but would make no prediction when the search would be concluded.[6]

Immediately after the attack on Pearl Harbor, thirty-six "American citizens of Japanese ancestry" at Oregon State College submitted a letter to acting president Gilfillan expressing their "unswerving loyalty to our country, and all her institutions." The students wanted to continue their academic programs, "subject to the new duties of citizenship imposed by the war" and to urge upon their parents an understanding "of the duties of citizenship" in the present crisis. The Japanese American signatories trusted that the present emergency would prove a unifying force for "Americans and their resident relatives from foreign lands." Gilfillan thanked the students for the value they placed on citizenship, but cautioned that it was "unavoidable that you shall face difficult and embarrassing situations."[7] Gilfillan and administrators at other colleges and universities on the West Coast were aware of the vicious news media hatred directed at the Japanese—whose worst fears would be realized in the coming months.

Life for Japanese Americans became increasingly perilous as winter 1942 moved into spring—in the total absence of spying or evidence of sabotage. Federal authorities required Japanese students to carry signed passes from the college for permission to travel. After President Franklin Roosevelt issued Executive Order 9066 directing the Department of War to "proscribe military areas . . . from which any and all persons may be excluded," the government further tightened travel restrictions. Although Executive Order 9066 made no mention of the Japanese, the order permitted General John L. DeWitt of the Western Defense Command (who had requested the directive) to remove all citizens of Japanese ancestry from the Pacific coastal region. In the interim, DeWitt's office allowed Japanese students to remain in Corvallis until the evacuation was announced.[8]

In the face of the pending evacuation, University of California president Robert Sproul suggested to California congressman John Tolan that Japanese American college students be allowed to continue their educational programs.

Sproul was impressed with the cooperation of Japanese students and their "willingness to make sacrifices cheerfully." It was essential, he told Tolan, to reciprocate their good behavior and provide them with the opportunity to continue their educations to protect against resentment and bitterness. Under those circumstances, the University of California was willing to offer its services to the federal government through a program permitting Japanese American students to continue their education.[9]

Sproul's plan, widely circulated among West Coast colleges and universities, attracted considerable attention, including the support of acting president Gilfillan. Estimating that 10 percent of the approximately 117,000 Japanese Americans were college students, Sproul proposed to offer students scholarships to attend school in "non-prohibited or non-restricted military areas in the country willing to receive them." For those unwilling to leave their families, he recommended extension classes be offered at internment camps either through specialized instruction or correspondence courses. Sproul's memorandum urged the appointment of a college committee to oversee the plan. Although the University of California offered to administer the program, all applicants would be cleared through the committee. The first step would be to survey prospective students to learn the academic facilities they desired, and whether such instruction should be in the camps or an institution away from the prohibited zone.[10]

Gilfillan praised Sproul's suggestion to Chancellor Hunter, indicating that college and university administrators would be in charge of the program. He regretted, however, that some institutions in the West and Midwest resented being asked to house Japanese American students. During that same week, two Japanese students asked OSC administrators for permission to travel home at the end of the school year. Raymond Hashitani, who had completed his graduation requirements, asked permission to travel to his parents' farm in Nyssa, Oregon, because his brother would soon be leaving for military service. The second request involved an American-born Japanese student from Hawaii, who the Southern Pacific Railroad Company advised could travel to San Francisco without special permission. However, the student needed to know if he could then proceed to board ship for Hawaii. While no record exists about Hashitani's request, the Hawaiian student was denied travel from San Francisco to his island home.[11]

The United States Commission on Wartime Relocation and Internment of Citizens reported in 1983 that the evacuation order meant that some 3,500 Japanese American students would be prohibited from attending colleges and universities in the three Pacific coastal states. The Western Defense

Command, however, had already released a few Japanese Americans to attend college or to harvest vegetable and orchard crops. Milton Eisenhower, director of the War Relocation Authority, organized the National Student Relocation Council to assist in transferring students to interior colleges and universities. In the end, federal authorities offered little support to students who relied on private philanthropy, especially from groups like the American Friends Service Committee. By the autumn of 1942, the council had placed some 250 students, a figure that totaled nearly five thousand by the end of the war.[12]

The Japanese American Citizens League (JACL), which supported Nisei (American-born persons whose parents emigrated from Japan) students in continuing their college education, asked West Coast institutions to determine the number of Japanese enrolled in classes and whether they had taken steps to transfer to schools in the interior West. With its central office in San Francisco, the JACL itself was preparing to move to Salt Lake City. To assist the Nisei, the National Student Relocation Council provided information to Japanese, Italian, and German students who were being evacuated. Buena Maris, professor of family relations at Oregon State College, served on the relocation council. Shortly after arriving at the North Portland center, three hundred Japanese men volunteered to help with the sugar beet harvest in Malheur County, where growers credited them with "tipping the balance" in saving the harvest.[13]

Evacuation involved a series of orders beginning in early May and continuing through early June. Authorities gave evacuees explicit details about the items they were permitted to bring with them: bedding and linens, toilet articles, extra clothing, and essential belongings. Under items that "*may* be taken" were flat irons, cribs, pillows, small radios (with limited kilocycle ranges), camp stools, portable sewing machines, typewriters, and cookbooks. The Oregon evacuations affected all Japanese west of the Cascade Mountains, who were ordered to report to the assembly center in North Portland. Assembly centers in other states included Manzanar, Santa Anita and Tanforan racetracks, Salinas, Tulare, and Turlock in California, and Puyallup in Washington.[14] When the University of Utah agreed to accept OSC students Tony Takashima and Jack Kato, the school requested permits to allow them to travel by train to Salt Lake City. Ernest Leonetti of the Wartime Civil Control Administration in Portland notified the Corvallis school that the students would have to evacuate with other Japanese to the assembly center in Portland and then present their case for moving to Utah.[15]

In the wake of Germany's invasion of Holland and Belgium and the capitulation of France in the summer of 1940, the nation's military services urged colleges and universities to begin enlisting students in reserve officer training programs. Invoking the "increased demands of the present emergency," the Marine Corps asked college administrators to identify 5 percent of the males in each graduating class who might be qualified for officers in the Marine Reserves. When OSC canvased its student body for men wanting "to serve their country during the emergency," the Marine Corps praised the response. One of its own graduates, Carl Larsen, was appointed the corps' liaison with the college, and the marines continued to praise the institution for selecting exceptional graduates for its officer program.[16]

With their lengthy histories at land-grant institutions, the navy and army were active recruiters on the Corvallis campus. Seeking to build its reserves with college graduates who had earned engineering degrees, the navy sent Rear Admiral H. E. Yarnell to speak to undergraduate and graduate engineering students. The college's cooperation would materially aid national defense, wrote Rear Admiral Chester W. Nimitz, later a major figure in the Pacific theater of war. The navy was interested in students majoring in aeronautical, chemical, electrical, industrial, mechanical, and marine engineering. Seniors who qualified would be commissioned ensigns and ordered to active duty after graduation.[17]

The National Roster of Scientific and Specialized Personnel developed an important presence on the OSC campus. Administered through the National Resources Planning Board, with the cooperation of the United States Civil Service Commission and the Selective Service Administration, the program was promoted at institutions with engineering schools. Shortly after Pearl Harbor, the national roster, which had already compiled a file of more than 250,000 individuals, asked the college to identify people with professional and scientific skills valuable for defense purposes.[18] To say that the federal government seized national institutions root and branch to pursue the war effort would be an understatement. The planning board's roster of cooperating agencies included the American Council of Education, the American Council of Learned Societies, the National Research Council, and the Social Science Research Council. The American Council of Education praised Oregon State College in late January 1942 for identifying personnel fit for defense-related research. It asked the college for students available for work immediately and the facilities it could offer for different training venues.[19]

Gilfillan wrote Paul McNutt, director of the War Manpower Commission, about the importance of making efficient use of trained personnel, such as seven staff members interested in war service. He insisted that there should be "a certain irreducible minimum" retained on campuses for teaching scientific and technical courses. Through the state director of Selective Service in Salem, Chancellor Frederick Hunter learned that Gilfillan could request that key faculty be exempt from the draft if their positions were "highly essential to the war effort." Hunter further suggested that male students should write the national roster to have their names added to the listings. Gilfillan's inquiry on behalf of his seven young staff members elicited a response when the War Manpower Commission reiterated that all young men with scientific training should register.[20]

To develop policy proposals for the State Board of Higher Education to present to the 1943 legislative session, Chancellor Hunter drafted "A Plan for Wartime" and sent the document to all institutions in the state system. To be effective during the war crisis, the state board and the chancellor's office should "be authoritative and clearly understood by all responsible executives." The board should submit to the legislature proposals that would focus on the war and the state's resources, and require institutions to be cooperative and understanding. Regarding the specialization of the state's institution of higher education, Hunter cited the Eugene school as a "comprehensive university," with its emphasis on the humanities and related disciplines. The state college, a typical land-grant institution, was a campus with "broadening and liberalizing courses in languages and social sciences," curricular offerings that should be expanded in the future.[21]

The chancellor's strategy addressed each institution's special interests. In subsequent meetings with OSC administrators he always gave the impression that he supported their larger aspirations. In the meantime, the board narrowed the list of candidates for the state college presidency, among them Dr. A. L. Strand, president of Montana State College. Board members, however, continued to procrastinate, with chairman Willard Marks insisting in June 1942 that his colleagues hoped to make a decision by September. By the summer of 1942, Dean Gilfillan had been filling the position for more than a year. It was late July before the board narrowed its choice to the Montana State College candidate, and even then the official announcement of Strand's hiring was put off until early August, when the board released its formal decision.[22]

Strand, a native-born Texan, had moved with his parents to Montana as a young boy. He graduated from Montana State College in 1917, where he excelled in writing for the student newspaper. After serving in the US Navy during the First World War, he attended the University of Minnesota, earning a PhD in entomology. He returned to his alma mater in 1931 to chair the entomology department and quickly emerged as a leader in faculty politics, talents that led to his appointment as president of the Depression-beleaguered

college in 1937. Before arriving in Corvallis, Strand issued a welcome to new
and returning students, quoting and paraphrasing from General Brebon
Somervell's recent address in Washington, DC, reminding Americans that
the nation was engaged in a "total war" being waged "on the battlefront, in the
factory and in the home. It is waged in every classroom throughout the nation." He urged students to make the college "a mighty citadel in our country's
service."[23] Strand, who would remain in office until 1961, witnessed the state
legislature elevate the college to university status the year he left office.

As the war crisis deepened, the Resources Planning Board accelerated its
recruiting of scientific and specialized personnel and solicited listings of students suited to research, industrial, or military appointments. President Strand
passed on to Gilfillan (once again dean of science) an urgent request from the
US Army's Officer Procurement Service in December 1942 for biochemists,
entomologists, parasitologists, research and radio engineers, and mathemati-
cians. Because the procurement office was having difficulty finding qualified
people, Strand believed the college could render a valuable service to the army.
The War Department added to the procurement frenzy in January 1943 when it
sought civilian specialists for its new Transportation Corps, Services of Supply.
In searching for engineers, architects, and production analysts, the department
cited the "scarcity of manpower" as the rationale for its request.[24]

    More pertinent (and potentially disruptive) to the campus were requests
to house special troops training in Corvallis. Anticipating such requests from
the military, housing director Melissa Hunter surveyed vacancies in men's dormitories and the dining capacity of the Memorial Union. The local chamber
of commerce provided details on rental apartments and houses and sleeping
facilities in clubs and lodges that could be converted to temporary sleeping
quarters. Before he left office, acting president Gilfillan had indicated to Navy
Department's Randall Jacobs the difficulty in finding such facilities in Corvallis, a town of eight thousand people and a campus of some forty-five hundred
students. Gilfillan wanted to know the precise number of students the navy
needed to house. Would it provide funding for extra buildings, equipment,
and teaching personnel? The campus, he noted, was already housing eight
hundred men with the 115th Horse-Mechanized Cavalry. As a land-grant institution, he told Jacobs, Oregon State College felt a responsibility to maintain
"an effective program of value to national defense."[25]

    After studying the Navy Department's request, Gilfillan determined
that ship-related instruction was not practicable at the college, because it
lacked a degree in naval science and tactics. Despite the institution's many

capabilities, it was impossible for the college "to meet all demands, especially in the field of technical training." George Peavy, the college's coordinator of war activities, advised Gilfillan that the Corvallis school was ill-equipped to handle the number of men involved "without turning over the major portion of the institution for this purpose." Peavy pointed to the following item in the navy's request:

> It is most desirable that the entire college be taken over for it
> will detract greatly from the purpose, morale and benefits of our
> program if our Spartanlike life of discipline and hard work is
> paralleled by a modern college life on the same campus.

The navy ultimately selected the universities of Iowa, North Carolina, Georgia, and St. Mary's College as the campuses for its aviation training centers. The navy again solicited bids to host six hundred preflight trainees in late 1942. After President Strand asked for more details, the navy abruptly excluded OSC, because it needed a location immediately.[26] Given the nature of the national emergency, the military services were in a great hurry to secure training sites.

The state college faced critical issues beyond its negotiations with the War and Navy Departments, because it had already lost forty-three staff members to the armed forces and defense industries. Twenty-three were reserve officers granted leave for the duration of the war, while others simply resigned their positions to join the military. The departures left remaining faculty and staff working overtime on national defense projects, especially in the schools of engineering, agriculture, science, and home economics. Engineering faculty taught sixteen college-level courses to defense industries in Portland under the Engineering, Scientific, and Management Defense Training (ESMDT) program. Three related engineering courses were also offered on campus: Radio Fundamentals, Chemistry of Explosives, and Ultra High Frequency Techniques. The president's biennial report for 1941–1942 indicated that certificates of achievement were awarded to more than a thousand persons under the program.[27]

The war crisis contributed to an enrollment drop of 11 percent in 1941–1942 from the college's all-time high of 4,759 in 1940–1941. Because the Selective Service and local draft boards recognized the need for specialists in technology, enrollment stabilized in 1942. Engineering students received deferments to complete their degrees, and engineering departments continued to attract the greatest number of students. Male students were encouraged to enlist in the reserve corps of one of the military services to ready them for active duty. President Strand reported that students were working as janitors, staffing offices on campus, and assisting at the experiment station. With faculty joining the military or taking jobs in defense industries, the college eliminated optional courses in several departments, streamlining operations to lessen instructional burdens.[28] The war skewed activities in the School of Home Economics, focusing on conservation, savings, and increasing food production. The foods and nutrition department offered programs in canning, preparing frozen foods, and seeking to preserve foods longer. The school urged consumers to buy lower-cost foods, to prevent waste, and to select food wisely. Laboratory instructors taught students to conserve food and to find substitutes for scarce commodities such as butter.[29]

Chancellor Hunter met with the administrative council in July 1942 and applauded the college's new curricula proposal for business majors. Although he thought the program "quite admirable," he struck one course, suggesting a more liberal option as a substitute, and forwarded the packet to the board for its approval. When Lower Division dean Ellwood Smith asked the chancellor for freedom to offer courses in language, social science, and art, Hunter responded that the college "ought not to try to duplicate what is at the University." On the other hand, he admitted that most land-grant colleges offered a broader array of courses than OSC, citing the examples of Kansas, Iowa, and Michigan state colleges. If Oregon State College wanted to revise its curricular offerings, he urged the council to "come through the proper channels." When the chancellor raised the question of financing in cash-strapped Oregon, one administrator suggested raising student fees. Hunter responded that the university and the college already had the highest student fees in the western states and added the striking reality—Oregon ranked at the bottom in legislative support for higher education.[30]

After A. L. Strand's selection as president (and before his inauguration), state college administrators sent their new chief executive a memorandum outlining the state board's decisions favoring the university. In a letter to the chancellor (with a copy to Strand), the administrative council explained that "many events of the last two years indicate a trend dangerous to the interests of the College."[31] The council focused its attention on the interinstitutional curriculum committee, which was considering the college's proposal to offer degrees in business administration. During the committee's deliberations, university representatives directed "partisan objections to practically every course suggested." Moreover, when the state board approved business courses, they "bore little resemblance to the College proposals." The administrative council suggested four system-wide changes to bring equity to the state college:[32]

(1) The interinstitutional curriculum committee required new leadership (university officials always served as chair).
(2) Interinstitutional deans, treated by the chancellor as representing the college, have consistently sided with the university on curricular issues.
(3) The state college president should participate in all board deliberations where its interests are involved.
(4) The state college president should have access to and control over an emergency budget.

Nearly two years had lapsed between President Ballard's illness in October 1940 and Strand assuming the presidency. Although Gilfillan, who filled in for Ballard until he was named acting president after Ballard's resignation, was an able administrator, the chancellor and state board found it convenient to ignore him when critical decisions were pending. Such were the shortcomings of not bearing the full mantle of president.

As summer moved into fall 1942, the registrar reported continuing decreases in enrollment, reflecting the attrition of students to war industries and military service. There were rumors of new initiatives—a large cantonment of troops to be located north of Corvallis (Camp Adair) and the creation of the Army Specialized Training Program (ASTP), a federal strategy to train men on college and university campuses similar to the Student Army Training Corps of the First World War. While those programs were taking shape, Corvallis leaders addressed air-raid instructions and coping with the arrival and departure of servicemen. Following a request from orchardists in the Hood River Valley, college administrators released three hundred students for a week of apple harvesting in late October. The work was to be incorporated with horticultural instruction, and Hood River orchardists were responsible for the student's transportation. The administrative council voted unanimously that "women not be allowed to leave the campus for the apple picking project."[33]

When Secretary of War Henry L. Stimson created the Army Specialized Training Program (ASTP) in September 1942, the military's objective was to accelerate the training of officers who were technically prepared for the war effort. The purpose of using colleges and universities as training grounds was to assure that troops would be taught in surroundings better equipped to prepare men for both the professional and scientific requirements for military duty. With the heavy drain of young men to the armed services, the ASTP also protected institutions of higher education from being impoverished by the lack of students. When the program was established in December 1942, it catapulted designated schools into a fever of preparation—finding adequate sleeping quarters, dining and classroom space, training grounds, and recreational facilities. With its emphasis on training scientific, engineering, medical, and linguistic specialists, the ASTP was "to prepare personnel for officer candidate school and for other military tasks."[34]

The City of Corvallis hurriedly set about seeking housing for the troop contingents. On campus, administrators considered using the fourth floor of Kidder Hall, the museum (now the Gladys Valley Gymnastics Center), the Barracks Shed (east of McAlexander Field House), and men's dormitories for sleeping quarters. With renovations and double bunks, the college found accommodations for more than a thousand men. Off-campus housing included the Julian Hotel (one hundred) and the old Kappa Sigma House (one hundred). Beyond those arrangements, the college provided ample space for military drill, tennis courts, men's and women's gymnasiums and pools, and athletic fields. Making use of folding chairs, the college identified adequate classroom space in its major buildings.[35]

The arrival of ASTP personnel brought major disruptions to campus life, with the administrative council frequently confronting unanticipated problems. Because the army contracted for daily use of the men's gymnasium, the college had to scramble to find space for regular convocations. Smoking was another issue, with administrators establishing more perimeter areas around buildings, identified with "orange markers," to accommodate ASTP personnel. President Strand confided to a former student in midsummer 1943, "we are pretty much 'in the Army' . . . with 1400 soldiers on campus." Instead of the normal four thousand or so regular students, the college expected only "about 1500, most of which will be women."

The ASTP troops were on active duty, subject to military discipline, and received regular army pay. The program fit well with OSC's twelve-week school calendar, with one week between terms. The ASTP divided soldiers into two programs, basic and advanced. The basic phase was roughly equivalent to a year and a half of college work (three twelve-week terms), with the advanced phase beginning with courses taken in the last half of the sophomore year. Advanced students gravitated to specializations that fit the army's needs. The demands of the program fell heavily on the Schools of Science and Engineering and the

Lower Division. Regular faculty, augmented with additional teachers to meet increased enrollments in certain fields, provided instruction. The college made a special effort to assure that students received regular "academic credit applicable at Oregon State College and other universities and colleges."[36]

Strand's first biennial statement reported the arrival, in March 1943, of 381 soldier-students of the Army Specialized Training Program. During the summer, ASTP numbers increased to 1,354; fall term 1,270; and winter term 1,260. Beginning with great fanfare and designed for the long haul, the program was drastically curtailed in early 1944 when General of the Army George Marshall ordered ASTP soldiers to withdraw from colleges to ready them for the pending invasion of France. There were only 167 ASTP troops on the OSC campus spring term 1944. Troops once expecting to become commissioned officers now faced a new reality as infantry privates. "For trainees," the Historical Division of the Department of the Army explained in 1948, the ASTP "was a series of disillusionments." The abrupt termination of the program was difficult to grasp for civilian educators, according to the Historical Division's assessment, and "seemed arbitrary, after repeated declarations by the War Department of the importance of specialized training."[37]

Although the ASTP lasted longer than the Student Army Training Corps of the First World War, its impact was transitory, flooding college campuses with large numbers of army personnel and then abruptly shutting down when military exigencies required troops elsewhere. Military authorities awarded certificates of completion to 365 soldier-students on the OSC campus. Curtis Jones, an ASTP student studying Arabic languages at the University of Pennsylvania, expressed disappointment when the army ordered his contingent to "general duty in the Pacific Theater." The end of their academic interlude, he wrote, "taught us a broader lesson: that the homily about best-laid plans going awry applies first and foremost to the military."[38]

The influence of the Specialized Training Program at other land-grant institutions paralleled the experience at OSC. Purdue University enrolled soldiers already in the army in advanced engineering and personnel psychology classes. Cornell University's involvement in the ASTP included preprofessional active-duty men preparing for medical college, language students studying Russian, German, Czech, and Chinese, and personnel psychologists and basic engineers. Both groups were on campus for only a short time. The fact that Cornell was teaching Russian to army personnel alarmed the New York *World-Telegram* enough to charge "Cornell Goes Bolshevist." Iowa State College participated in the ASTP in one of its key areas of expertise, veterinary medicine. By the time the program ended in mid-1944, the school had turned out 220 veterinarians. In

East Lansing, Michigan State enrolled one thousand troops in several programs. Madison Kuhn, author of the college's history, believed the program influenced faculty to see "virtue in the prescribed courses of the Army program."[39]

For the Corvallis community, the opening of the large army training facility seven miles north at Camp Adair was far more important than the Army Specialized Training Program on campus. The War Department had been searching for a suitable place in the Pacific Northwest to establish a training facility since early 1941. The department's requirements were open land, access to a good water supply, a railroad, and cheap electrical power. With the lobbying of state college engineering graduate John Gallagher Sr., the army chose the site near Corvallis in September 1941 and began construction at the cantonment that became Camp Adair. Although construction was delayed until after Pearl Harbor, college administrators were aware that the big camp might have some effect on campus activities. To coordinate discussions and to take advantage of defense funds that might be available, the college wanted to be "in on the ground floor" to assist the new training facility. The ambitions to partner with Adair mostly turned up empty, except for faculty in the School of Engineering, who contracted to oversee construction.[40]

To make way for Camp Adair's buildings and training grounds, residents in the area, many of them farmers, were forced to sell their land and move elsewhere. A cemetery with 414 gravesites, some dating to the 1850s, had to be moved as well. In frenetic construction activity beginning in mid-spring 1942 and lasting until fall, four large construction companies put up some 1,700 buildings—barracks, dining halls, kitchens, a bakery, movie theaters, stores, an infirmary, and a large field house sufficient to fit three full-size basketball courts. Local merchants thrived, selling foodstuffs, lumber, and other building supplies. The camp required the construction of freshwater and wastewater treatment plants, a central heating facility, warehouses, firing ranges, an airfield, and much more. According to John Baker's *Camp Adair*, eight thousand men labored through the summer of 1942 to complete the facility.[41]

The School of Engineering was significantly involved during the construction phase at Camp Adair. Department of Mechanical Engineering chair Samuel Graf reported that his faculty participated in thirty-two separate activities at Camp Adair, with Graf himself serving as liaison in hiring construction engineers. Graf's work involved heating installations; inspecting refrigeration, mess hall, and steam plant equipment; designing the water filtration plant; supervising and inspecting all mechanical facilities; and myriad other activities. The engineering faculty carried out those responsibilities while they were consulting with other clients involving airports in the Northwest, the

Medford army cantonment at Camp White, the Umatilla Ordnance Depot, Willamette Valley Project dam construction, the Bonneville Power Administration, and Portland shipyards.[42] The college's engineering staff was more involved in war-related work than any other school on campus.

The military units trained at Camp Adair included the 96th Infantry Division (August 1942–August 1943), the 104th Infantry Division (June 1943–July 1944), and the 70th Infantry Division (November 1943–March 1944). The first unit to occupy the camp in August 1942, the 96th, saw combat in the Philippines and later at the climactic battle for Okinawa launched on April 1, 1945. The 104th spent ten months fighting in Belgium, France, and Germany, crossing the Rhine River in March 1945, capturing many German troops and taking several towns along the way. The 70th Division began training at Adair in June 1943 and left for the European theater the next year, seeing heavy fighting for eighty-six consecutive days in Italy and France. During their stay at Adair, troops occasionally fought forest fires and assisted with fruit and vegetable harvest in the Willamette Valley.[43]

Camp Adair's brief history was similar to that of other temporary training camps, where buildings were thrown up overnight and thousands of troops matriculated through training sessions, and then after a period of two years or so, they were all gone. Summer winds whistled around vacated buildings at Camp Adair by July 1944, with the US Navy using the infirmary/hospital to treat wounded sailors. One section of the camp housed Italian and German prisoners of war between 1944 and 1946 (although few local people were aware of the prisoners' presence). Sixty-two thousand acres of Adair property was deeded to Oregon State College and became the northern Dunn unit of McDonald-Dunn Forest. The college acquired several of the naval hospital buildings (Quonset huts), temporary structures that were moved to campus for administrative, academic program, and faculty offices. The college also made use of some of the barracks buildings in 1946 to house veterans until similar facilities were built on campus. The US Air Force operated a radar station on the Adair site between 1955 and 1969. The officers' residential homes provided the nucleus for Adair Village, incorporated in 1976.[44]

Beyond military enrollees on campus, the number of regular students continued to trend downward, falling to 3,262 students for the academic year 1943–1944, of which 1,279 were ASTP enrollees. Enrollment fell again in 1944–1945, to 2,375 students. Despite declining numbers, students continued to win scholarships and fellowships, although some awards designated for men went without recipients because of the dearth of candidates. Students

Ava Milam (1884–1976) came to Oregon Agricultural College in 1911 as head of the Department of Foods and Nutrition. She served as dean of the School of Home Economics from 1917 to 1950, overseeing Oregon's nutrition program during the Second World War. During her tenure, she traveled to several Pacific Rim nations establishing home economics programs and consulting at institutions of higher learning. Her many achievements garnered her OSU's Distinguished Service Award in 1966. Courtesy of the OSU Special Collections and Archives Research Center.

majoring in specialized fields (physics, chemistry, medicine, and pharmacy) could take advantage of loans up to $500 per year to pay their way through college. Because of the drop in enrollment across the state system, the Board of Higher Education adopted a budget that led to the release of 104 faculty among the six state schools. The Oregon College of Education in Monmouth took the largest reduction, with 20 percent of its faculty discharged.[45]

The war left nothing untouched on campus. At the request of the War Department, the Lower Division offered introductory language classes in Chinese, Portuguese, and Russian, and courses in foreign cultures. One ASTP contingent in the summer of 1943 was detailed to "foreign area and language study." As the troops arrived, many of them with college educations, they were tested for assignment to appropriate levels of instruction. Dean of Science F. A. Gilfillan was one of two Russian-language professors. The Lower Division also created courses in Asian geography and economics. More than any other unit on campus, the Department of Military Science was transformed from educating ROTC students to a department responsible for supervising and providing room and board and military education to virtually all male students. The department was heavily involved with ASTP troops beginning in the spring of 1943, working closely with President Strand, who created a dean of administration position to oversee campus organizations and instruction, and to coordinate the ASTP presence.[46]

Campus women provided significant war services, especially Ava Milam, dean of the School of Home Economics, who headed the Oregon Nutrition Committee, representing business and educational groups. Through news releases, public talks, radio programs, classes, fair exhibits, and other forums, the committee preached good nutrition as a vehicle to assist national and international food problems. The committee organized nutrition clusters in each of Oregon's thirty-six counties. For those who argue that the United States was unprepared at the time of the attack on Pearl Harbor, it should be noted that Ava Milam answered President Roosevelt's call and attended the inaugural National Nutrition Conference in May 1941. As the nutrition committee's principal organizer, she worked for four and a half years to carry the national nutrition program to the people of Oregon.[47]

Other women, among them Lorna Jessup, assistant dean of women, issued ration books to students during the early part of the war and created the hostess league, which organized recreational programs for servicemen, including dances at Camp Adair. Her secretary, Mabel Winston, oversaw the hostess program when Jessup was away, chaperoned hostess parties to Adair, and scheduled entertainment on campus. Maud Wilson in the School of Home Economics arranged rooms for war guests with local families willing to rent unused bedrooms to war workers. One imagines that large numbers of construction workers at Camp Adair in 1942 made use of Wilson's service. She gathered data on age, sex, occupation, and other information important to homeowners willing to rent. Wilson attempted to pair people of similar ages and dispositions.[48]

Under the direction of librarian William Carlson, the college library continued its normal routine, but in other ways increased its conventional services. The library cooperated in Victory Book Drives in 1942 and 1943, collecting books on behalf of the American Library Association, the Red Cross, and the United Service Organizations. The second drive collected 884 books with the assistance of local bookstores, the newspaper, and radio station KOAC. The college library extended its hours and remained open evenings during the summer for the Army Specialized Training Program. It cooperated with the Army Map Service, providing rare maps for the army's use. Several library staffers—five women and one man—resigned to take similar positions with the army and navy. The library acquired several army newspapers and made them available during the war, and it began saving duplicates of periodicals and books to offer to war-ravaged libraries following the war.[49]

Among campus administrative units, the School of Agriculture suffered unprecedented retrenchment. Enrollment dropped from 524 students in the fall of 1942 to sixty-four one year later. Although the ASTP did not include courses in agriculture, the school's faculty taught classes with the science and engineering staffs. The extension service, in contrast, was heavily involved in promoting "urban and non-farm rural gardens" to increase food production.

The Victory Garden program was an immense success during the war years. At the direction of Congress, extension was charged with recruiting, training, and placing farm laborers to the tune of 180,000 workers. Among Oregon's emergency labor pool were some 4,600 Mexican nationals recruited under the federal government's Bracero Program agreement with Mexico. Approximately eight thousand Japanese evacuees provided another valuable workforce in the fields and orchards east of the Cascade Range. Extension also reported placing sixty thousand youths in various sectors of agricultural work.[50]

Faculty in the School of Science were inundated with requests for information about "fields not previously covered," analyzing thousands of bacteriological samples—"water, milk, food, and pathogen specimens." The chemistry department cooperated with the Office of Civil Defense to protect the public against gas attacks and provided advice to military officials at Camp Adair about chemical warfare and sanitation. The Department of Entomology offered information about pest control to citizens who were growing victory gardens. Newspapers and radio programs provided forums for circulating the information.[51]

Oregon State College took a respite from military-related work in October 1943 to celebrate the diamond anniversary of its founding as a land-grant institution. The *Oregonian* believed the college, under the firm leadership of President August L. Strand, was "among the top few technical schools of the country" and a "steady source of military strength for the nation." The *Oregonian's* John Burtner wrote that Oregon State College and its land-grant peers, in keeping with the purposes of the Morrill Act, had provided the nation with trained officers, the nucleus for the modern military. The college was "a center of important military developments," whose graduates were wresting "conquered lands from the axis invaders." The festivities on campus took place amid patriotic music, flags, and khaki uniforms, and featured Oregon governor Earl Snell, OSC's president Strand, and University of Idaho president Harrison Dale as speakers.[52]

College administrators were turning their attention to the postwar period by late spring 1943, a time that promised great challenges. Although the future would be unpredictable, President Strand thought the college well-equipped to handle a larger, more diverse student body and to assist the increasingly industrialized Pacific Northwest. "The war is placing its mark on us all," Strand reported, with veterans requiring "rehabilitation" and the college nurturing military personnel who were worried about "lost time." Faculty committees and administrative personnel had already been gathering statistics and trying to formulate suitable postwar policies for the institution.

The president indicated that Linfield College, a private liberal arts school in McMinnville, was offering a course in postwar planning.[53]

Responding to an American Council of Education questionnaire on postwar planning, Oregon State College reported that it was considering an industrial, semiprofessional curriculum requiring more facilities than those available on campus, with suggestions that it should acquire Camp Adair when it was deactivated. The administrative council thought it prudent to accelerate programs to enable servicemen "to make up for lost time." President Strand questioned whether the postwar era would see greater specialization or a shift to more comprehensive academic programs. Expecting a deluge of students, the president believed acquiring competent staff would be as important as classroom space.[54] The sheer numbers of students at the end of the war would force the college to chase frantically after additional faculty and classroom buildings.

Because of declining enrollment in Oregon's higher education institutions, the State Board of Higher Education reduced the system's budget by $141,000 for the 1944–1945 biennium. Looking to the future, the board approved building plans for its two flagship institutions, some of it self-financed, with construction to begin as soon as structural materials became available. To resolve deferred building and the need to accommodate more students, the board developed a ten-year plan. The state college was in line for a new women's dormitory, expansion of the agricultural and engineering buildings, and an industrial building. Realizing that the large number of veterans would require more living space, the board added a men's dormitory to OSC's construction plans in midsummer 1944.[55]

The state system had limped along during the Depression, with federal assistance, student fees, and fund-raisers financing the only construction activity on campus. While California had appropriated $10 million for new college and university buildings and Washington $5.7 million, Oregon lagged badly, putting up only $100,000 for new buildings. Understanding that enrollment in Oregon's institutions was certain to increase sharply, the *Oregonian* followed closely the state board's trials in dealing with more students. The big challenge for Oregon's public colleges and university would be during the immediate postwar years when veterans hit the state's campuses. The newspaper thought the board underestimated enrollment, because there were approximately twenty-five thousand Oregon servicemen and women who would be eligible for federal assistance. The Board of Higher Education had a responsibility to do more than the "minimum program" outlined in its ten-year plan.[56]

If Oregon's beleaguered prewar economy provided limited resources for education, when the war moved toward its bloody conclusion, the *Oregonian* demanded that lawmakers provide more support for public schools and colleges. Tax collections from business profits and individual earnings were up, and considerably so by 1944. Oregon's incoming revenue indicated a greater per capita percentage increase than many states. Although the war severely disrupted rural communities, defense industries such as Portland's Kaiser Shipyards drew thousands of people to high-paying jobs. The city's big shipyards, and another across the river in Vancouver, employed as many as 120,000 workers at peak production. The Kaiser facilities made an early commitment to hiring women for welding work, paying good wages, and providing equal pay with men for similar work and pride for women in holding jobs that formerly were reserved for men.[57]

Labor-saving advances in the agricultural and wood-products industries helped resolve some labor shortages. With the assistance of the Oregon State College Extension Service, Polk and Yamhill County prune growers used mechanical tree shakers in the fall of 1944 to assist with their harvests. Although no damage to trees was evident, the extension office indicated that further study was needed. To fund additional labor-saving advances for agriculture, the *Oregonian* argued, experiment stations needed increased funding for technical investigations. Several Oregon State College specialists addressed those issues at a Portland meeting in January 1945, including Stephen Wyckoff, director of the forest experiment station, and Paul Dunn, dean of the College of Forestry.[58]

As longtime members of the Association of Land-Grant Colleges and Universities, Oregon State College officials followed closely congressional measures affecting higher education. As legislative bills worked their way through Congress, the association asked member institutions for their preferred plans to support veterans, and for the number of public colleges and universities in each state, average rates of tuition and fees, and tuition costs for in-state and out-of-state students. The association was collecting data on land-grant schools to present to congressional committees and wanted replies to ready itself for a "*very heavy schedule* beginning in January 1944."[59]

The principal veterans' bill before the 78th Congress in 1944 (S-1946) would appropriate $97.5 million for vocational and technical training and college education. The association valued the $24 million available to member schools that were technical institutions, but worried that a clause "of less than college grade" would extend provisions to secondary schools and conflict with programs in land-grant colleges. At the association's request, President Strand wrote Oregon congressman James Mott that the term "vocational technical education" in S-1946 lacked clarity. The bill should provide for mathematics, science, and English, which "need some kind of shot in the arm if they aren't to be crowded out altogether."[60]

When President Roosevelt signed the Servicemen's Readjustment Act—the GI Bill—into law in June 1944, the legislation was a watered-down version of his State of the Union address calling for "an economic bill of rights" guaranteeing every citizen a job at living wages, adequate housing, health care, education, and "protection from the economic fears of old age, sickness, accident, and unemployment." The GI Bill offered returning veterans federal funding to attend vocational schools and colleges, support for health and housing expenses while enrolled as students, and low-interest loans for purchasing homes or businesses. Fearing that the nation would fall into a recession similar to the one following the First World War, lawmakers acted with dispatch. "Anxiety," Ira Katznelson argues, propelled Congress to develop strategies to avoid a return to prewar conditions: If war ended the Depression, what would happen when the federal government withdrew its unprecedented investment and spending?[61]

College and university administrators offered the only significant opposition to the GI Bill. The University of Chicago's reform president Robert Maynard Hutchins was among the opponents, charging that universities would be "converted into educational hobo jungles. And veterans . . . will find themselves educational hobos." In a seemingly generous act benefitting veterans, race discrimination reared its ugly head when Mississippi congressman John Rankin amended the bill with a provision that mandated administrative decentralization. As a consequence, 4.4 million of the fifteen million veterans participating in the GI Bill earned college and university degrees. Still others attended vocational schools and obtained bank loans to start businesses or purchase homes. Because local officials directed the programs—making bank loans and overseeing college admissions—the GI Bill effectively preserved "the Southern way of life" in the segregated states of the Old South. Black veterans were refused admission to all-white universities and colleges and were excluded from technical training programs that would lead to good-paying jobs. Matters were only marginally better for black veterans in the North, where less discriminatory Ivy League schools like the University of Pennsylvania listed only forty-six black students in 1946 out of a total enrollment of nine thousand.[62]

For schools like Oregon State College, an institution perpetually strapped for financing, the GI Bill was a welcome program. President Strand believed the bill would be a great boon for veterans' education, bringing the institution around $300 per year for each enrolled serviceman. If the president was optimistic—believing the college well-positioned to handle the inrush of students—Japan's quick surrender in August 1945 and the rapid demobilization that followed rent asunder many carefully planned reconversion strategies. The Oregon State Board of Higher Education anticipated greater difficulties ahead, an intensification of efforts to meet the needs of returning veterans. The effects on Oregon's system of higher education were apparent a full year before V-E Day, when discharged servicemen, many of them recovering from wounds, began to appear on state system campuses.[63]

The state board collected data on sixteen thousand alumni and students who had served in the military from Oregon's public institutions. That figure represented a sizable percentage of the 145,000 Oregonians who served in the armed forces. More than 8,500 OSC alumni and students had served in the military by the end of the war, with 275 of those making the ultimate sacrifice. Among the predominantly male group were young women graduates who had enlisted in the WAVES, WACS, marines, and SPARS, many of them achieving officer's rank. While much was made of the Army Specialized Training Program at Oregon State College and the University of Oregon, a less heralded cohort involved five hundred women in the US Cadet Nurse Corps who had trained at the University of Oregon Medical School in Portland and Eastern Oregon College of Education in La Grande. The purpose of the Nurse Corps was to assure that the United States had a sufficient number of trained nurses to care for civilians at home and those in the military.[64]

"It is a sobering fact," President Strand stated in his first biennial report following the war, that the Oregon State College campus "is not much better than it was twenty years ago." With the support of the GI Bill, men and women were entering a college grounds where Quonset huts and other makeshift structures provided cover from the elements. Deferred maintenance was obvious everywhere—buildings in need of fresh paint, roofs requiring repair, and other signs of physical decay. Since the onset of the Great Depression, the chemistry and health services buildings—funded with federal money—were the only significant additions to the campus. Because of its limited physical facilities, the president wrote, "the campus [was] unprepared for its task."[65]

Rather than focusing on the past, the president's report addressed the future, emphasizing again the college's inadequate "preparation for the tremendous task that faces us in these postwar years." Confronted with thousands of students seeking admission, the institution's physical facilities

limited the numbers it could accommodate. The wartime curriculum, however, had advanced the college's course offerings in foreign languages and cultures. "The necessity of a world view has increased interest in foreign cultures
and economy," Strand reported. With the addition of the Navy ROTC unit,
the college offered a new social science sequence, "Foundations of National
Power," a requirement for the navy program and an elective for the entire
student body.[66]

Strand was the first president to significantly address the imbalance
in the institution's educational stricture, the absence of a commitment to
the liberal arts. The college, he observed, always had students seeking both
a liberal education and preparation in a professional field, "but never more
keenly than now." The majority of Oregon State College professors were in
the professional schools, and while they supported a liberal education, most
were absorbed in their own fields of specialization. While professional faculty wanted students to have a liberal education, Strand believed their chief
responsibility was to their profession.[67] Faculty in the humanities and social
science were the central issue, according to the president, because teaching
lower-division "service" courses limited their class time with students. Although the practices were embedded in the land-grant tradition, the creation
of the Oregon State System of Higher Education in 1929 and its directives to
eliminate the duplication of courses between the University of Oregon and
Oregon State College solidified those divisions.[68]

Resolving the disparity between the professional schools and the liberal
arts would become more difficult with each passing year, Strand argued. In
one of its first investigations, the new faculty council, created in March 1945
and forerunner to the faculty senate, addressed the institution's area requirements for majors and degree programs. The council learned that students
were required to take a minimum of course work in three groups: language
and literature, science, and social science. When the council asked for a larger
inquiry into the college's course requirements, the president directed the curriculum council to review the institution's "general-education objectives and
procedures." As part of that investigation, Strand asked the college to send
representatives to attend the Northwest Conference on Higher Education to
gather information.[69]

The end of the two-ocean war in 1945 ushered in a dramatic changing of the
guard in students attending Oregon's public colleges and university. When
allied forces bludgeoned Germany into unconditional surrender on May 8,
1945, the student population in the state system consisted "largely of girls,

seventeen-year-old boys, and a sprinkling of discharged veterans" (number-
ing about four hundred in all institutions). After Japan's surrender in August,
1,085 veterans were enrolled in the state system, a figure that grew to 3,039
in the winter term 1946 and 4,201 in the spring. College registrations, which
dropped to a low of 2,375 during the 1944–1945 academic year, rebounded to
3,126 at the end of 1946 and then more than doubled to an astounding 7,133
students in the spring of 1947. Ex-servicemen and women explain most of
the huge boost in numbers, with 4,494 enrolled fall term 1946. As a group,
the veterans were more mature, serious, and had definite objectives in mind.
The college's worst bottleneck was housing. Although the school made use of
surplus war barracks moved to campus to house students, additional apartment units at Camp Adair would not be ready until 1947.[70]

The crush of veterans registering at Oregon State College in the fall of
1946 pushed enrollment to a postwar high of 7,498 in 1948, which then tailed
off to fewer than six thousand students in 1950. Even with Quonset huts serving as classrooms and offices, the college struggled to find room, often resorting to ill-suited basements and storerooms for extra space. During the frantic
search for housing, one University of Oregon official indicated that students
often signed up for dormitory reservations in several colleges to make "sure
they will be able to attend one." Students looking for places to live in Corvallis
often found rooms with townspeople; others traveled to campus from nearby
communities such as Philomath or, in a few cases, as far away as Salem.[71]

The GI Bill was only one component in the dramatic expansion of higher
education in the United States during the postwar years. Rising birthrates and
a westward-migrating population brought dramatic enrollment increases in
western states, with California adopting a master plan in 1960 to provide access to its tiered public institutions. Junior colleges in California that predated
the Second World War boomed after 1945, providing students with two years
of postsecondary education leading to a terminal degree in professional and
occupational fields or transferring to a four-year college or university. By
the late 1950s, junior colleges had morphed into community colleges, with
Oregon joining the ranks in the late 1950s.[72]

8
Campus and Community in the Cold War

Writer David Halberstam has called the 1950s the black-and-white decade, a period captured in still photographs and reflecting the growing number of television sets in American homes. The 1950s launched the "baby boom" and a quest for material well-being as citizens reached for the American dream. Traditional systems of familial reckoning and authority continued, and at least on the surface, people imitated those standards. Beneath the sheen of growing affluence and seemingly omnipresent conformity, however, were restive signs, especially among the nation's African Americans, many of them veterans who chafed at timeworn discrimination. While the brutally segregated South was a canker on the body politic, discrimination in housing, employment, and access to higher education existed elsewhere, including the State of Oregon with its overwhelming white population.[1]

With the nation at large, Oregon witnessed the onset of the Cold War in the late 1940s, a euphemism that describes more than four decades of confrontation between the Soviet Union and the United States in which the American nation, according to historian David Kennedy, became "a virtual garrison state." With the dark forces of National Socialism and the Japanese military caste down for the count, the former allies engaged in a protracted struggle over spheres of influence, first in Europe and then Asia and elsewhere. For many Americans, long fearful of socialist and communist influences, the US-Soviet encounter symbolized good versus evil, a phenomenon that penetrated every aspect of national politics. Although the roots to the conflict date to Russia's Bolshevik Revolution of 1917, the years following the Second World War witnessed proxy clashes in Italy, Greece, several European countries, and eventually American intervention in Korea and Vietnam to stymie Soviet advances.[2]

The Cold War reverberated across the Oregon State College campus, buttressing its reputation for training military officers, sending scientists abroad to advance agriculture in Third World nations, and influencing academic freedom and hiring and firing decisions. The administration, faculty, and townspeople approved—like much of the nation—questioning the loyalty of those who challenged Cold War, anticommunist precepts. The postwar years also witnessed thousands of people in Oregon and elsewhere fleeing rural settings for cities and towns. Oregon's farm population of 258,751 in 1940 dropped to 221,399 in 1945 and continued to fall precipitously as rural families took advantage of labor-saving technologies. Oregon's population of 953,786 in 1930 had grown to 1,089,684 during the Depression, a 14 percent increase far outstripping the national rate of 3.5 percent. Between 1940 and 1950 its population grew nearly 40 percent, to an astounding 1,521,341. The Willamette River community of Corvallis experienced a similar increase—a population of 7,585 in 1930, 8,392 in 1940, and a leap of 93 percent to 16,207 people in 1950.[3]

Bill Tebeau, a graduate of Baker High School in 1943, moved from the small eastern Oregon community to Corvallis to attend college in the midst of the war. Tebeau, the first African American male student to graduate from Oregon State College, was awarded a degree in chemical engineering in 1948. Carrie Halsell, the first African American to graduate from the institution, earned a degree in commerce in 1926. Tebeau's graduating class of 1,184 students, the largest to that date, included a large veteran contingent. He remembered a normal college experience, except for difficulty in finding housing and an administrator's suggestion that he enroll at the University of Oregon where he might feel more comfortable. A woman operating a boardinghouse for foreign students befriended Tebeau and found him a basement room in a fraternity where he tended furnace in exchange for the room. Tebeau's experience points to another reality of immediate postwar Oregon—the state's population was more than 98 percent white, a ratio that would decrease when increasing numbers of Hispanics and Southeast Asians began migrating to the Pacific Northwest after 1970.[4]

As the flood of veterans began to ebb, Oregon State College president A. L. Strand indicated that, during the previous half century, "the chief factors affecting enrollment at the State College have been wars and economic depression." The president was concerned that the college would suffer lost income from the decline in veterans under the GI Bill. For the foreseeable future, he believed high school graduates seeking a college education would increase because of the surge in the state's population. In addition, rising graduate enrollments would mitigate the declining number of veterans. The graduate school enrolled 509 students in 1948–1949 and 602 in 1949–1950, the latter representing a 70 percent increase over the previous decade. And for the first time in the history of the institution, the president reported a seminar in college and university teaching, indicating the faculty's interest in improving their teaching skills.[5]

If there were an end to the old and a beginning of the new at the college, it would be the retirement of longtime Dean A. Ellwood Smith, who had headed various iterations of the humanities and social science departments since 1919. Administering programs that were caught in the curricular battles between the University of Oregon and the State College, Smith went about his responsibilities with insistent and purposeful attention. Oregon Agricultural College hired Smith in 1919, with a PhD in English literature from Harvard University, to serve as dean of service departments, an understated reference to the non-major courses students took in their first two years. Three years later, the Service Departments became the School of Basic Arts and Sciences. The newly appointed board of the Oregon State System of Higher Education, established in 1929, jointly administered the Lower Division and Service Departments at both institutions. Smith served as dean of both units, with the college's Lower Division serving as a terminal, two-year certificate program, or as a springboard to one of the institution's professional majors.[6] For three decades Smith administered departments and programs that supported ("serviced") important majors in the sciences and professional schools.

Smith appears to have found a sympathetic ear in Strand, when the president began drawing attention to Oregon State College's unbalanced educational offerings and citing the importance of the humanities and social sciences in his biennial reports. That issue became more evident in the postwar years, reflecting tensions in the State System of Higher Education's long-standing division of curricular responsibilities between the university and the college. The board had muddled its original allocation when it restored sciences to the university in 1941 and allowed the college to reinstitute a few business courses the following year. Although the university and college were busy with war-related matters after 1941, the struggle to expand course offerings and majors at the two schools continued to simmer.

At the end of the 1940s, the Oregon State College catalogue dutifully repeated the state board's 1932 organizational plan for distributing degrees among its public institutions. To the uncritical eye, the arrangement appeared to be a seamless, smoothly functioning system. The university and college were elements "in an articulated system, parts of an integrated whole," providing students with the opportunity to pursue a general education and then "to center on a particular campus [for] specialized, technical, and professional curricula." Students could complete lower-division work in the humanities and sciences at either of the major institutions. From there they could enroll in specialized degree programs offered on the Eugene or Corvallis campus. President Strand admitted that "practical aims dominate, but liberal aims . . . have a place" in the Lower Division and to some extent in the schools of science and home economics. Overseeing this unified arrangement was Chancellor Paul Packer, who replaced Frederick Hunter in 1946. Under the chancellor's office were the presidents of the University of Oregon and Oregon State College, David Baird and A. L. Strand, respectively. The system also had a centralized business office, extension division, and libraries. William Carlson, the state college librarian, also held the state system's title, director of libraries.[7]

The college's dean of the Lower Division and Service Departments administered instruction "not included in the major departments and schools," except military science, naval science, and physical education. The University of Oregon offered majors in arts and letters, architecture (and landscape architecture), journalism, music, and social science. The Oregon State College catalogue for 1948–1949 urged students to enroll in the institution where they intended to major, but they could also take the first two years at the university and transfer to the state college in their junior year. The college's lower-division departments were divided into two groups, arts and letters and social science, disciplines associated with the liberal arts.[8]

Chancellor Packer added his voice to retiring Ellwood Smith's career-long effort to promote the humanities. In his biennial reports and public statements, he cited the importance of technology and vocational education but stressed the need to place greater emphasis on the humanities and social sciences. He believed the liberal arts, which had been slighted in the twentieth century, were important to understanding the need for "moral support for our form of government." Reviewing the previous twenty years under the state system, the chancellor praised growing graduate student numbers at all institutions, the building program launched in 1945, and statistics predicting that enrollments would double in the next ten years.[9] The quest to achieve equity between sciences and humanities at the state college would be a persisting theme in the institution's story for several decades.

From 1947 until the collapse of the Soviet Union in 1990, Cold War events simmered among the world's nations, occasionally bursting forth into full-scale conflict. In the midst of veterans flooding the Corvallis campus, President Truman went before Congress in March 1947 asking for military assistance for Greece and Turkey, two nations resisting "subjugation by armed minorities," a reference to communist insurgencies. Dubbed the "Truman Doctrine" in Cold

War literature, the president's statement reflected the apocalyptic rhetoric that came to define Soviet-American relations. The dictatorial, suspicious, and paranoid Soviet premier Josef Stalin viewed those initiatives as a direct threat to the Russian nation. The Soviets escalated tensions with the communist coup in Czechoslovakia in February 1948, and four months later, their blockade of land traffic into West Berlin. Those events, and Secretary of State George C. Marshall's previous announcement of a huge economic assistance program to assist European nations recover from the ravages of the Second World War—the Marshall Plan—brought the Cold War to fever pitch.[10]

The coup in Czechoslovakia and the Berlin blockade galvanized witch-hunting campaigns in the United States against public figures—politicians, entertainment stars, and liberal-minded college and university faculty—well before Wisconsin senator Joseph McCarthy launched his bombastic hunt for communists. Among Pacific Coast institutions, the University of Washington was the first to purge its faculty of professors accused of being members of the Communist Party or sympathetic to the party line. Following the Washington legislature's infamous Canwell Hearings in the summer of 1948, the university's investigations led to charges against six faculty members and the dismissal of three of them, including renowned social psychologist Ralph Gundlach, a noncommunist professor committed to social justice causes. The University of Washington Tenure Committee recommended Gundlach's firing because his political activities were "a more effective agent for communism than the re-spondents who admit Communist Party membership." The committee's report, critics charged, was an astounding assault on academic freedom. University president William Allen carried out the recommendation in January 1949.[11]

The next month Oregon State College joined the ranks of Cold War controversy when President Strand informed young chemistry professor Ralph Spitzer and economics professor Laurent LaVallee that their annual tenure contracts would not be renewed. The activities of Spitzer, the more prominent of the two, suggest the perilous nature of straying from political orthodoxy during the Cold War. Spitzer's hounding as an academic liberal was much more than a local story, reverberating through national scientific organizations and involving the US State Department. A student of Oregon State College's most renowned alumnus, Linus Pauling, Spitzer had earned his PhD at the California Institute of Technology in the early 1940s and then worked in war-related research before joining the chemistry faculty at the college in 1946. His dismissal came in the midst of the biennial session of the Oregon legislature, which passed a measure prohibiting anyone "linked to Communists" from state employment.[12]

A protégé of Linus Pauling, who described him as an "unusually able man," Ralph Spitzer joined the Oregon State College chemistry faculty in the fall of 1946, and his wife Terry enrolled as an undergraduate student. In the midst of the emerging Cold War between the Soviet Union and the United States, the Spitzers were outspoken proponents of world peace, a dangerous view, as it turns out, with the onset of Communist hysteria in the United States. Because of their activism, President A. J. Strand terminated Ralph Spitzer's appointment in the spring of 1949. With Ralph unable to land another teaching position in the United States, the Spitzers emigrated to Canada and settled in British Columbia where they both enjoyed professional careers. Courtesy of the OSU Special Collections and Archives Research Center.

Although the Spitzer case was drawn out and complicated, the young chemistry professor's essential sin was supporting former vice president and secretary of commerce Henry Wallace when he ran for president in 1948 under the banner of the Progressive Party. The contest pitted third-party candidate Wallace against Democrat president Harry Truman and Republican aspirant New York governor Thomas Dewey. Wallace, the "peace" candidate, favored negotiating with the Soviet Union and recognizing Russia's legitimate spheres of interest in Eastern Europe. Spitzer's wife, Terry, an undergraduate student activist and leader of the campus Young Progressives of America, unknowingly made her husband's situation more tenuous when she championed Wallace's candidacy in letters to the *Barometer* and at campus events. Copious documents reveal that Terry's outspoken political positions angered the largely conservative Corvallis community and unquestionably figured in President Strand's decision to dismiss her husband.[13] In this instance, Henry Wallace served as a scapegoat for ridding the campus of faculty who failed to meet domestic Cold War ideological prerequisites.

Ralph Spitzer was an idealist interested in the social consequences of the scientific enterprise and deeply concerned about policies regarding the atomic bomb and avoiding an armaments race. Because scientists were responsible for creating such destructive weapons, he believed they had a responsibility "to inform the public about the results of mistaken policies." In an increasingly simplified black-and-white world, Ralph and Terry Spitzer's support for world peace found little space in the political discourse settling over many American communities. When Spitzer appealed his case to the college's Committee on Review and Appeals, the committee supported the president's decision, which was based on "the culmination of various consultations on departmental, scholarly, and institutional levels extending over a period of several months."[14]

Although Strand initially gave no detailed reason for Spitzer's dismissal, the escalating media attention prompted him to launch a full-blown assault on the chemistry professor. What followed was the US State Department asking Strand to declare that Spitzer's dismissal involved "a long record of activities in support of the 'party line.'" Such a declaration would allow the department to effectively counter claims that the United States was censoring teaching and research. From that point forward, Strand responded in spades, charging that Spitzer had "been engaged in a very active campaign . . . the last few months on behalf of the Progressive Party but all the time in behalf of the communist viewpoint." The president settled into a pattern of addressing Spitzer's sympathies with the Communist Party line in the absence of any evidence to the contrary—unless one presumes him guilty for supporting Henry Wallace, a noncommunist, for president in 1948.[15]

When Spitzer applied for a position as chemistry department chair at Ripon College in Wisconsin in 1953, Strand wrote to Ripon's president explaining that Spitzer's outside activities interfered with his college duties. The president mentioned Terry Spitzer's questionable activities on campus and concluded that neither of the Spitzers was "campaigning for Henry Wallace, which would have been all right." Instead, "they were campaigning for the Communist party line." Strand's letter made copious use of the handwritten notes of a student spy, "Vern," who attended Young Progressive meetings in the Spitzer home after Ralph was fired. The conspiratorial gatherings involved discussions about unions, peace, and listening to the folk music of Earl Robinson[16]

Two international developments in 1949 dramatically heightened Cold War tensions—the Soviet Union's detonation of an atomic bomb in late August and the victory of Mao Tse-tung and the communist People's Republic of China. Those events spurred American military preparedness and boosted Oregon State College's ROTC program. When communist North Korean forces crossed into the Republic of South Korea on the night of June 25, 1950, the United States became embroiled in a "hot" war. The Korean conflict (June 1950–July 1953) roused patriotic fervor on the Corvallis campus, prompting *College Now*, a campus publication welcoming students, "to meet the obligation to your country . . . to defend her future." *College Now* urged physically fit persons to enroll in ROTC and emphasized the need "for trained minds. . . . to make the American Republic a standard which the free world can meet and respect." Employing military metaphors, the pamphlet praised American colleges for "moving into the front line of the government's long-range preparedness program."[17]

The Korean emergency triggered the mobilization of the nation's military and educational resources. As a longtime member of the Association of Land-Grant Colleges and Universities, Oregon State College cooperated with initiatives to improve military preparedness and provide technical and research services. The association supported mandatory military service for able-bodied males between the ages of eighteen and twenty-six to provide trained men to meet the military's needs. State College administrators worked with the land-grant association to strengthen campus ROTC and engineering programs.[18]

"The shadows of war fell again upon both students and young faculty members," Chancellor Paul Packer wrote in his June 1952 biennial report. The state's faculty had contributed to the war effort, using their talents and scientific expertise to aid the military. Because the Korean conflict involved a potential nuclear war with the Soviet Union, colleges and universities were fully involved in the mobilization effort. When the National Conference for Mobilization of Education and the American Council on Education solicited information from institutions, OSC responded with research projects involving the schools of engineering, science, forestry, and agriculture, with proposals ranging from chemistry investigations to wood and cellulose research critical to the war emergency.[19]

One of the more intriguing projects—and a prototype for future environmental investigations—was a biological survey of the Columbia River. Oregon State College proposed to join the Public Health Service and the Atomic Energy Commission to survey the Columbia River downstream from the Hanford Nuclear Reservation to study radioactive pollution in the waterway. The inquiry would involve safeguards to protect air and water from radioactive contamination. Other research investigations involved the bacteriological and biological sciences—the study of pathogenic organisms, the production of antibiotics, the better understanding of sanitizing agents, and joining with the Atomic Energy Commission to investigate the effects of radiation on viruses and aquatic biology.[20]

Although America's modern mobilization for war dates to the late 1930s, the Korean conflict added a new sense of urgency because the Soviets possessed the atomic bomb and North Korea was a client state. In an age threatening nuclear destruction, the Federal Civil Defense Administration directed states to disseminate disaster preparedness information to county officials. Oregon State College cooperated with the Benton County Civil Defense Agency to prepare for civil defense emergencies. The county's planning document cited a litany of international events that could lead to war: the Berlin blockade, the Soviet possession of the atomic bomb, the communist takeover of China, the Korean War, and a world "filled with fear that Russia plans to make war on all free people." County agencies were merely reflecting national and state administrators who were urging local governments to prepare for military attacks. Benton County's civil defense office circulated an "Official U. S. Booklet" on biological warfare, air raids, and advice to citizens in case of an attack ("Be Quick But Calm"). Homeowners were advised to purchase the government document, "Survival Under Atomic Attack."[21]

State college administrators submitted a bid to the air force to train 450 women clerk-typists, with the School of Business and Technology handling the instruction. The air force also sought programs to train some six thousand airmen in preventive medicine. The three- to five-month sessions were subject to consultation with the National Research Council. The air force expected field experiences to be part of the training regimen. Responding for the college, Dean of Administration E. B. Lemon indicated the institution's interest, citing its experienced public health and sanitary engineering staffs, and its close working relationships with Oregon's public health and sanitary agencies.[22]

Super-heated Cold War anticommunism struck the OSC campus in a peculiar way in the early 1950s when a national right-wing organization attacked Frank Abbott Magruder's social studies textbook, *Magruder's American Government: A Textbook on the Problems of Democracy*. A Virginia native, Frank Magruder was educated at Princeton University, when he published the first edition of *American Government* in 1917. The book would undergo multiple editions. Magruder, who taught political science and international relations at OSC for thirty years, died in 1949. William "Bill" McClenaghan, a young colleague, took over as editor of the popular text. The incident placing the book in the crosshairs of anticommunist zealots was Edna Lonigan's scurrilous 1949 review, charging that the text promoted "communistic teachings." Conservative radio broadcaster Fulton Lewis Jr. followed with a program devoted solely to quoting from Lonigan's review. In the next several months school boards, district superintendents, and journalists indicted the book for being receptive to socialist and communist viewpoints.[23]

School district attacks extended from Houston, Texas, Atlanta, Georgia, and the Midwest, to small towns in Washington and Montana. Worried about socialist or communist reading material, school administrators wrote President Strand, asking whether his staff had examined the book to determine if the charges were substantive. Henry Ruppel, superintendent of Deer Lodge City Schools in Montana and a member of the OSC faculty for four years, remembered Magruder being highly respected on campus. Although Montana's Department of Public Instruction had not criticized the book, Ruppel thought a letter from Strand would help the district fend off a self-appointed woman from the local American Legion Auxiliary, a "busybody who does more to help the cause of Stalin by her misguided zeal than she does to help the cause of democracy."[24]

Only two years removed from dismissing chemistry professor Ralph Spitzer in February 1949, Strand defended Magruder in a strongly worded telegram to Ruppel:

> If Magruder ever had slightest tinge of communism in his
> teachings, his life, or any of his associations, then I am Joe Stalin's
> uncle. Accusations against Magruder [are] founded on two or
> three sentences where he was talking about ideal communism.
> These [have been] removed from later editions. Magruder was as
> good and patriotic American citizen as I have ever known.

Strand sent another telegram to the secretary of the Deer Lodge schools describing Frank Magruder "as good a citizen and as patriotic an American as anyone can find." As a charter member of the Gallatin post of the American Legion during his years in Bozeman, Strand called the charge against Magruder malicious and said the "perpetrators should be prosecuted for libel." If Magruder wrote anything negative about American government, "they are not nearly as bad as what Republicans have been saying for years."[25]

McClenaghan worked closely with Strand in aggressively defending the Magruder book, indicating where critics misquoted or selected passages out of context to distort the text. Strand, in turn, shared Montana news clippings with McClenaghan, including one from Butte's *Montana Standard* reporting that Magruder's was a "widely condemned textbook." The newspaper reported that numerous groups in the state—the American Legion, Daughters of the

American Revolution, and Kiwanis—were looking for subversive materials in such books. Strand immediately rebuked the editor, accusing the *Standard* of duping the people of Montana. "Did you ever read it?" The president reproached the editor for omitting words, running paragraphs together, and quoting passages from a World War Two edition of the text "when most Americans were praising the valor of the Russian people in their defense of Stalingrad." Frank Magruder, Strand noted, was a respectable member of the Corvallis community and a man of unquestioned loyalty. The *Standard's* editor denied that he intended to question Magruder's loyalty, but insisted that the book needed revising. Who, he asked, was McClenaghan, the person charged with revising the text? The present edition, he insisted, included "fuzzy, unclear statements."[26]

The respected *Atlanta Constitution* featured the Magruder textbook controversy—"McCarthyism in the Classroom"—in a late October 1951 article. The American people, the newspaper declared, were being introduced to a big lie, one that threatened the freedom of students to think and express themselves. The Georgia newspaper praised Atlanta's superintendent of schools for retaining the textbook, and reviewed the defamatory attacks against it and found them without merit. Despite the *Constitution's* defense, the Georgia State Textbook Commission refused to approve the book for use in state high schools. In an ironic twist, McClenaghan told the president that his cousin, Mrs. Julius Talmadge, condemned the book because it supported the United Nations. "S'help me," McClenaghan wrote, "that's her stated opinion. She is chairman of the Textbook Commission."[27]

The Magruder book-burners continued to attack *American Government* even after McClenaghan's revised edition appeared in 1952. Although McClenaghan vehemently denied that earlier editions contained subversive passages, the *Oregonian* thought the revision reflected "some sensitivity to the bigoted attacks." The newspaper observed that those who attacked Magruder could "find much that would be suspicious to them in the Declaration of Independence and the U.S. Constitution." The book, however, continued to receive mixed receptions beyond Oregon. The Indiana textbook commission dropped Magruder from its list of approved texts in December 1952 for being sympathetic to socialism. And nearby, Washington's *Tri-Cities Herald* made life difficult for educators in Kennewick, Pasco, and Richland who continued to use the text.[28]

As criticism of Magruder faded, McClenaghan published an article in the *Saturday Review* tracing the history of the book, its widespread adoption in high school government classes, and point-by-point responses to its critics.

In Houston, Texas, site of the first attacks, school board–appointed teachers unanimously voted to retain the book, and 80 percent of Texas schools were assigning the book in government classes in 1952. A reviewing committee in New Haven, Connecticut, referred to Magruder as an "unbiased, impartial, fair presentation of the facts." A committee of five teachers in Council Bluffs, Iowa, critiqued the Lonigan review of *American Government* and declared it without merit. McClenaghan explained that the text had been revised many times since 1917 to recast the narrative "in more understandable language." The story of American government, he wrote, "does not lend itself to static or stereotyped treatment." If Magruder were to be faulted for its subversive content, the book should be judged on its merits rather than misquoting passages and falsifying its narrative.[29]

Bill McClenaghan never faced the doubts and suspicions cast upon Ralph Spitzer, the chemistry professor committed to international peace and supporter of Henry Wallace for president. McClenaghan hewed closely to Cold War orthodoxy, insisting that textbooks "openly or insidiously" supporting communism or socialist sentiments did not belong in American classrooms. The same standards applied to teachers, he wrote in *Saturday Review*, who advocated socialism or communism: "Especially is this true of the Communist, for he fails the most essential test—his mind is closed and he can no longer be objective." McClenaghan's closing lines in the *Review* closely parallel President Strand's statements when he dismissed Ralph Spitzer three years earlier.[30]

In the midst of cold and hot war distractions, students and student life remained at the center of Oregon State College. With veterans flooding the Corvallis campus after 1945, enrollment rose to more than seven thousand students for each year beginning in the fall of 1946 and continuing through the graduating class of 1949. Fall term enrollment for 1949 fell to 6,793 and continued to drop through the fall of 1953 when the college reached a low of 4,848 students. Admissions did not rise above the seven thousand figure until fall of 1957, attaining an all-time high of 7,981 in 1958. The fluctuating student numbers meant a hiring and construction bonanza in the late 1940s and then a decline in the instructional force when registrations tailed off in the early 1950s. In addition to veterans, postwar students differed in the growing number of foreign students registering for classes. There were 121 foreign students representing thirty-seven countries enrolling in the fall of 1951 and one hundred from thirty-five countries the following year. Three of those registering in 1951 were listed as stateless. To assist the newcomers, the college created the position of Foreign Student Counsellor.[31]

Following the Second World War, there was a sharp increase in graduate enrollees, rising from fewer than 2 percent of students in 1925 to more than 10 percent in 1952. The graduate school, responsible for coordinating students working toward advanced degrees, became important to the institution, overseeing general research and preparing graduates for occupations in professional fields. Oregon State College joined four other Northwest colleges and universities, cooperating with the General Electric Corporation's Graduate School of Nuclear Engineering in Richland, Washington, where students could earn credits toward advanced degrees. Another cooperative program with the nuclear facilities in Los Alamos, New Mexico, permitted two students to obtain PhDs with research projects carried out at the southwestern site. And beginning with the academic year 1952–1953, the college began offering doctoral degrees in pharmacy.[32]

Although demographers had predicted an increase in college and university enrollments, the anticipated "bulge" did not affect the Corvallis campus until the fall of 1955 when registrations surged more than 25 percent. The sharp rise reflected a greater number of returning students, a 29 percent increase in new enrollees, with veterans rising from 662 to 1,184 students, mirroring the ceasefire on the Korean peninsula and the demobilization of military personnel. The increase across classes and schools is revealing:

Percent Increase by Class		Percent Increase by School	
Frosh	29	Home Economics	5
Sophomore	34	Agriculture	11
Junior	39	English	43
Senior	11	Education	56

While a new curriculum in elementary education explains much of the increase in that program, rising enrollments in engineering continued a postwar trend, making the school the largest on campus.[33]

The swelling enrollments of the mid-1950s reflected the American Council on Education's prediction of a long-range upward trend. The respected American Society of Foresters forecast the largest enrollment increase for OSC's School of Forestry of any comparable program in the United States, a judgment reflecting Oregon's booming lumber industry. The dean of Oregon State's graduate school characterized the large numbers of undergraduates as the "lull before the storm." Because of the increase in students, the faculty council considered limiting enrollment, revising the curriculum, and adjusting teaching loads and salary. President Strand feared that more students would lead to larger classes and more advisees, threatening the quality of instruction and advising. In the face of those challenges, he urged faculty to keep the welfare of students in mind.[34]

Oregon State College's land-grant mission is writ everywhere across its seminal texts. When President Strand signed off on his biennial report for 1951–1952, he praised the institution's distinguished faculty and "a campus great and beautiful," reminding readers that the college was more than gracious lawns and brick-and-stone buildings—it was "the very spirit of the State."[35] With educational and professional experiences rooted in Montana, he was a cheerleader for good relations between Oregon State College and the people of Oregon. The idea that land-grants were "people's colleges," Strand wrote in 1958, was even more fitting in the present day. The state college addressed the needs of industry, agriculture, and forestry, and provided expertise on nutrition, consumer affairs, domestic budgets, and child development. OSC's footprint extended to cooperating with state boards and commissions, who looked to the institution for its know-how. As the state's land-grant school, its reach extended through the eleven western states, where it was preeminent in several fields.[36]

College administrators paid increasing attention to the quality of educational programs through the mid-1950s, especially the need to enrich experiences for superior students. Preoccupied with teaching large classes, faculty sought ways to enhance opportunities for talented students, challenging them to achieve intellectual excellence. The Lower Division created trial sections in a few liberal arts courses to provide thought-provoking environments for high-performing students. The college's undergraduate classes focused on teaching effectiveness and student counseling, posing questions about proper approaches to education, with some faculty emphasizing improvements in teaching. To foster such progressive approaches, the graduate school published a quarterly, *Improving College and University Teaching*, in 1953. The college's committee on the advancement of teaching began recognizing outstanding teachers and conducting symposia on classroom instruction in 1955.[37]

Oregon State College developed a program in elementary education in the mid-1950s involving many participating disciplines to provide students with a liberal education. The program for secondary school teaching required students to take a major subject field and a minor. The college also developed a joint degree program in medical technology requiring students to take three years on the Corvallis campus and one year at the medical school in Portland. Another new program, a cooperative veterinary medicine degree, required three years of course work on the OSC campus and a transfer to Colorado State College, where students would receive a bachelor's degree after completing a year in Fort Collins.[38]

The college benefitted when the State Board of Higher Education contracted with Dr. Earl Anderson, an Ohio educator, to advise the Oregon system on teacher-training programs. Anderson's report in 1952 recommended establishing elementary and secondary teacher preparation degrees at all state institutions. When the board adopted Anderson's proposal, it marked a sharp departure from the long-standing policy of limiting elementary education degrees to the three colleges of education, and secondary education to the university and state college. Adding fuel to the fire, the board approved liberal arts courses for the colleges of education to strengthen their secondary education programs. While four institutions endorsed the board's decision, University of Oregon president Harry Newburn called the move a departure from the university's responsibility for the liberal arts: "This says in effect, we are prepared to make regional colleges of liberal arts of these schools." Newburn was also the only president who objected to the board's decision allowing Portland State College to grant liberal arts degrees.[39]

The board's new policy, the *Oregonian* suggested, required those privileges be extended to Oregon State College. Although the Corvallis school offered general studies courses, it lacked degree-granting authority. The board was moving away from the "rigid compartmentalization" that had been its guiding principle, the newspaper observed, because population growth and changing educational standards mandated more flexibility in allocating courses and degrees. Board member A. S. Grant thought the university was wrong to oppose the board's decision· "There is overwhelming evidence that to get good teachers, you educate them together. . . . If we are to have good institutions (the teacher colleges) we should make them strong, not treat them like poor cousins."[40]

If there were a magic point of movement in the restoration of liberal arts at Oregon State College, it began with longtime lower-division dean A. Ellwood Smith, who persistently argued for greater balance in the college's degree offerings. His successor, Ralph Colby (with the support of President Strand), raised expectations in his first biennial report, insisting that the institution should offer liberal arts degrees in the humanities and social sciences to better serve students. Colby deplored the situation "forced upon students" who completed two years in the Lower Division and then needed to transfer to the University of Oregon to finish a liberal arts degree.[41]

Colby challenged the state board's allocation policy, arguing that no school should monopolize four-year liberal arts degrees. While five state institutions conferred such degrees, only Oregon State College was prohibited from offering majors in the humanities and social sciences. The college had the students, a well-qualified faculty, and the courses and facilities to offer such degrees. A survey of lower-division students in 1956 indicated that more than 60 percent would remain in Corvallis if a general studies degree program were available. President Strand repeated Colby's assessment in his report to the board, emphasizing that it was "logical *now* for Oregon State College" to have the same degree privileges enjoyed throughout the state system. With President Strand presiding at the faculty council meeting on January 20, 1956, administrators adopted a unanimous resolution supporting liberal arts degrees:

> The Faculty Council, recognizing the need for a vigorous liberal arts program on our campus, go on record in support of liberal arts degrees for Oregon State College, and that the Faculty Council strongly urge the administration, together with the faculty to take all possible action to secure liberal arts degrees (in fields where they are not offered) for Oregon State College in the very near future.[42]

In what appeared to be a trial balloon, the lower-division policy committee spent much of 1956 preparing a modest general studies degree proposal. The broadly structured program required course work in four interrelated fields—humanities, social science, communications, and natural science—all of them involving the human condition. Students would do major and minor work in those fields, with flexibility left to advisers and each student's special interests. The committee sought advice from several deans, the college curriculum council, and the president. Although Strand supported a liberal arts degree, he urged Colby to focus on general studies and avoid departmental majors. The chief obstacle to any liberal arts degree at the state college would be the University of Oregon. Through this entire process, policy committee chair Walter Foreman, head of the English Department, and Dean Colby proceeded cautiously, recognizing the division's "obligation . . . in the service of the other schools on our campus," a euphemism suggesting they were not challenging the supremacy of their own professional schools.[43]

To promote general studies degrees, the Lower Division sponsored a campus lecture series, "Liberal Arts in an Age of Technology." Vernon Cheldelin, director of OSC's Science Research Institute, gave the initial talk, citing the importance of liberal arts to the educational development of scientists and engineers. Most of the State Board of Higher Education's attention to expanding liberal arts, however, focused on granting such degrees to newly minted Portland State College. The rapid growth of the Portland school indicated that the state board would have to contend with an increasingly powerful third voice in the allocation of courses and degrees.[44]

The Lower Division's push for a general studies program ran aground on internal college disagreements, making it impossible for President Strand to forward a proposal to the chancellor's office. Despite the enthusiasm of the Lower Division's policy committee, the initiative reached a dead end when the college's curriculum council withheld its approval. Although the curriculum council's minutes are vague about the proposal, it is reasonable to assume that the council's professional school representatives feared the budgetary consequences of such a move. When Dean Colby and Foreman appeared before the curriculum council in 1957, one member accused them of being self-serving and not looking to the best interests of the institution.[45] Colby and Foreman again acknowledged the division's responsibility to provide "services" for the professional schools. That sentiment among the Lower Division's administrators would have a long shelf life.

Oregon State College finally submitted a proposal to the state board to offer divisional majors in the liberal arts in the spring of 1959. When the board deliberated the issue in September, University of Oregon president O. Meredith Wilson delivered an hour-long argument in opposition, urging the board to maintain the special functions of each school. If the board allowed liberal arts degrees at OSC, Wilson threatened a quid pro quo: "You will have before you our application for a major in environmental science." President Strand countered that OSC was the only state institution without a liberal arts degree. The tit-for-tat continued, with Wilson accusing the college of misleading students with false advertisements in its bulletins, suggesting that it offered liberal arts degrees. The problems between the two schools "could better be resolved," he suggested, "by adjusting recruiting methods than by a change in allocations."[46]

The state board adjourned without making a decision, deferring action on the liberal arts proposal until it had studied the educational and economic impact of courses and majors among member institutions. Board chair Cheryl MacNaughton promised that the allocation question would be continued at the October meeting. Chancellor John R. Richards told departing members that the problem of allocating courses and majors among colleges and universities was common to most states. Of the organizational strategies at play in states with major universities and colleges, Richards noted, the trend has been for colleges to develop more comprehensive and diverse programs: "The college develops ambitions for complete duplication of the university."[47] Although OSC's effort to expand its liberal arts programs remained in limbo, Chancellor Richards was the first to articulate the ultimate objective.

When the State Board of Higher Education met in October 1959, Chancellor Richards announced that it was the board's consensus that the college could change its Lower Division to a school of liberal arts and that it be permitted to offer general degrees in the humanities and social sciences. Its new liberal arts programs would be general in nature and not disciplinary, and the college would continue to emphasize the sciences—engineering, forestry, agriculture, and pharmacy. University of Oregon president Wilson called the decision unsatisfactory, a move that would cause greater polarization between the schools. Placing itself above the fray, the *Oregonian* declared the consensus decision sufficient: "The State System would not be justified in duplicating the University of Oregon's liberal arts program 40 miles away at Oregon State College." It recognized, however, that the Corvallis faculty members, like those at Portland State, would want to upgrade general studies programs into disciplinary degrees. By approving the college's request, the board made it difficult to refuse the school's next effort to relax allocation decisions.[48]

Dean Colby thought the new degree programs would improve classroom instruction and build student and faculty morale. Liberal arts students would be equal to their classmates in the sciences and professional schools. Earning a liberal arts degree would require students to complete minors in the sciences or science technology, including courses in agriculture, forestry, and home economics. The educational philosophy of the new degrees, Colby argued, was forward-looking and encouraged a broad intellectual experience at the undergraduate level. The University of Oregon's president Wilson held a contrary view—the social science and humanities degrees would lead to departmental majors. He cited courses already offered in several departments at Oregon State College and thought they provided ample work for a major. Wilson complained about new geography courses taught at the college and worried that the board's actions would make his faculty apprehensive.[49]

Except for Cornell University—the only private university with a land-grant mission—OSC's development of liberal arts degrees lagged behind public land-grant institutions. At President Strand's previous administrative stop in Bozeman, Montana State College's humanities departments provided conventional service courses for professional schools through the Second World War. Following the war, however, several departments—philosophy, political science, and history—began offering degree programs, with history granting a master of science in 1954 and master of arts in 1970, both decades ahead of OSC. Michigan State College was even more advanced, offering both bachelor's and master's degrees in the arts in 1924 involving eight majors ranging from English to history and modern languages. Students in the program were required to take two years of a foreign language. Although the institution achieved university status in 1955, its full title was Michigan State University of Agriculture and Applied Science, abbreviated to Michigan State University in 1964.[50]

For the first half of the twentieth century, Iowa State College's arrangement was similar to OSC's, where a professional survey in 1915 mandated that liberal arts served to support technical degrees. In a major restructuring of its agricultural college in 1959, the Iowa legislature elevated the college to university status and created the College of Sciences and Humanities, which offered students full-fledged degrees in most departments. Renamed the College of Liberal Arts and Sciences in 1990, it is Iowa State University's largest college, offering students an array of disciplinary majors. In that sense, Iowa State was approximately a decade ahead of OSC in becoming a comprehensive university. Purdue University became a comprehensive academic institution under renowned President Frederick Hovde (1946–1971), strengthening its graduate school and adding several new schools—Veterinary Science and Medicine (1957), Management (1958), Humanities, Social Science, and Education (1963), and Technology (1964). Liberal arts departments, which had been in the School of Science, Education, and Humanities since 1954, offered their first bachelor of arts degrees in 1959.[51]

While the humanities and social sciences struggled for parity in Corvallis, older and better-endowed schools forged ahead in the postwar years, taking advantage of an expanding economy to increase enrollments and attract research grants in a wide array of professional/technical fields. At Oregon State College, the schools of agriculture, forestry, engineering, home economics, and pharmacy flourished, offering new majors and degree programs and working with experiment stations and extension on a variety of outreach issues. With the nation's home-building industry operating in overdrive, the construction industry had a profound effect on the School of Forestry. The demand for lumber powered Oregon timber harvests to an all-time high of more than nine billion board feet in 1955, a market that remained strong, with brief downturns, until the early 1980s. The belief that the nation's saw timber would be exhausted was a powerful incentive for forestry schools across the country to develop more efficient harvesting and reforestation strategies, to curb wasteful practices, speed production processes, and eliminate forest fires. Under Dean Walter McCulloch (1955–1967), OSC's forestry school was preeminent among Pacific Coast institutions in addressing those issues. Mc-Culloch emphasized the school's mission to prepare students "for the great social and technical complexities of the future and [to] fire them with zeal to enhance the forest resource while enhancing their professional positions."[52]

McCulloch anticipated forestry's future in intensified forest management, harvesting practices, and use of wood products, developments that would require skilled forestry graduates. He initiated revisions in the forestry curriculum, including forest engineering courses requiring a five-year program. Working closely with the timber industry, McCulloch announced three enhanced fellowships: the Weyerhaeuser Company doubled two graduate fellowships from $1,000 to $2,000; Crown Zellerbach Corporation added another $500 to its undergraduate fellowship; and the Louis W. and Maud Hill Family Foundation added another $1,000 to an existing fellowship. McCulloch reported in 1958 that the forest experiment station was now part of the agricultural experiment station's Forest Research Division, a cooperative enterprise advancing research in forest soils, forest pathologies, and forest entomology.[53]

Passage of a timber harvest tax in 1947 helped fund the Oregon Forest Research Center in 1957 (renamed the Oregon Forest Research Laboratory in 1961). The new center, McCulloch believed, would raise the prestige of Oregon State College as a widely respected center for advancing studies of genetic variation and strategies for propagating Douglas-fir. The forestry school built a "forest insectary" in 1958—laboratories and greenhouses to provide entomologists with the tools to study insects. In a tribute to the school's alumni, McCulloch noted that graduates were staffing positions at the new forestry school in Humboldt State College in Arcata, California. Looking to the future, he touted the school's undergraduate and graduate enrollment increases. He was proud, too, of the forestry faculty's expertise, with several individuals taking leave to earn doctoral degrees at Syracuse, Yale, and the University of Washington.[54] These were truly the go-go years for OSC's production-oriented forestry programs. Beyond the campus—in the woods and mills—the monthly production figures of sawmills made headlines in national newspapers.

Like the School of Forestry, the School of Science also expanded rapidly in the postwar years. "Recent international developments have focused attention upon our field of endeavor," Dean F. A. Gilfillan wrote in 1958, a reference to the Soviet Union's successful launch of *Sputnik* in October 1957, the first satellite to orbit the earth. *Sputnik*, David Halberstam argued, heralded "a kind of technological Pearl Harbor," with the United States responding in January 1958, launching its own satellite, *Explorer I*. Those events marked the onset of the space race between the two superpowers, and—to underscore Gilfillan's remark—provided an enormous boost to scientific research and education in the United States. With its eleven departments and the Science Research Institute, undergraduate and graduate enrollment in the School of Science grew apace, reflecting "a tremendous wave of interest in science and engineering." The most dependable indicator of the school's prestige was the number of research contracts it was attracting.[55]

Two years after the launch of *Explorer I*, Gilfillan praised the completion of the new physics-chemistry building (Weniger Hall), a large structure providing classroom and office space for undergraduate and graduate students, the latter coming "out of dark, unventilated interior closets originally built for storage rooms." Earlier facilities, such as Cordley Hall (occupied in 1958), had improved instruction in botany and entomology. Housing the herbarium in the same building was a boon to graduate research projects. Up-to-date laboratory equipment for undergraduate instruction, however, remained a lingering problem. The institution's new Department of Oceanography, a "guest" in the Food and Technology Building, was awaiting federal support for its own quarters.[56]

Expanding studies of the world's oceans gained stature at Oregon State College when Wayne Burt, with a doctorate from the Scripps Institution of Oceanography, arrived in 1954. Burt taught a new course, Introduction to Physical Oceanography, and began a research program involving coastal bays and estuaries. Operating with a $25,000 budget, most of it courtesy of grants from the Office of Naval Research (ONR), Burt was teaching three oceanography courses by 1958. His boundless energy (and luck) coincided with the decision of ONR's Geophysics Branch to contract with ten universities to advance oceanographic research. Burt approached Dean Gilfillan seeking support to expand oceanography, a plan that would involve continued ONR funding and the need to create a new department. With additional funding from the National Academy of Sciences and the creation of the Department of Oceanography in July 1959, Burt's program was off and running. The navy's initial funding to OSC and other participating institutions was explicitly tied to the Cold War and the need for underwater research related to submarine defense.[57]

Wayne Burt's program, which eventually earned OSC designation as a Sea Grant institution, expanded quickly. Working with the ONR, the department acquired the *Acona*, a newly outfitted research vessel equipped to conduct research in coastal waters and large enough for extended voyages during the summer months. Burt's staff of three expanded to seven in the fall of 1960 and continued to grow with additional research grants. Enrollment in oceanography courses increased to more than one hundred students in 1959, with eight students using the program's credits as a minor for master's degrees. More than a dozen students were expected to major in oceanography in the fall of 1960.[58]

With the increasing bureaucratization of colleges and universities following the Second World War, institutional executives limited their deliberations to the most significant functions. The twice-monthly meetings of OSC's administrative council bear this out. Administrators had already delegated authority over student disciplinary cases, faculty requests for leave, and other routine matters. Questions about tenure and promotion, clearly the province of the council, required regular attention. The council deliberated proposed regulations for academic staff in May 1951, clarifying time in service for assistant professors before they could be tenured and promoted, the length of appointment for instructors, and exceptions for research positions unrelated to regular advancement.[59]

Loyalty oaths, deeply embedded in Cold War hysteria—requiring public employees to swear fealty to federal, state, and local governments—were occasionally on the council's agenda. President Harry Truman led the way in March 1947 when he issued Executive Order 9835, a loyalty program prohibiting federal employees from membership in the Communist Party or being in "sympathetic association" with such groups. Truman's initiative snowballed between 1947 and 1956, with some forty-two states and thousands of local governments adopting loyalty programs requiring public employees to sign oaths. The loyalty laws and constitutional amendments allowed Congress and state legislatures to investigate, interrogate, and humiliate anyone whose politics or activities were deemed questionable.[60] Although the Oregon State University archival holdings are largely mute on loyalty oaths and faculty dismissals, the administrative council referred to such oaths on two occasions in 1953. The first was President Strand, reading a directive from the chancellor's office "regarding the oath of allegiance required by state law." One month later,

Dean of Administration E. B. Lemon reported that staff and faculty needed to sign the loyalty oath before receiving their annual appointments.[61]

The administrative council passed judgment on college committee proposals related to curriculum, academic requirements, commencement, the functions of department chairs, and other matters. The council discussed group requirements for undergraduate degrees in September 1952, with Deans Colby and Gilfillan, heads of the two largest schools, Science and Lower Division, asking for greater clarity, because their faculties taught the largest number of students. The council exercised greater flexibility on faculty attendance at commencement exercises, ruling in May 1953 that all faculty members were expected to attend commencement unless excused by the president.[62]

Claire Langton, longtime director of the Division of Health and Physical Education, delivered an important report to the administrative council in April 1955 to clarify relationships between the administrative council and the faculty council. Under "conditions and established facts," Langton indicated that the state board held legislative, administrative, and executive powers, many of which it delegated through officials—the chancellor, institutional presidents, deans, and department chairs. The nature of those relations, therefore, gave the president discretionary powers in legislative, administrative, and executive matters. Based on President Strand's recommendation in 1945, the administrative council had adopted legislative powers for itself.[63]

Langton advised the administrative council to delegate minor decisions to the faculty council. All administrative functions, however, were reserved to the president and his chief administrators. ("The Administrative Council is an extension of the centralized authority of the President.") The faculty council held general and limited legislative powers. Although it established policy related to faculty affairs, Langton determined that the president could veto faculty council measures. The faculty council's province was curriculum, teaching, and research. With the exception of appeals to the state board, Langton concluded: "The President is the personification of the College. He represents it to the people. He defends its policies. He provides the vision to inspire its major developments and statesmanship to lead it through changes that these developments involve."[64] Langton's report underscored the unprecedented power of the institution's chief executive.

After nineteen years as OSC's president, August L. Strand passed the executive baton to James H. Jensen in 1961. During his presidency, Strand oversaw a building program paralleling that of William Jasper Kerr. Gill Coliseum, completed in 1950 and constructed without internal supports, was reputedly

Oregon's largest building at the time. Three years later, the college dedicated a new football field—Parker Stadium—to replace Bell Field (which was turned into a track and field facility). Other major buildings completed during Strand's tenure included Wiegand Hall (1951), Withycombe Hall (1952), Azalea House (1953), Gleeson Hall (1955), Cordley Hall (1957), Weatherford Dining Hall (1957), Snell Hall (1959), and Weniger Hall (1959). The college's student population grew from 4,359 in 1942 to 9,039 in the fall of 1961, and shortly before Strand left office, the State Board of Higher Education elevated the college to university status.[65] Although Strand dealt with the disruptions and great sacrifices of OSU students and graduates in the Second World War and the lesser conflict in Korea, he presided over a relatively complacent and quiet campus, conditions that would change dramatically with the social, civil, and cultural revolutions of the 1960s.

9

Civil Rights, Campus Disorder, and Cultural Change

The Pacific coastal states of California, Oregon, and Washington have always been strategically important to American interests because of their geographic location at the crossroads of the nation's relations with the Pacific Rim. Although the Korean War had reached a stalemate by 1953, with a US troop garrison remaining in South Korea, during the 1960s, events in Southeast Asia would consume the energies of the nation's political leadership and military forces on a scale that would dwarf the Korean police action. As the conflict in Vietnam heated up, an American president was assassinated and civil rights protests erupted across the segregated states of the South. The history of the turbulent and strife-torn decade of the 1960s is writ in dynamited churches in the South, rioting and torched inner cities in the North and West, body counts from Vietnam, and flawed national statesmanship. With new President James H. Jensen at the helm, Oregon State University navigated its way on the periphery, yet inescapably part of those disruptions.

The "Age of Aquarius," as one writer dubbed the 1960s, witnessed a spate of progressive legislation in the wake of President John F. Kennedy's death that would have a significant effect on Oregon State University. The new federal initiatives included aid to education, Medicare, Medicaid, immigration reform, the Civil Rights Act, the Voting Rights Act, and the creation of two seminal agencies, the National Endowment for the Humanities and the National Endowment for the Arts. Beginning with the University of California, Berkeley, in 1964, the "free speech" movement hit college and university campuses, resonating with greater fervor at elite institutions and affecting others to a lesser degree. The assassination of Kennedy in 1963, the parallel violence of pro-segregationists in the South, and blacks rioting in the Watts section of Los Angeles in 1965 (five days after President Lyndon Johnson signed the Voting Rights Act) prefaced the assassinations of Martin Luther King Jr. and Senator Robert Kennedy in 1968. The escalation of America's intervention in Vietnam between 1965 and 1968 provoked demonstrations on campuses across the nation, including Oregon State University.[1]

Corvallis was still a quiet college, farming, and logging community in the early 1960s, with its twenty thousand people, more than half of Benton County's 39,163. The 1960 census listed Oregon's population at 1,768,687, an increase of some 240,000 since 1950, but considerably less than the state's growth during the 1940s. Forest products and agricultural goods were the state's economic mainstays. Mill towns from Coos Bay and Roseburg to Bend, Burns, and Baker City provided relatively stable, if seasonal, work. Vegetable and fruit growers in the Willamette, Hood River, and Rogue Valleys provided a limited number of year-round jobs and a large labor force, many of them migrants, during the frenzied harvest season. Oregon's resource-based economy would remain strong through the 1960s and 1970s and then begin a transition toward greater diversification during the 1980s. A severe recession in the early 1980s, and an uneven recovery favoring urban centers in the Willamette Valley, left many sawmill towns struggling with an uncertain future. Those starkly contrasting economic stories would heavily influence academic programs at Oregon State University.[2]

The year 1961 was auspicious for Oregon's land-grant institution. In March, young Republican governor Mark Hatfield signed legislation conferring university status on the school, indicating that it continued to enjoy political clout in Salem. Five months later, the State Board of Higher Education named James Jensen, provost at Iowa State University, as the institution's tenth president. A native Nebraskan, with bachelor's and master's degrees from the University of Nebraska and a PhD in plant pathology from the University of Wisconsin, Jensen held honorary doctorates from North Carolina State University and the University of Nebraska. In overseeing the transition from college to university, Jensen addressed the theme, "the university in our society" at the Faculty Day gathering, September 14, 1961. His message—land-grant institutions "should not try to be all things to all people"—was qualified, urging the university to accelerate research and leadership on technological and academic issues.[3]

James Jensen inherited a thriving, growing, increasingly sophisticated institution. During President Strand's last year in office, college officials established the Water Resources Research Institute to fund and coordinate faculty investigations in related disciplines—agriculture, geosciences, fisheries and wildlife, entomology, and civil engineering. An ideal fit for land-grant institutions, the institute would expand during the ensuing years to embrace geothermal research, the relationship between boating and stream-bank erosion, the impact of the Mount St. Helens eruption of May 1980 on streams draining the mountain, the restoration of Sauvie Island's polluted Sturgeon Lake, and studies of non-point pollutants in the upper Willamette River. The Water Resources Research Act of 1964 funded much of the institute's research. In the twenty-first century, the agency morphed into the Institute for Water and Watersheds.[4] Its significance has been its ability to coordinate research from many disciplines to examine common problems.

Shortly before Jensen took office, the administrative council established the framework for the Oregon State University Press (OSU Press). J. Kenneth Munford, an Oregon State alumnus, editor, and director with the college's Office of Publications, led the charge to establish the press, whose imprint would be used to publish biology colloquium proceedings, forestry papers, and its own publication, *Improving College and University Teaching*. Its immediate problem would be building sales to the point that the enterprise would be self-sustaining. Munford believed the press would increase the institution's prestige as a center for scientific studies.[5]

The OSU Press published eight books during its first year, including the standard textbook for high school and college classes, *Atlas of the Pacific Northwest*. (The press has published several editions of the atlas during its fifty-five years and counting.) Another classic, Helen Gilkey and Patricia Packard's *Winter Twigs: A Wintertime Key to Deciduous Trees and Shrubs of Northwestern Oregon and Western Washington*, appeared in the first list and remains in print with updated information using the most recent scientific findings. Gilkey, the primary author and a botanist, earned a master's degree at Oregon Agricultural College in 1911 and a PhD from the University of California, Berkeley, in 1915. She joined the college faculty in 1918 and curated the institution's herbarium until 1951. Thousands of students, teachers, amateur botanists, and others have used *Winter Twigs* to identify plants during the winter season.[6] Targeted for elimination during a budget crunch in the early 1990s, the OSU Press survived and remains the leading publisher of quality regional books in the state.

Although the university's predecessors kept records dating from the school's inception, the institution gave no professional attention to its growing archival files until Harriet Moore's appointment in 1961. Beginning in 1950, the library's Archives Committee provided general oversight for record-keeping, an assignment that accelerated in 1959 when it gave more attention to the technical and professional scope of archiving. Before Moore's appointment, the committee defined archives as "the organized body of records made or received in connection with the transaction of its affairs by each OSU agency and preserved for records purposes in its custody. Collections may include . . . all materials relating to its history and activities." Moore, who was not a professional librarian, had been active with the Benton County Historical Society and was knowledgeable about local history.[7]

The collection was housed in the basement of Gill Coliseum, and Harriet Moore's archival work began with business office records and grew until the collected material counted 7,300 items. She accumulated boxes of photographs, records from the president's office, and an overwhelming quantity of other items. Rod Waldron, associate librarian, estimated that the twelve boxes of photos and two boxes of negatives included about twenty-five thousand photographs. Moore labored with student help and a shoestring budget in the Coliseum until 1964, when the new Kerr Library was completed. At that point she inherited the "Science Room" in the old library (Kidder Hall) as the archives new home, and even then, library items occupied much of the shelf space. Despite operating in cramped quarters, former librarian William Carlson observed in 1966 that Moore's "archival program began to assume the outlines of a true and major division of the Library."[8]

The university's archives assumed more professional dimensions in 1965 when the administration established an archival council to oversee "the legal, educational, administrative, and historic values inherent in any body of records they may consider." The archivist, a qualified professional, would be an ex officio member and secretary to the council, responsible for managing the archives, enforcing rules and regulations, and performing other duties associated with archival record-keeping. In addition to institutional records, the archives would be a repository for the records and papers of "organizations, memorability, or the personal papers of individuals" associated with the institution. The archival program would involve collecting, inventorying, and making available to interested parties "all obtainable archival material" relating to the operation and history of Oregon State University.[9]

Courtesy of a legislative appropriation in 1961, OSU president Jensen held groundbreaking ceremonies in May 1962 to begin construction on a new library that would be twice the size of the old building. The $2,225,000 four-story structure (with nearly five hundred thousand volumes) nearly doubled library use, according to librarian William Carlson. The library was named in honor of the late William Jasper Kerr, and the dedication ceremonies featured Oregon congresswoman Edith Green, a strong proponent of federal aid to education. The late president's son, Robert Kerr, spoke for thirty-six Kerr relatives who attended the occasion. Vacated Kidder Hall, constructed in

1918 with a wing added in 1941, underwent a major remodel to house foreign languages and mathematics offices and classrooms.[10]

When Wayne Burt's growing Department of Oceanography acquired the eighty-foot *Acona* in 1961, Oregon State University solidified its ties with the Office of Naval Research (ONR), an agency with heavy investments in Cold War–related research. The National Science Foundation augmented ONR funding to properly equip the *Acona*. The Navy, writes historian Craig Biegel, was interested in "research applicable to submarine warfare, including acoustics, optics, and sea bed features." From the department's former practice of chartering fishing boats or hitching a ride on Coast Guard vessels, the *Acona* was a major advance in research capability. Literally overnight, the department extended its research horizons to 165 miles offshore.[11]

The *Acona*, however, proved difficult for conducting research at sea. The vessel rode high in the water, subjecting its crew and researchers to rough cruises. In turbulent seas it listed as much as sixty degrees, with some researchers characterizing its seaworthiness with "a very high retch factor." Despite those deficiencies, the *Acona* averaged 180 days at sea, setting baseline studies of the ocean floor during its three years with the OSU program. Those early cruises included researchers of many types—biologists, chemists, geologists, and physicists. John Byrne, who later became the university's fifteenth president, served aboard the *Acona* and recalls working with scientists from other disciplines as "an opportunity to do things that became interdisciplinary."[12]

The Department of Oceanography graduated from the questionable seaworthiness of the *Acona* to the much larger *Yaquina* in 1964, a converted 180-foot Second World War vessel equipped with two winches capable of plumbing depths to thirty thousand feet. The *Yaquina* logged some fifty-two thousand miles and 492 days at sea during its first two years, ranging as far as three thousand miles from its home port. Oceanography added tugboats to its growing fleet—the thirty-foot *Shoshone* in 1963, replacing it with the *Sacajawea* in 1967, both operating on the Columbia River. For estuarine and near-coastal research, the department acquired two smaller craft, the *Paiute* and *Cayuse*, the latter designed to conduct continental shelf research. To round out its research capabilities, Wayne Burt successfully sought funding to build shore facilities in Newport, with the first section of what became the Marine Science Center completed in 1965.[13]

As the university was slowly developing into a modern institution, there was much that was traditional and mundane in its operation. The administrative council dealt with routine matters such as Homecoming, determining whether to cancel Friday afternoon classes the day before the big event. In the fall of 1961, Dean of Men Dan Poling remarked that students needed time to prepare for Homecoming activities—building the bonfire, constructing house signs, and preparing meals and other events for alums. Dean of Administration Milosh Popovich sought to establish a long-term policy so that the council would not have to debate the issue every year. Following its timeworn practice, the council directed Poling to form a study group to determine the proper approach to Homecoming. University traffic regulations, with recommendations from the Campus Traffic Committee, was another perennial item before the council—identifying parking areas, special permits, appropriate fees for faculty and students, after-hours parking, hourly parking zones, and entry points to campus.[14]

Although student conduct may not have been a routine matter to administrators, like western Oregon's winter rains, problematic student behavior recurred every academic season. In James Jensen's first year as president, the administrative council urged students to conduct themselves with "honesty, and integrity." Those who failed to meet acceptable standards of behavior would be subject to discipline ranging from warnings to expulsion. As members of an academic community, students were "expected to dress and conduct themselves at all times in accordance with standards of decency and maturity." The guidelines stipulated specific visiting hours for living groups, provided that an officially designated representative of the dean of men or dean of women was present:[15]

Monday through Thursday	1:00 p.m. to 10:30 p.m.
Friday	1:00 p.m. to closing
Saturday and Sunday	12:00 noon to closing

Students were prohibited from possessing or using alcoholic beverages on university grounds and at social functions "where such possession, serving, or use may reflect on the name and reputation of the University." Violating the regulations would result in the probation or suspension from school of the offending student group. Student regulations also covered theft, falsification of records, and business integrity. Other rules prohibited hazing, including "the practice of taking students on 'rides'" into the countryside. Punishment included probation, suspension, or removal from office for officers of off-campus living groups. A final article, vandalism, required offending parties to be responsible for damages to university property, with the perpetrators subject to suspension.[16]

Cold War matters occasionally occupied the council, with the university's commitment to civil defense—"in the event of a disaster of major proportions"—the subject of one meeting. General Joseph Berry, the president's adviser on ROTC matters, told the council in August 1961 that two two-hundred-bed hospitals were stored in the basement of Gill Coliseum with electrical generators housed in the physical plant. Drugs were kept in cold storage in the food technology building. There were additional repositories of food that could be allocated in emergencies. In case of a disaster involving Salem's state office buildings, all government offices would be moved to the OSU campus.[17]

The council addressed the timeworn smoking issue again in November 1967, in this instance, students and faculty smoking in classrooms. From early-twentieth-century prohibitions banning all smoking, the biblical camel now had its head firmly fixed in campus buildings where people smoked with reckless abandon (except in areas prohibited by the fire marshal). Dean of Administration Popovich reported numerous complaints from students and faculty objecting to residue left in classrooms and the cost of maintenance. The major issue, Popovich noted, was the absence of any regulations to control smoking. Rather than resorting to rules, he asked everyone to use common sense to ameliorate the problem, urging deans to seek voluntary compliance to end smoking in classes.[18]

President Lyndon B. Johnson's expansive federal education and Great Society programs began to affect administrative council deliberations in the mid-1960s. Those initiatives marked the beginning of federal policies that would dramatically affect admission standards, gender equity in hiring, pay, and sports programs and, beyond the academy, environmental measures such as clean air and water legislation, the establishment of the Environmental Protection Agency (1970), and the Endangered Species Act (1973). The historic Civil Rights Act of 1964, passed in the aftermath of the assassination of President John F. Kennedy in November 1963, was among the most significant federal measures. Title VII of the act prohibited discrimination in employment, identifying specific categories of sex, race, color, religion, and national origin. It established the Equal Employment Opportunity Commission, an agency overseeing federal enforcement of gender equality. When President Johnson signed the Civil Rights Act, Senator Everett McKinley Dirksen—the Republican minority leader of the Senate—famously paraphrased Victor Hugo: "No army can withstand the strength of an idea whose time has come."[19] Most notable for Oregon State University would be affirmative action programs.

The Economic Opportunity Act of 1964 established several lasting programs: VISTA (Volunteers in Service to America), Job Corps, Head Start, Senior Centers, and Meals on Wheels. Less heralded, but important to higher education, were "work-study" programs, providing support for colleges and universities to hire needy students. Because the legislation required students to meet certain qualifications, Dean of Students Robert Chick told the council that the greatest difficulty would be identifying those who would meet federal standards. OSU acted quickly, embracing work-study financial aid as a valuable part-time student employment strategy, with the university establishing one of the earliest and largest work-study programs in the nation, garnering $413,000 in federal allotments for 984 participants in its first year of operation (1965).[20]

Another Great Society measure, the Higher Education Act of 1965, included funding for several programs that excited President Jensen, who saw opportunities if the university pursued the steps to become eligible. Because multiple federal programs affected higher education, Jensen appointed a person to keep track of such opportunities. Reporting to the state board, the president observed that "federal agencies, federal laws, and federal funds" would have an increasing influence on the future of the Corvallis school.[21] Within a few months, OSU housed several offices responsible for administering federal programs.

At the request of the State Board of Higher Education, Jensen commissioned university planning consultants L. A. DeMonte and A. R. Wagner to draft a long-range development plan to guide the physical expansion of the university. The president wanted to preserve the visual integrity of the campus and to promote that idea with the public. After an extensive survey of academics, research, housing, student activities, and other components of the institution's life, the firm turned in a report projecting an anticipated enrollment of eighteen thousand students by 1971–1972 and twenty-five thousand students by 1982–1983. The preamble to the document emphasized that an "orderly and beautiful" physical environment would promote the university's teaching, research, and extension services. DeMonte and Wagner proposed developing dormitories in three clusters around the periphery of campus within a short distance of central buildings. Classroom and office buildings would continue to be grouped around the campus core, the Memorial Union and the new library. Because the City of Corvallis and the university had developed in tandem, the report cited the importance for the campus to "reach a balance between the essential land needs of the University and the limited land resources of the City."[22]

Long before historic preservation became a watchword for protecting architectural structures, the DeMonte-Wagner plan urged the university to use existing buildings as long as they were useful and could be remodeled at realistic costs. Older structures should be replaced only if they were unsafe, could not be remodeled at reasonable cost, or if they interfered with important development projects. The report singled out Strand, Kidder, Apperson, and Waldo Halls as "buildings that cannot be retained permanently." Benton Hall, a building "of special historical worth," however, should be renovated and preserved. Building heights in the campus core should not exceed four floors, including basements, and for visual purposes, tall structures should be placed apart from one another.[23] The height restriction for central campus was breached early on with the construction of the six-story Kerr Administration Building.

For an academic institution's "learning-living" environment, DeMonte-Wagner recommended housing most students on campus. The university should provide housing for approximately 40 percent of single students and build additional accommodations for those who were married. All facilities should be within easy walking distance of the central campus, with married-student apartments accessible to nearby shopping and public schools. Housing should "not be provided for faculty or civil service staff." Beyond the recently opened library, the study saw no need for departmental or branch libraries. The development plan proposed other facilities to enrich campus life—"an auditorium-theater, a conference center, a faculty club, and additional student union facilities."[24]

In a section, "Landscape and Open Spaces," the document underscored the importance of a beautiful campus. A well-designed plan should have a unifying effect, providing open spaces, malls, a plentitude of trees, and redesigning streets into campus ways. On the central campus, the "Quad" would remain prominent, with walkways leading to educational clusters. DeMonte-Wagner mirrored the Olmsted design of 1909 in proposing attractive university boundaries, "as in the case of the large green near the easterly end of the campus." Efforts to preserve such spaces "must be carefully coordinated with City Plans." Strategies for placing new buildings should take into consideration the beauty of surrounding hills. Planting shrubs and trees indigenous to the Willamette Valley should be used to screen the rail lines passing through campus.[25]

There was more to the development plan—the placement of fields and courts for classes and recreation purposes. Outdoor space devoted to physical education should be located in proximity to the two gymnasiums; conversely, areas adjacent to Parker Stadium and Gill Coliseum would be reserved for intercollegiate athletics. The principal access points to campus would have a familiar ring to future visitors. Three routes intersecting the university grounds should remain open, providing access to campus—"14th–15th Streets, 30th Street (The Mall, in part), and 35th Street." As the university and community grew, DeMonte-Wagner anticipated great improvements in public transit. President Jensen praised the proposal for its potential to protect the "visual qualities and the traditional amenities that have so long characterized Oregon State University."[26]

By the mid-1960s, the state system had backed away from its internal skirmishes of previous years. Chancellor Roy Lieuallen reported in 1966 that students were better informed, faculty better paid and more knowledgeable, and Oregon's public campuses larger and more modern. There was a downside, however: students were more numerous, faculty worked under difficult conditions, and campuses were more crowded. More than 42,219 students were enrolled in state schools in the fall of 1965, an increase of nearly six thousand over the previous year. Because the higher education system anticipated only thirty-nine thousand students, budgets were readjusted to accommodate the additional numbers. Modest increases in the fall of 1966 brought enrollment to 44,030. Although a single biennium in the life of the state system is not that significant, the events and circumstances of 1965 and 1966 were noteworthy.[27]

Despite the burst in enrollment, the chancellor's office reported expanded opportunities for studying world cultures. Portland State College established programs in Central European and Latin American studies and a master of arts in German, including a year's study at a German university. The University of Oregon entered the second year of a student-exchange program in business with an institution in the Netherlands. The state board authorized Oregon State to grant a master's degree in business administration, and more significant, to offer undergraduate degrees in English, history, art, economics, speech, political science, and Russian studies, a significant departure from the curricular model of 1932.[28] Although the School of Humanities and Social Sciences continued to provide service courses for the institution's professional schools, its faculty was slowly building credible academic programs.

The university's new undergraduate majors, Jensen argued, were "curricular improvements," programs that would advance the institution's liberal programs. Responsible for more than a third of the university's credit hours, the School of Humanities and Social Science anticipated the approval of additional majors. The university should be proud, Jensen believed, for a new PhD in statistics and new undergraduate degrees in aerospace, bioengineering, and metallurgical and nuclear engineering. Other innovative programs included a PhD in biophysics and a master's program in the history of science. The campus also offered a unit to challenge high-achieving students, a university-wide Honors College. Originating in the School of Science in 1959, the honors program enrolled 431 freshman and sophomores during its first two years of operation.[29]

Student tuition across the state system for the 1965–1966 biennium remained unchanged, $110 per term for Oregon residents, $300 for nonresidents, and $110 for graduate students (resident and nonresident). The chancellor indicated that Oregon's tuition ranked in the middle among comparable state colleges and universities. The state system would begin assessing prospective students a $10 fee beginning January 1966 to compensate staff for evaluating applications. Dormitory charges, the most significant expense, increased from approximately $740 to $790 per year for multiple occupancy rooms in typical residences. At the front end of the state's income/expense ledger for higher education, the legislature approved significant salary adjustments: 9 percent for 1965–1966 and 4.5 percent for 1966–1967, the latter adjustment distributed on the basis of merit and promotion and tenure.[30]

Oregon's outlier institutions—beyond the two flagship universities—cried foul over the chancellor's allocation formula. Portland State College (PSC) and Southern Oregon College (SOC) students believed they were being "gypped." In divvying out state funds, the chancellor's office allocated $770 per student at SOC and $789 at PSC for 1966–1967 biennium. In contrast, the University of Oregon received $1,089 for every student and Oregon State University $1,242. Administrators at the smaller institutions and a few legislators called the allocation formula antiquated. Chancellor Lieuallen defended the UO and OSU allocations because those schools were running advanced operations. He conceded, however, that PSC and SOC were being shortchanged and that his office would revise its calculus for funding each unit's need per student.[31]

State board member J. W. "Bud" Forrester raised another red flag in 1966 regarding the low tuition charged to nonresident graduate students. He was upset that out-of-state graduate students paid the same rate as in-state undergraduates ($330 per year), while out-of-state undergraduates were charged $900 per year. Forrester believed it unnecessary for Oregon to "hold out the carrot any longer." Oregon enrolled some 5,600 out-of-state graduate students in 1966 (most of them at the UO and OSU), indicating that graduate education in Oregon colleges was attractive. Speaking for the board, Chancellor Lieuallen supported the status quo, because graduate students were valuable to the state system. Presidents Arthur Flemming of the UO and James Jensen of OSU both pointed to the importance of graduate students to academic programs and to the state economy.[32]

The likelihood of tuition increases—only hinted at in previous board meetings—gained momentum in October 1966, when Chancellor Lieuallen and board president Charles Holloway pointed to the state system's need for more revenue to meet increasing costs. Oregon spent less money on higher education than twelve comparator schools in the western states, and since 1963 the cost of education had risen considerably without comparable increases in revenue. Lieuallen and Holloway anticipated there was a "real probability" that tuition would increase in the fall of 1967. Holloway contended that state schools had experienced significant enrollment increases in recent years and needed more funds to meet the increasing work load.[33] It is clear, however, that the unified system was alive and well in the mid-1960s, with the Oregon State Board of Higher Education allocating degree programs, salary increases, and setting tuition and dormitory rates for every public university and college. The state's two flagship universities and rapidly growing Portland State College navigated cautiously through those crosscurrents.

The Oregon State University library was the center of academic life on campus. In his biennial report for 1967–1968, librarian Rodney Waldron issued a plea common to administrators in his position: "No Librarian is ever satisfied; No Library is ever large enough or provided enough funds, but considering all facets of this biennium, it has been a time of growth, cooperation and change." The holdings in newly minted William Jasper Kerr Library had expanded from 283,807 to 564,295 volumes, and the library staff of forty had nearly doubled in the previous decade. A perennial and troubling reality for the library, Waldron indicated, was unstable support, with sometimes wildly fluctuating funds available from one year to the next. Rising costs for books and journal subscriptions compounded the problem.[34]

The library was playing "'catch-up' in a losing race" to fill long-neglected titles in humanities and social science. It faced a monumental task in strengthening those collections, "because the base from which we started was so far behind." New and expanding programs in the humanities and social sciences were placing an extra burden on the library's budget. Title II of the Education Act of 1965, however, provided $32,945 for purchasing library materials. Other federal initiatives made the library a depository for United Nations documents, federal and military specifications, and reports and publications associated with the Commercial Fisheries and Development Act and the Anadromous Fisheries Act. Waldron was also grateful to Friends of the Library for enriching university holdings.[35]

In the midst of those fiscal restraints, the OSU library launched a long-range effort to improve its services through automation. Working in cooperation with the campus computer center, the library hired a systems analyst to determine operations that were amenable to computerized processes, such as acquisitions, serials, and cataloguing. The university applied to the US Office of Education for a grant to install an online technical processing application. The pilot program was successful, and the library set about computerizing important procedures.[36] Purchasing books and periodicals with limited funds, however, put this strategy in a perpetual bind. The budget emphasized the immediate needs of faculty and students, with no funds available to overcome basic deficiencies—"Our only reliable instrument for change," Waldron wrote, "is University needs." Funding questions aside, he believed the library made progress when it implemented automated procedures and developed an information services center for business and industry. A modern institutional library, Waldron insisted, should coordinate planning with other libraries in the state and serve all citizens. For the university, the library remained "the basic resource for teaching and research."[37]

Oregon State University restructured its administration in the mid-1960s, creating dean positions for research and university relations. Roy Young, chair of the Department of Botany and Plant Pathology, was named the first dean of research. The appointments gave the institution four executive deans (including the deans of administration, faculty, and students), who constituted the president's "cabinet." The consensus among university administrators was that the director of university relations, unlike the dean of research, would have little to do with academic policy; therefore, the president should feel free to appoint a person of his choosing. Because research was closely linked to academics, however, the faculty should be invited to make nominations for the position. Because the schools of engineering, home economics, and science units were unhappy with OSU's ability to compete with other institutions for contracts, the president retained a highly qualified public relations person to improve the university's ability to attract grants.[38]

The university advanced its academic outreach during the 1960s through the state's new community college system. With increasing numbers of students transferring from community colleges, the schools of engineering, agriculture, and home economics developed articulated arrangements with several two-year schools. Community colleges were a recent development, and OSU expanded those relations, especially with nearby Linn-Benton Community College, founded in 1966. The university was also heavily invested in the Division of Continuing Education (DCE), an outgrowth of the Oregon State System of Higher Education's extension service. Intimately linked with the land-grant tradition, DCE extended educational services to the citizens of the entire state. The agency's unique structure enabled departments and schools to offer courses, either as informal or accredited college classes, anywhere in the state.[39]

The DCE office made use of university services to deliver courses through KOAC radio and TV, information services, the office of audio-visual instruction, and the Corvallis Center for Continuing Education. DCE developed strategies for delivering instructional materials to professional groups distant from Corvallis. An early technological innovation—anticipating future distant-delivery courses—was the "telelecture," in which instructors delivered telephone lectures from campus to distant locations. At the distant site, a discussion leader provided visual aids and met with student groups. President Jensen reported in 1966 that discussions were under way to combine DCE with OSU's Cooperative Extension Service. In the coming decades, distance education would explode to the point that a candidate for the OSU presidency in 1996 would proclaim that the university's campus was the State of Oregon.[40]

Oregon State University overseas programs were increasingly active by the late 1960s, especially projects with the Agency for International Development (AID). With other land-grant institutions, Oregon State had been involved earlier with overseas ventures related to Cold War programs in less-developed countries. Through the auspices of the US government, Oregon State College engaged in a cooperative agreement in 1954 with Kasetsart University in Bangkok, Thailand, to help the country diversify its agricultural economy. The subtext to OSC's participation in the Southeast Asian nation was to mitigate the influence of communism in the region. James R. Beck of the OSC Extension Service directed Kasetsart's technical assistant program, focusing on teaching, research, and extension outreach to Thai farmers. Between 1954 and 1960, nineteen different college staffers worked in Thailand for periods up to two years. In return, fifty-nine Kasetsart faculty and staff spent time studying in the United States.[41]

During the 1950s and continuing through President John F. Kennedy's creation of the United States Agency for International Development (USAID) in 1961, international aid was an extension of US foreign policy. From Oregon State University, agricultural personnel were working in Latin America, offering technical assistance in weed control programs that could be extended to other countries. A team of twelve faculty and three advisers in Turkey assisted with new and improved varieties of wheat. Jensen estimated that during the 1968–1969 biennium upward of thirty-five faculty had been involved in projects around the globe, a matter of pride, prompting the administration to compile an inventory of personnel with international experience.[42] President Jensen would spend time in both Thailand and Iran on agricultural projects after he left the presidency.

As one of thirty-three universities in the nation offering training in all four military branches—US Army, US Air Force, US Navy, and Marine Corps—the university's ROTC program has always been vital in training officers for military service. This was especially true when America's intervention in Vietnam escalated after the US Senate passed the Gulf of Tonkin Resolution, in August 1964, granting President Johnson carte blanche powers to deter military aggression in Southeast Asia. The university restructured its training program when Congress passed the Reserve Officers Training Corps Vitalization Act, legislation requiring students to train at military bases before their junior year (in lieu of taking ROTC basic training during their freshman and sophomore years). The alternative two-year program retained the traditional four-year training with scholarships for some students. Oregon State's ROTC successes were stunning, with President Jensen reporting in 1966 that fifty-nine students were commissioned in the air force, 113 in the army, fifty-four in the navy, and six in the marines.[43]

As one of the most controversial military ventures in American history, the Vietnam War generated protests on college campuses across the nation, with students in larger population areas the most active dissenters. Although events at the Corvallis campus were less volatile than those taking place at the University of Oregon and Portland State College (elevated to university status in 1969), a small cohort of OSU student and faculty activists participated in Vietnam Days activities (October 15–17, 1965) in Salem, an event that was part of nationwide campus protests. When an OSU administrator questioned the legitimacy of posters being put up around campus, Dean of Students Robert Chick indicated there were no prohibitions against such postings as long as they conformed to conventional use. Chick added that a student organization, Students for a Democratic Society, sparked the movement.[44] News about Vietnam would continue to infuse campus life, with OSU graduates serving in the officer corps and as enlisted personnel, some becoming prisoners of war and still others never returning home. Campus protests continued to grow, especially after 1969.

With the university's centennial as a land-grant institution approaching in 1968, J. Kenneth Munford, director of publications, urged President Jensen to commission a written history of the school. He advised the president to appoint a committee to oversee the project and manage the publicity and distribution of the prospective book. Munford believed that "ends of periods of time, such as years or centuries," provided occasions to explain the past and anticipate the future. Although he fused the proposal with annual Charter Day activities and presentations of distinguished service awards, Munford thought a publication would highlight the university's story. If Jensen commissioned a history, timing was of the essence.[45]

The administration approached George Carson, chair of the history department, with a $30,000 proposal to free a faculty member for two years to research and write the history. After consulting his faculty, Carson, a Russian historian, told the president that the department was "very heavily loaded with instructional duties" and could not take on the project. Steady research over a number of years, with modest funding assistance from the university, would better serve the history staff. Another proposal, Carson suggested, would be a volume of essays on topics related to the history of the university; however, he would continue to encourage the history faculty to pursue aspects of such a study without the pressure of having to complete a book by 1968.[46]

Jensen pursued Carson's second alternative, a "research undertaking by a number of individuals with a real interest in the subject." There would be no deadline for the project. To facilitate the work, the president asked each department to prepare a timeline describing its chronological history, including photos and other illustrations. He suggested a due date of January 1967. Although several departments submitted reports early, the president sent a reminder in November 1966 that the chronological histories would "become important parts of our major Centennial publication." Jensen's emphasis on the significance of the outlines, however, was misplaced, because no one made use of the departmental submissions for the centennial. Moreover, the reports were uneven, some of them detailed and interesting, others haphazardly thrown together.[47]

Rodney Waldron, appointed director of OSU libraries in 1965, chaired the centennial steering committee charged with preparing a booklet for Charter Day activities in 1968. Waldron estimated that twenty thousand copies of an attractively designed publication could be reasonably produced. President

Jensen pushed Waldron to a broader agenda, asking him if there were some "firsts" that the university could use in its effort to convince the US Post Office to issue a commemorative stamp. Waldron responded that Oregon State was the fourth land-grant college in the nation to offer courses in home economics, and it was the first to do so west of the Rocky Mountains. To the president's suggestion that Oregon State might be the farthest west of all the land-grants, Waldron said yes, adding facetiously: "We are now checking to see if Oregon State University is the wettest Land Grant institution in the 48 states."[48]

Waldron's committee labored on several fronts—raising funds, preparing 37,500 brochures of seventy-two pages each, approving released time for English professor James Groshong to write the historical narrative, planning symposia, constructing birch display cases, and recommending that the university confer five distinguished service awards during the centennial year. To the committee's delight, Portland's KGW-TV agreed to show a twenty-eight-minute color documentary of the university, and the campus educational television network was preparing short vignettes from the institution's film archives for occasional showing.[49] The committee fell short on several of its objectives—it printed a twenty-four-page *Charter Day Convocation* booklet; James Groshong published *The Making of a University, 1868–1968*, a brief but well-written history of the institution; and KGW-TV produced its promised show, *The Possible Dream*—but the Postal Service did not produce a commemorative stamp and no one knows anything about birch display cases.[50]

Centennial fever appeared to be spreading across the Pacific Northwest, according to the *Oregonian*. The State of Oregon celebrated its centennial in 1959; Lewis & Clark College commemorated one hundred years of education with a magnificent program to mark its centennial in 1967; and Oregon State University, the state's oldest public institution, was preparing to celebrate its one-hundredth anniversary as "the agricultural college of the State of Oregon." The university had already designated the freshman class of 1965—seniors in October 1968—as "The Class of the Century." The *Oregonian* commended the institution for serving every corner of Oregon "with a minimum of conflict among regions or communities." The Oregon State University Press announced that it would publish Ava Milam Clark's *Adventures of a Home Economist* in the spring of 1968. Milam Clark, who served as dean of Home Economics from 1917 to 1950, collaborated with Ken Munford to write a history of the School of Home Economics and the home economics movement. Copies of the book would be available by OSU's Charter Day, October 27, 1968.[51]

The City of Corvallis and Benton County scheduled a Centennial Year Celebration Day prior to Sunday's Charter Day activities. Because Benton

County citizens funded construction of the first campus building (Benton Hall), President Jensen invited people to visit the campus on Saturday to strengthen ties between the university and surrounding communities. With Governor Tom McCall as grand marshal, leading the parade in a 1933 Rolls-Royce touring car, the day was a rousing success. President and Mrs. Jensen, outfitted in late-nineteenth-century dress, followed the governor in a separate vehicle. Thousands of people lined the parade route, which ended in front of Benton Hall. The governor's trophy for best parade entry went to the First Baptist Church for its huge open Bible float. Among the *Oregonian*'s illustrations featuring the Saturday festivities was a photograph of Governor McCall, Mrs. Jensen, and OSU graduate, former forestry faculty member, and timberland owner, T. J. Starker.[52]

Sunday's Charter Day activities provided several celebratory events, including a convocation in Gill Coliseum. With President Jensen presiding, the OSU-Corvallis Symphony Orchestra played George Bizet's *L'Arlesienne Suite No. 1* as people were being seated. The processional, with Professor Thomas Roberts performing, was Ernest Bloch's *Four Marches for the Organ*. J. W. Forrester, president of the Oregon State Board of Higher Education, offered greetings and introduced Wilson Foote, who presented the centennial awards. The capstone to the presentations was the Alumni Association's Distinguished Professor Award to Wayne Burt, the internationally acclaimed leader of the university's oceanography program and the individual responsible for Oregon State University's designation as a Sea Grant institution. Following the centennial address, Robert Walls led the audience in singing "Alma Mater."[53]

Fred Harvey Harrington, president of the University of Wisconsin (a land-grant school) gave the centenary address, "A Look at the Next 100 Years." Before the packed crowd in Gill Coliseum, the prominent Wisconsin executive praised the timelessness of land-grant institutions—an inexpensive education, serving the public through applied, practical, and theoretical research, and "providing a spirit of freedom." Both the University of Wisconsin and Oregon State University, among the original land-grants, were also "pioneer Sea Grant universities." Because the war in Vietnam was putting strains on federal revenue, Harrington feared that low-cost education was in a crisis, threatening historic low tuition rates for the poor. The early promise of an inexpensive education had eroded and was "pricing some people out of higher education."[54]

Because state legislators were calling for law and order in the wake of campus violence, Harrington worried that freedom of expression in the academy was in jeopardy. Dissent that turned into anarchy, however, was anathema to higher education. Harrington's testimonial reflected on one of the most turbulent years in recent history—the assassinations of Martin Luther King Jr. and Robert F. Kennedy in the spring and then the spectacular violence at Chicago's Democratic National Convention in August. His address was striking, warning of the dark forces of anarchy at academic institutions, while urging caution "that we do not, in the process destroy other freedoms which are fundamental and without which the American campus would have little meaning." Harrington praised activists, "because that is our tradition." He envisaged a future of lifelong learning, where "the campus will be everywhere" and college life will be indistinguishable from everyday living. He closed with the words of a critic who remarked that Americans were still living in the age of Chaucer. "If we are," Harrington mused, "there are many good days ahead, and this university will help to create them."[55]

In "A New Century Begins," Jensen's first report following the centennial, the president praised the institution's tradition of educating young people, cutting-edge research, and services to the public. There would be challenges confronting the school in its next century, especially social restiveness and the increasing complexities of the modern world. The most far-reaching development bestowed on the university in recent years was the National Science Foundation (NSF) and President Lyndon Johnson designating Oregon State University as one of the nation's three Sea Grant institutions. Similar to the land-grant precedent in 1868, the Sea Grant designation would provide knowledge about uses of food from the sea and other research findings. With congressional support, the NSF awarded OSU $553,000 in its initial funding cycle (with the Oregon legislature providing $500,000 in matching funds). Jensen anticipated larger federal grants in the future.[56]

In its centennial year, the university's School of Science hosted a new Department of Biochemistry and Biophysics, offering both master's and doctoral degrees. The School of Humanities and Social Science was offering seventeen undergraduate degrees, fourteen departmental majors, an interdisciplinary degree in Russian studies, and divisional majors in humanities and social science. The school had devoted much of its time to evaluating courses and programs, including a joint major with the School of Education to certify preschool teachers. The School of Engineering was taking advantage of telelecture and teleconference equipment to enhance its graduate offerings in Portland, and OSU expanded its summer term courses, with enrollment expected to surpass 4,500 students in 1968.[57]

President Jensen worried about student unease across the land—"They were terrifically bothered by Vietnam" and wanted a greater voice in university policies and decision-making. Student demonstrations, dissent, and unrest beyond Corvallis sometimes overshadowed life on campus. "But," the president proudly observed, "the administration and the faculty listened, as they traditionally have on this campus." Jensen pointed to the student-faculty council created in 1967 to build trust at the institution and the appointment of student representatives to more campus-wide committees. Despite the president's assurances that all was well on campus, he sent a circular to academic and executive deans in the summer of 1968 about mimeographed sheets found in classrooms—Carl Davidson's "University Reform Revisited." Davidson, a former officer of the Students for a Democratic Society, was warning about the evils of corporate presences on college campuses. Jensen, suspicious of such documents, thought "it may help us understand some of the things that are going on."[58]

The chancellor's office expressed similar apprehension, citing student unrest as one of the most vexing issues on college and university campuses. The "Berkeley Affair" of 1964 and the "Columbia Fiasco" of 1968[59] set the table for student disruptions at major urban universities. Chancellor Roy Lieuallen referred to a "sleep in" at the University of Oregon as the primary local example of such activity. The chancellor attributed student discontent to factors over which institutions had little control—Vietnam, poverty amid plenty, and barriers to minority student participation in the nation's life. Many students argued that college courses were irrelevant to their interests and that grading systems were arbitrary and outdated. The chancellor urged administrators to be aware of those tensions and to engage students in policymaking, but advised them to act promptly to isolate disruptive behavior.[60] Two years hence, Lieuallen and Jensen would submit more pessimistic reports.

With events on other campuses capturing national headlines, OSU's administrators established protocols for student disturbances and demonstrations. The university's eighteen-member police force would be the front line in the event of a campus emergency. Should disturbances occur near residence halls, police were to remain on the periphery and leave communications to residence hall directors and the dean of men. "Care must be taken," the protocol declared, "to determine the difference between a disturbance and a 'demonstration.'" Police should stand clear of the central activity, keep an eye on the severity of the action, and follow the procedure of watchful waiting in cases of demonstrations. Should a demonstration get out of control, off-duty police should immediately report for assignments to protect strategic buildings.[61]

By the fall of 1968, the university had developed more urgent strategies to cope with campus disorders. Following the guidelines of "'College and

University Business' (Aug. '68)," C. H. Blumenfeld proposed a master plan to assure efficient coordination and control. Operating under State Board of Higher Education statutory provisions, institutional presidents were responsible for the state's property and welfare. Blumenfeld urged the university to establish a committee to intercede and keep everyone talking to avoid hostile confrontations. Comprising deans, the group would serve as a command post, isolating the president, who would be free to act independently. Blumenfeld's statement included provisions for police operations, communicating with the state board, details on student discipline, and punishment for those who violated the code of conduct.[62]

A cascading series of national and international events reverberated across college and university campuses in 1968 and 1969. Following a decade in which young people increasingly demanded peace, justice, and racial equality, events began spiraling out of control in the late 1960s. President Jensen did his best to stay in front of campus disturbances, addressing the university's failure to recruit American Indian, Mexican American, and black students in his Faculty Day talk in September 1968. To advance minority recruitment, he appointed a person to canvass minority communities to identify young people with college potential and to help them with financial assistance. Jensen's initiative followed escalating racial tensions in the wake of the assassinations of Martin Luther King Jr. and Senator Robert Kennedy in May and June of 1968, and the riots at the Democratic National Convention in August.[63] Three months after Jensen's address to the faculty, OSU black students organized the fifty-five-member Black Student Union (BSU).

In truth, student and faculty protests had been heating up on campus. English professor Robert Jones had derided "white ghetto merchants and landlords" for exploiting inner-city blacks, the brutality of white troopers in the South, and the "dilapidated, ill-equipped, overcrowded and poorly staffed" schools in black communities. If those problems were not solved, Jones wrote for the *Barometer*, "we will see riots and destruction and death in every major city in the country." The *Barometer* carried other articles bearing on race issues during the summer of 1968, including a review of Jack Olsen's extraordinary five-part series, "The Black Athlete," in *Sports Illustrated*. Olsen cited black athletes in several sports who were dissatisfied and disillusioned with their experiences on college campuses. He pointed to a "carefully concealed" truth about black athletes—few of them graduate from college.[64]

The formation of OSU's Black Student Union in November 1968 stirred citizens in overwhelmingly white Corvallis to think of the militant Black

Panther Party, which originated in Oakland, California, in 1966. Although the BSU may have seemed combative to some in the community, the organization's purpose was constructive and mundane, "to develop black consciousness" and advocate for the educational needs of black students. BSU's public statements addressed tutorial support for black students and better recruiting strategies to attract minorities. Although the university participated in Chancellor Roy Lieuallen's "three-percent program"—admitting 3 percent of every freshman class with students who could not meet the minimum grade-point requirement—no blacks were among students admitted in the fall of 1968. Moreover, there were significant weaknesses in the "three percent" initiative—students were given no tutorial assistance.[65]

The BSU submitted a proposal in mid-January 1969 addressing the difficulties that black students confronted on campus—the university had "opened its doors but closed its eyes" to the academic difficulties of "less-well prepared black students." Although the university employed a black adviser for athletes, it ignored other students of color. The institution expected black students to fit seamlessly into programs for people whose backgrounds gave them a reasonable chance for success. Yet, at the end of every marking period, according to the BSU statement, black students failed or were suspended for academic deficiencies. The BSU provided examples of institutions providing assistance to "educationally disadvantaged black students."[66]

In the midst of meetings between the BSU and university administrators, James Farmer, cofounder of the Congress of Racial Equality, spoke to a large audience in Gill Coliseum. President Jensen cancelled classes during Farmer's address, "The Black Revolution." At a panel discussion the same day, George Carr, BSU's vice president, praised the administration for agreeing to provide tutorial assistance for minority undergraduates and to develop a stronger recruiting strategy for black students. One of the problems in recruiting black students, Carr told the audience, was Corvallis's reputation as a conservative community and a place "slow to change." Students had difficulty with housing and experienced "social discomfort in the community." There had been improvements, however—when he first arrived in 1963, there were only nine black students on campus, seven of them athletes. In a nod to radical black organizations elsewhere, Carr believed "bad publicity" gave local people the wrong idea about student unions: "Their purpose is not disruption but aiding black students in obtaining a good education."[67]

All appeared to be going smoothly in deliberations between administrators and black student activists. The president appointed Karl Helms director

Linus Pauling (1901–1994), America's only double Nobel Prize winner (Chemistry, 1954, and Peace, 1962), is Oregon State University's most prominent alum. In this photo, Pauling was preparing to give an address at Oregon State University's Gill Coliseum in February 1969 when Black student activists asked President James Jensen for permission to speak briefly to the audience. Jensen and Pauling graciously stepped aside. Courtesy of the OSU Special Collections and Archives Research Center.

of the new Office of Minority Affairs, and in mid-January the *Barometer* published the Black Student Union's "General Statement, Provisional Program, Remedial Program, Tutoring Program, Special Advisor-Counsellor, Recruitment, Athletic Program, and Housing." Under the athletic section, the statement noted that coaches ordered black athletes to cut their hair or otherwise practice good grooming. "We, in this union," the statement declared, "feel that it is not the responsibility of any Department on campus to define for a black student the word 'neatness.'" If it did not affect the person's performance, the athletic department should not mandate a person's hairstyle.[68]

As the winter rains wore on, the Office of Minority Affairs implemented a tutorial program for students needing academic assistance, with some eighty people volunteering as tutors. More assistance was needed, especially qualified students willing to tutor in English composition, math, and science. Helms indicated that his office defined minorities broadly—"social, economic and academic"—factors not restricted merely to skin color. The relatively quiet and benign campus changed dramatically in late February, however, when assistant football coach Sam Boghosian observed black linebacker Fred

The signal event on the Oregon State University campus—suggesting that OSU had joined the burgeoning civil rights movement—involved the school's football coach, Dee Andros, ordering linebacker Fred Milton to shave his goatee during the off season or forfeit his position on the team. The divisive incident on the nearly all-white campus prompted Black students en masse to walk off campus in protest in March 1969. Courtesy of the OSU Special Collections and Archives Research Center.

Milton sporting a mustache and goatee. In the absence of head coach Dee Andros, who was out of town, Boghosian ordered Milton to shave his facial hair. When Andros returned, he supported Boghosian's directive, telling Milton to be clean shaven by the following Monday or lose his athletic scholarship for the next year. The erstwhile peaceful Corvallis institution, bereft of the disruptions and turmoil at the University of Oregon and Portland State, became an instant national story, with Andros accused of discriminating against a black football player.[69]

Charges and countercharges escalated. The BSU accused Andros of denying Milton's freedom to express his fundamental human rights as a black person. Andros disagreed, insisting that prohibiting facial hair was a coach's prerogative, a matter of team discipline. Like his peers on other campuses, OSU English professor Michael Oriard writes, Andros "seemed to welcome the opportunity to draw a line in the sand." The Black Student Union accused Andros and the athletic department of racism. The day following the coach's mandate, black football player Rich Harr commandeered a microphone and asked to speak at the centennial convocation in Gill Coliseum, where Oregon State's famous alumnus Linus Pauling was about to speak. President Jensen, on stage with Pauling, allowed Harr a few minutes to address the audience, but before the microphone was turned on several catcalls were heard, including one student shouting, "Go home you—nigger." With the microphone on,

Harr and BSU president Mike Smith argued that their cause was much greater than Fred Milton's dismissal from the football team; it involved housing, social discrimination, and much more.[70]

Black athletes compounded the university's difficulties when they announced they would no longer participate in sports until the administration took steps to alleviate discrimination. BSU president Smith accused the athletic department of discrimination against black athletes and infringing "on their rights as individuals and athletes." The university should not be defining a person's cultural values. The BSU protest gained further momentum when the group voted to boycott classes. Outsiders added their support when John Carlos, Olympic bronze medalist in the four-hundred-meter run in Mexico City the previous summer, spoke before a noon rally. (Carlos and gold medalist Tommy Smith gained international fame—and were expelled from the games—when they raised their fists in a black power salute at the awards ceremonies.) The feisty Carlos urged the OSU crowd to "get rid of those athletic dictators." Simultaneously, a much larger crowd of four thousand people turned out in front of the Memorial Union to cheer Andros and other coaches.[71]

The dueling war of words escalated when Athletic Director James Barratt accused the BSU of plotting to embarrass the athletic department. Speaking to a packed faculty-senate forum on March 6, Barratt charged the BSU with using football and the athletic department as a "premeditated target" to attack. The Milton incident was never "a case of racial discrimination," Barratt declared, because the athletic department had received hundreds of supportive telegrams from alumni and the general public. According to the *Oregonian*, many of those attending the faculty forum disagreed with Barratt's impassioned defense of the athletic department.[72]

The *Oregonian's* respected journalist Wayne Thompson underscored one clear truth emerging from the controversy: "The black student crisis at OSU did not start with Fred Milton's beard, and will not end when or if he shaves it." The campus revolt reached its high point on March 5, when black students declared they would leave school. The issue was not explicitly racial, Thompson wrote, "but in fact it must be considered such." Despite the denials of the athletic department, racial overtones ran everywhere through the events of late February and early March. Thompson quoted BSU president Michael Smith, who grew up in Corvallis, reporting that he felt discrimination "in one form or another every day." Some black athletes believed the athletic department's discriminatory policies were not premeditated but "a painful consequence of Coach Dee Andros' militaristic policy." Thompson learned that ten anonymous phone callers reported Milton's facial hairs to the athletic department, despite the fact that, during the off-season, several white players grew long hair and sideburns. The *Oregonian* journalist faulted OSU officials for "limited vision" that alienated people on both sides of the issue.[73]

Fred Milton left Oregon State and completed his undergraduate degree at Utah State University. Of the black students walking off campus on March 5, only eighteen enrolled for spring term. Among the five black members on the football team in the fall of 1968, only two showed up for spring practice. Recruiting black football players became difficult, Michael Oriard and others argue, and contributed significantly to the decline of the football program. Beginning in 1971, the team suffered through twenty-eight consecutive losing seasons (most of them long after Andros was removed as coach and elevated to the athletic director's office). One important and significant consequence of the Milton-Andros episode, however, was the university's heightened awareness of cultural, ethnic, class, and, eventually, gender differences among its students and faculty.[74]

Under acting president Roy Young, who replaced James Jensen when he retired in June 1969, an ad hoc minority affairs committee recommended hiring an experienced director, establishing protocols for recruiting minority students, and providing a framework for remedial classes and tutoring. The committee advised breaking free of tradition-bound curricula and developing courses appropriate to minority issues.[75] Those initiatives would accelerate in the next decade, many of them responding to federal mandates and executive orders related to discrimination based on race, ethnicity, gender, or disability. The Oregon State University of the future would look very different from the institution that James Jensen headed in the 1960s. In that sense, the courageous Fred Milton served as an important point of departure between the old and the new, between an older vision of homogeneous Corvallis, and its university as pure and innocent, and a newer, different perspective that slowly grasped the value of diversity and cultural difference.

10
Federal Policies Become Preeminent

No one captured the bifurcated nature of Oregon politics in the midst of the civil rights and Vietnam War protests better than Governor Tom McCall. When the articulate large-framed governor addressed the Annual State Lions Convention in Salem on May 22, 1970, he confessed that it had "not been a Victorian lawn party at the Capitol lately." He complained of the pending arrival of unwanted nerve gas at the Umatilla Army Depot and the seeming inability of people to get along with one another. There had been turmoil on Oregon campuses, with disruptive and occasionally violent clashes at the state's institutions. Equally worrisome, administrators warned the governor that more could be expected when students returned in the fall. He told the Lions Club that he had already ordered Oregon State Police to Eugene on two occasions, and the recent disorders at Portland State required sending in fifty state police for more support. Because small groups of students and nonstudents were the perpetrators, McCall assured the Lions that "no radical band of anarchists" was going to close the universities, adding that most students were working within the nation's cultural and political traditions.[1]

McCall shared a story about a recent incident at the capitol, when a student group presented the governor with five demands: denounce President Nixon for sending troops into Cambodia; call out the National Guard to prevent rail shipments of nerve gas to Oregon; bring Oregon's congressional delegations home to discuss current problems; support Senator Mark Hatfield's amendment restricting the president's ability to wage war in Vietnam; and call for the release of Black Panther leaders imprisoned on false charges. The governor told the Lions that his response brought catcalls from the group, "not the sort of appearance which makes a public official feel a sense of accomplishment." The governor's real fear, however, was that student behavior would hurt public support for Oregon's colleges and universities.[2]

War abroad and disorder at home, the watchwords of McCall's address, characterized the American nation's state at the onset of the 1970s. The normally lively governor, up for reelection that fall, was in a gloomy mood, telling the Lions that he would call a special meeting with the State Board of Higher Education and key legislators to consider policy changes to deal with campus unrest. McCall was not in a charitable mood, suggesting the need to clearly define the rights of faculty and staff to participate in political protests. Responding to public requests, he would ask the board to review tenure to limit abuses of academic freedom, clarify the rights of students under criminal law, evaluate how administrators should be held accountable, and limit nonstudent access to campuses. He was "*not* ordering a witch-hunt or sponsoring a white-wash," but wanted to find a way to peacefully operate the state's colleges and universities. He chuckled at the thought that his critics—who thought "40 students, not 4, should have been shot at Kent State"—would censure him.[3]

McCall's appearance before the Lions took place three weeks after the first truly violent activity on the OSU campus. Early on the morning of May 1 (International Workers' Day) someone threw a Molotov cocktail through the second-story window of the OSU Armory, causing $560 in damages. Before Corvallis police arrived, a maintenance worker and campus policeman put out the fire. A few days later, the following handwritten letter arrived in the offices of the *Gazette-Times* and *Barometer*:[4]

> May Day, 1970
> Dear People of Corvallis,
>   We fire bombed the R.O.T.C. armory early this morning to show our solidarity with the Vietcong and other freedom fighters in Cambodia, Laos, and Vietnam who are fighting against U.S. imperialism.
>   U.S. imperialism also jails and even murders Black Panthers and other black, brown, and red men who resist their oppressor. We express our solidarity with all oppressed people by our action against R.O.T.C. which turns college students into hired killers for greedy businessmen, imperialists.
>   The only way that anyone can be truly free from imperialist war and institutionalized racism is to join the World Revolution as an active participant on the side of the oppressed peoples of the world.
>   "DIG IT? DO IT!"

The bombers were not finished, firebombing both the ROTC Armory and the National Guard Armory on the early morning of May 25. A short section of the campus building was scorched and a window broken. Damage to the National Guard structure was more extensive. Four firebombs thrown through a window damaged chairs, a desk, and clothing lockers. In the case of the ROTC building, a janitor extinguished the flames outside the structure. When fire was reported at the ROTC building, police were immediately dispatched to the National Guard Armory and put out the flames.[5]

Oregon was in good company in the contagion afflicting college and university campuses. National news events stirred student protests in 1970, one of them the conviction of five members of the Chicago Seven for inciting violence at the 1968 Democratic National Convention. Even uglier was the violence that occurred at Kent State University on May 4, when national guardsmen killed four students and wounded nine others who were protesting the United States invasion of Cambodia. The reverberations of the Kent State tragedy were felt on all Oregon campuses. Portland State joined the University of Oregon in calling for the cancellation of nonessential campus commitments to memorialize the Kent State victims. Student groups at those institutions and elsewhere were planning other activities, with the Eugene campus calling for a strike. Governor McCall refused student requests to lower flags to half-staff, telling a reporter the Kent State killings should be memorialized as a "matter of individual reflection of compassion and concern." Similar actions took place on Washington campuses.[6]

Responding to the Kent State tragedy, acting president Roy Young cancelled classes on Friday, May 8, for students and faculty to reflect on the increasing incidents of violence on the nation's campuses. The university scheduled a memorial service for Kent State victims and for young Americans who had died in Southeast Asia, and faculty and students held forum discussions and several teach-ins. Hewing to the university's conservative roots, on May 9 a group calling themselves "The Majority Coalition" demanded an end to the disruptions and cancellation of classes, which denied them services they had paid for. Declaring they had no position on Vietnam, Cambodia, or Kent State, the coalition objected to shutting down the university, accusing administrators of bowing to pressure. Their spokesman, Lon Wall, argued that what protestors did was their right, "so long as they don't interfere with the rights of other students."[7]

The coalition's demands were not the last word on student antiwar protests. The *Barometer* reported in mid-May the results of an engineering students' opinion poll involving five questions, with advice from a statistics faculty member. With 350 volunteers, students circulated the questionnaires in classrooms and solicited responses from 8,997 students out of an enrollment of 13,838 (65 percent). Campus organizations supporting the poll, included student chapters of the American Society of Civil Engineers, Association of General Contractors, Institute of Electronic Engineering, and Blue Key. While there were no controls over the circulation of the questionnaires and the potential for duplication raised questions, the student findings bear attention:[8]

1. Should ROTC be available to students?
Available—7,495 Not available—914
2. Do you favor or oppose use of off-campus police?
Favor—3,975 Oppose—3,860
3. Do you favor or oppose closure of a university?
Favor—3,035 Oppose—5,168
4. Which of the following are acceptable means of protest?
Petition the administration—8,166
Boycott classes—4,006
Classroom disruption—590
Sit-ins—3,353
Violence—205
5. What is your gender?
Male—5,650 Female—3,265

Student-body treasurer Charlie Larson, who opposed disruptive campus protests, asked the chancellor's office to investigate outside agitators who were "attempting to incite students to violence." He told Chancellor Lieuallen that most OSU students believed that violence was not the route to peace. Although a small minority of young people was responsible for the bad behavior, Larson thought the press exaggerated such events. The *Barometer* added to the acrimony, reporting that an anonymous petition was circulating through campus civil service offices seeking signatures for a "firm stand" against demonstrators. The petition's grievances complained about protestors attacking the free enterprise system, large corporations, and American workers, and asked that troublemakers be run out of town. Still other employees objected to political activity taking place in university offices.[9]

The late 1960s and early 1970s marked a transition for the nation's colleges and universities, one in which federal policies and programs loomed ever larger in institutional life. Affirmative action principles, growing out of the Civil Rights Act of 1964, principally Title VII banning gender discrimination in employment, were beginning to influence faculty hiring and student recruitment.

Those initial affirmative action programs would multiply in the coming years, prompting administrators to scramble to satisfy both federal requirements and college alums. None would be more vexing for Oregon State University administrators than Title IX, commonly referred to as the Education Amendments of 1972. Oregon representative Edith Green and Indiana senator Birch Bayh pushed the measure through the House and Senate with language that would give college and university officials fits:

> Section 1681. Sex (a) Prohibition against discrimination; exceptions. No person in the United States shall, on the basis of sex, be excluded from participation in, be denied the benefits of, or be subjected to discrimination under any education program or activity receiving Federal financial assistance.[10]

The growing environmental movement also heightened the federal presence in the academy. Seminal texts that heralded growing threats to the planet were Rachel Carson's classic, *Silent Spring* (1962), Paul Ehrlich's *The Population Bomb* (1968), and Barry Commoner's *The Closing Circle* (1971). The first Earth Day, celebrated on April 22, 1970, following the Santa Barbara oil spill, marked an intuitive beginning to environmental alarms. Congressional environmental legislation contributed to the development of new and innovative curricular and research programs at institutions of higher education, including Oregon State University. The most important federal law was the National Environmental Policy Act (1970), important for establishing the Environmental Protection Agency (EPA). Other significant pieces of environmental legislation followed—creating the Occupational Safety and Health Administration (1970), and passing the Clean Air Act (1970), Federal Water Pollution Control Act (1972), and a strengthened Endangered Species Act (1973).[11]

Collectively those federal initiatives would generate new programs in the biological and earth sciences and, with the passing years, elevate the term "ecosystem" to a household word. With its extensive research programs in forestry, agriculture, fisheries and wildlife, and oceanography, Oregon State University would be at the center of a wealth of groundbreaking research opportunities. The *Barometer* regularly reported on environmental issues, welcoming speakers such as John Hessel, a Stanford University population biologist who addressed global population problems in April 1970. Later that month, three OSU panelists spoke in Gill Coliseum about the relationship between human communities and ecological problems. Professor of History

William Appleman Williams stressed the importance of ecological balance in the environment and equilibrium among people. Creating truly human communities, he insisted, was the route to environmental health. The morning session in Gill included agricultural economist Joe Stevens, and Richard Boubel from mechanical engineering. After a break for lunch, the program reconvened in the Home Economics Auditorium, where speakers addressed problems with waste disposal, the mechanics of reuse, and air and water pollution.[12]

Environmental issues increasingly influenced university academic and research programs, eventually reaching to distant places through expanding oceanography investigations and, in the forest sciences, through research at the HJ Andrews Experimental Forest in an upstream drainage of the McKenzie River. Established within the Willamette National Forest in 1948, the Andrews would become the foundation for basic research into a variety of ecosystem functions—investigations into vegetation, nutrients, and the complex relationships between forests and streams that are being carried on to the present. During the 1970s, the Andrews became a popular site for field research, with interdisciplinary imperatives that emphasized monitoring sites to sustain long-term knowledge about ecological relationships. A two-hour drive from Corvallis, the Andrews has served as an evolving collaborative laboratory for multiagency, interdisciplinary research.[13]

Before he left office in June 1969, President James Jensen appointed a three-member commission on university goals to provide the institution with a clear definition of the purposes and objectives of planning. Professors Emery Castle, chair of agricultural economics, Warren Hovland, chair of religious studies, and James Knudsen, associate dean of engineering spent several months fact-finding and interviewing people to develop strategies for long-range planning. The commissioners, who spoke to the chancellor's office, deans, faculty, student groups, and alumni, completed their report in September 1970, the first planning document in the institution's long history. Summaries of the report appeared under various headings: General Recommendations, Academic Affairs, Administration and Business Affairs, Extension Education and Service, Research and Advanced Studies, Student Affairs, University Relations, School Structures, and the State System of Higher Education. While many recommendations were routine, one powerful statement stands out under the State System of Higher Education heading: "The commission believes the rigidity of this system [duplication of courses] is a major obstacle to Oregon State University realizing its potential contribution to the citizens of the state."[14]

Among the commission's principal recommendations was establishing a center for the performing arts and strengthening administrative support for the president's office. The latter suggestion included new vice presidents for academic affairs, administration, extension, research, student affairs, and university relations. Reflecting the campus turmoil during the preceding months, the commissioners advised creating an Emergency Campus Disturbance Committee, whose purpose would be to advise the president in case of campus disruptions. To the faculty's delight, the report recommended following the standard faculty–student ratio when the university was operating on a fixed budget.[15]

Under academic affairs, the commission recommended greater flexibility in degree requirements, with special attention to interdisciplinary programs, increased use of pass/fail grading, and department responsibility "for instruction, research, and extension education." The university's administrative structure should be upgraded, with the president's council including the vice presidents, deans, and directors of service units. To carry out the commission's proposals, the report advised establishing a president's planning commission to monitor progress in implementing its recommendations. In a major administrative revision, the commission suggested merging the Division of Continuing Education and the Cooperative Extension Service, with the proviso that schools and departments administer disciplinary extension programs.[16]

Perhaps to the faculty's chagrin, the commission urged the administration to fund the student government to implement "and publish" course and instructor evaluations. The administration should also appoint student government officers to the president's cabinet and the planning commission, and hire a student ombudsman. Under school structure, the report called for the School of Humanities and Social Sciences to develop plans to reach parity with other schools, an effort to blend science and liberal arts cultures. Finally, the commission recommended that the School of Agriculture upgrade its title to reflect new programs that departed from traditional agriculture.[17]

Goals commission member Emery Castle observed in a delightful memoir, *Reflections of a Pragmatic Economist*, that the traditional model of land-grant institutions was outmoded: "A homogeneous clientele no longer exists; multiple viewpoints must be taken into account. Both intended and unintended consequences need to be considered." Castle, whose career was steeped in land-grant traditions, indicated the changing parameters of land-grants in his work on the commission. While the three members were assembling their report, the world of land-grant institutions was changing before their eyes. The advent of the first Earth Day in April 1970 and new environmental legislation prompted an increasing number of scientists to join writers such as Wendell Berry in questioning the production-at-all-costs model of natural-resource exploitation. Public policy questions were becoming more complex, puzzling, and seemingly beyond simple solution.[18] This was the provocative and challenging atmosphere that Robert MacVicar joined when he assumed the presidency of Oregon State University in July 1970.

Montana-born and growing to adulthood in Wyoming, MacVicar graduated from the University of Wyoming in 1939, earned a master of science in biochemistry at Oklahoma State University, and then entered the doctoral program at the University of Wisconsin. An ROTC cadet since his days at Wyoming, MacVicar was called to active duty shortly after Pearl Harbor. He returned to Wisconsin after the war, completed his doctoral degree, accepted a biochemistry appointment at Oklahoma State, and rose through administrative ranks, eventually becoming dean of the graduate school and serving as vice president of academic affairs. Southern Illinois University hired him in 1964, first as vice president for academic affairs and then as chancellor of the Carbondale and Edwardsville campuses in 1968. With an outstanding record as a research scholar and sound administrative abilities, Oregon State University appointed MacVicar its fourteenth president in the early summer of 1970.[19]

The goals commissioners delivered their report to MacVicar, recommending policies that would move the university toward developing more comprehensive programs that would provide students in professional fields with a better understanding of the social, political, and cultural spheres of their disciplines. To meet that objective required liberal arts to achieve parity with the professional units on campus. MacVicar, who agreed that the School of Humanities and Social Sciences was underdeveloped, remarked that a careful reading of the commission report did not mean "Ph.D.'s in every department in H & SS." While the president supported accelerating general education programs, more money for the library, and building a performing arts center, he thought the increased costs would limit expansive programs in the humanities. In deference to the state board's allocation policy, Dean of Administration Milosh Popovich argued that the liberal arts would be featured elsewhere for the present.[20] Despite the goals commission charge that the School of Humanities and Social Sciences achieve parity with the professional schools, little forward movement would take place during MacVicar's tenure.

During his first two years in office, MacVicar's correspondence reflects a tough-minded approach to campus disorders, unquestionably a reaction to protests and violence at Southern Illinois University in the wake of the Kent State shootings in May 1970. The Carbondale police made liberal use of tear gas, 1,300 National Guard troops were called out, and Chancellor MacVicar forbade student gatherings on campus of more than twenty-five people. The Carbondale mayor prohibited sales of alcohol and established curfew between 7:30 p.m. and 6:00 a.m. Student protestors marching through Carbondale streets on May 12 threw rocks at the home of the Southern Illinois president's house and then repeated the same at the building housing the president's office while MacVicar was visiting. Because of the student riots, MacVicar and his staff closed the school until the beginning of summer term.[21] The State Board of Higher Education, mindful that legislators would be watching carefully the selection of OSU's next president, likely saw the tough-minded MacVicar as the right person for the job.[22]

Responding to Governor McCall's request that the Oregon State System of Higher Education address campus disorders and abuses of academic freedom, the chancellor's office ordered reviews of administrative procedures related to those issues. MacVicar received a copy of the chancellor's revised rules for personal conduct just as he was settling into his new office. After reviewing the document, he told the chancellor that its language lacked precision and would be open to abuse. Because the statement seemed too general, he hoped the chancellor would agree to "more specific language" in the OSU faculty handbook.[23]

MacVicar, however, followed the board's directive for student behavior, a decision he explained to a disgruntled alumnus who reproached him for adopting liberal conduct policies. The president disagreed with the state board's administrative code placing adjudication with the faculty. He personally favored vigorous action against students, faculty, and staff who interrupted university business. The board was mistaken, he believed, for placing complicated adjudication protocols in the hands of the faculty. MacVicar hoped the university could avoid the more serious problems plaguing other institutions.[24]

Through the summer and fall of 1970, MacVicar drummed home the idea that colleges and universities were vulnerable, subject to rogue elements among young people who had chosen such places to vent their protests against the social order. Newsletters from the National Association of State Universities and Land-Grant Colleges warned about reactions from angry congressmen and women who wanted to withdraw federal support for student aid.

One association circular alerted presidents to be wary of President Nixon and his cabinet, who were blaming campus violence on lax administrators. Although institutions should defend themselves vigorously against such attacks, the circular noted that disorders were widespread and not restricted to college campuses; violence was a uniquely American phenomenon.[25]

Eighteen months into his presidency, MacVicar wrote Emeritus President James Jensen about the university's budget struggles and Oregon's troubled tax system. Aside from financial exigencies, he thought the fall season was "close to normal, although conditions in Corvallis had always been quieter than other places." With excellent student leaders, he hoped the university would be able to avoid future social unrest. There was a particularly worrisome problem looming on the horizon, however: a federal Department of Health, Education, and Welfare directive prohibiting discrimination in employment against minorities and women. He thought the university's response would not be sufficient, "particularly when it is obvious that the individuals who are making the inspection are biased in the first place."[26]

The Department of Health, Education, and Welfare (HEW) and its Civil Rights Division launched an equal employment opportunity, affirmative action initiative with colleges and universities in 1971. One of the more contentious and wide-ranging reform enterprises in the history of American higher education, HEW's decision to implement Executive Order 11246—originating in the Civil Rights Act of 1964—would enforce equal opportunity in employment, access to higher education, and, eventually for public schools at all levels, equal funding for sports facilities and programs irrespective of gender. The mandate triggered long and rancorous conflict in hiring and sports programs in colleges and universities and left few institutions unaffected. For many schools, the federal initiative pushed sports programs, which had never been central to administrative policy decisions, to the forefront of controversies involving fairness and gender equity. Equal employment and affirmative action policies affected Oregon State University root and branch, implementing procedures over time that would affect every department and unit on campus, as well as the institution's outreach divisions, extension, and experiment stations. Working with HEW's regional office in Seattle, MacVicar directed all administrative units to implement procedures to put into effect equal opportunity/affirmative action policy directives.[27]

Oregon State University filed its Equal Opportunity Affirmative Action Compliance Plan with HEW in June 1971. In his foreword to the document, the president committed the university to providing equal employment opportunities for everyone and to eliminating discrimination in all university operations. Although much foot-dragging took place in many institutions, OSU's compliance statement was comprehensive, outlining academic procedures for recruiting, promotion, wage considerations, grievance procedures, monitoring the program's progress, and a legal framework.[28]

To assess the university's compliance, HEW's Seattle office sent a team to interview and collect data from OSU in November 1971. Marlaina Kiner, director of the Seattle Civil Rights Division, responded early in 1972, commending Oregon State's efforts to establish credible equal employment policies. However, her letter pointed to deficiencies in the affirmative action plan and recommended procedures to rectify shortcomings. The review's most important section charged that departments had made no effort to recruit minorities. Too many units still used the "grapevine" strategy for recruiting, which reinforced hiring white employees. Kiner urged the university to reach out to predominantly minority institutions for every job opening, to keep records of applications by race for each vacancy, and to report its efforts to recruit minorities to the affirmative action office.[29] There were subsets to the HEW directive, but the major deficiency was the absence of efforts to recruit minorities.

There were significant salary differentials between women and men among the deficiencies in OSU's affirmative action program. The HEW review directed the university to account for those differences across every department and required action: eliminate inequities between females and males, with attention to time in service, time in rank, accomplishments, and professional standards. It faulted OSU for failing to provide upward mobility for women, keeping some of them in research appointments for an eternity. The report recommended establishing an affirmative action office to oversee such deficiencies.[30] Recruiting minorities was a separate issue, requiring time to develop procedures to attract underrepresented groups to campus. To meet compliance standards, the administration provided departments with information on collecting materials related to job vacancies—the applicant's ethnicity, efforts to attract minority and female candidates, and evaluation criteria. OSU departments deluged administrators with questions about "level of effort" in applying affirmative action in filling positions. HEW's response: there should be no limit to time and effort to improve hiring women and minorities.[31]

In its response to HEW, the university gathered data on salaries and other matters. MacVicar's letter to Marlaina Kiner, with numerous appended documents, provided details about discrimination in hiring and wage differentials. As a consequence of an in-house survey, the university determined that the salaries of sixty faculty women would be adjusted. The reviews and actions taken, the president noted, represented the university's commitment to affirmative action as an ongoing process. As outlined in the university's affirmative action plan, the president appointed an antidiscrimination board to adjudicate complaints and investigate discriminatory procedures.[32]

When the president announced appointments to the antidiscrimination board, Margaret Lumpkin, professor of education and member of a women's study group, protested that there were no women—the university's largest minority—on the board. The panel that would hear complaints about discrimination added to the problem "in the appointment of all men to represent them on the board." The composition of the board brought into question the university's compliance with the affirmative action program. In less than two months, the president appointed five more people to the board, four of them women.[33] Another complaint from Juan Mendoza, president of the Chicano Student Union, charged that the president had appointed no blacks, Chicanos, or Indians. MacVicar's most difficult problem, however, was responding to HEW's review of discriminatory hiring involving women and minorities, issues that would foster sharp exchanges between Marlaina Kiner and the president.[34]

HEW circulated an update to Executive Order 11246 in the fall of 1972, requiring institutions to develop nondiscriminatory hiring procedures and to identify groups that had previously been denied employment or advancement. Karla Brown, OSU's acting affirmative action official, urged the president to take the directive seriously, because OSU still used traditional word-of-mouth recruiting strategies for hiring. Brown indicated that HEW required "*extra* efforts to recruit women and minorities through *new* and *different* channels." She urged the university to adopt a campus-wide recruiting policy, include women and minorities on search committees, and to allow a minimum of thirty days in announcing job openings.[35]

The next communication from Seattle's HEW office confirmed Brown's worries. Kiner wrote MacVicar in November 1972 that the university's plan did not satisfy the requirements of Executive Order 11246. The university should revise its recruiting procedures and include an analysis of minorities available for every job. Moreover, the institution, not the federal government, was responsible for seeking qualified females and minorities.[36] It is important to know that Executive Order 11246 did not stipulate that requirements be waived to accommodate women and minority hiring, a common misunderstanding then and today. The order simply mandated that job requirements be applied equally across the board to all candidates. Implementing affirmative action, according to Peter Holmes, director of HEW's civil rights office in

Washington, DC, should never be used "to restrict consideration to minorities and women only." Status as a member of a preferable group was disallowed in advertising for job openings.[37]

With the vantage of hindsight, it is clear that HEW's Office of Civil Rights and OSU administrators were seeking common ground on achieving equal employment opportunities for women and minorities. Because land-grant institutions were heavily involved in federal contracting, it was prudent to accommodate the new hiring, promotion, and wage schedules. MacVicar's subsequent communications with Kiner provided detailed responses to specific sections and subsections of affirmative action guidelines. In one letter he expressed frustration in collecting data on minorities, but noted that the university was pressing forward and continuing to add to its statistical profile. There was another looming issue, he told Kiner: the legislature was meeting in the spring of 1973, and budgetary adjustments for new hires depended on legislative action.[38]

The compliance exchanges with HEW's Seattle office became more positive with the passage of time. Region X civil rights director Kiner upheld the institution in two discrimination complaints filed against the university, although in the same letter Kiner indicated that the athletic department had failed to implement the institution's affirmative action plan. Ronald McClain, who became OSU's first official affirmative action director in 1973, drafted the university's compliance plan in 1975. The last section of the document listed "Problem Areas," with the highest percentage of "underutilization" of female faculty in the colleges of Liberal Arts and Science. The two colleges were also slow in minority hiring, with extension facing similar problems.[39] Aside from ongoing issues involving the athletic department and Title IX, Oregon State University reached a full conciliation agreement with the office of civil rights in September 1978.[40] Meeting the provisions of Title IX, however, would be a much more difficult, rancorous, and drawn-out undertaking.

From its inception, Title IX was a broad decree affecting all institutions receiving federal funding, embracing all aspects of education, employment, and cases of sexual harassment. The preamble to Title IX was succinct:

> No person in the United States shall, on the basis of sex, be
> excluded from participation in, be denied the benefit of, or be
> subject to discrimination under any educational program or
> activity receiving federal financial assistance.

Rooted in Executive Order 11246, Title IX met little resistance when it worked its way through Congress as part of the Education Amendments in 1972. Because the legislation was a civil rights measure, HEW's office of civil rights was again the primary enforcement agency. Three other civil rights measures, all affecting colleges and universities, followed Title IX: the Rehabilitation Act (1973), prohibiting discrimination because of disability; the Age Discrimination Act (1975); and Title II of the Americans with Disabilities Act (1990), banning public agencies from discriminating on the basis of disability.[41] While those measures all affected Oregon State University, Title IX would have the greatest impact.

Although HEW did not issue its Title IX regulations until May 1975, OSU officials established three new women's intercollegiate sports programs in golf, swimming, and gymnastics, adding to crew, the sole women's intercollegiate sport. Three other women's sports quickly followed: softball in 1975 and basketball and volleyball in 1976. Establishing women's intercollegiate sports was more than an exercise in complying with federal law. Texas senator John Tower introduced an amendment in 1974 exempting revenue-producing sports from Title IX requirements. The Senate compromised and adopted a requirement that HEW regulations should make "reasonable provisions considering the nature of particular sports."[42] Reactions to Title IX on the Corvallis campus and at many other institutions brought much wailing and gnashing of the teeth.

In a modest effort to press forward with Title IX requirements, President MacVicar appointed Pat Ingram to a half-time position as director of women's intercollegiate athletics (with a part-time secretary). To mitigate financial strain on the athletic department, he urged Ingram to make use of existing staff in health and physical education. Aware of the additional costs of Title IX, Oregon governor Tom McCall was unsuccessful when he asked the legislature for $300,000 to fund women's athletics at the state's three major institutions. "Hanging over our schools," he wrote Washington governor Dan Evans, "is the possibility of HEW withholding millions of dollars in Federal higher education grants unless . . . good faith efforts are made to give women's sports parity with men's." Calling for a meeting of Northwest college and university presidents, McCall worried about the disparities in TV income between the region's schools and those in California. He strongly believed that both men and women's nonprofit sports were worth saving.[43]

When the National Collegiate Athletic Association (NCAA) proposed a merger with the Association for Intercollegiate Athletics for Women (AIAW), MacVicar disputed the notion that NCAA rules should apply to all intercollegiate programs. He cited club sports—crew, sailing, rugby, "and women's

OSU's affirmative action officer from 1976 to 1987, Pearl Spears Gray guided the university's first Title IX compliance self-study in 1976. She drafted guidelines to help the university avoid sexist terminology in publications, assisted in recruiting African-American graduate students, and always was a strong proponent of attracting students of color to OSU. Pearl Gray was on the local board of the NAACP, the Governor's Commission on Black Affairs, and the Oregon Public Health Advisory Board. Courtesy of the OSU Special Collections and Archives Research Center.

athletics"—implying that women's teams were akin to club sports. In the face of tight budgets, he advised "thoughtful study rather than hasty, unilateral action." The most serious problems were Title IX regulations regarding athletic scholarships and OSU's efforts to remain in compliance. John Davis, faculty athletic representative, juggled the proportional allocation of scholarships between men's and women's sports, fearing that funding women's programs would hurt football scholarships. "The effects of Title IX," he told MacVicar, "could be very pronounced."[44]

In the midst of those challenges, there were disparities in the treatment of male and female athletes and coaches on campus. Male athletes in football, basketball, baseball, and track received academic credit for participating in the sport, and the Department of Physical Education compensated their coaches, out of instructional funds, for the student credit hours they generated. That arrangement did not extend to women's sports, prompting Charlotte Lambert in the Department of Physical Education to describe the tradition as a "questionable practice," arguing that paying coaches and giving athletes academic credits for sports participation should end. Lambert pressed the issue with health and physical education dean James Long, citing the double compensation for male coaches in football, basketball, baseball, and track and the absence of similar provisions for women coaches. The university was out of compliance with Title IX, she argued, because it was paying male coaches for their instruction in several sports in addition to their regular salaries.[45]

Paying men's coaches out of health and physical education instructional funds continued into 1977 when Jack Rainey, administrative assistant to the Department of Intercollegiate Athletics, reported to affirmative action director Pearl Spears Gray that baseball, basketball, football, and track and cross-country coaches (all males) received 75 percent of their salary from the athletics department and 25 percent from health and physical education. The football coach's duties, according to Rainey, involved teaching a varsity football class in the fall and spring for one credit and a "football coaching" class in the spring for two credits. Resolving the issue would be difficult, because physical education had a vested interest in the allotted credit hours.[46]

The university created the Women's Intercollegiate Athletics Board (WIA) in 1973 to accommodate the expanding women's sports programs. The women's board reported significant advances in 1975, hiring Sandy Neeley as full-time director, as well as two full-time coaches; upgrading the positions of other coaches; and obtaining the services of a full-time trainer. The WIA also met with the men's athletic board to address common concerns. The WIA concluded its second annual report on an upbeat note, pleased that women participating in intercollegiate sports at OSU ranked among the highest with schools of comparable size.[47]

President MacVicar—a competent administrator by most accounts— struggled with Title IX issues during the remainder of his tenure. The university's Intercollegiate Athletics Board (men) and the institution's booster organization, the Beaver Club, were reluctant to loosen purse strings to achieve gender parity. The elevation of football coach Dee Andros to director of athletics in the fall of 1975 was another complication. Following Andros's several dismal seasons as football coach, MacVicar appointed him athletic director despite other excellent applicants and mixed support from those close to OSU. Whether the president regretted the decision is unknown, but the many letters opposing Andros must have given him pause. The usually gracious MacVicar would spend his remaining years as president trying to find his way through budget shortfalls, struggling to comply with Title IX, and dealing with an athletic director who only grudgingly agreed with the federal mandate.

Implementing Title IX proved a long slog for Oregon State University, with progress taking place in fits and starts over several years. MacVicar and most college and university presidents contended with institutional inertia, largely conservative alumni, and powerful revenue-producing sports. Even if MacVicar were personally aggressive in pushing Title IX, it is doubtful the university could have achieved compliance in more timely fashion. MacVicar moved cautiously, seeking alternatives for funding women's sports, in the midst of stringent budgetary conditions, without taking from men's programs. The president insisted that parity between men's and women's sports needed to be settled at the national level. If OSU were to achieve equity among men and women athletes, it would have to "sharply curtail contributions to male athletes or substantially increase them to female athletes." MacVicar hoped courts would resolve the problem.[48]

Revenue-generating sports were the center of acrimony on the Corvallis campus, in the Pacific-8 Conference, and across the nation. For Northwest members of the Pac-8, that meant negotiating with Marlaina Kiner in HEW's Seattle office. When MacVicar filed a university self-evaluation with Kiner in July 1977, he explained that including revenue-producing sports data would subvert the policies of the State Board of Higher Education, which had forbidden universities to use state funding for non-revenue-producing sports. When Kiner questioned the exclusion of men's basketball and football from the self-evaluation, MacVicar referred to a state board directive dividing intercollegiate sports into two categories, those that produced revenue and those that did not. Since no women's sports were revenue-producing, they were in the same category as "non-income" men's sports. Although the university and other state institutions had appealed to the legislature to enhance women's sports programs, he told Kiner, lawmakers refused the request.[49]

If Oregon State University was guilty of sandbagging in its commitment to Title IX, it had lots of company. Title IX prerequisites were challenged in virtually every session of Congress following its enactment in 1972. The NCAA enlisted the testimony of several big-time football coaches who claimed Title IX would ruin men's sports. A congressional bill to exclude revenue-producing sports failed in 1976 and again in 1977. In the midst of political debates at the national level, Oregon State University administrators considered merging women's and men's athletic programs, a union that Athletic Director Dee Andros feared would jeopardize profit-making men's programs that should be exempt from Title IX.[50]

Slowly the worm began to turn toward supporting women's athletics—with the Beaver Club agreeing in December 1977 to raise funds for women's sports. In a meeting with President MacVicar and Andros, acting director of women's athletics Sylvia Moore recommended reorganizing the Beaver Club to include supporters of women's programs. In the interim, the committee deliberating the merger of men's and women's programs produced ambiguous recommendations, voting six to five to merge, but questioning the viability of women's athletics.[51] William Kirkpatrick believed most committee members

Sylvia Moore joined the faculty in physical education in 1966, served as gymnastics coach, 1967 to 1975, and director of women's athletics, 1975 to 1977 and 1980 to 1982. Moore was deputy director of intercollegiate athletics from 1983 to 1985 after the merger of women's and men's athletics. When President John Byrne removed Dee Andros as athletic director in 1985, Moore served as interim athletic director until the appointment of a permanent director. Moore brought a more assertive voice to women's athletics, praising progress but pointing to glaring inequities between men's and women's intercollegiate sports. Courtesy of the OSU Special Collections and Archives Research Center.

wanted to defend the current system, with "personalities" intervening and subverting efforts to structure a new model. Ruth Stiehl, who voted in the affirmative, made clear what bothered Kirkpatrick, having "Mr. Andros and his staff . . . administer athletics for women." The present staff would never promote women's sports "at the least expense to men's athletics." Craig Fletcher opposed the merger because women's sports would be "swallowed up" in a system different from their own.[52]

Sylvia Moore introduced a new tone for women's athletics in her annual report for 1977–1978, praising progress in the program yet bluntly pointing to deficiencies and inequities between men's and women's sports. She cited modest advances in women's scholarships, more equitable salaries for women coaches, travel funds for qualified athletes, and the president's promise of an advisory board that would fairly serve men's and women's programs. In another memo to MacVicar, Moore indicated that support for men's non-revenue-producing sports was "vastly superior" to that for women. While the president continued to rank men's football and basketball over women's sports to protect their income, Moore pointed to alarming discrepancies in non-revenue-producing athletics, where conference and regional levels of competition favored men's sports.[53]

In a February 1978 letter to HEW's civil rights office in Washington, DC, MacVicar argued that OSU should have autonomy to manage "its programs in the best interests of the students," including the ability to choose its competitive sports. The president hoped the civil rights office would operate on principles of "equity and fairness," recognizing the difficulties of institutions with modest resources. In a message five months later to HEW secretary Joseph Califano, MacVicar invoked the State Board of Higher Education's administrative rules mandating nondiscrimination in intercollegiate athletics. Without reference to football or basketball, he asked the secretary to approve the university's "alternate form of achieving compliance." The president conveniently ignored that his own institution's figures contradicted his public statements that OSU was moving toward compliance. Financial support for athletes for the academic year 1979–1980 reveals striking disparities between men and women (table 10.1). The total funds awarded coincided with the number of athletes on scholarship—men, $462,335, women, $89,017.[54]

Title IX policy shifts would continue through the remainder of MacVicar's term and beyond. Central to the deliberations were HEW's guidelines outlining three options for meeting requirements: improved conditions for women athletes, evidence that women athletes were treated fairly, and evidence of "proportionality"—women holding scholarships in the same percentage as they were represented in the student body. Politics at the national and state level, court cases, and the powerful NCAA shaped the contours of compliance with Title IX. Enforcement lagged during the 1980s, when the US Supreme Court limited Title IX requirements to athletic scholarships in *Grove City v. Bell* (1984). The court reversed the decision in 1996, reinstating the "principal of proportionality" as a vehicle for colleges and universities to show compliance. Through those legal vicissitudes, women's programs made progress toward parity with men's non-revenue-producing sports. Revenue-producing

Table 10.1. OSU NCAA Division I Athletes Supported, 1979–1980

Men	No. Supported	Women	No. Supported
Baseball	26	Basketball	13
Basketball	17	Softball	22
Crew	41	Crew	35
Cross Country	50	Cross Country	16
Football	95	Gymnastics	8
Golf	13	Golf	6
Track and Field	50	Track and Field	44
Wrestling	41	Swimming	24
		Volleyball	12
		Tennis	13
Total	333	Total	193

programs, however—football and basketball—remained above the fray, expanding and enhancing facilities, while non-revenue-producing men's sports suffered cuts to provide greater support for women.[55]

More than any other president during the twentieth century, Robert MacVicar fought "Daemon Rum," using his powers as chief executive of Corvallis's largest employer to lobby the Oregon Liquor Control Commission and city council to oppose issuing alcoholic licenses to Monroe Street businesses. Taverns adjacent to campus, he feared, would contribute to blighted neighborhoods. He prefaced his letters with worries that student leaders would request beverage licenses for the Memorial Union, a move he would oppose unless the legal age for purchasing alcoholic drinks was substantially raised. MacVicar's outgoing correspondence from 1973 until retirement consistently opposed the sale of beer, wine, and liquor in proximity to the university.[56]

The president's opposition to alcohol is revealed in a letter to a Corvallis woman who was concerned about newspaper reports that one-third of the faculty regularly smoked marijuana. MacVicar thought the report a "gross exaggeration"; alcohol was the more insidious and dangerous of mood-altering substances. On the other hand, when an influential Salem restaurateur proposed converting the old Citizens Bank building on Second Street into a high-end restaurant with liquor services, MacVicar was fully supportive. One year later (1978), he wrote the liquor control commission supporting the Class Reunion, a new restaurant in a renovated cannery on Ninth Street, praising the investor for creating an environment promising excellent cuisine in an aesthetically pleasing setting. Oregon State University had an interest in the venue, because the community lacked quality restaurants.[57]

Proposals to open restaurants serving alcohol on Monroe Street, however, were a different matter. When the new La Creperia restaurant on Fifteenth and Monroe applied for a beer and wine license, MacVicar reminded the commission of his long-standing opposition to such licenses. Monroe's commercial environment was sensitive to deterioration; moreover, a new branch of Citizens Bank attracted elderly citizens, making it important to limit the commercial zone to small shops and offices. MacVicar insisted that it would be inappropriate to locate a "tavern" in the vicinity of religious centers—Westminster House, Canterbury House, the Newman Center, Christian House, and Luther House.[58]

Times were changing, however, as MacVicar recognized when the liquor control commission issued a beer and wine license to La Creperia, with the proviso that a meal be served for those purchasing an alcoholic beverage.

When Nearly Normal's Vegetarian Cuisine applied for a beer and wine license in 1982, MacVicar indicated that he would support a license similar to the one issued to La Creperia (subsequently transferred to Clodfelters, operating at the same location).[59] The SuperDeli at 2525 Monroe presented a new challenge for the OSU president when it applied for an alcoholic beverage license in the summer of 1982, with the proviso that it would sell several items constituting a "bona fide" meal to meet the food requirement. In response to a question from the city, MacVicar indicated that anyone ordering that quantity of food would certainly not be attempting to escape the license requirement simply to purchase beer and wine. MacVicar, in effect, lived up to his self-appraisal in a letter to Hattie Williams of Portland in 1979—"I really don't consider myself a modern Carrie Nation," telling Williams that, if he were sensitive to all criticisms, he would be an unhappy person, and he was certainly not rendered unhappy when a reporter referred to him as old-fashioned.[60]

MacVicar was the first president to face politically sensitive environmental issues—field burning, nuclear energy, cattle grazing in national refuges, herbicide spraying of forestlands, and pollution in Oregon waterways, issues vitally important to Oregon citizens and OSU researchers. As a scientist, MacVicar took a conservative view of environmental problems, arguing that in most instances industries would use best practices, making regulations unnecessary. The autumn burning of grass-seed fields emerged as a public controversy in the mid-1960s and developed to the point that Governor Tom McCall declared a ten-day moratorium on burning in August 1969 when winds blew clouds of acrid smoke into the Eugene-Springfield area. The smoke blanketing the southern Willamette Valley that day prompted the state legislature to grant the Oregon Department of Environmental Quality (DEQ) authority to prohibit burning on marginal days.[61]

Burning grass-seed fields originated with Oregon State College in the late 1940s, when USDA plant pathologist John Hardison determined that burning ryegrass fields after harvests eliminated the fungus-like blind-seed disease as well as ergot, infestations that threatened the quality of the crop. After Hardison's findings, burning ryegrass fields proved strikingly successful in controlling diseases and weeds. Field burning, an Oregon State University Extension publication reported in 1989, "has historically been the most effective practice used for volunteer control." There was one major problem—the greatest acreage burned took place amid more than 70 percent of the state's population. Beginning in the mid-1960s OSU scientists began studying environmental conditions affecting burning, and then, bowing to legislative threats to end burning in 1975, the agricultural experiment station developed an alternative "thermal treatment" with propane burners to protect against seed diseases.[62]

Several Oregon State University departments—soil science, crop science, and the agricultural experiment station—were involved in searching for options to burning fields. After years of research on open field burning, MacVicar told Medford *Mail-Tribune* editor Eric Allen in 1977 that controlled burning was still the most effective tool in sanitizing seed-grass fields. Although open burning remained a common practice, farmers reduced field burning from a high of 315,000 acres in 1968 to an average of 220,000 acres in the 1980s. And then tragedy struck on August 3, 1988, when a field burn near Harrisburg torched grass adjacent to I-5, engulfing traffic in blinding smoke. When the air cleared, twenty-three wrecked vehicles were strewn across the highway. Seven people died and thirty-seven were injured from collisions. From that point forward, legislators sharply reduced field burning into the twenty-first century, until burning was banned on all but fifteen thousand hillside acres on the periphery of the valley.[63]

In the midst of Oregon's booming timber harvesting following the Second World War, foresters sought a multitude of techniques to speed reproduction in western Oregon, where fast-growing Douglas-fir dominate. To keep newly planted clear-cuts free of brush, private timberland owners and state and national forestry officials used a variety of herbicides, especially 2,4-D and 2,4,5-T, to kill competing hardwoods such as vine maple and alder. The US Army had also tested 2,4,5-trichlorophenol as a defoliant during the Second World War. Following the conflict the federal government registered the herbicide for domestic use, and the chemical quickly became popular for controlling weeds and brush. When evidence indicated that 2,4,5-T caused deformities and birth defects in rodents in the late 1960s, the EPA prohibited its use on human food crops. The Forest Service and industrial foresters had no such restrictions.[64] The jury was still out, however, as protests increased in the 1970s over the use of the dioxin-contaminated phenoxy herbicide.

Siuslaw National Forest to the west of Corvallis—the most productive in the entire national forest system—was at the epicenter of the controversy. The dispute over 2,4,5-T centered on the contaminant, TCDD, a highly toxic dioxin and by-product of the production process that could potentially cause cancer, birth defects, and miscarriages in humans. Protests over the use of phenoxy herbicides originated in the early 1970s and then escalated in 1978 when an EPA study revealed a significant correlation between women having miscarriages and the aerial spraying of 2,4,5-T in the vicinity of the small logging community of Alsea. At a media seminar in June 1977, Oregon State University scientists defended use of the herbicides. Michael Newton, a forest science professor, told reporters that the dangers of the herbicides were "negligible." Controlling brush with the use of the chemical sprays was more economical than cutting it by hand. OSU toxicologist Frank Dost joined Newton in emphasizing the safe use of 2,4,5-T. George Streisinger, a University of Oregon molecular biologist, argued otherwise, indicating that laboratory tests "quite conclusively" showed that TCDD accumulated in organisms.[65]

Newton, an enthusiastic proponent of using the herbicide, attempted to acquire some of the US Air Force stockpile of Agent Orange—a mixture of 2,4-D and 2,4,5-T—to eradicate brush in western Oregon and Washington timberlands in 1973. Agent Orange had been widely used as a defoliant in Vietnam during the 1960s, but the Defense Department ended its use in 1970 when reports circulated that it caused widespread birth defects and miscarriages in humans. Newton claimed that the dioxin level in a significant portion of the stockpile was low enough to qualify it for commercial application. Because the EPA had not registered Agent Orange for domestic use, the air force treated Newton's proposal as "premature." The EPA subsequently denied air force requests to register Agent Orange for commercial purposes and forbid the sale of the chemical compound to Latin American countries.[66]

When the EPA suspended the use of 2,4,5-T in 1979, the decision attracted a firestorm of criticism from the forest products industry and several OSU faculty. Michael Newton insisted there was "near universal agreement among scientists in the weed science and toxicology fields that 2,4,5-T is safe to use." Jim Witt in agricultural chemistry called the EPA's studies inaccurate and dishonest. OSU faculty opposing the herbicide's use thought the university had sacrificed its credibility in assuming the role of an advocate. Willamette Week's editor Phil Keisling cited the university's long tradition of supporting studies on the use of herbicides. In the wake of the delisting of phenoxy herbicides (2,4,5-T and silvex), College of Forestry researchers John Walstad and Frank Dost reviewed the scientific literature on the health risks of the herbicides and concluded that 2,4,5-T and silvex did not pose "an appreciable risk to human health." They attributed the delisting to inaccurate news stories, "sensationalized reporting," and "a discrepancy between perceived and actual risks of herbicide use."[67]

President MacVicar defended university faculty and the extension service against charges that they were practicing a "pro-herbicide bias." When Lawrence Langdon of Cottage Grove made this accusation, the president responded that herbicides were only one means of controlling weeds and

brush in crops and forest environments. In a follow-up letter, Langdon accused toxicologist Frank Dost of ignoring the hazards in the use of toxic
materials. MacVicar responded again that a preponderance of the scientific
community agreed with Dost that, when properly used, herbicides presented
no hazard to "warm-blooded animals, including human beings." To another
writer who argued that herbicides posed a health hazard to humans, the
president indicated that Oregon State University scientists had been leaders
in providing reliable information on the use of herbicides in forest and field
environments. Their work had "been objective and deliberate in both the
design and execution of their experiments."[68] It is important to remember
that these exchanges were taking place just as Vietnam War veterans were
building their case for disability benefits as a consequence of their exposure
to Agent Orange.

The School of Humanities and Social Sciences curricular programs posed
vexing problems for President MacVicar throughout his tenure. He wrote
Emeritus President James Jensen in 1971 that "a small group of dissidents"
wanted more dramatic changes than were "feasible or desirable." The president
believed the faculty's "terrible inferiority complex" unlikely to reverse itself
in the near future. He questioned their scholarship amid the plentitude of
doctoral candidates available and wondered why they were unable to appreci-
ate that teaching "undergraduates was an honorable profession." MacVicar
thought the school's middle-age faculty had been conditioned to believe that
unless their disciplines had graduate programs, they lacked status. He had
similar problems with the Division of Health and Physical Education, where
he had been "pushing and shoving and generally being mildly obnoxious" in
an effort to merge the physical education departments for men and women
into a single unit. He believed such a move would bring prominence to an
area that had been mediocre.[69]

Humanities and Social Sciences, renamed the College of Liberal Arts in
1973, had affirmative action problems in the late 1970s when data indicated
disparities between minorities applying for positions in the college and the
percentage being hired. MacVicar notified Dean David King that HEW's
Office for Civil Rights would be keeping an eye on tenure-track appointments in the college, looking especially at screening requirements to assure
that departments were following regulations when minority candidates were
finalists. In a different tone from his exchanges with HEW, MacVicar told the
liberal arts dean that OSU had one of the few approved affirmative action
plans in the Northwest, and that he was anxious to maintain cordial relations

with HEW's Office for Civil Rights. If liberal arts departments used greater care in screening candidates, it would help maintain the university's positive relations with HEW.[70]

Unlike his two predecessors, A. L. Strand and James Jensen, MacVicar made little effort to bring greater parity between liberal arts and the professional schools. Moreover, his reactionary attitude may have slowed advances in the humanities and social sciences. When Associated Students vice president Cleora Adams introduced a bill in the student senate to raise the standards in the College of Liberal Arts to that of the School of Science and the professional schools, the president demurred, remarking that in "institutions of our type," graduate studies in liberal arts were interdisciplinary. "Standards," he reminded Adams, "should be related to the mission of the institution and the mission of the College of Liberal Arts as defined by the governing board." It was inappropriate, he believed, to compare OSU with universities whose responsibilities differed from land-grant schools. Although he agreed that liberal arts programs should not be substandard, MacVicar insisted that the college should be compared with those in similar institutions.[71]

The problem for MacVicar and his administrators was allocating scarce resources in an institution perpetually struggling to fund programs. When OSU's long-range planning committee recommended creating programs to enhance research opportunities for liberal arts faculty, the president approved a one-time allocation of $25,000 "on an experimental basis" to determine the faculty's response and the quality of their research proposals. Future allocations would depend on faculty publications and the availability of funds. The president asked planning committee members to review the program's success, which "must be highly productive if it is not to create serious internal stresses between other units of the University which have been deprived of resources."[72]

MacVicar's executive decisions show him to be a land-grant institutionalist, who fully agreed with State Board of Higher Education guidelines allocating degrees and majors among the state's universities. In a 1976 letter to Miles Romney, vice chancellor for the state system, MacVicar explained that it was difficult to discuss OSU's liberal arts program in the face of the board's broad policy decisions. Although the state board and the legislature had been inconsistent in adhering to the allocation adopted in 1932, he had "always promoted the non-duplication principle which presumably is state policy." MacVicar asked Romney to prepare documents indicating the degree to which "the principle of non-duplication" had been eroded, urging the board to confront the issue at its next meeting "in a forthright manner."[73]

When College of Liberal Arts Dean Gordon Gilkey announced his retirement in the fall of 1976, MacVicar's job posting described the college as inheritor of a lengthy tradition of divided curricular responsibilities that limited graduate degrees to a single interdisciplinary program. "This rather unusual circumstance," the president announced, required a person with a commitment to undergraduate education and an understanding that there was an opportunity to develop graduate programs highlighting interdisciplinary approaches. The president emphasized the same point in a letter to Mansel Keene of the California State University System, accentuating the need for a dynamic leader who understood the parameters of operating in a system with "non-duplicative programs of graduate education."[74]

For the remainder of his presidency, MacVicar believed that state board guidelines largely adhered to the non-duplication principles of 1932. In a note to Emery Castle, former dean of OSU's graduate school, whom he visited in Washington, DC, in 1977, MacVicar remarked that the state board had reaffirmed its opposition to graduate programs for the College of Liberal Arts, with the chancellor and vice chancellor in full agreement. When pressed by constituents about the absence of graduate programs in the behavioral sciences, the president would defer to state board policies to explain the constraints on such graduate degrees. Although OSU's failure to develop social science graduate degrees was embedded in long-ago decisions, he regretted that "rural sociology," offered in many land-grant schools, did not develop at Oregon State.[75]

Robert MacVicar was a personable, old-fashioned, hands-on president. He was direct and straightforward in communicating, even when he disagreed with someone. From all indications he loved Oregon, traveling about the state to visit experiment stations and extension offices, and forming delightful insights that he would pass on to friends. Visiting Baker City in eastern Oregon shortly after his arrival, he described the countryside as beautiful and rivaling in some respects "the more pretentious coast and Cascade Range." He was forthright about his administrative style, describing it as one that fit well with the looser organizational style Oregonians were accustomed to. MacVicar was mistaken, however, when he told a friend in 1972 that he delegated authority and responsibility to a greater degree than most institutional executives. He also acknowledged that, of the two campuses at Southern Illinois University, he found the liberal arts people on the Carbondale campus "difficult to cope with" and always felt more comfortable at the "free-wheeling" atmosphere in Edwardsville, the land-grant school.[76]

MacVicar's hands-on habit was illustrated when he told Gil Polanski, representative of the Oregon State Employees Association, that he greatly appreciated his organization, because it was not a labor union, admitting that organizations "adopting union tactics" distressed him. Rather than communicating by letter, MacVicar urged Polanski to phone and discuss matters in person. One of the problems with communication was the absence of informal contact. Endless correspondence could drive the president to frustration, as it did when a disgruntled father kept complaining about the omission of his daughter's photo in the *Beaver* yearbook. Yet another letter prompted the president to "be redundant in my response. . . . I regret sincerely the error and have expressed regret repeatedly through you to your daughter." He repeated again his willingness to refund the cost of the yearbook, "an offer in the past you refused to accept."[77] None of MacVicar's successors ever delved so intimately into institutional policy.

Nearing the end of his presidency, MacVicar reflected on student unrest beleaguering college campuses in the late 1960s and 1970s. He placed those circumstances in a national and global context, citing the Cultural Revolution in China, "The Great Leap Forward," Mao Zedong's effort to modernize the Chinese economy. His experiences on the Carbondale campus and at Oregon State convinced him that students used issues such as racial discrimination, social injustice, and the Vietnam War to challenge authority, with academic institutions a "convenient vehicle" to attack. College students "were caught up in a phenomenon that did not have [a] strong intellectual basis but was clearly one of great emotional intensity." The effects of those events rested in policy statements, the appointment of commissions, and "statutory and regulatory requirements," but the "passion . . . has gone out of the situation." In the end, he preferred leaving the question of historical significance to "historian[s] and others more competent than I."[78]

11
Becoming a Modern University

When John Byrne succeeded Robert MacVicar as president in November 1984, Oregon was in the midst of a severe recession in the wood-products industry and a downturn in agricultural prices, both standard-bearers of the state's economy. Although the state's natural-resource sectors had suffered brief slumps following the Second World War, the spring planting season and renewed logging following winter storms usually righted the economy and put people back to work. At the outset of the 1980s, however, the closure of labor-intensive old-growth sawmills devastated western Oregon towns like Coos Bay and Roseburg and the central and eastern Oregon communities of Bend, Burns, and Baker. A parallel recession in agriculture and the technological displacement of workers in both sectors added to the state's distress. People living along Oregon's natural-resource byways witnessed mill and cannery closures and support service jobs disappearing.[1]

The four counties with the highest unemployment in 1984 were timber-dependent: Curry, 20.7 percent; Coos, 15.4; Baker, 14.2; and Douglas, 13.7. Beyond the I-5 corridor, technological and capital shifts and increased mechanization in the woods and on the farm left in its wake high unemployment, blighted communities, and persistent efforts to restructure local economies. Those economic troubles, most pronounced in southwestern Oregon and forested counties east of the Cascades, rubbed raw historic divisions between rural and urban Oregon. With Portland's emerging high-tech sector leading the way, the lower Willamette Valley economy had begun to recover by the mid-1980s, prompting economist Charles Allcock to fear that worsening political and cultural differences between country and city would become an increasingly "divisive factor" in Oregon politics.[2] Those conditions set the stage for the turbulent future that John Byrne would experience as president.

Byrne's affiliation with the university dates to 1960, when he joined the oceanography department as a marine biologist, becoming chair in 1968 and the first dean of the School of Oceanography in 1972. Byrne later served as dean of research from 1977 to 1980 before leaving for Washington, DC, in 1981 to head the National Oceanic and Atmospheric Administration (NOAA). After four years with NOAA, he returned to Corvallis as OSU's fourteenth president. Before assuming office, Byrne let it be known that he would restructure the university's administration, asking President MacVicar to fill positions on an acting basis only. Byrne's objective was to free the president from routine and mundane time commitments.[3]

His predecessor, Robert MacVicar, did not have a second-in-command, a provost, which left him with the everyday responsibilities as chief operating officer. He met regularly with deans, responded directly to their requests, and signed out-of-state travel vouchers. "For Mac, that management style worked," Byrne acknowledged, but "that was not the manner in which I planned to occupy my time as president." When he arrived in Corvallis, Byrne remembers many people wanting time with the president, because MacVicar responded to issues "to the satisfaction of the *individual*." Advice for the new president came from every direction, some of it, Byrne admitted, helpful.[4]

The *Oregonian* predicted Byrne's NOAA experiences would serve him well. His first problem was the struggling football program, again in search of a coach to bring an end to fourteen losing seasons. Athletic Director Dee Andros wrote Byrne—still in Washington, DC—citing the urgency of hiring a football coach should Joe Avezzano be dismissed after five losing seasons (six wins and forty-six losses). Andros advised completing the hire by December 6 to meet recruiting deadlines, insisting that the screening committee be limited to three people to avoid the "drawn-out, cumbersome, and unsatisfactory selection system following affirmative action guidelines." Byrne indicates in his memoir that he wanted to hear Avezzano's side of the story.[5]

This frustrated Andros, who thought the president should act quickly on the athletic board's advice. Andros fueled the rumor mill, leaking to reporters a potential candidates list. "The thing I cannot read right now is what Dr. Byrne is really thinking," Andros told an *Oregonian* beat writer. When Byrne decided against retaining Avezzano, he bypassed the athletic board and announced the appointment of a "specially constituted advisory group"—faculty, students, athletic department members, and community supporters—to draft a list of candidates for head football coach. He hoped to have the new coach aboard by mid-December. To satisfy the media, Byrne reported that the advisory group was identifying and evaluating candidates. He made clear who was in charge of the search and the need for confidentiality to attract highly qualified coaches. Byrne further upset convention, declaring that the university's Intercollegiate Athletics Board would not be involved in the selection.[6]

The next few weeks turned into a comedy of errors, with Andros testing Byrne's mandate for confidentiality. Early in December, University of Idaho coach Dennis Erickson let it be known he was a candidate, as did California State Fullerton coach Gene Murphy. While the athletic director acknowledged the names of some candidates, he told a reporter on December 5, "We'd like to be able to name a new coach this weekend," acknowledging that the president would be making the decision. Erickson, who visited campus on December 4 and 5, was annoyed at the spectacle, because it was hurting recruiting on the Idaho campus. "I just wish Oregon State would make up its mind."[7] The rumor circus continued while Byrne was traveling, including a stopover at the Pac-10 Conference meeting in San Francisco. In the interim, the *Oregonian's* respected George Pasero predicted on December 12 that Dennis Erickson would be the next coach. Two days later Gene Murphy withdrew his candidacy and Erickson followed suit the next day.[8]

When Byrne returned to Corvallis, he deplored the lack of confidentiality, commending the press "for its ingenuity in finding out what's going on." Andros blamed affirmative action for holding up the search and claimed that Erickson was his first choice. There were recriminations beyond the university, some of them directed at the president. Beaver Club president Harry Teel questioned Byrne's qualifications for selecting a football coach. Pete Pifer, OSU's leading all-time running back when he graduated in 1966 and a member of the search committee, resigned in protest, telling Pasero that the university was embarrassing itself. Pifer chastised Byrne for going against the wishes of the Beaver Club and athletic director and listening to "others who have little or no experience to offer."[9]

In the midst of the search, but unknown to the media, President Byrne asked for Andros's resignation as athletic director, reprimanding him for "unacceptable and inexcusable" behavior in hiring a coach, failing to follow affirmative action guidelines, breaching confidentiality, and discouraging the president from having a voice in the selection. Byrne cited the facts involving Andros and the botched pursuit to fill the coaching vacancy, especially the athletic director's behavior in a search to be "conducted with the utmost confidentiality." That failure cost the university an opportunity to hire a young coach of good character.[10] The president had clearly made his point about decision-making to the power brokers involved with OSU's football program.

Despite his devoted supporters, "The Great Pumpkin," as Andros was known, had been a polarizing figure for more than a decade, causing divisions among alumni and athletic board members who opposed his appointment as athletic director in 1975 and the renewal of his contract in 1979. When Coach

Craig Fertig was dismissed in 1979, critics urged President MacVicar to send Andros packing as well. Those opposing his reappointment cited a litany of shortcomings and complaints: the absence of "strong moral leadership at the top;" the need for a "complete housecleaning in order to turn the program around"; the "lack of athletic department leadership"; the athletic director "manifests a mediocre leadership style"; "who runs OSU? You or him"; and Andros "never should have been hired in the first place." Some negative letters were ill-tempered and lacking in grace, but others carried a clear message: "He appears to meet many people well and has a certain following in the valley area but if he has the qualifications as an athletic director for this large of a university, they are not evident."[11] Byrne's decision to remove Andros drew on two decades of memory about OSU athletics.

The university announced the hiring of Utah State University athletic director Dave Kragthorpe as the next football coach in late December 1984. Byrne first offered the job to Sam Boghosian, a former assistant to Andros and now an assistant coach with the Los Angeles Raiders. Although he was not Byrne's first choice, the fifty-one-year-old Kragthorpe came with impressive credentials and praise from Brigham Young's celebrated coach LaVell Edwards. To flesh out OSU's athletic department, Byrne appointed Sylvia Moore interim director of intercollegiate athletics. Moore, the director of women's athletics, had solid recommendations from across campus to guide the athletic department until a permanent director was hired.[12]

The president released a public statement in early January announcing Andros' appointment as special assistant for athletic development, a position where his talents would be used as a fund-raiser. Byrne reported that the two had agreed on the arrangement to promote the best interests of the university's athletic program. "Mr. Andros and I have differences in philosophy, standards and methods of operation concerning both the role and responsibility of an athletic director" that required changing the leadership in the department. Andros, who would receive an increase in salary, the president announced, had "collaborated and agreed on the contents of this statement."[13]

In a letter to NOAA colleague John Carey, Byrne confessed that his first weeks in office were hectic, although the pace had slowed from "full throttle to 7/8 throttle," allowing him to attack unanswered letters. While his years with NOAA were busy, Byrne's brief stint as president had exceeded the pace in Washington. There were important differences, however: while social gatherings at NOAA were optional, as president of Oregon State University they were mandatory. He quickly learned there was little discretionary time for personal matters. At the moment, he told Carey, he was waiting for the report of three administrators who had just visited campus to look "under all sorts of administrative rocks." The review team included Harold Enarson, retired president of Ohio State University; Charles Sturtz, vice chancellor of administration at the University of Maryland; and Robert Clodius of the National Association of State Universities and Land-Grant Colleges. As they were leaving, they told Byrne that far too many people were reporting directly to the president. That would change, he wrote Carey, pending approval of the State Board of Higher Education.[14]

Byrne's experiences in reorganizing NOAA prompted his efforts to streamline and improve the efficiency of OSU's administrative structure. In a letter to the reviewers, he included an organizational chart to illustrate the problem. With many top administrative positions vacant or the incumbents close to retirement, the time seemed opportune for action. He sought advice on a wide range of issues—"academic programs, continuing education, personnel functions, external relations, international activities, [and] communications." Byrne was interested in delegating authority and responsibility and holding officials accountable. He asked the reviewers for their observations and suggestions.[15]

With a firm understanding of Robert MacVicar's hands-on administrative style, the consultants' reports were remarkably appropriate. Ohio State's Harold Enarson cautioned against criticizing the previous administration—they should be "*respected*," because they may have been a good fit for the person and the time. He agreed with Byrne's initial observation—too many people had access to the president. Institutions, he wrote, outgrow their leaders, and "organization matters"; therefore the first change should be creating the office of provost and vice president for academic affairs and appointing a trusted associate to fill the position on an acting basis (to allay the fears of the faculty). The provost would act on all matters academic and be "second-in-command" to the president. Enarson recommended a strong budget office, with an experienced person in charge and with similar functions grouped together. Under this arrangement, the president would need to deal directly with vice presidents.[16]

Enarson's report abounded with the wisdom of one who had been chief executive of a major university. "Sleeping dogs and sleeping bureaucrats offer possible hazards," he cautioned, warning Byrne that "power is slippery stuff." He believed that faculty deserved interest in "the strictly academic part of the enterprise"—therefore, the need for a vice president for academic affairs. Byrne should appoint the provost and vice president for academic affairs first, because academic issues were primary. Other vice presidents should include student services, finance and administration, research and graduate studies, and university relations. The alumni office should be watched carefully, because it served the president's interests. While the alumni would involve time and energy, their power was "grossly exaggerated." Enarson added a final warning—when presidents add staff and salaries, the media will pounce and accuse him of extravagance. In those instances, Byrne would be left alone, with the faculty standing mute or joining the chorus of naysayers.[17]

While there was some symmetry among the reports, Enarson's was the most substantive. Charles Sturtz, with the University of Maryland system, complimented Oregon State's physical environment: "Your campus is far and away the best kept, cleanest, and most environmentally attractive that I have experienced in a long time." The president should treasure its beauty and not tamper with it. Like Enarson, he advised a second-in-command—a provost/vice president structure—with vice presidents for academic affairs, administration, and finance representing the core offices. Robert Clodius, who represented the perspective of the association of land-grant universities and colleges, repeated the suggestion about cabinet administrators, with a model mirroring Enarson's suggestions. A vice president for finance and administration should be a first-class person, and he urged Byrne to appoint vice presidents at an early date and give faculty a voice in screening but not final selections.[18]

Byrne acted quickly on the consultants' recommendations, sending an April memorandum to administrators and the faculty senate executive committee, advising them of the administrative reorganization "to render faster and more efficient service." He enclosed an organizational chart, bringing attention to vice president positions and their responsibilities and asking for written comments on the proposal by May 15. The tentative plan included five vice presidents (two already existing): academic affairs and provost, research and graduate studies, finance and administration, student affairs, and university relations. In addition to the consultants' recommendations, Byrne assigned the legal counsel, affirmative action officer, and athletic department to the president's staff, the latter reflecting a national move "to reassert oversight" over athletic programs. The restructured administration, according to the *Oregonian*, indicated that Byrne would keep "athletics squarely in his hand."[19]

As the consultants predicted, Byrne heard from those who disagreed: one respondent to an OSU fund-raising caller questioned the need for additional vice presidents in the face of strained legislative budgets. Under present arrangements, Byrne responded, students, faculty, and staff needed the president's approval for virtually every activity. The restructuring would enable the university to better "serve the people of Oregon."[20] The State Board of Higher Education approved the new administrative structure, announcing that three existing administrators would be appointed vice presidents with different titles—Theron Parsons, vice president for finance and administration; Jo Anne Trow, student affairs; and George Keller, research and graduate studies. The remaining two vice presidents, academic affairs and provost and university relations, would be filled on an interim basis, pending the conclusion of a national search.[21]

The administration's second major initiative, reflecting President James Jensen's commission on university goals, would establish guidelines for long-range planning. Unlike Jensen's three-member commission, which spent several months fact-finding and interviewing people, Byrne wanted everyone involved in the planning process. The dust had barely settled over administrative restructuring when he appointed the Long-Range Planning Commission. For the president, planning involved "a rationally conceived plan," a malleable blueprint to improve an institution over time. Planning would be no pie-in-the-sky idea, but would focus on developing realistic and dynamic principles to assist in preparing budgets and to use as a tool to implement goals and objectives.[22]

To achieve the objectives, the president and the faculty senate created three committees—the external environment, the institution, and missions and goals—each to draft documents for the strategic plan. He gave the committees a six-week window to complete their work, which they accomplished before the deadline. From that point, the planning commission solicited ideas from faculty, students, alumni, and constituencies interested in OSU's future. Subdivided into committees and task forces, the Long-Range Planning Commission prepared a review draft in March 1987, "Preparing for the Future: Strategic Planning at Oregon State University." Byrne presented the document to the faculty as a process that would undergo revision at regular intervals.[23]

The president emphasized that the planning document would help guide budget priorities and schedules for accomplishing objectives, with primacy given to academic and operational planning. The academic component mandated a comprehensive review of curriculum, especially of co-curricular offerings. On the operations side, the highest priority would be providing competitive salaries for faculty and staff. Beyond those issues, the president listed improving the university's facilities, especially the library, and advancing OSU's computing capabilities. While those objectives depended

After several failed efforts, proponents of capping Oregon property taxes succeeded in narrowly passing a property tax limitation measure on November 6, 1990, prompting student protests. Measure 5 reduced support for all state programs, including higher education. The measure required the state to make up the revenue that local school districts lost through limitations on property taxes. Courtesy of the OSU Special Collections and Archives Research Center.

on legislative appropriations, others could be initiated immediately. Byrne's planning document would undergo revision in 1990, with an updated title, "Creating the Future," and when the administration readied a third effort, it faced the daunting task of the fallout from Ballot Measure 5, Oregon's severe tax limitation initiative.[24]

Enrollments in America's public institutions of higher education reflect external environments—wars, recessions, social conflicts—issues that affected colleges and universities with specialized programs. Contrary to popular belief, college enrollment often increases during economic downturns, based on the perception that an academic degree would be an asset in the job market. What happened to enrollment in Oregon's public colleges and universities between 1970 and 2000 would muddy all such correlations. The most striking instance of enrollment flatlining may well be Oregon State University, with 15,509 students registered in 1970–1971 and 16,788 for 2000–2001. The University of Oregon had only slightly larger growth numbers during the same period, 15,249 in 1971 and 17,843 in 2001. It is not an oxymoron to say that the State of Oregon has been less than charitable in its support of education at any level.[25]

Much of this period embraced the presidencies of Robert MacVicar and John Byrne. Enrollments during those years do not reflect the quality of their administrations; rather, they highlight a parsimonious legislature and a public that mistrusted spending on education. Those limitations circumscribed Oregon State University's operations for nearly three decades. During those years, the state shifted from an economy dependent on labor-intensive lumbering and agriculture to an economy requiring an educated work force in high-tech industries and technologically sophisticated natural-resource industries. An important reckoning point in Oregon's calculus is the intersection of white- and blue-collar occupations, which crossed somewhere around 1960 when sawmill and agricultural processors began centralizing facilities and employing fewer workers.[26] With major workforce changes originating in the early 1980s recession and the restructuring of the timber economy, the Oregon public was caught in the warp of a troubled present and an uncertain future.

Although the state's problematic economy forced President Byrne to modify his plans to modernize the university, the administration allocated funds where most needed in the budget cycle for 1985–1986. Under the disbursement formula, the president redirected funding upgrades to the library, computing, and the Educational Opportunities Program. The library had been underfunded for years, and Byrne intended to increase its budget over the next few years. Computing was in a similar fix, placing the university "woefully behind" other institutions in computer technology. The Educational Opportunities Program was important to a university with an increasingly diverse body of students, many of whom needed assistance if they were to survive in an academic environment. Byrne ordered a reduction of 10 percent in all college budgets, with the reallocated savings distributed among the library, computing, and educational opportunities.[27]

The president's funding strategy succeeded, but it would be the only successful budget reordering during his presidency. As the next funding cycle approached, newly elected governor Neil Goldschmidt tightened the reins on spending to stave off threats of a tax limitation measure similar to California's Proposition 13. The governor decided against raising taxes to fund state programs and directed state agencies to grant employees a 2 percent salary increase for each year of the biennium—to be funded internally. The governor's decision created, Byrne wrote Chancellor William Davis, an immediate budget crisis and shortchanged the university's land-grant mandate. The policy would have "a very serious *long lasting* negative effect on Oregon State University." The move stunned department heads, who were forced to cut their budgets and provide salary increases at the same time.[28]

The Byrne administration adopted a variety of approaches to achieve internal savings to fund payroll requirements. Departments were eliminated, others were merged, faculty members close to retirement were offered early severance packages, and hiring was frozen to achieve the university's reduction of $2.26 million. Referred to in administrative memoranda as the "2% Goldschmidt cuts," OSU's reductions were greater than those at the University of Oregon and Portland State University. Although the process was unpleasant, Byrne characterized the university's response as reasonable and orderly— giving proper attention to the institution's mission; protecting the integrity of teaching, research, and service; preserving important academic programs; and maintaining affirmative action programs and the tenure system.[29]

When the higher education board moved to change from a quarter to a semester system in the spring of 1987, department and college committees launched the tedious work of converting courses designed for three ten-week terms to two sixteen-week semesters. Because of significant resistance at Oregon State University, the faculty senate asked the state board to suspend the conversion to a semester system until June 1989. The faculty wanted time to examine the advantages of conversion because of other priorities facing higher education. In a cover letter to Chancellor Davis, President Byrne agreed that this was not an opportune moment to shift to a semester calendar. When Governor Neil Goldschmidt appointed new members to the State Board of Higher Education, the new board reversed the conversion to a semester system. President Byrne was blunt about the sudden change, a pronouncement "made in response to *political* forces in the absence of any overwhelming *academic* reason."[30]

In another important event, the university commissioned a team of fifteen academics from the Northwest Association of Schools and Colleges who visited OSU between February 27 and March 2, 1990, as part of the institution's accreditation evaluation. The survey team praised the university's significant changes since its last review in 1984, especially hiring consultants to advise on reorganizing the administration, with an emphasis on "delegation and decentralization of authority." Despite the abortive effort to change from a quarter to a semester system and the governor's mandate to cut budgets and provide salary increases, the reviewers commended the university for its strategic planning, producing two "milestone documents," *Preparing for the Future* and *Creating the Future.* Under "Facilities and Equipment," the team found that the university, like other land-grant institutions, had used maintenance funds to continue basic operations. The consequence was a great backlog in maintenance, especially for poorly designed structures built in the 1960s.[31]

The academic side of the accreditation review singled out the library for special attention. Its materials budget fell far short of membership requirements in the Association of Research Libraries. Two bright notes, however, were the $25 million fund-raising campaign to expand the library and the recent acquisition of Linus Pauling's personal papers. The team praised agricultural sciences, forestry, and engineering for forward-looking approaches to facilities and research. Support for instruction in the College of Science was "spotty," a problem that required the attention of the administration. The reviewers devoted more space to the College of Liberal Arts than any other unit. Facilities and equipment for music and theater did not meet Northwest Association standards, and faculty salaries were very low. The team applauded the emphasis on research and scholarship in the humanities, although department chairs and the dean should provide more resources for research. The report commended the reduction in teaching loads for liberal arts faculty from three to two courses per term, the university standard. Those reservations aside, the commission reaffirmed OSU's accreditation.[32]

The ink was barely dry on Goldschmidt's 2 percent reduction/salary increases when the university faced another athletic program budget crisis. Because the State Board of Higher Education required intercollegiate athletics at OSU, the UO, and PSU to be self-supporting, they were forbidden to use state general funds for athletics and had to reimburse their institutions for services such as physical plant support. Those policies caused all three athletic departments to run significant deficits. In a memorandum to Chancellor Davis in April 1987, Byrne indicated that only two of OSU's intercollegiate sports contributed funds to athletics—men's basketball and football. While he was reluctant to eliminate any sport, he intended to drop women's softball and fund crew from outside sources. Within a year, however, the administration suspended both men's and women's track and field programs. Although costs per participant for track and field were low, the number of athletes involved made the sport expensive.[33]

One of President Byrne's regular correspondents during this period was Jud Blakely, a former OSU student-body president and OSU grad (1965), who had served in Vietnam. After military service, Blakely formed a consulting firm, writing speeches and coaching corporate executives in the art of public presentations. Byrne wrote candidly about problems funding intercollegiate athletics and whether the university could continue to compete successfully in the Pac-10. OSU athletics were "in deep trouble," Byrne reported in the summer of 1988, with the odds of increased funding and a quick turnaround in the football program "not good on any count." With the smallest budget in the Pac-10 and the need to balance men's and women's sports, he worried that the university's diminished athletic program would damage the institution's prestige. If it were possible to maintain academic associations with UCLA, Stanford, Berkeley, and other Pac-10 schools "without being involved in the intercollegiate athletic maelstrom, we might have an entirely different situation." No one had an answer to that problem. While it might be preferable to seek more support for academic programs, Byrne thought it necessary to "pay our dues of time and effort for these 'non-academic matters' before we can enjoy the benefits of those other more enjoyable conflicts." Writing to Blakely two months later, Byrne cited the legislature's "generally negative" attitude toward higher education as a serious problem.[34]

The Athletics Advisory Board held fast to certain principles in the face of the funding crisis—OSU would remain in the Pac-10; football, women's volleyball, and men's and women's basketball were inviolate; and the university would meet the NCAA's minimum number of required sports. The advisory board believed the institution should support a few strong competitive programs, holding fast to the importance of gender equity in sports.[35] Oregon's funding difficulties with college and university athletics improved a bit when the 1989 legislature created the Oregon Sports Lottery authority to permit betting on National Football League games. Under the program, 88 percent of lottery funds would support athletics, and 12 percent would support scholarships for athletes. The State Board of Higher Education changed the formula in 1992, mandating that 30 percent of the money should support revenue-generating sports, with 70 percent going to non-revenue programs (50 percent of each institution's appropriation would be for women's athletics). Sports lottery funding for university and college athletics continued—with some changes in distributing funds—until January 2007, when the legislature disbanded sports betting and replaced the revenue with regular lottery money from the economic development fund.[36]

When Governor Neil Goldschmidt unexpectedly decided not to run for a second term, Oregon's gubernatorial contest in 1990 featured two well-known political figures, Democratic secretary of state Barbara Roberts and Republican attorney general Dave Frohnmayer. Ultraconservative candidate Al Mobley complicated the race when he entered as an independent, with political pundits predicting correctly that he would damage Frohnmayer's prospects more than Roberts's. Ballot Measure 5, the property tax limitation measure that threatened to drastically diminish funds for public education and other services, loomed in the minds of many. When voters delivered their verdict, Barbara Roberts had won the governor's race, and the tax limitation measure passed 574,833 to 522,022.[37] Ballot Measure 5 would mean continuing struggles with the state's tax system.

The title of President Byrne's report to the chancellor's office for 1990–1991 and the two epigrams that follow serve as powerful representations of the struggles that Ballot Measure 5 would entail:

Crossing the Divide to New Realities

"These are the times that try men's souls."
　　　　　　　　　—Thomas Payne

"It was the best of times; it was the worst of times."
　　　　　　　　　—Charles Dickens

Byrne predicted the budget cuts would bring greater change to Oregon State University "than anything that has taken place in recent decades." The fiscal emergency that ensued created "unprecedented levels of uncertainty and unrest." For faculty and staff during the late winter and spring of 1991, the hemorrhaging was apparent everywhere—the elimination of the College of Education and the Honors College; "discontinuing" the Departments of Religious Studies and Journalism and the Program in Broadcast Media in the College of Liberal Arts; discontinuing the General Science Department in the College of Science; eliminating the Department of Management Science in the College of Business and suspending its program in hotel, restaurant, and tourism; Agricultural Sciences merged the Departments of Poultry and Animal Sciences and reduced its majors; and the Department of Forestry eliminated its pulp and paper program and reduced courses elsewhere. Other colleges—Home Economics, Health and Human Performances, and Veterinary Medicine—reduced course offerings and programs, and cut administrative staff. University-wide cuts included one dean, five associate deans, and eleven department chairs. The university's popular Horner Museum, located in the basement of Gill Coliseum, was targeted for closure (with its holdings eventually transferred to the Benton County Historical Museum in Philomath).[38]

Similar to long-standing efforts to dismantle Oregon's land use planning system, property tax limitation measures were not new to the state's voters. Patterned after California's Proposition 13, the Oregon measure, a constitutional amendment, became effective in the 1991–1992 tax year and would cut local property taxes by 51 percent by 1995–1996. When unhappy citizens passed a more restrictive Measure 47 in 1996, the legislature referred Measure

50 to voters to correct its technical flaws. For estimating local property taxes, Measure 50 limited growth in assessed value to 3 percent annually. Under the new fiscal arrangements, the legislature was expected to replace lost revenue to local school districts.[39] The property tax limitations marked the onset of steady decreases in state funding for higher education.

Higher education's share of general fund appropriations declined from 12.2 percent in the 1987–1989 biennium to 7 percent in 1999–2001. During the same period, the general fund grew from $3.7 billion in 1987–1989 to $10.7 billion in 1999–2001, with higher education appropriations increasing from $456,745,165 to only $755,074,000. The legislature's increasing responsibilities for public schools explains the percentage decrease in state support for higher education. The repercussions of Measure 5 extended far into the future, with Oregon spending less per capita on higher education at the outset of the twenty-first century than any other western state and ranking forty-fourth nationwide. To sustain academic programs, Oregon institutions raised resident undergraduate tuition and fees, with the largest uptick coming after Measure 5.[40]

Although Byrne expected tuition to increase as much as 40 percent, he confided to Jud Blakely in January 1991 that the university would survive "a different but hopefully stronger institution." He hoped to find ways to improve liberal arts and the institution's computing processes. Less than a month later, he wrote Blakely again with the gritty details of the mandated reduction in state funds—$12.2 million for the first year of the biennium. Byrne estimated the loss of 154 faculty and seventy-one staff positions, "one of the most difficult tasks ever undertaken at OSU." The cutbacks would mean some two thousand fewer students. The president pointed to an irony—"Oregon is not an impoverished state"—its economy was growing, indicating that it could improve its support for education at all levels.[41]

Athletics, once peripheral to the central operations of Oregon universities, now involved all major institutions, faculty senates, and the vigilant eyes of administrators and alumni. In an effort to provide budgetary relief, in October 1991 the state's Interinstitutional Faculty Senate encouraged the state board and the chancellor's office to seek alternative funding for athletics outside the general fund. OSU's faculty senate endorsed the measure, sharing its frustration that athletics should not be supported at the expense of academics. While athletics had symbolic value to higher education, academic needs should be a funding priority. David Schacht, retired science and technology librarian, supported the faculty senate resolution, telling President Byrne that after years of underfunding, OSU's library continued to cancel important scientific and technical journals. He agreed with the president that women's athletics should be funded, but criticized supporting "an expensive football team with a meager academic record."[42]

Ray Leidich, a former collegiate athlete and casualty of Measure 5, thought it insensitive to fund athletic programs with tax dollars. As the former head of OSU Academic Services, he was familiar with the subpar grades and SAT scores of many football and basketball players. He urged Byrne to support academic programs rather than those favored by a "smaller, yet more vocal, minority." Janet Meranda, a staff member and a graduate student, was even more forceful, accusing the chancellor's office of planning "to steal money from academic programs . . . to finance intercollegiate athletics." Finally, Arnold Appleby of crop science indicated that the athletic department was "different," following its own set of rules. Unlike the athletic department, "the rest of us are not allowed to exceed our budgets."[43]

Measure 5 compounded the difficulty of funding athletics. When Weldon Ihrig of the chancellor's office reviewed OSU's proposed athletic budget for 1990–1991, he thought it would balance if "the assumptions made about revenues and expenses are reasonable." Although he questioned "under-budgeted" items for recruiting and shortfalls in revenue, Ihrig believed the department could defend those estimates. Seven months later, athletics department head Dutch Baughman reported declining revenue from the Pac-10 and "several projections that will not develop." In a memo to the Beaver Club in May 1991, Baughman indicated the need to cut $500,000 from the budget. By October he was rallying university athletic supporters to ask the state board to provide $1.5 million to Oregon State University and the University of Oregon and $350,000 to Portland State. Lottery funds would not solve the funding problems, and Baughman feared those opposing athletics had already "bent the first ear of the board." He urged Beaver Club members to contact state board members asking them to support athletics.[44]

Baughman's appeal to Beaver supporters triggered a trove of letters to the board and President Byrne urging increased state support for athletic programs. One writer insisted that "professors and narrowly focused students" should recognize that their futures depended on enrollment. College athletics was "BIG BUSINESS," and the state needed to support its athletic programs. Investing in athletics would attract new students, increase gate receipts, and increase local tax revenue. Glenn Klein, an OSU professor emeritus, supported the chancellor's efforts to fund athletics, because it was "an important part in the life of all major universities." Meeting in October

1991, OSU's Athletics Advisory Committee acknowledged that the timing of its funding request was unfortunate, because it "pits academic units against non-academic units." Zoe Ann Holmes, who served on the athletics committee and was president of the faculty senate, advised the athletic department to avoid adding to its debt.[45]

Eight years into his tenure as president, Byrne appointed a task force to review the university's sports and athletics programs. Chaired by Sally Maleug, associate dean of the College of Liberal Arts, the committee would explore the value of sports to the university, the public relations aspect of athletics, the academic prospects for sport and athletics, appropriate roles for nonathletic faculty in sports, and how to communicate those ideas to the OSU community. The task force report delivered in May 1992 stated unequivocally that the survival of athletics at the university depended on state financial support. The historic, intangible benefit of athletics to the university was the critical issue.[46]

The task force pointed out that state support for college and university athletics was fraught with disagreement. The benefits to college communities were contested by those who thought intercollegiate athletics detracted from obligations to academic excellence. Those contrasting narratives loomed ever larger in an age where football and basketball were becoming billion-dollar sports. In the end, the task force concluded that athletics brought immeasurable benefits to the university, worthy of state support. To disengage from athletics would do more harm than good. The report closed with a series of recommendations: survey students, faculty, and alumni about the value of athletics; urge the athletic department to improve its communication with the rest of campus; strengthen the academic mission of intercollegiate athletics; develop degree programs in other colleges related to athletics; elevate the athletic director as a key university administrator; and provide greater autonomy for the Athletics Advisory Committee.[47]

In a parallel move, the State Board of Higher Education appointed a special task force in February 1992 to investigate athletic funding problems at the three universities. Comprising board members, legislators, student representatives, and a university president (John Byrne), the committee met three times and drafted recommendations to provide athletic programs with stable funding: add a surtax of one dollar on all ticket sales; advise athletic departments to cut their budgets by 2 percent for 1991–1992; forgive the deficits of the three athletic departments ($6.3 million); and allow institutional funds to support women's athletics, men's and women's non-revenue sports, or charge in-state tuition for athletes. Byrne observed in his memoir that the state board accepted the recommendations at its May 1992 meeting, ushering in "a new era for intercollegiate athletics at the three universities."[48]

If John Byrne's presidency was a succession of budget misfortunes, those headaches did little to deter his successes at fund-raising. Although Robert MacVicar's achievements with donors were considerable, Byrne's efforts surpassed all previous presidents in attracting support for building projects and academic programs. The most significant construction in the early 1980s was building the Cultural and Conference Center at the southeastern corner of Twenty-Sixth Street and Western Boulevard. Renamed the LaSells Stewart Center to honor the principal donor, the center's Austin Auditorium (1,200 seats) was capable of hosting major speakers and performing arts ranging from dance to concerts. Built at the end of MacVicar's presidency, it represented the hard work of the OSU Foundation and became integral to the university's built environment.[49]

President Byrne moved beyond MacVicar's legacy with a tireless traveling schedule to garner support from donors he considered friends. With his long tenure and high visibility among OSU faculty before becoming president, he had certain advantages. Ten days after assuming office, he exchanged correspondence with Robert Lundeen, an alumnus and chairman of the board of the Dow Chemical Company. Lundeen was interested in promoting Project Foursight, a MacVicar fund-raising initiative, with one component targeting support for the humanities. Lundeen supported the initiative, because he expected to sustain the humanities with generous contributions through the remainder of Byrne's tenure as president. Byrne told Lundeen in 1986 that if Lundeen made unrestricted funds available to the university, Byrne's first priority would be to complete the humanities portion of Project Foursight and then shift to the Linus Pauling laboratory, the library expansion, and advancing campus computer networks. Per the Dow executive's suggestion, the president placed 90 percent of Lundeen's contribution that year with the university's Center for the Humanities.[50]

When OSU initiated its library expansion fund-raising campaign in 1989, Lundeen provided a "critical catalytic role," according to Byrne, promoting public and private support for the big-money project. Because Lundeen contributed $600,000 to the library expansion, Byrne urged him to write Governor Neil Goldschmidt to ask the legislature for $780,000 to develop plans and designs for the project. As it turned out, Lundeen was not the only alum associated with Dow Chemical who contributed to OSU projects. When Byrne visited the company's headquarters in Midland, Michigan, in

June 1990, he met OSU graduate Keith McKennon, president of Dow Chemical USA. Through McKennon, Byrne met eleven other employees, all OSU
alumni. When he returned to Corvallis, he urged the development office to
maintain close contacts with McKennon, who was "very enthusiastic" about
the university.[51]

F. Wayne and Gladys Valley, who lived in the San Francisco Bay area,
were among Byrne's earliest donor contacts. Both attended Oregon State College in the 1930s, with Wayne finishing his business degree at the University of
Oregon (after the state board eliminated such programs in Corvallis). Gladys
Leibbrand graduated in 1933 and worked as a secretary for the School of
Science until she married Wayne in 1940. After working in Portland, Wayne
Valley returned to the Bay Area, where he became immensely successful as a
residential home builder following the Second World War. One of the original owners of the Oakland Raiders and the first president of the short-lived
American Football League, Wayne Valley began giving to charitable causes
in the 1970s and formed the Wayne and Gladys Valley Foundation in 1977 to
manage the family's philanthropic activities.[52] They were avid Beaver sports
fans and interested in OSU's welfare.

The president's first meeting with the Valleys took place at a "social"
dinner in a San Francisco restaurant in late 1985. The next morning he
met with Wayne Valley to discuss university fund-raising efforts, including
Project Foursight. Valley told Byrne about their foundation, and that he and
Gladys were determining where they should allocate $200 to $300 million
in the endowment. While he was less interested in Project Foursight, he was
willing to fund athletics and other developments important to the university.
Byrne met with Valley two months later and again pressed funding for Project
Foursight. Valley expressed little interest in the program but was willing to
contribute elsewhere to OSU's benefit. Although much of his money was tied
up in a building enterprise merger with the Singer Corporation, he told Byrne
that he would make a major gift of stock in Singer amounting to about $1
million. Byrne wrote Valley in January 1986 expressing the thanks of liberal
arts faculty for the Valley Foundation's significant donation to the Center for
the Humanities.[53] The president had obviously made a persuasive argument.

Byrne's good relations with the Valleys persisted through the summer
of 1986 as Wayne Valley was suffering through a lengthy bout with cancer.
In mid-July, Shirley and John Byrne traveled to San Francisco to have dinner
with Wayne Valley and special guest Paul O'Connor, soon to join the Valley
Foundation. It was obvious that Wayne Valley was failing, but the gathering
went well, and the president established good rapport with O'Connor. Valley

told Byrne that the University of Oregon was also courting him, using his UO business degree as an opening for discussions. Valley remarked that for the moment he was "holding them off." Byrne wrote both Valleys in September about hiring his full administrative team, the university's academic achievements, and construction activity on campus. He told the Valleys that contributions to the OSU Foundation had increased, attributing much of that success to his conversation with Wayne Valley in December 1984, which "helped to get me started on the right track. The advice and confidence you expressed had a great impact on me. . . . The changes in athletics came about directly as a result of my conversations with you."[54] Wayne Valley died one month later.

Although Byrne established significant friendships with other donors and foundations, the Wayne and Gladys Valley relationship was special. The Valley Foundation would be a major contributor to the Center for the Humanities, the Valley Football Center, the Gladys Valley Gymnastic Center (formerly Mitchell Playhouse), and, most significantly, the Valley Library. The naming rights for the expanded library were not finalized until 1995, when Byrne received a phone call from the Valley Foundation asking what it would cost to earn naming rights to the building. The president remembered a figure of $5 million in earlier conversations with the Valley Foundation, but with John Evey of the development office nearby, he held his hand over the phone and asked again. According to Byrne, Evey held up both hands, indicating that Byrne should ask for $10 million. After deliberations on the Valley Foundation end, the deal was struck, and the refurbished building would be the Valley Library.[55] The trend for large donors in recent years to insist on naming rights for buildings is a marked departure from previous practices, in which donors asked that new structures be named after a popular teacher or administrator.

The OSU Foundation had served as Oregon State's fund-raising arm since 1947; however, with expanding donor contacts, the foundation's functions were becoming increasingly convoluted. A development fee of 10 percent charged on funds coming into the foundation caused antagonisms among the faculty and potential donors and prompted Byrne to suggest a "handling fee" of 1.5 percent on money received. To clarify responsibilities, the administration established the Office of Development, whose mission would be fund-raising. The foundation continued as a nonprofit, managing funds with a smaller staff, while the development office housed professional fund-raisers and devoted its energies to raising money. The restructured plan was in place in October 1987, with the foundation designated "custodian of funds" and the

Office of Development charged with the full portfolio of fund-raising—gift receiving, public relations, and coordinating and soliciting funds.[56]

The Valley Foundation's funding for the library expansion required Byrne to work with Paul O'Connor, still in the formative stages of assembling the endowment two years after Wayne Valley died. In the interim, Gladys Valley determined the distribution of gifts while O'Connor settled the estate and set up the foundation. Byrne learned that O'Connor was an accomplished equestrian, a graduate of the United States Naval Academy, and had spent most of his life in the Northeast. At O'Connor's suggestion, Byrne invited him to campus to attend a basketball game (Coach Ralph Miller's team was highly ranked) and visit the Marine Science Center. "If we spend some time with Paul O'Connor," Byrne wrote for the record in late 1988, "we can be very helpful to him and at the same time develop a relationship which will be to the long-term benefit of Oregon State University." The president kept in touch with Gladys Valley as well, inviting her to football games and to a whale cruise to Mexico in 1990.[57]

Other donors were no less significant than the Valleys in funding OSU initiatives. Byrne enjoyed cordial relations with Tom Autzen, a major University of Oregon donor who took pride in advancing OSU projects, such as funding an elevator for Parker Stadium. Byrne hosted a get-acquainted dinner with Autzen at Portland's Heathman Hotel in July 1986 and invited him to the annual civil war game in Corvallis that fall. Three years later, the president's friendship with Autzen was rewarded when Autzen's foundation provided major support for humanities programs.[58]

Bohemia Lumber Company brothers Faye and Loren "Stub" Stewart were also important contributors to OSU programs. Faye Stewart told the president on one occasion that he had given a quarter of a million dollars to the football program during coach Joe Avezzano's tenure and wished he had given the money to Dave Kragthorpe. In addition to bequeathing money to earn naming rights for the LaSells Stewart Center, the brothers made matching donations of $250,000 for Project Foursight's Center for Gene Research. That investment would be used to help the university leverage more than $3 million for the project, including a proposal to the Kresge Foundation for a half-million-dollar match. The president thanked Stub Stewart for his gift, telling the Bohemia executive that the university hoped it would "never abuse your generous giving commitment to OSU." Both Stewarts also supported renovations to Gill Coliseum and Parker Stadium.[59]

When Linus Pauling, Oregon State's most prestigious alumnus, announced in April 1986 that he would donate his papers and the papers of his late wife, Ava Helen Pauling, to Kerr Library, the news set in motion a series of developments that would redound to the university's academic prestige. Inventorying the Pauling papers would prove a daunting task, prompting the university to request $266,000 from the William and Flora Hewlitt Foundation to inventory and organize the extensive collection. Librarian Melvin George indicated the project would require storage rooms, working space, and staff knowledgeable about Pauling's work—a full-time special collections librarian and a clerical assistant for two years and two part-time graduate students. When the library expansion was completed in 1999, the Pauling papers became the centerpiece for scholars doing research in the fifth floor special collections room. The location of the papers at OSU influenced the Linus Pauling Institute to move from Palo Alto, California, to Corvallis in 1996.[60]

When he became president in 1984, John Byrne wanted to "create an atmosphere of change and the pursuit of excellence" at Oregon State University. This meant strengthening the liberal arts, improving the morbid condition of the library, advancing international education, and broadening the visibility of extension in university life. The library was substandard by virtually every measure. A faculty senate report in 1989 ranked OSU last in collections and support services among sixteen comparator land-grant institutions—before the passage of Ballot Measure 5. The Association of Research Libraries (ARL), the organization representing major research universities, ranked OSU close to the bottom in library collections, a principal reason the university lacked qualifications for membership in ARL and the honor society, Phi Beta Kappa. The faculty senate indicated that library funding continued to trend downward. In the biennium for 1987–1988, the legislature appropriated a 7 percent increase for its materials budget, while material costs for that period increased 15 percent. The *Barometer* added its voice to the chorus, placing library improvements as the university's most significant problem.[61]

Because Kerr Library was a bottom-feeder in state board funding, President Byrne worked externally and internally to improve its base budget. He reallocated university funds to augment the library collections and its computer system and quietly transferred unrestricted gifts to colleges to the library account. University librarian Melvin George worked closely with the president in fund-raising and developing architectural plans for the building's expansion, expected to cost some $40 million. Although estimates for projecting future enrollments were "all but impossible," George advised in 1988 that a more important factor would be acquiring collections that required more space. He anticipated that the university should build its collections to two million by 2012, which translated to an average of forty thousand volumes a year. If the president wanted to dramatically improve the library's budget over the next few years, that project should be included in the planning process.[62]

As the OSU library campaign proceeded, Oregon senator Mark Hatfield suggested to Byrne that the library become a repository for federal documents, providing an opportunity for OSU to qualify for federal support. Byrne relayed the idea to George, suggesting that areas in natural resources might represent such an opportunity. Two major events put the OSU library campaign over the top. Most important was the Valley Foundation's pledge, in June 1995, of $10 million for naming rights; the second was Oregon governor John Kitzhaber signing a legislative measure for a second $10 million, bringing the fund-raising total to $35 million. To push the aggregate closer to the $40 million objective, the chair of the OSU Foundation board, Martin Kelley (and his wife Judy) pledged a cash gift of $1 million. With two pledges of $500,000 from OSU's Associated Students of 1991 and 1995, the campaign was close to the finish line.[63]

The public and private gifts to support the expanded and renovated library totaled $47 million. More than nine thousand alumni, students, staff, and friends partnered in the gifting. When Valley Library opened in 1999, *Library Journal* designated the building "Library of the Year." Remodeling and expanding the library was the Byrne administration's greatest achievement. The president's effort involved years of fund-raising and persuading state legislators to support the expanded library. The achievement fit Byrne's objective of raising the university's profile as a major research institution. With the Pauling papers and natural-resource and scientific documents as attractions, the number of scholars visiting the research room has risen sharply. Mel George's 1988 prediction that the library's collections would reach two million volumes by 2012 was remarkably accurate. Those collective achievements highlight John Byrne's belief that a library should be "the intellectual heart of the university."[64]

The library's abysmal holdings in humanities and social sciences through the mid-1980s reflected the State Board of Higher Education's grand bargain adopted in 1932—designating the University of Oregon home to the arts and humanities and Oregon State College to the sciences and professional schools. That compromise left the Corvallis school without degrees in the liberal arts until the early 1960s, and even then the board limited OSU to bachelor's degrees only. With a few significant exceptions, the faculty's published scholarship in the old School of Humanities and Social Science was limited, a trend that continued through the early years of the College of Liberal Arts. Those circumstances began to change in the mid-1980s, when the university's curriculum committee revised the baccalaureate core requirements, mandating more undergraduate courses in liberal arts. At the same time, the state board approved graduate programs in English, applied anthropology, economics, and scientific and technical communication.[65]

Byrne's provost, Graham Spanier, initiated another move that proved to be a major advance for liberal arts faculty. A trained sociologist with expertise in human development and family studies, Spanier reduced annual liberal arts teaching loads from twenty-seven to eighteen hours, the university standard (roughly two classes per term). College of Liberal Arts faculty agree that Spanier, appointed vice president for academic affairs and provost in 1986, was the driving force in what turned into a significant morale booster. In pursuing the change, the provost had the full support of President Byrne.[66]

Establishing the Center for the Humanities ranks as another significant achievement in John Byrne's promotion of liberal arts. The background to the center rests in the skills of its founding administrator, English professor Peter Copek, and his department chair Richard Astro. The center originated in a National Endowment for the Humanities (NEH) grant in 1975 that funded the Humanities Development Program, largely run out of Copek's office in Moreland Hall. With participating College of Liberal Arts faculty, the program offered interdisciplinary certificate programs in marine and maritime studies, Pacific Northwest studies, and twentieth-century studies. A component of Project Foursight fund-raising when it received the NEH challenge grant, the Center for the Humanities began hosting OSU faculty and fellows from other colleges and universities who would spend designated periods pursing research projects. The center also sponsored conferences, seminars, lectures, and an international film series.[67]

The Center for the Humanities was without a physical home until the Byrne administration acquired a turn-of-the-twentieth-century Tudor-style former sorority house on Jefferson Avenue midway between campus and downtown Corvallis. The Autzen Foundation funded the purchase and President Byrne—aware that the University of Oregon was very proud of its Autzen football stadium—thought it appropriate to have the name Autzen House on a building located on the main thoroughfare to campus. The Center for the Humanities thrived in the location, first under Peter Copek, and then, after his death in 2001, under David Robinson of the English Department. In retirement, President Emeritus Byrne has held an office in the building where he did much of the writing on his memoir. The university's Honors College, another Byrne initiative that fell victim to Measure 5, was resurrected in 1993 and eventually earned state board approval as a degree-granting unit. Byrne attributes the Honors College's success to its first dean, Joe Hendricks, and a cohort of colleagues who valued its presence on campus.[68]

The onset of the environmental age profoundly influenced Oregon State University, inspiring and expanding a network of innovative research projects and placing the university president in the crosshairs of controversies between major natural-resource industries and university scientists. Like Robert MacVicar before him, Byrne walked a tightrope through prickly issues—controlling woodland insects, timber harvesting practices, stream pollution, grazing in eastern Oregon, and other matters. With Oregon's powerful lumber and agricultural businesses playing watchdog over environmental regulations, the president navigated his way through the demands of industry and the findings of OSU scientists. The campus units most affected were the College of Forestry and the Department of Fisheries and Wildlife in the College of Agriculture. Those environmental conflicts reflected a sea change in university research. Until the 1970s, forestry and fish and wildlife research focused on production— growing bigger, faster-growing trees, increasing hatchery production of anadromous fishes, and controlling predators to augment deer and elk populations. Because of the growing interest in and sophistication of ecosystems data, old scientific paradigms came under attack, with some university researchers accused of environmental advocacy and of sacrificing scientific objectivity.[69]

One of the more extended and contentious issues involved university fisheries biologist Chris Frissell's research on the relationship between logging and stream sedimentation in southwestern Oregon. At the invitation of the Siskiyou and Umpqua national forest supervisors, Frissell and doctoral candidate Richard Nawa wrote assessments of draft environmental impact statements (EIS) in the late spring of 1988. When Troy Reinhart of the Douglas Timber Operators noticed the letters were written on OSU stationery, he wrote Byrne that using such stationery gave the impression that the letters represented the official position of the university.[70] What ensued were letters from Byrne to Reinhart, to Carl Stoltenberg, dean of the College of Forestry, and to Richard Tubb, chair of the Department of Fisheries and Wildlife, inquiring about the propriety of Frissell's letters on OSU stationery. Although the president did not intend to prevent Frissell from expressing his views, he thought "official correspondence on such highly controversial issues would hold to a higher standard of objectivity in presenting scientific information," including judgments of personal values.[71]

Frissell's name resurfaced a few months later involving stream classifications and how land use practices affected waterways and riparian zones in southwestern Oregon. At the invitation of the Powers Ranger District (Siskiyou National Forest), Frissell provided comments on the effects of a timber sale in the Sixes River basin and the purchaser's willingness to relinquish his rights to harvest trees in the headwaters of the Dry Creek drainage. The issue involved Port Orford (white) cedar and the spread of a root fungus that had devastated the species along the southern Oregon coast. Logging roads spread the root disease, and the Forest Service plan to build roads in the Dry Creek drainage would spread the root syndrome. There was "a simple solution," Frissell noted: accept return of the timber sale and avoid any further road-building in the area.[72]

Dennis Hayward of the Eugene-based North West Timber Association protested to President Byrne that Frissell was threatening to close public lands to resource users. Hayward charged that "scientists dealing with emotional issues such as old growth and wildlife" were abandoning objectivity in lieu of political values. Moreover, Frissell had used university stationery and was criticizing the Siskiyou National Forest for refusing to cancel a timber sale.[73] Before the president could respond, Frissell and his research supervisor Bill Liss sent Byrne an extended report on the ecological uniqueness and importance of the Dry Creek watershed. The letter provided background on OSU's ongoing stream research in southwestern Oregon, especially the harmful effects of logging on fish habitat. Dry Creek was the last large coastal watershed bereft of logging activity that still hosted healthy runs of salmon and steelhead in the Sixes River system. Equally important, from a research perspective, Dry Creek had "a continued fish research data base dating to the 1960s."[74]

Department chair Richard Tubb fully supported Frissell and Liss. Frissell was proper in commenting "on areas within his competency" and in using letterhead stationery when answering requests related to his expertise. In his communication with the president, Tubb included a supporting document from Curry County's Board of Commissioners as an example of the requests the department received. Because the southwestern Oregon encounter was developing into a hot-button media issue, Byrne asked forestry dean Carl Stoltenberg for advice. Stoltenberg's response was blunt—the president should respond directly to Frissell and Liss, with a copy to Hayward, that "clearly supports the faculty." It would be unwise to prevent the faculty from responding to requests, because if their letter became public, it would make them martyrs and be bad for the university.[75] The president rode out the storm, defending

Hayward's questions about Frissell's comments going beyond his professional expertise and urging Frissell to "continue to speak clearly and constructively as a representative of the University."[76]

The sledgehammer budget cuts between 1988 and those associated with Measure 5 (1990), prompted the legislature to review the administrative costs at all state system schools. Lawmakers appointed an administrative review committee to help institutions develop guidelines for budget reductions of 10, 20, and 30 percent. The committee contracted with a private-sector consulting firm KPMG Peat Marwick to advise the review process. At Byrne's suggestion, Oregon State volunteered to be the first institution to undergo the review, assigning a university committee to work with Peat Marwick in examining its administrative structure. In a memorandum to faculty and staff in May 1992, Byrne believed the institution would need to eliminate and consolidate campus units to operate more efficiently.[77]

Following the review team's belief that restructuring the administration would minimize reductions to academic programs, Peat Marwick delivered its report in July 1992. The university committee and Peat Marwick offered six recommendations: (1) reduce leadership and management positions; (2) reduce the number of vice presidents and consolidate academic support units; (3) consolidate/merge academic departments and colleges; (4) consolidate and centralize business processes; (5) outsource or eliminate some internal functions; and (6) upgrade central computing. Certain Peat Marwick recommendations were notable—reducing vice president positions, recognizing the provost as chief operating officer, enhancing the extension service's statewide work, and strengthening its relationship with university research. Recommendation 5, to achieve cost savings, would outsource the bookstore, food services, printing and mailing, and some physical plant operations. Horner Museum, OSU Press, OSU's Portland Center, and the public aquarium at the Hatfield Marine Science Center were also targeted for elimination.[78]

To a Corvallis resident who charged that OSU's priorities were misguided, Byrne responded that these were desperate times, with the elimination of Horner Museum, the OSU Press, and the College of Veterinary Medicine an "indication of our desperation." Until the state recognized the importance of higher education, "we may have to take desperate steps." The potential elimination of veterinary medicine turned into a mini-circus of a kind not seen in Oregon in decades. When Byrne informed the vet med community that the college was targeted for elimination, he asked for whatever help they could offer to avoid closing the college. Following the meeting, the faculty and staff

Established as the Marine Science Center in 1965 and renamed in 1983 for Oregon governor and senator Mark Hatfield, the Center developed into a prominent marine laboratory with research partnerships that are truly global. Federal research agencies present at the Center include the Environmental Protection Agency, Fish and Wildlife Service, National Marine Fisheries Service, National Oceanic and Atmospheric Administration, and the National Coastal Resources Research and Development Institute. The Hatfield Center serves as an educational hub for all levels of learning. Courtesy of the OSU Special Collections and Archives Research Center.

contacted every veterinarian in the state asking for assistance. What followed were people appearing at the capitol in Salem with llamas and other pets, asking the legislature's Joint Ways and Means Committee to fully fund the college. Similar strategies were employed later when veterinary medicine at the college continued to struggle financially. Byrne was informed on the latter occasion that pygmy goats were brought into the hearing room to persuade reluctant lawmakers.[79]

The second stage in the effort to reduce the university budget and streamline its administration was the president's appointment of a leadership implementation team to provide guidance on executing the recommendations.[80] The team held five campus forums and distributed some 5,500 copies of survey forms to gather input for reorganizing the university. When all the chits were in, Byrne announced in February 1993 that the restructured administration would have the provost overseeing the everyday operations of the university. The provost would then appoint an associate provost for academic affairs, associate provost for information services, and the chief business officer. The positions of dean of agriculture and director of the agriculture experiment station would be combined. Vice Provost of Student Affairs Jo Anne Trow reported, in the fall of 1993, a major renovation of the

Memorial Union Commons, a move that would outsource food services, bringing in franchises such as Taco Bell.[81]

John Byrne placed his stamp on the university's administrative structure immediately upon entering office. He would leave the presidency with another major reorganization mandated by the State System of Higher Education. There were more significant markers of Byrne's eleven years as head of the institution, especially his skills in setting the table for the university's dynamic fund-raising capabilities and the explosive building enterprises that followed. Byrne was an innovator who understood the prerequisites for a truly modern, comprehensive university. While Oregon State University was playing catch-up to other Pac-10 schools, Byrne's emphasis on the strategic importance of the library and computing moved the institution closer to parity with other conference universities. His promotion of the humanities, the Honors College, and related matters was an important subset to modernizing the academy.

12
Student Life, 1940–2010

In the midst of violence spreading across Europe and Asia in the late 1930s, the Oregon State College campus remained quiet, as state and national economies slowly recovered from the Depression. Seattle-born Andy Landforce bridged the worlds of depression and war, graduating from high school in the mid-1930s and following work north to Alaska, where he manned hydraulic cannons to sluice away gravel from hillsides in search of gold. "To find a way out of common labor," he enrolled at Oregon State College in 1938, majoring in agriculture and playing football, including the school's first Rose Bowl game in Durham, North Carolina, three weeks after Pearl Harbor. Landforce was a member of the Blue Key National Honor Society, and as an ROTC student, he joined Scabbard and Blade, a national honor society in military science. Commissioned in the United States Army after graduation, Landforce served in Alaska and later captained an all-black transportation troop in England from September 1944 to May 1945. After V-E Day, the army transferred his unit to the Philippines to prepare for the invasion of Japan when the war ended. He joined the OSU Extension Service in 1946, serving in multiple capacities until he retired in 1977.[1]

Andy Landforce's Depression-era employment, educational experiences, military service, and professional trajectory paralleled that of many contemporaries. Serving as student-body president in his senior year (1941–1942), he was part of an "independent" trend (students not affiliated with fraternities or sororities) that gained momentum when independents captured three of seven student-body offices in 1938–1939. While Hitler's armies were advancing in Eastern Europe and military preparedness was under way at the state college, most students went about their business oblivious to the gathering war clouds. Despite the seeming insignificance of those events in student life, the 1941 yearbook captioned a series of photos of the fall 1940 water carnival, "Blitzkrieg in a Bathtub."[2] Campus life during the Second World War, however, presented new and dramatically different experiences for students.

With the nation fully engaged in war in the spring of 1942, the yearbook welcomed the next freshman class—"Stumbling into Oregon State's most turbulent fall term." Summarizing the previous months, the *Beaver* recalled surprises, thrills, and jubilation, "war with its blackouts," a Red Cross fund-raiser, the "Nickle Hop," Andy Landforce addressing the Oregon Student Leaders Convention, and ROTC's Colonel Maylon Scott warning students to take war seriously. Before Pearl Harbor, students went about their normal routines, attending classes, gathering in the Memorial Union Wednesday afternoons for home football rallies, new students attending a picnic in Avery Park, and others participating in circus parties, "rookie rumpases," sings, teas, and open houses. Those activities changed after December 7, 1941, with Corvallis and the OSC campus subject to periodic blackouts. The *Oregonian* reported that students busied themselves to keep fear at bay, and young people were sleeping longer hours. With the holiday season approaching, sorority and independent women toured residential halls serenading dormitories and fraternities with Christmas carols and "sweetheart songs."[3]

The war prompted the college to offer new defense-related engineering courses in Portland on ship construction and design. Students taking civilian pilot training at nearby Corvallis Airport had their program suspended when the US Army grounded all civilian flying from the Cascade Range to the Pacific Ocean. The University of Washington, University of Oregon, and Oregon State College attended a Civil Aeronautics Division hearing in Portland, declaring their interest in training civilian pilots. The state college began offering war-service classes for women in medical fields (technicians, nursing, medical entomology, pharmacy), secretarial science, dietetics, nursery school work, foreign languages, engineering, and auto mechanics in late 1942. The demand for nurses topped the list, with the National Council of Nurses urging women to enter nursing programs. Oregon State was already enrolling women in engineering programs and courses in auto mechanics, and the School of Home Economics was training students for nursery and nutrition jobs related to national defense. [4]

The Associated Women Students (AWS), an umbrella organization for women's groups established in 1924, raised funds for war bonds, the Red Cross, and other charitable activities. To coordinate campus defense efforts, AWS played a seminal role in opening the OSC Victory Center in the Memorial Union in October 1942. As a fund-raiser, the center sponsored popular "Nickle Hops," where male students paid a nickel for dancing with women from sororities and residence halls. The OSC Victory Center sponsored a college rally in Portland on October 24 prior to the Oregon State–Washington

State football game. The program included sorority and fraternity skits, student speakers, vocal performances, and the OSC ROTC band. Intended as inspirational, the venue involved a navy recruiter and an alumnus with the war bonds staff.[5]

Although male students left in droves for military service, the campus maintained a semblance of social life. With coeds moving from sorority and residence halls to fraternity houses to prepare for what the *Oregonian* termed "an army school," women continued to sponsor dances, concerts, and other social events. Male forestry and engineering students sponsored dueling "annual balls" in January 1943, the competition directed at attracting coeds. The president of the Interfraternity Council, however, cancelled the fraternity sing for spring term 1943, because the arrival of the Army Specialized Training Corps had inundated campus with military personnel.[6]

The pages of the *Beaver* reflected a sea change in the otherwise happy face of the yearbook. With Jean Floyd as editor, the 1943 issue featured a photograph of military personnel marching with flags and arms on the campus parade grounds. The facing page included a photo of war wreckage, with the following epigram:

> While the Beavers crouched in the
> hell holes of the Solomons . . . . some
> ferried bombers to Europe . . . . and
> some tramped the sun-parched desert,
> we stayed in school to prepare for the
> battle. This is the story of a college at
> war as we lived it.

A photo of bombing destruction follows with the caption, "Time went faster . . . our pace was geared higher." The yearbook referred to the shortage of automobile tires, food rationing, meatless days, rolling Red Cross bandages, male students running obstacle courses, war bond sales, "Dancing in the Dark," and khaki uniforms. "There's Something About a Soldier" captioned an image of five army personnel on the Memorial Union steps.[7]

With enrollment at colleges and universities hitting rock-bottom in the winter of 1942–1943, Oregon State students economized, with Campus Weekend of 1943 billed as a "war-tailored" event, having "fun without a dollar sign." Student concerts and talent shows replaced paid entertainment. The OSC Victory Center publicized the importance of purchasing war bonds, and the Student

War Council organized blood donations and helped arrange work crews for farmers needing help during fall harvests. OSC alum Marion Carl, a fighter pilot who shot down sixteen enemy aircraft over Guadalcanal, visited campus in the spring of 1943 and addressed a capacity crowd in the museum (now the Gladys Valley Gymnastics Center). Carl's appearance helped sell $14,000 worth of war bonds. Although the campus was heavily vested with army agendas, student social life continued with the help of an army-sponsored dance in the Memorial Union ballroom in November 1944. A San Francisco dating bureau paired coeds with soldiers.[8]

Intercollegiate sports were casualties of the war. With men entering military service, colleges and universities had difficulty fielding competitive teams. OSC fielded a football team in 1942 and intended to do so again in 1943, with only one letterman returning. The problem in the Northern Division of the Pacific Eight Conference (Washington, Washington State, Oregon, and Oregon State) was the league's declaration that army trainees were not eligible to play. Football coach Lon Stiner expected twenty to twenty-five players to turn out for fall practice. Only twenty players showed up at the first practice on September 16. Then the chips began to fall—first, the University of Oregon announced that it was dropping football. Three days later, Idaho and Washington State cancelled football for the 1943 season. Although Oregon State had enough players to field a team, Athletic Director Percy Locey cited the absence of opponents in the Northern Division and cancelled the football season. Little had changed in 1944, and the Northern Division again cancelled all football games.[9]

With the surrender of Germany in April 1945 and Japan the following August, the annual gridiron classics returned to college and university campuses. The restoration of football in Corvallis came in the midst of a swirl of veterans registering for classes. Taking advantage of the GI Bill, discharged servicemen and women began enrolling in larger numbers in 1944, their numbers escalating over the next two years. Although there were few male students on campus, returning military personnel filled the complement of males for all-campus dances. A sign of changing customs took place in May 1945, when freshman engaged in the early "burning of the green," the caps (men) and ribbons (women) students were required to wear until the adornments were burned in a ceremony occurring on Junior Weekend. In a fit of revenge, the student government cancelled three traditional events for that weekend.[10]

As military victory neared, the School of Forestry prepared for increased enrollments. The School of Science also readied for postwar reconstruction programs, turning "swords into plowshares." Students enrolling in the Lower Division looked forward to new courses for returning servicemen, emphasizing democratic traditions and the American way of life. The yearbook for 1945–1946 captured a very different student clientele—older, more mature, self-directed, many of them married. The military still had a significant presence in Corvallis, participating in parades, in addition to regular drill practices. The 1946 *Beaver* praised the war's end but cautioned of "new problems in the effort to return to peacetime valuations and brighter prospects." Photos of older students in assorted civilian clothing styles and family settings with small children filled the volume. In a signal moment for the nearly all-white school, the yearbook included photos of blackface comedy under the caption, "Sophomores All Turned Black."[11]

High school graduates enrolling at Oregon's institutions after the war were treated to a rapidly changing world of new consumer goods, improved transportation, and the rapid mechanization of the agriculture and lumber industries. The use of automobiles grew exponentially as new federally funded highways spread across the land. OSC students increasingly relied on automobiles as rail travel declined. Students were proud of college alums who were shaping the new environment of consumer goods, exclaiming in the 1951 yearbook that graduates had "won distinction in scientific, industrial, commercial, and administrative pursuits." One alumnus, Douglas McKay, was governor of Oregon, another was editor of a major newspaper, others were writing fiction and producing movies, and Linus Pauling was doing path-breaking research in chemistry.[12]

Ex-servicemen flooding college campuses tempered and brought an end to some student traditions. The annual tug-of-war and other Junior Weekend activities diminished in importance, while the carnival, part of spring festivities, gained in popularity. Sponsored by the Associated Women Students, the carnival became part of Junior Weekend in 1945 and quickly became a big attraction. Veterans, with little patience for what they viewed as absurd customs and traditions, brought change to many activities. The "rook" tradition of freshman wearing green throughout the school year had already been limited to the first week of fall term. With most veterans graduating by the late 1940s, however, older traditions returned in modified form. Benny Beaver, the institution's human/animal mascot, emerged as a presence at athletic events and rally assemblies. Although wearing green had disappeared from campus by 1960, the affable, smiling Benny would continue to be a vital part of student life into the future.[13]

Fall term's Homecoming Weekend experienced changes through the years as well, with its first Homecoming court selected in the 1930s (no queen was chosen until 1953). OSC graduates initiated the popular Alumni Barbecue in 1946 as "The Reunion After Tokyo," with alums handing out donuts, a tradition lasting into the 1990s. Homecoming organizers revived the noise parade in 1948, including a loud compressor-powered air siren. And, well into the 1960s, big-name concert artists appeared regularly—Dionne Warwick, Doc Severinsen (born in Arlington, Oregon), and Henry Mancini. In the midst of the civil rights crusade and growing antiwar movement in the late 1960s, Homecoming Weekend became more benign when planners ended the long-standing bonfire ritual in deference to air pollution concerns. Although the bonfire eventually returned, big dances declined in popularity, and in the mid-1990s the tradition of electing Homecoming royalty came to an end.[14]

Writing for the *Oregon Stater* in 1989, Betsy Krause observed that "wars, changing technology, new laws, civil liberties, and liability cut a swath through many of OSU's traditions." The Second World War was a major factor in introducing changes at the state college. Students coming from high school mixing with war veterans "screwed it all up," Crawford "Scram" Graham told Krause. Placing seventeen- and eighteen-year-olds with men who liked booze "changed our thinking on the residence halls." While class-related mores—wearing green, freshman building bonfires and showing deference to upper classmen—fell by the wayside, others continued, especially Moms and Dads Weekends and Homecoming. The mainstay of all traditions, class reunions, persisted through the decades.

OSC students continued to host headline entertainers and speakers during the 1950s—the all-black Depaur Infantry Chorus, crooner Vaughn Monroe, singer and actor Nelson Eddy, famed humorist Bennett Cerf, movie star Rock Hudson, the Robert Shaw Chorale, the piano team Ferrante and Teicher, bandleader Stan Kenton, a lecture by distinguished nuclear physicist J. Robert Oppenheimer, soprano Leontyne Price (*Porgy and Bess*), the National Ballet of Canada, the Portland Symphony Orchestra, the Boston Pops Orchestra, Mantovani "and his New Music," the Philadelphia Symphony Orchestra, and many others. Folk dances celebrating other cultures and early American music, football rallies, talent shows, intercollegiate rodeos, students heading for the snowy slopes of the Cascades, campus theater, and the still-current Sadie Hawkins Day Race were representations of student life during the 1950s.[15]

Other student activities shifted with the social habits of the times, none more than lighting up a cigarette or pipe. For much of the institution's early history, having a cup of coffee and a smoke before going to classes would have been grounds for being expelled from college. Until the 1930s the "no smoking" rule prevailed everywhere on campus. There was, however, a breach in this policy during football games, when visitors in the stands were smoking. Meeting in October 1930, the college administrative council agreed that the rule was unenforceable and that smoking should be allowed at football games. Those urging the change believed there would be no difficulty enforcing the rule at other times. Three years later—having permitted smoking in the Memorial Union's men's lounge and in the dining area "when women are not present"—the council rejected a request to allow smoking everywhere except in the main lounge. But with the camel's nose pushing into the institutional tent, President George Peavy asked deans and department heads to make certain faculty were adhering to campus smoking regulations.[16]

Peavy further refined campus smoking regulations in March 1939, announcing that smoking would be prohibited outside campus buildings within the perimeter of the inner campus (marked with orange stripes on sidewalk entrances). Faculty and staff were not to smoke in the presence of undergraduates, and the college would provide fire-resistant receptacles for ashes and cigarettes for those who did. The president repeated again that deans and department heads were responsible for enforcing smoking regulations. While Peavy realized that attitudes about smoking had radically changed since earlier in the century, he thought the institution should uphold its reputation for conservatism and exercise restrictions on "personal appetite and habit." The future would show that smoking habits had loosened, and yearbooks in the 1950s included photos of male students smoking pipes while studying and "lighting-up" as they left the library.[17]

Students arriving in the fall of 1951 were treated to a college catalogue that praised the town of sixteen thousand people, its "pure mountain water, modern sanitation, good schools, numerous churches, and strong civic and social organizations." The catalogue applauded landscape architects John C. Olmsted and A. D. Taylor for developing a campus "in accordance with a permanent plan." In a statement that might surprise twenty-first-century visitors, prospective students were informed that arranging the campus in quadrangles enabled expansion to "take place without injury to established buildings and campus areas." New buildings to meet postwar student enrollments would soon be replacing temporary structures from Camp Adair and elsewhere. The 1951 catalogue concluded with bucolic word pictures of the quadrangles surrounding campus, with students passing through walkways "planted with ornamental trees and shrubs."[18]

The hefty 476-page catalogue included information about the library (nearly 257,000 volumes), admission requirements, placement examinations, fees and deposits and board and room (about $835 per year), student living (dormitories, sororities and fraternities, cooperative houses, private homes, and housing for married students), and student automobiles. Warned about congestion on campus, students were urged to leave their automobiles at home. The catalogue included information about extracurricular activities—lectures, concerts, forensics and dramatics, sports and athletics, student publications—and provided statistics for the 1949–1950 academic year: 6,705 undergraduates and 602 graduate students, for a total enrollment of 7,307.[19]

A decade later, the 1961–1962 yearbook listed the Corvallis population at 21,253. The climate remained "equable," with an average annual precipitation of thirty-nine inches, most of it occurring during the winter months. Descriptions of campus parroted accounts from the previous decade. Library collections had grown to 390,000 volumes, and fees for room and board had risen to an average of $1,204 for resident students. Enrollment had increased slightly, with 7,456 undergraduates and 899 graduate students registered for fall term 1959. The General Extension Division enrolled thousands of students, most of them for one or two courses. The Portland Center tallied the greatest number of enrollees, with the remaining extension courses offered at sixty-nine centers across the state. Although the extension division listed 21,399 students taking courses, many of them were regular enrollees at one of Oregon's public institutions. The division's data does not indicate the student credit hours involved.[20]

Freshman entering Oregon State University in the fall of 1971 could expect an inviting array of foreign study options in France, Germany, and Japan. Those opportunities originated when Dean Gordon Gilkey of the School of Humanities and Social Sciences (soon to become the College of Liberal Arts) pioneered the university's first study-abroad programs in 1968–1969 at the University of Stuttgart in Germany and Waseda University in Japan. With those initiatives under the auspices of the Oregon State Board of Higher Education, Oregon State opened a new French study center at the University of Poitiers in the fall of 1971, offering two semesters for fully integrated students. Like other study-abroad programs, Poitiers was open to students from all disciplinary majors who had completed two years of undergraduate courses (with two years of French). Prior to beginning the regular school year in Poitiers, students took a four-week language and orientation class.[21]

The objectives of international education were to provide a broader understanding of people and nations in the global community. The university's director of international education invited faculty interested in participating in study-abroad programs, and the foreign student adviser arranged travel to overseas study sites for students. Those qualifying for Poitiers could choose engineering, pharmacy, medical, business, legal, economics, arts, and Latin American studies majors. Professor Odette Cadart-Ricard was appointed the first director of the French study center. At Gilkey's instruction, Cadart-Ricard worked with the French Ministry of Education to set up the program while she was teaching for the American Heritage Association in France in 1968. She thought Poitiers would be an appropriate setting because of its strengths in art, history, and architecture, and its superb faculty and wide-ranging curriculum.[22]

The original student-exchange arrangement between the University of Stuttgart and Oregon State University has evolved into a nation-to-nation arrangement involving more than twenty colleges and universities, including exchanges of students, faculty, and administrators. Referred to as the Oregon/Baden-Wurttemberg Exchange Program, the vibrant union of cultures and peoples is one of the most successful of its kind in Europe and the United States. Operating out of the University of Stuttgart until 2002, it moved to the University of Tübingen, where it now has a permanent resident director. Under the Oregon University System (OUS)—successor to the State System of Higher Education—the German Academic Exchange Service honored the Baden/Wurttemberg program as a "flagship of state to state cooperation." All OUS institutions and Willamette and Pacific universities are participants, as well as fifteen German universities.[23]

The Oregon State University Office of International Education, through the Northwest Interinstitutional Council on Study Abroad, provided other opportunities for students wishing to study in foreign lands. The consortium of Northwest colleges and universities had cooperating liberal arts study centers in Avignon, Paris, London, and Stockholm. In the late 1970s, the international study programs transitioned to partnership exchanges in which foreign students began coming to OSU in greater numbers. Over the years, student interest led to programs in Australia, China, Denmark, Ecuador, Ireland, Korea, Mexico, Thailand, and several places in the United Kingdom. As dean of International Programs in 1996, Jack Van de Water secured federal funding through the Peace Dividend Program to initiate an international education, experience, and employment strategy for graduate students desiring work experiences in foreign countries. An OSU faculty member and an on-site supervisor would administer the program. Two-thirds of the work experiences eventually took place in the developing world. [24]

Oregon State University has always been home to a strong sorority and fraternity system. Among the more than forty chapters on campus in 2015, most were established between 1910 and 1930. To oversee the men's organizations, and to present a common front to Oregon Agricultural College, fraternity chapters formed the Interfraternity Council in 1927. Its counterpart, the sororities' Pan Hellenic Council, was established in 1917 as the Women's Interfraternity Council (renamed in 1919). Although wars and economic depressions have always affected the number of Greek houses, Oregon State has been recognized for the strength of its Greek system. While the houses gave way to military personnel during the Second World War, they quickly recovered regular enrollments in the 1950s.

Always conscious of their grade-point averages (GPA) vis-à-vis the general student population, Greeks were quick to bring attention to improvements in their academic work and regularly provided news releases to the *Oregonian*. In most instances, sororities earned higher GPAs than fraternities, although the Sigma Phi Epsilon fraternity usually held the highest GPA for Greek houses. That honor, however, went to the sorority, Kappa Kappa Gamma for their achievement during fall term 1950. By the end of the academic year, however, Sigma Phi was back on top with a GPA of 2.99, and Pi Beta Phi led sororities with a 2.91 mark. Less celebrated, veterans attending OSC on the GI Bill topped all general student groups, with a 2.73 GPA, well above the college average. Those comparisons continued through the 1960s and well into the next decade.[25]

When Oregon State College fraternities pledged 333 men in the fall of 1950, the figure broke the previous high of 314 pledges. What was interesting—and this is a tribute to the Interfraternity Council's public relations efforts—was listing the names and home towns of the 333 pledges in the *Oregonian*. Without a collective voice, veterans and other groups received no such recognition. Fraternities and sororities worked hard for respect. When 1,600 high school seniors descended on campus during "Beaver Preview" in April 1951, Greek chapters held open houses through the long weekend to welcome the visitors. Not all the news about fraternities was positive, however, especially when houses were placed on academic probation. When six men's living groups earned this distinction early in 1958, four of them were fraternities—Phi Kappa Psi, Lambda Chi Alpha, Alpha Sigma Phi, and Theta Chi.[26]

Other problems surfaced among the Greek houses from time to time. Writing for the *Oregonian* in the spring of 1954, Paul Ewing charged that fraternity and sorority students in Eugene and Corvallis were immature and lacked stability. Those issues were important, he wrote, because Greeks were prominent in student affairs. On the University of Oregon campus, fraternities constituted 37 percent of undergraduate men and sororities 33 percent of all women in 1954. At Oregon State the percentages were much higher—fraternities made up 49 percent of undergraduate men and sororities an astounding 60 percent of women. Because student fads were more noticeable in Greek houses, they were also difficult to regulate when they overstepped the norms of reasonable behavior. Oregon State's dean of men, Dan Poling, believed postwar students were less mature than earlier generations and prone to exhibit boorish behavior. To mitigate behavioral problems, administrators considered requiring fraternities to hire house mothers to counter the void in student leadership. Unlike the University of Oregon, where freshman were required to live in dormitories, OSC had no such rule. If house mothers failed to resolve those difficulties, Poling thought deferred Greek living would be adopted at OSC.[27]

Far more serious issues—deeply embedded in the nation's history—were discriminatory racial and religious prohibitions in national fraternity and sorority councils. When the State Board of Higher Education directed the University of Oregon and Oregon State University to survey the regulations of Greek houses for the existence of such clauses, OSC reported that five of its thirty-one fraternities had exclusions in national chapter regulations and three of seventeen sororities had the offending prohibitions. At the UO, four of twenty-one fraternities had such clauses, while sororities were free of such restrictions. Presidents A. L. Strand (OSC) and Meredith Wilson (UO) hoped national organizations would remove those prohibitions at their annual conventions. The *Oregonian*'s Malcolm Bauer thought it important "that the dirty bath water be tossed out without losing the baby, because the physical plants of Greek houses were worth millions of dollars."[28]

Despite the state board's mandate "to oppose and prevent . . . all discrimination based on race, color, or religion," the problem persisted into the 1960s. An *Oregonian* editorial charged that some Oregon fraternity chapters were hiding behind national bylaws requiring that selecting members must have unanimous approval, "one black ball and out for the applicant, whatever his color." This "convenient rule of evasion" for living organizations, the newspaper insisted, enabled some Greek houses to skirt the Board of Higher Education's antidiscrimination efforts. What individual fraternities did was their business, the editorial contended, but citizens should support the board's effort to make certain that local chapters, not fraternity headquarters in the Old South, set membership policies.[29]

The civil rights movement and opposition to the Vietnam War created membership problems for fraternities and sororities in the late 1960s and early 1970s. Jeff Elder, a rush chairperson, cited external factors for difficulties in attracting pledges: "People think we are in some way prejudiced about pledges. And they are concerned about fraternal secrecies." Those criticisms were no longer valid, he insisted, because today's Greek houses were trying to create modern fraternities, "what a fraternity is, not was." The downturn in memberships continued, however, with entering freshman at the University of Oregon and Oregon State having fewer houses to choose from in 1971. Oregon lost five fraternity houses because of financial difficulties, and Oregon State lost one fraternity and one sorority. The Corvallis school, the great stronghold for Greek chapters, had already turned the corner in the fall of 1971. The membership problem had reversed by the mid-1970s, and University of Oregon and Oregon State Greek houses were gaining members and new chapters were opening. Bill Brennan, fraternity adviser at Oregon State, believed student moods had changed, and the desire to live off-campus "to do your own thing" was wearing thin. Oregon State University continued as the pacesetter for Greek membership in the 1980s, with twenty-eight fraternities and fourteen sororities housing some three thousand members (21 percent of undergraduate students).[30]

Violations of a state law prohibiting student hazing, and Corvallis police reports about raids on two fraternities for liquor and gambling abuses, suggested ongoing problems. Jeffrey Boyd, a senior in health care and former Beaver football player, singled out the isolation that black students felt on campus—he was the only black student in all of his classes. He told reporter Pat Kight that if he missed a class, everyone knew it. "This is a Greek oriented university," with sororities and fraternities having functions every weekend. But, if you are not a member, "you won't be able to go." Among Oregon State's twenty-seven fraternities, Kight indicated, there were only four black members.[31] Perception, of course, matters in the telling of those stories, because most white students would see little harm to minority students in such situations. If they walked the paths of the approximately 180 black students in the mid-1980s, however, they might see the world differently.

Several Greek houses experienced interesting transitions during their existence, with local chapters linking up with various international fraternities for a charter. Delta Chi traces its origins to 1920 as local fraternity, Delta

Kappa. Partnering with Theta Delta Nu, the fraternities petitioned for a char-ter, and in 1931 the international headquarters approved the Oregon State chapter of Delta Chi, which subsequently experienced fluctuating member-ships. Delta Chi sponsored a calendar, "Women of OSU," with models that it introduced at the Clackamas Town Center on consecutive evenings in 1982. To highlight the event, the chapter featured football coach Joe Avezzano and athletic director Dee Andros with the coeds. Within two years, Delta Chi underwent a major reorganization, with members from the previous year leaving and new enrollees and fresh leadership moving the chapter in a differ-ent direction. As part of the reorganization, Delta Chi disbanded its women's auxiliary, "Sisters of the White Carnation." The chapter struggled through the 1990s and closed in March of 2000 because of low membership. Leaders from the international headquarters, however, visited Corvallis in 2003 and enlisted enough support to reopen Delta Chi, a chapter that lived on with a full house of forty members in 2015.[32]

Amid ribbon-cutting ceremonies and welcoming festivities, Greek Row introduced a new house in the fall of 2011, when Phi Kappa Psi celebrated its opening. Built on the grounds of a structure destroyed when a boiler exploded in 2008, the house was the first new building on Greek Row since 1960. After living in scattered locations for three years, members welcomed having their own rooms again. Donations and members' dues defrayed construction costs of some $3 million. Unlike chapters recruiting freshman, Phi Kappa Psi re-quires prospective members to prove themselves as students before joining. With success in academics a priority, Phi Kappa Psi promotes scholarship and positive ethical behavior, and awards success with scholarships.[33]

During the 1990s, students returning for the annual fall "work week," turned what was to be labor and hard work into an interlude of merrymaking, creating problems for Corvallis police, who made hundreds of arrests. Cap-tain Dave Henslee told a *Gazette-Times* reporter that it was time to change the behavior of the houses. Beginning in 2001, the department assigned an officer to each house to create a pipeline of communication to avoid unpleas-ant conflicts. Referred to as the "liaison program," city councilors and the federal Office of Juvenile Justice praised its success. Having created a suc-cessful model, the Corvallis Police Department now offers strategies to police forces as far away as Florida.[34]

The Greek community has changed since the flush decades following the Second World War when the sororities and fraternities were noticeable for the sheer percentages of their presence among the student body. In the second decade of the twenty-first century, some forty-five Greek chapters are represented in three governing councils; however, they make up only about 12 percent of Oregon State's undergraduate population. As always, sororities and fraternities continue to provide leadership in student government, with *Barometer* staff members participating in varsity athletics and other university functions. Whether those students are more or less mature than their predecessors is left to the eye of the beholder.[35]

External events, especially the civil rights movement and the Vietnam War, challenged Oregon States' reputation as an island of tranquility in a state where other public universities were centers of turmoil, rioting, tear gas, and student arrests. Contemporaries who believe that Oregon State University was largely free of disruptions ignore evidence revealing a campus, community, and county going through the throes of cultural and political change. The early 1969 incident involving football coach Dee Andros kicking linebacker Fred Milton off the team for growing facial hair is notable for attracting the attention of national media. Given the spike in student and faculty activism, there was more afoot on campus and in the community than Beaver lore acknowledges. President James Jensen's sudden resignation in mid-1969 may reflect a desire to distance himself from the increasing discord at OSU. Interim president Roy Young, who served until Robert MacVicar arrived in autumn 1970, witnessed the continued escalation of campus protests, sit-ins, arrests, and other demonstrations.

In addition to the Black Student Union boycott and parade off-campus in March 1969, there were other demonstrations and protests. The university hosted the annual meeting of the Pacific Conference on Higher Education in the summer of 1969 under the theme "Confrontations." The gathering featured hot-button topics of the day: "Minorities/Majorities," "Rights/Responsibilities," and "Change/Establishment." Other events witnessed that summer were the arrest on campus of fourteen students and nonstudents protesting the university's refusal to grant tenure to English professor Frank Harper. Those arrested were occupying the office of humanities and social science dean Gordon Gilkey, seeking an explanation for the Harper decision. The incident followed similar demonstrations when students protested the dismissal of another English instructor, Alan Young. Both were popular with students and active in campus antiwar groups.[36]

Turmoil on the Corvallis campus became more intense following the National Guard killing of four students on the Kent State University campus on May 4, 1970. Flyers appeared, "The Draft: Hassle It To Death, Take *Legal*, Non-violent Action." Model copies of letters to US senators were circulated urging students to support resolutions opposing the Vietnam War and praising Corvallis citizens for demonstrating their disapproval of the Kent State shootings. A Veterans for Peace group planned a massive Armed Forces Day parade on May 16. The parade would rally in the quad and march downtown to the Safeway parking lot, where speakers would address issues of the day. A flyer reported that the crowd would return to the quad to avoid violent confrontations with law enforcement personnel. Safeway was linked to the protests, because it sold produce grown and harvested by farmworkers who lacked sanitary facilities and clean drinking water when they were in the field.[37]

Although the *Barometer* provided reasonable coverage of campus disruptions, a better gauge of cultural changes in the community were underground newspapers challenging the status quo. Some of the alternative papers were crudely put together, such as the *Spark*, which lasted for only two or three issues, while others gained more visibility and stature on campus and in the Corvallis community. The *Scab Sheet*, first published in March 1969, focused on the experiences of the university's black students, with its last issues hewing heavily toward opposition to the Vietnam War. Another paper, the *Daily Planet*, published from November 1970 to May 1971, was a bit more sophisticated, carrying advertisements. Like the television comedy *Saturday Night Live*, launched in October 1975, nothing was sacred to the underground scribes. They pilloried the established press, political figures near and far, OSU administrators, student government, coaches, and sororities and fraternities, and offered creative sketches of the objects of their disdain. Printed in Corvallis, the publications were the creation of student activists.[38]

The *Scab Sheet* was the collective effort of the Student Action Committee, a group supporting the Black Student Union's quest for change. Adopting the motto "5c for the truth" as a metaphor for challenging convention, the committee printed approximately a thousand copies per issue and sold every print run. Articles in the *Scab Sheet* were anonymous "because of the fear of harassment and repressive action." In presenting alternative interpretations of events, the *Scab* believed it provided a service to students. Its first issue, appearing amid the campus turmoil over the dismissal of Milton from the football team, accused the football coach of bullying the university administration. Individuals whose interests extended "no further than Jock straps and Tartan Turf" were intimidating the president's office. The paper ridiculed a three-hour faculty senate meeting for adjourning empty-handed, failing to support human and cultural rights. Although the *Scab Sheet* was a simple mimeographed publication, the writing was clear and assertive.[39]

Subsequent issues described black students walking off campus through the historic wrought-iron gates at the east end of campus. The artwork on the front cover of issue number four featured an Athenian-like athlete wearing a tie (President Jensen), kneeling and holding aloft a globe-sized likeness of the Great Pumpkin's head (Coach Andros). The issue included more about the stalemated faculty senate and a letter (titled "Broken-Hearted Melody") reporting that the *Barometer* was threatening to sue the *Scab Sheet*. The newspaper loved Junior Carnival, praising its originality, "a moving extravaganza designed to please beings of all ages, abilities, desires, and frustrations." The weekend promised ten rides that would "carry you to the outer reaches of reality," skill booths, foods of every description, and free music in the evening. It printed a full page of artistry advertising carnival events to take place in Parker Stadium.[40]

The *Scab Sheet* interrogated the English Department's promotion and tenure policies for failing to renew the contracts of three popular instructors. The department's guidelines listed teaching ability as first in importance, yet "in practice it weighted a big, fat ZERO!" In one of its last issues, the *Scab* told of four students traveling south on Ninth Street coming abreast of a vehicle in the curbside lane driven by Dee Andros, "the famous personage himself." While passing the black and orange car, the students all flashed the universal sign for peace. The football coach's "immediate and unfailing response was to flip the universal sign for . . . well, you know what for." The incident prompted the *Scab* to reflect a bit of wisdom—freedom to be obnoxious "is not a right."[41]

The *Daily Planet* differed from the *Scab*—it was more expensive (ten cents) and offered advertising rates. The staff and management of the paper wanted to "tie together the roots of an emerging life culture," seeking contributors, news columns, opinion pieces, stories, articles, photography, and money. It solicited information about public events for future issues and urged those interested to help sell the paper. The *Planet*'s maiden issue featured psychedelic guru Timothy Leary "and people who find freedom outside the laws," and included articles on racism and women's liberation. Under the slogan "Sisterhood is Powerful," a woman who had just learned about the expression praised women's potential for overcoming insecurities to bring about changes in society. The writer was upset that a system offering women unequal pay expected them to keep house and raise children.[42]

Under "People Rock . . . The People Tremble," the *Planet* addressed the myopic behavior of the Student Activities Council for proposing a screening committee to review musical groups performing at the university. Council members had argued that "hard" and "acid" rock performers were attracting unsavory people to campus and creating conditions violating state and federal laws. The council wished to avoid rowdy behavior such as crowds attending the rock group Jefferson Airplane displayed in 1968, when Gill Coliseum reportedly suffered $3,000 in damages. When the concert sponsors threatened to sue the activities council for distorting the cleanup costs, the figure was revised downward to one normal for a crowd of that size. After Jefferson Airplane's appearance, the administration killed invitations to Sly and the Family Stone and Iron Butterfly, decisions the *Barometer* also criticized. The *Planet* featured a news article on the opening of The First Alternative Co-op on Northwest Fourth Street, praising the store's novel view of free enterprise and its opposition to "ripping off their patrons."[43]

Although American military ventures abroad occasionally roiled the Corvallis campus, tensions lessened after the fallout from the disturbances at Kent State. Violence of a different order, however, stalked Oregon State when National Merit Scholar and freshman Nancy Wyckoff was found dead in her room from a stab wound to the heart in the early morning hours of February 8, 1972. At approximately 3:30 a.m., Poling Hall friend Nancy Lundeen heard screams from across the hall and found Wyckoff bloodied and dying. Several other residents heard the screams and sounds of someone running, but no one saw the intruder. Law enforcement investigators found an eight-inch knife and a red flashlight in Wyckoff's room and removed a blood-stained doorknob at the end of the floor leading to a stairwell. Wyckoff's murder, the first in the 105-year history of the institution, put the campus on high alert. The incident was even more traumatic because two other coeds had been attacked in the nights before the murder.[44]

Although Nancy Wyckoff's mother absolved the university of blame in her daughter's death, others in the community were willing to find fault. In a letter to the *Gazette-Times*, Louise Weidlich, president of Mothers for Children, cited the new coed living arrangement, allowing male and female students to live in "sin," as the culprit. She believed students should have less voice in dormitory living arrangements. Another writer thought the university should "return to better moral standards, to good old-fashioned discipline and effective punishment." A male resident of McNary Hall reminded Weidlich that the year was 1972, that coed dorms were not immoral, and that many men and women students enjoyed sharing the same dormitory. But on the third floor of Poling Hall, coeds locked their doors at night and several protested that they were not free to do as they wished. To a person, however, they were adamant that coed living was not the problem. One woman remarked, "We feel safer because there are boys here."[45]

While Poling Hall residents forged ahead with projects to memorialize Nancy Wyckoff's memory—including a tree with a bronze commemorative plaque at its base—Corvallis police were quietly assembling evidence under the guidance of district attorney Frank Knight. With new district attorney James Brown succeeding Knight when Brown retired on February 15, a city and county legal team continued a series of repetitive interviews that finally achieved success when two officers arrested seventeen-year-old engineering student Marlow Buchanan, who confessed that he committed the crime. A graduate of Lake Oswego High School, Buchanan was a brilliant student at all levels of education, including a 4.0 average thus far in his freshman year. In the subsequent trial, the defense portrayed Buchanan as a person with a "schizoid personality," raised by a domineering mother and passive father, and exhibiting behavior that doubted his masculinity. With the defense and prosecution largely agreeing on those details, circuit court judge Richard Mengler found Buchanan guilty of manslaughter and sentenced him to ten years in prison.[46]

Students registering for classes at Oregon State University in the 1980s entered a far different environment than did their parents' generation. Absent from the *General Catalogue* for 1981 were the glowing descriptions of Corvallis, its health-giving qualities, and the bucolic nature walks adjacent to campus. The catalogue was different, more detailed, and businesslike, providing information about "academic programs and policies, faculty, and services." For the first time in its long history, the catalogue included legalese, warning readers that the statements herein did "not constitute a contract between Oregon State University and its students or applicants for admission." Next in order was a declaration of the institution's compliance with federal civil rights and affirmative action programs, with the proviso that it did not discriminate "on the basis of race, color, national origins, religion, sex, age, or handicap." In keeping with the format of catalogues published since 1932, it described the member institutions of the State System of Higher Education, while muting the curricular divisions between the University of Oregon and Oregon State ("specialized, professional, and technical programs are centered at specific institutions"). The catalogue urged international students to ask for an interinstitutional booklet, "It's Your Decision," listing fields of study at system institutions.[47]

The 1981 catalogue listed "estimated" fees and tuition, with yearly totals of $1,200 for residents. Students could also register for courses at other state institutions or the extension division at no added cost, unless they took more than eleven credit hours. Meal charges varied depending on the number of meals and whether students required a specific diet. The catalogue offered housing options, with facilities in West International House exclusively for graduate students of either sex or those over the age of twenty-one. Married students' housing was available in the Orchard Court apartments for $115 to $145 per month. Twenty-seven fraternities and fifteen sororities offered small living-group experiences as housing options. The catalogue cited "principles of friendship, scholarship, mutual respect, helpfulness, and service" as guiding tenets of Greek houses.[48]

Using a puzzle theme, the *Beaver* yearbook for 1981 asked "Where do I fit in?" and portrayed campus activities, performances, weekend celebrations, and other special events. The annual opened with a photo of a military draft rally on the Memorial Union steps featuring veteran codirector Tom Motko protesting President Jimmy Carter's call for a military draft. Motko wanted no more of fighting "for the multinationals and their fat bank accounts." Student-body president Jeff Mengis disparaged the apathy of the 1970s and thought "maybe now in the '80s people are ready to start caring again." With a nod to global events, the yearbook devoted a page to Iran's release of fifty-two American hostages seized by students in Teheran in November 1979 and held in captivity for 444 days.[49]

Lighter events for 1980–1981 included a record-breaking kiss-off in Parker Stadium involving 1,746 students (an even number!) who took part in "a simultaneous, continuous kissing contest" on Valentine's Day. The chairperson of the "kiss-off" promised that the event would make the Guinness Book of World Records. The students formed a giant heart as NBC television crews recorded the kiss. On "Cow Day" there were milk chug-a-lug contests, crowning a dairy princess, egg tossing contests, mechanical bull-riding, and photos of the Mount St. Helens eruption on May 18, 1980, with an estimate of casualties. Moms Weekend featured activities captured in photos from the musical "A Chorus Line" and medieval warriors dueling for a "fair maiden" as part of Renaissance Fair. The latter turned the MU Quad into a marketplace of goodies for sale: ceramics, flowers, jewelry, candles, and food. The featured performer for the weekend was tenor Anne Murray, who charmed a sellout crowd.[50]

The 1981 yearbook included a section on the university's Studio Theater Program, a venue combining "opportunity, experience, [and] free entertainment" to provide students the opportunity to practice drama and its role in education. Students could be actors, directors, stage hands, and producers in an apprenticeship environment; although faculty members were available for consultation, students ran the show. In a refrain that would be repeated in annuals for the next few years, the *Beaver* referred to budget cuts of $2.9 million that affected all colleges, the library, and physical plant operations.

The stringent fiscal environment created havoc for students registering for classes at the beginning of the school year. Students protested cutbacks in Kerr Library hours, a decision eventually rescinded during fall term. Despite those difficulties, the university graduated 3,437 students at the end of the year.[51]

The yearbook returned to celebrating "tradition and pride" in the early 1990s—the Homecoming spirit parade, Dads and Moms Weekends, the OSU Foundation's seventeenth annual (student-operated) Super Telefund, the NCAA National Gymnastics Championship in Gill Coliseum, and the Oregon Newspaper Publishers Association Award of General Excellence to the *Barometer*. Homecoming Weekend revived the spirit parade and bonfire. Fate, however, intervened and disrupted events when rain fell on the weekend, dampening the turnout for the Friday parade and evening bonfire. Earlier in the week, student-body president Shahid Yusaf won a pie-eating contest, with his hands tied behind his back. In the spring, students celebrated the twentieth anniversary of Earth Day, featuring a rally, lectures, and a dance at McAlexander Field House. The university's three cultural centers presented open-house venues, introducing students to unfamiliar cultural worlds. The Black Cultural Center sponsored distinguished lectures during the academic year, including the appearance of Congressman John Lewis of Georgia, a civil rights activist and confidant of Martin Luther King Jr. The Hispanic Center proudly focused on Hispanic cultures, celebrating Cinco de Mayo and its cultural heroes at an open house sponsoring a Mexican dinner and folklore dancers. The Native American longhouse, incorporated in 1969, sponsored educational activities and its annual November Powwow in the Memorial Union Ballroom.[52]

Hints of war returned to the yearbook in the wake of the First Gulf War in the spring of 1991. Two photos symbolized public opinion on the commitment of American troops to force Iraq to end its occupation of Kuwait—a huge sign, "Support Our Troops," draped over the entrance to a Greek house, and students and townspeople holding a "NO WAR" banner across the entrance to the Benton County Court House. The *Beaver* celebrated "Thursday Nights," featuring a new McMenamins on Monroe Street and the old standby, Clodfelters. For the more rowdy, Murphy's Tavern on South Third offered another option. According to one student, Thursday was the best night to roam the town and meet friends: "I don't have many classes the next day, so I like to go out on Thursday night and try to forget about school." The 1991 *Beaver* carried news important to the university's future—the beginning of massive construction projects that would remake the physical parameters of the campus. The building programs under way included the library expansion, the

OSU Child Care Center, the Family Study Center, and the Agricultural Sciences II Building.[53] This marked the onset of construction activity that would continue for two decades and beyond.

While yearbooks highlighted student experiences, college and university catalogues explained institutional requirements and student expectations. Changing times and expectations affected what college administrators deemed important for inclusion in catalogues. Over the decades, OSU catalogues illustrate the enormous academic, moral, and cultural transitions that students experienced. While four faculty members taught at the institution when the State of Oregon assumed control of the college in 1885, students enrolling in the fall of 1990 faced a full-time faculty of 2,160. They could also choose from five thousand courses, 120 different undergraduate programs, and more than seventy graduate degrees. Students had access to 350 social, athletic, academic, and honor societies, and in the evening and on weekends there were athletic events and cultural and social activities—concerts, lectures, recitals, dances, and other venues. Where two students from each Oregon county could attend college free of charge in 1884–1885, in the fall of 1991 full-time tuition for resident undergraduates was $933. Room and board rates would have been unrecognizable to nineteenth-century students (indeed to those graduating in 1980). Unlike the 1880s, when administrators permitted men and women to socialize on limited occasions, by the 1990s they could live in the same dormitories, although on separate floors.[54]

Freshman registering in the fall of 1991 could expect "excellence and quality," the university's watchwords for expanding knowledge and research and assisting people "through a commitment to service," acknowledging OSU's land-grant mission. The catalogue assured students that OSU's highly qualified faculty, excellent library, research accomplishments, educational opportunities for the disadvantaged, and extracurricular activities provided opportunities for everyone. The catalogue touted the quality of its engineering graduates, its exceptional accounting programs, and the university's College of Forestry, "the first of its kind in the nation." Other claims to excellence included the Honors College, which offered intellectual challenges through colloquia, seminars, and research projects for superior students. There was much more—ROTC, study abroad, the National Student Exchange (within the United States), and the Experimental College, offering more than two hundred courses.[55]

The implementation of baccalaureate core undergraduate degree requirements in 1990 dramatically affected the courses students were expected to take. The new curricular program likely baffled prospective students when they read the formidable new course requirements. Under three broad categories—skills, perspectives, and synthesis—the baccalaureate core emphasized "writing, creative thinking, cultural diversity, the arts, science, literature, life-long fitness, and global awareness." The curricular mandates were central to the university's land-grant mission to provide the basics of an educated citizenry: "curiosity, rigorous observation, tolerant understanding, and a commitment to lifelong learning." Pie-in-the-sky objectives, a few critics muttered, the requirements directed students to clusters of courses that previous generations had never experienced.[56]

A perusal of the *Beaver* published in the spring of 2001 portrays a joyous campus during the previous year—Homecoming, Dads and Moms Weekends, the civil war football game, a dance marathon, and a litany of musicals, plays, and visiting performers. In a year that culminated in the climactic events of 9/11, the yearbook summarized the controversial presidential election of 2000, left undecided until the US Supreme Court decision confirmed Republican candidate George Bush the winner over Democrat Al Gore on December 12. At the civil war football game in Parker Stadium on November 18 (after the election and before the court decision), a sign-carrier evoked the sentiments of some in the crowd:

> 4 President
> ☐ Bush/Cheney
> ☐ Gore/Lieberman
> ☑ Smith/Simonton
> GO BEAVERS [57]

Students returned to Corvallis in the fall of 2001 with the dust still settling from the terrorist attack on New York's World Trade Center on September 11. With six pages of Associated Press photos and accompanying narrative, the 2002 *Beaver* published images of panic, heroism, dismay, sorrow, and destruction. "It was a day no one will ever forget," Samantha Hudson wrote, with people donating blood and doing what they could after the shock of the attacks subsided. Administrators established a gathering place for students in the Memorial Union, and on September 14 the university community took part in the National Day of Prayer and Remembrance. Athletic Director Mitch Barnhart cancelled Saturday's September 15 football game with Montana State, the unprecedented tragedy making the game insignificant.[58]

When President George Bush sent military forces to Afghanistan to strike at terrorist training camps, 9/11 would have lasting influences in other ways. The president's decision set in motion what war correspondent Dexter Filkins refers to as a war without end: ongoing violence in Afghanistan, Iraq, and elsewhere that seemingly had no end. American military ventures would once more involve graduates from OSU's ROTC programs and members of the National Guard and military reserves. With the onset of the Arab Spring in the Middle East in 2010, and the evolution of some of those protests into radical Islamic movements, American forces initiated air strikes to deter Islamic advances and committed troops to train Iraqi forces and Syrian freedom fighters.[59]

With other colleges and universities, OSU regrouped from the New York City tragedy. The Corvallis school carried on with traditional celebrations, including the nationally televised civil war football game played at the University of Oregon's Autzen Stadium on December 1, 2001. The *Beaver* observed that tension was thick before the game, with "neither side compromising the faith that this year their team will come out on top." Despite leaving Eugene disappointed, Beaver fans had high hopes for next year, when the Ducks would be "playing in Beaver territory." Oregon State was coming off its best year ever in 2000–2001, when the team finished 11–1, defeating Notre Dame 41–9 in the Fiesta Bowl. Oregon State's one hundred and thirty-third commencement in June 2002 graduated 3,558 students. The degree recipients represented thirty-five of the state's thirty-six counties, forty-five of the fifty states, and forty-six foreign countries, truly an eclectic and diverse group.[60]

Four years after the controversial 2000 presidential election, OSU's student government sponsored a voter-registration drive, stopping students in the MU Quad, clipboards in hand, with the timeless question, "Are you registered to vote?" The nonpartisan, festive fall event featured live music and a beer garden (for those of age). Although there was no mention of the number registered, the *Beaver* reported a great turnout on a beautiful fall day. For the once-conservative campus, the 2004 fall season featured another important event: the gay, lesbian, bisexual, and transsexual community celebrating the grand opening of the Pride Center in a newly renovated building. With President Ed Ray doing the ribbon-cutting, pride members heralded the center as a secure place for LGBT students and an opportunity to promote acceptance among the general population.[61]

OSU's twenty-first-century students were increasingly adventurous, with the Rainbow Continuum sponsoring its third annual Drag Show. Although the *Beaver* failed to mention previous shows, the 2005 yearbook devoted two pages to the event, reporting a packed nightclub, loud music, an enthusiastic audience, and "sexy women in high heels." The Club Escape venue, with a sold-out crowd of three hundred, featured men and women switching gender roles and lip-synching to dance music. The evening proved popular, selling out for the second year running. The previous year's "Queen of the Beaver," Lucilla DeMore (aka Luke Sugie) performed "Santa Baby." Sugie told the *Beaver* reporter that he had been doing drag shows for two years, finding the experience fun "with people that made me feel comfortable." He had played both king and queen in previous performances, finding the latter the most time-consuming to prepare for.[62]

For Dads Weekend in November 2004, the Improv All Stars—Drew Carey, Colin Mochrie, Greg Proops, and four others—entertained at Gill Coliseum with ninety minutes of hilarious comedy. Carey opened the show with "What's up Beavers?" and then proceeded to mock Paris Hilton, Democrats, and international politicians. Before the improv group ended its show, Greg Proops wished the Beavers well in their football game the following night against USC. "We all live in southern California," he told the crowd, "but none of us are from there, so we hope you win." Playing against the number one team in the nation, the Beaver footballers played through a thick fog the following night, leading 13–0 at one point, but then the Trojans fought through the adverse conditions on their way to a 28–20 win. The high point for the visitors was Heisman candidate Reggie Bush's sixty-five-yard punt return for a touchdown. Two weeks later the Beaver football team sent their loyal fans home happy, beating the Ducks in the annual civil war game 50–21 and becoming bowl eligible.[63]

In a year of firsts, Oregon State University restored its women's cross-country program in 2004. (Men's and women's teams had been disbanded in 1987.) The athletic department hired Kelly Sullivan, who left a successful track and field program at Willamette University to launch the women's team that fall. Twenty-six students, a few freshmen and a mix of upper classmen who simply enjoyed running, turned out for fall practice sporting shirts with the words "We Are Back." Coach Sullivan reported that nineteen members of his first team were women who had attended informational meetings or may have read advertisements in the *Barometer*. With one scholarship to award, most of the runners were walk-ons. In its first meet in early October at Eastern Washington University, the squad placed second against competition from smaller schools. Later that month the Beavers hosted their first home cross-country event in seventeen years, with junior Katie Magnuson placing fifteenth of sixty-four runners. At the major NCAA

West Regional Championships in November, the Beaver women surprised everyone, placing sixteenth among twenty-nine teams.[64]

Students attending freshman orientation—Connect Week—in the fall of 2010 were treated to a new spirit slogan, "Powered by Orange." The university launched the campaign with posters, banners, bright orange spots on sidewalks and buildings, and a free lunch in the MU Quad. "Once students set foot on campus this year," Ben Sunberg wrote for the *Barometer*, "they will be seeing the world through orange-tinted glasses." The program originated with the Office of Student Life, in 2009, whose mission was to provide support services for students. The Powered by Orange catchphrase was an attempt to revive campus traditions associated with the university's culture, to build a sense of community, and to advance socializing among students from different classes. The new Office of Student Life developed an elaborate administrative language that would have been unfamiliar to recent alumni and other supporters of the university.[65]

The Office of Student Life administered multifaceted programs: Career Services, Child Care and Family Resources, Disability Access Services, the Healthy Campus Initiative, the ASOSU offices of advocacy and student advocate, Human Services Resource Center, New Student Programs and Family Outreach, Student Conduct and Community Standards, Student Care, and Veterans Services. Despite its dizzying portfolio, the office's initial report addressed on-campus issues—personal crises, mental health problems, and academic difficulties. Important responsibilities included addressing the growing friction between the university's rapid growth and disgruntled residents in surrounding neighborhoods. Reflecting "town and gown" concerns, the university hired a person to serve as liaison between OSU and its neighbors. The Office of Student Life also promoted diversity, strengthening community through greater cultural awareness and celebrating difference, because "Everyone Matters."[66]

Although the successes of the student life initiative remains an open question, conventional student practices continued, with the Powered by Orange logo used to advertise the 2009 Homecoming, "haunted by orange." Around campus the sounds of workers resonated—operating jackhammers, backhoes, and cement trucks to upgrade access to buildings for people with disabilities and improving parking lots and sidewalks. Construction on the Linus Pauling Center was under way in 2010, as well as the Hallie Ford Center for Healthy Children and Families and a new dormitory for international students.[67] With its sesquicentennial looming a few years hence, the campus was in the midst of a huge building boom, with ever-greater numbers of students, circumstances that would further exacerbate tensions between the university and the community. For the foreseeable future, student activities would need to navigate carefully through those tensions.

13
Into the Future

Between 1980 and 2010 Oregon's population grew from approximately 2.6 million to 3.8 million, an impressive 46 percent, with in-migrations accounting for much of the increase. During the same period, Benton County grew from 68,211 in 1980 to 85,817 in 2010, and the City of Corvallis from 40,960 to 54,338. The stunning feature of those figures is that Oregon's public colleges and universities show no comparable enrollment increases until the twenty-first century. Statistics for Oregon State University reflect a relatively flat profile between 1970 and 2000, with the university enrolling 15,509 students in 1970 and 16,788 at the onset of the new millennium. In the next decade, however, state system institutions exploded to 96,960 students in 2010, with the Corvallis school increasing to 23,761 (approximately seven thousand additional students).[1]

Although the university added only 1,279 students between 1970 and 2000, the blueprints for expansions to accommodate the stunning enrollment growth in the next decade were being put in place during the 1990s. A host of new buildings and programs initiated in the late twentieth century set the table for growing student numbers in the new century. The Oregon State University Foundation was forging ahead of the University of Oregon and Portland State University in fund-raising in the early 1990s, bringing in some $27.1 million in the fiscal year ending in 1993. Renovations to existing structures and groundbreaking for new buildings abounded during John Byrne's final years as president and continued apace under Paul Risser. Construction began on the $40 million expansion of the soon-to-be renamed Valley Library and the CH2M-Hill Alumni Center in the spring of 1996. The College of Forestry's new Richardson Hall was dedicated in the spring of 1999, along with the completion of Valley Library. Another event important to OSU's future was the relocation of the Linus Pauling Institute of Science and Medicine to the Corvallis campus in 1996. In March of the following year, the university launched OSU Statewide, a distance-learning module operating through community colleges and other locations around the state to enable students to earn college degrees.[2]

The renovated and expanded Valley Library, named to honor donors E. Wayne Valley and Gladys Valley in 1996, was formally dedicated in 1999. President John Byrne, who led fund-raising for the $40 million project before he left office, had the donor agreements in hand for construction to begin in the spring of 1996. The new Library provides study spaces on all six floors, group study rooms, and research rooms available by reservation. Contemporary Northwest art is displayed throughout the building. The main branch of OSU Libraries, Valley Library also houses Ecampus, home to the university's on-line degree programs. Courtesy of the OSU Special Collections and Archives Research Center.

The *Oregon Stater* set the tone for the university's ambitious building activity, observing in June 1996 that construction costs for that year would be close to $88 million. In addition to the library, the Industrial Building was being rebuilt after a devastating fire destroyed much of the structure in 1992. The expansion of the Valley Football Center was under way, and a major remodeling project was taking place at the Hatfield Marine Science Center in Newport. The most intriguing story about those ventures was funding—the state was no longer a significant player in bankrolling costs. Private giving and state bonds shared equally in financing the $40 million, 147,000-square-foot addition to the library and upgrading its delivery services. The $6.5 million CH2M-Hill Alumni Center, completed in 1997, was privately funded, along with the $5.5 million expansion of the Valley Football Center. While insurance covered the new Industrial Building, the federal government paid for the renovated Hatfield Center and for upgrading and expanding its docking and supply facilities.[3]

Oregon State University was moving aggressively to extend its historic mission to reach citizens distant from Corvallis. No initiative would surpass its efforts to establish a satellite program in Bend. OSU's presence in central Oregon originated with a few upper-division courses in the mid-1980s,

televised microwaved classes taught live in Corvallis and delivered simultaneously to students in the growing liberal studies program on the Central
Oregon Community College (COCC) campus in Bend. Those one-way visual
and audio courses initiated the delivery of liberal studies classes to central
Oregon and eventually elsewhere. The State Board of Higher Education formally awarded OSU jurisdiction over its four-year Bend program in February
2001. Classes were to begin on the COCC campus the following September,
offering dual enrollment for COCC students leading to twenty bachelor's and
graduate degrees. With the attack on the World Trade Center buildings on
September 11, 2001, Oregon State cancelled the grand opening of its Cascades
campus, scheduled for September 16.[4]

Oregon's three major universities were part of a larger phenomenon, the
increasing corporatization of higher education enterprises. State support for
colleges and universities nationwide had fallen sharply beginning in the early
1980s. After passage of Oregon's Ballot Measure 5 in 1990, private sector funding has played a larger role in the state's three principal universities, turning
components of conventional academic life into market-oriented objectives not
always consonant with traditional educational programs. Escalating student
debt for tuition, fees, books, and living expenses, the hallmarks of modern
higher education, have plagued students in public and private institutions,
with a few high-profile cases of cozy relations between college loan officials and
private-sector lenders. Athletics, especially football and basketball programs,
fixtures at most major institutions, is another critical piece of the corporate
university. Although larger schools feature football and basketball as money-
making propositions, respected Harvard University president Derek Bok
observed that "many do not, especially if the capital costs of their facilities are
accurately counted." Critics James Schulman and William Bowen reported in
2001 that athletics was "bad business" if it was expected to be a money-making
proposition.[5] This is not to suggest corruption or wrongdoing on the Corvallis
campus, but to indicate that OSU administrators and policymakers—like their
counterparts at other institutions—have been operating in an increasingly
corporatized environment for nearly four decades.

The accelerating construction activity on the Corvallis campus in the later
years of Byrne's presidency continued apace through Paul Risser's seven years
in office. Risser, who taught at the University of Oklahoma, directed the Illinois Natural History Survey, served as an administrator at the University of
New Mexico, and was president of Miami University in Ohio before accepting the OSU job. A well-known and widely published grasslands ecologist,

he assumed the presidency in January 1996. During his first five months in office, the new president took part in two ribbon-cutting ceremonies—the library expansion and the CH2M-Hill Alumni Center.[6]

In the midst of this busy activity, the administration restructured the university's fund-raising apparatus, with most of the reorganization taking place between 1996 and 1998. The Office of Development, under the Byrne administration's decision in 1987 to separate fund-raising from the OSU Foundation, had successfully raised millions of dollars to support major building programs. At first, those fund-raising strategies were centralized, with a few individuals coordinating most of the footwork. By the early 1990s, however, individual campus units—colleges, centers, and directors of special programs—were doing considerable fund-raising themselves. When Risser arrived, unhappy persons in the development office began pushing the administration to restructure the university's gifting solicitations.[7]

The director of development, John Evey, wrote the president in February 1996 outlining a centralized plan for development that he had shared with Byrne and Provost Roy Arnold. He told Risser that his responsibilities were to "raise major gifts so that OSU can construct important buildings and endow chairs." Evey believed he had successfully carried out that mission. "Never," he added, "have I been told to focus on making the deans happy." The problem was obvious—individual unit fund-raisers were competing with each other and thereby harming the institution's interests. "Continued compartmentalization is not the solution," Evey wrote, "nor is competition among units for budget dollars or donor prospects." And, if he were to stay at OSU, Evey wanted fair compensation in return for the millions of dollars he had raised for the university.[8]

There was also considerable dissension in the university's fund-raising enterprise. According to Evey, Gene Kersey, head of the OSU Foundation, and Bob Bruce, interim head of Institutional Advancement and director of University Relations, thought keeping the deans and their fund-raisers happy "equates to productivity." Because of its built-in redundancies, that approach was inefficient in soliciting gifts. If the president wanted a fund-raising growth rate equal to that of the past decade, OSU's development strategy needed to change. Evey was upset that Bob Bruce, who was unfamiliar with donors, was trying to undo what he had accomplished. In a related issue in late January, the president had already reprimanded Bruce for making "unilateral personnel changes" in his absence: "Under no circumstances is a cabinet officer to make decisions at this level without discussion with me and approved by me."[9] While Evey's letters to the president were presumptuous and self-serving, the university would soon adopt a fund-raising strategy very much in concert with his proposal.

Another fund-raiser, Cliff Dalton, informed the president that the present system had evolved over many years from a centralized strategy "to a mixed model with both central and unit development components." In the interim, there was discord between the development office (especially John Evey) and other university units vying for the same funding sources. Those problems, according to Dalton, "were further compounded by the territorial posture of the deans." Although John Byrne never took a strong position on development, Evey devoted most of his time to fund-raising rather than managing the development office. Dalton called Evey "an excellent major gift fund raiser," but faulted his management shortcomings and not being a team player. To improve gift solicitations, he advised Risser to shift the strategy "from unit to university" and allow donors to determine what their gifts should support.[10]

President Risser moved forward with a revised plan in April 1996—"University Development—*Creating a Unified Approach*." An earlier draft—"Realignment of Institutional Advancement"—explained the failures of previous development strategies, missed opportunities, duplication in fund-raising, and ineffective use of time and effort. Risser's final draft called for "a unified approach to development and university/alumni relations" to increase financial support without hiring additional personnel. The key to the new structure would be three related units—Development and University Relations, University Communications and Marketing, and the University Development Council.[11]

Gene Kersey, now director of the Office of Development, issued a memorandum to implement the president's plan to streamline development office communications and relations with the campus community. To assure respectful approaches to donors, Kersey drafted new management policies for field personnel and urged more efficient use of staff. John Evey, who would soon be departing for the University of the Pacific, suggested to the president that he work through the summer with major donors with whom he had developed good relations during the previous decade. Evey asked, in return, for an enhanced salary through September 20, 1996, vacation pay, and time to make brief trips to the University of the Pacific at its expense.[12]

With a better grasp of development priorities by the spring of 1998, and with university-wide gift solicitations centralized, Risser directed the OSU Foundation to assume full responsibility for fund-raising. The move redefined OSU Foundation responsibilities, including recruiting a CEO responsible for appointing a first-class development organization while continuing to oversee its asset-management enterprises. With the approval of the OSU Foundation's board, development responsibilities were collapsed back into the foundation's everyday tasks, restoring a separation that had existed for a decade.[13]

While the president wrestled with university fund-raising strategies, the institution expanded its use of interactive television and online classes to offer liberal studies degrees through the state system's University Center at Central Oregon Community College (COCC). By the fall of 1996, OSU staff members were teaching in Bend on evenings and weekends, providing weekday televised classes, and offering online Internet and individualized directed learning (IDL) courses. Because the programs were popular, promoters in Bend began lobbying the state board to establish another four-year state college in central Oregon. The *Bend Bulletin* reported that Chancellor Joseph Cox thought such an option might provide good results in a decade or so. COCC president Bob Barber disagreed, telling the *Bulletin* that central Oregon's needs for a four-year school were immediate and pressing.[14]

With legislative support, the chancellor's office expanded Bend's University Center in June 1997 to assist industry and business, establish undergraduate and graduate degrees, provide continuing education and professional development, and coordinate degree programs among participating institutions. The University Center would coordinate several public and private schools offering bachelor's and master's degrees and certificate programs. The center's Dick Markwood sent a memorandum to President Risser and Chancellor Cox suggesting the need for a "work group" to develop a long-range strategy to present to the next legislative session. Such an approach, he believed, would focus on central Oregon's needs and fit with "OSU's strategic agenda to serve the State."[15]

Through the summer and fall of 1997, OSU administrators worked with central Oregon legislators, COCC officials, the Oregon Business Council, the US Forest Service, and the State Board of Higher Education to establish a four-year college. Forrest Rogers, who represented the university in central Oregon, suggested to Risser and Provost Arnold that OSU consider transforming the University Center—reputedly the chancellor's project—into a separate unit. His proposal advanced when OSU signed a memorandum of agreement in early 1998 to assign a full-time extension service faculty to teach at COCC's Chandler Center. Those efforts to establish a four-year institution in Bend created friction among institutional players, with the *Bulletin* reporting that OSU, the UO, and Eastern Oregon University were involved in turf wars for entry into a lucrative educational market.[16]

Central Oregon supporters continued to seek a long-term commitment from the State Board of Higher Education. COCC president Bob Barber echoed that sentiment, and Bend resident Marilyn Beem worried that the University Center was being fed "leftovers from the [state run] schools." Chancellor Cox moved the central Oregon project forward in September 1998 when he released a draft document, "'Central Oregon University': The Compelling 20 Year Vision," declaring the need for a university offering upper-division courses focusing on areas important to central Oregon. A *Bulletin* editorial followed with the observation that the region's citizens "find themselves at an educational crossroads," with the promise of a four-year school looming somewhere in the future. To achieve that goal, COCC officials should serve as supporting players and central Oregonians should be less worried about local control.[17]

Oregon State University's commitment to central Oregon gained traction over the next several months, when COCC's Board of Directors declared its support for a four-year institution, and Chancellor Cox appointed an advisory board to guide the development of higher education in the region. At the chancellor's request, President Risser appointed a committee to draft a plan for a branch campus in Bend. The coup de grace for OSU was the president's message to the faculty and staff on February 7, 2001—the chancellor's recommendation that Oregon State University be awarded a branch campus in central Oregon. Describing the decision as "a major event in the evolution of Oregon State University," the president applauded the institution's land-grant tradition: "When the people of Oregon are served, we can take pride and share in a sense of accomplishment." The state board ratified the chancellor's recommendation one week later.[18]

The capstone to OSU's Cascades campus rests in an exchange of letters between Arthur Golden of Eugene, who had "an intimate and emotional . . . interest in the Bend campus," and President Risser. Golden observed that University of Oregon president Dave Frohnmayer and wife Lynn were pleased that the UO would be a participant in the undertaking. Golden hoped for even greater cooperation between the two universities—"After all, wouldn't this be the best of two worlds?" Risser appreciated the note and thought mechanisms were in place for cooperation between the institutions. He believed the state board had selected OSU because of its innovative proposal and its "long-time and deep commitment to Central Oregon."[19]

In another manifestation of its mission to serve Oregon citizens, OSU had already upgraded its instructional services across the state when President John Byrne placed the extension service and the Office of Continuing Education into the new Office of Extended Education. Under the direction of a dean who would report to the provost, the new unit would have equivalency with the eleven academic colleges. Byrne's initiative reflected the strategy spelled out in Emery Castle's report, *On the University's Third Mission: Extended Education* (1993). The integrated unit would create a responsive and customer-driven system to provide Oregonians with greater access to university resources. "Implementation of a new approach to extended education," Byrne declared, "will fundamentally change the University."[20]

The Office of Extended Education fit the university's blueprint for delivering instructional programs to citizens living in remote geographical locations. The new unit's reports emphasized OSU's long-standing commitment to the land-grant tradition and dovetailed nicely with the Oregon State System of Higher Education's distance education policy (1995). Its planning principles included the assumption that part-time students would have access to courses comparable to regular enrollees on campus. The state system's distance education directive raised significant planning issues: "blending" campus and off-campus instruction, dividing and coordinating responsibility among member schools, and whether Bend's University Center model should be pursued elsewhere.[21]

Oregon State University had been involved in distance education since the early 1980s, believing that the institution's resources were important to the state's economy. The university expanded that view in its Distance Education Plan, a strategy developed in early 1997 to deliver fourteen degree programs, certificate and licensure courses, and high school classes to locations throughout the state. The plan emphasized the university's statewide commitment to deliver instructional resources broadly, all of it "founded in its mission as a Land Grant institution." To assure the success of its ambitious distance education project, its programs would provide on-campus services to off-campus students and assist faculty in developing instructional strategies to fit distance education environments.[22]

By the fall of 1997, OSU hoped to provide every Oregonian with access to an education "as convenient as their home computer, telephone or mailbox." The university established an Alumni College, allowing former students to enroll in classes to strengthen their degree programs and to keep their e-mail address for a lifetime. President Risser repeated the genesis of remarks he made as a candidate for the OSU presidency: "This is the first time . . . a university in this country has made the entire state its campus by providing these kinds of courses and curriculum across the state." While the president's statement may have been exaggerated, OSU announced that it would partner with other state system schools and community colleges to offer new degree programs. Its broad geographic scope would extend through Willamette Valley cities from Portland to Eugene, coastal communities from Astoria to Coos Bay, and to Medford, Pendleton, Hood River, The Dalles, La Grande, and Ontario.[23]

The distance education initiative would mean closer relations between the extension service and academic units on campus. Extension service faculty were assigned to appropriate disciplines in departments and colleges. Seeking to expand course offerings, the Office of Extended Education published an *OSU Statewide Catalogue* to publicize the opportunity for people to complete baccalaureate degrees. As part of its rapidly evolving distance education programs, the university replaced "Extended Education" with "OSU Statewide" as the new unit title for its outreach courses. OSU Statewide's umbrella was broad, embracing long-standing units—the Extension Service, Agricultural Experiment Station, Forest Research Laboratory, Hatfield Marine Science Center, Portland Center, Capitol Center (Beaverton), the OSU Center in Medford, Alumni College, and the High School Outreach Program. OSU Statewide created two new administrative positions, the Dean of Distance and Continuing Education and the Dean and Director of the OSU Extension Service.[24]

One critical component in this explosion of academic delivery programs to distant places involved the question of responsibility for the academic integrity of courses. Early on in this ambitious enterprise, Provost Roy Arnold stipulated that academic colleges and departments were responsible for degree programs: "The faculty of the academic colleges design courses, curriculum and degree programs, and deliver them throughout Oregon with support from Distance and Continuing Education." The issue was a cardinal moment for departmental control of courses to be taught and the people selected to teach them. Former Harvard University president Derek Bok warned in 2003 that the money-making potential for extended education programs would circumvent traditional faculty oversight and responsibility for the courses taught. The chronic need for money, he cautioned, would move some institutions into ill-considered decision-making.[25] At Oregon State, faculty retained control over those who taught distance education courses.

As OSU moved into the twenty-first century, the university celebrated OSU Statewide in its "Good News Talking Points," the administration's strategy for highlighting electronic services to students through campus information "kiosks" and providing Internet access to dormitory rooms. The American Productivity and Quality Center named OSU the preeminent institution in the United States and Canada for providing electronic connections to its constituents. The highlight to OSU's "Talking Points," however, was OSU Statewide and its curricular delivery to twenty sites around the state. An important component of the program was its availability to students on the Confederated Tribes of the Warm Springs Reservation, enabling native students to complete a baccalaureate program without leaving the reservation.[26]

Along with Robert MacVicar and John Byrne before him, Paul Risser faced continuing problems with the troubled athletic department. Athletic Director D. Thomas "Dutch" Baughman and football coach Jerry Pettibone, both holdovers from the previous administration, failed to reverse the university's long stretch of losing seasons in football. When Risser arrived, critics of the football program abounded, with many calling for a complete housecleaning, to include the AD and the entire football coaching staff. There were also bothersome issues unrelated to competence on the sporting field, some of it reaching the sports pages of the Portland *Oregonian*. There had been rumors through the early 1990s that Baughman, an evangelical Christian, judged a coach's credentials based on religious persuasion. Coach Pettibone, like his boss, was an evangelical Christian. Those were sensitive issues for presidents Byrne and Risser, because they involved significant donors to athletics who praised Baughman and Pettibone for running "clean" programs.[27]

Newspaper reports and rumors about religious influences in OSU athletics prompted the faculty senate to ask Dutch Baughman to address the issue. Referring to accusations in the *Oregonian*, Baughman told the senate that when he recently addressed a private meeting of the Fellowship of Christian Athletics, he was unaware that reporters were present. If he had known otherwise, he would have been more careful about his remarks. He denied rumors that religious persuasion played a role in hiring coaches. Senator Robin Landau, however, pursued the religious issue, asking why coaches, who have faculty status, were leading athletes in prayer in public facilities while they were on the job? The athletic director admitted that prayer was taking place in the football program and that he had asked Coach Pettibone to end the practice. He told the senate that he had sought counsel on matters of church and state and what was permissible as an employee of the university.[28]

The football program's most critical problem in the fall of 1996 was a team in the midst of its twenty-sixth consecutive losing season. In his sixth year as coach, Jerry Pettibone was coming off a one and ten record the previous year, and as the losses mounted in 1996—with the school in the midst of a fourteen-game losing streak—the voices calling for his ouster grew louder. With the Beavers 0–4 in early October, the *New York Times* reported that Pettibone promised that Oregon State would win in 1996. After yet another loss, he praised the team for playing well, remarking, "There were so many good things we did in that game." For teams on long losing streaks, the *Times* observed, "even a close loss can be turned into an emotional victory." The *Oregonian's* respected sports columnist Dwight Janes was less charitable after another loss, with the Beaver offense totaling 187 yards, with eight fumbles, four interceptions, and 286 yards in penalties. Most annoying to Janes were Pettibone's comments after the game—"I feel good; we can have a good team." The columnist wrote that the entertainment sold on Saturday "was consumer fraud."[29]

At the conclusion of the two and nine season, it seemed clear that the football coach, and perhaps the athletic director, would be dismissed. But then a torrent of letters landed on President Risser's desk asking him to retain Pettibone and Baughman for another year. Because most of the letters referred to "integrity," "character," "moral ethics," "leadership," "loyalty," and "good citizen"—interspersed with frequent allusions to God, spiritualism, and prayer—it is fair to assume that the inch-thick folder of correspondence was orchestrated. The letters echoed John Fagan's early November column in the *Gazette-Times,* in which he asked, "Do we want to turn out the O. J. Simpsons, Michael Irvins, and Isaiah Riders or the A. C. Greenes, Jeff Harts, and Congressman Steve Largents?" Many of the letters included copies of Fagan's article. A Portland writer, Jonathan Weaver, who knew Baughman, called for the dismissal of both the football coach and athletic director. The reasoned tone of his letter went beyond wins and losses, faulting Baughman for lacking business acumen and fiscal management, fund-raising, and marketing skills. Because the program was "dull, humorless and a failure," Weaver urged Risser to assert "leadership" and reverse the downward spiral.[30]

A few weeks after another civil war loss to Oregon, Jerry Pettibone "retired," with the university negotiating a settlement of $200,000 for the remaining two years of his contract. That move prompted some who supported Pettibone's dismissal to refuse to renew their annual pledges to the Beaver Club. One disgruntled alum told Risser that if he ever left "the football/ entertainment business (at which you are third rate) and get back into the education business, I will be happy to resume contributions." The *Oregonian* commended Pettibone for his players' accomplishments in the classroom, but the newspaper thought OSU had mortgaged its future when it awarded Pettibone the retirement package: "Why give him a $200,000 golden parachute in gratitude for a job that was poorly done?" Baughman lasted only a few more months as athletic director, resigning in August 1997, telling reporters that he had wearied of the criticisms. Success for the football program, he believed, was critically important to his job. "I don't know if you can put too much emphasis on how important." [31]

With new football coach Mike Riley on board in December 1996, the athletic department had still not turned the page on its troubles. Its long-standing struggle with budget deficits, ranging between $2.5 million and $2.8 million in the early 1990s, increased to $3.2 million in 1996, $5.8 million in 1997, and was projected to reach $8.9 million in 1998. The department noticed an increase in the deficit in the last half of 1996, a fact confirmed following an extensive audit in mid-1997. The department cited growing costs for scholarships, decreases in gifting, and a commitment to Title IX compliance—scholarships for female athletes—to explain the upward-spiraling debt. To cover those expenses, the university raised yearly resident tuition to $1,445 in the fall of 1996.[32]

The head of finance and administration, Lee Schroeder, appointed interim athletic director when Baughman resigned, repeated the accepted rationale for the deficit—the investment of significant funds in women's sports and scholarships to meet Title IX compliance. The declining competitiveness of OSU's revenue-producing sports meant a sharp drop in ticket sales. Schroeder argued that the only way to climb out of the deficit was "to increase income and cut expenditures." Mark McCambridge, in the finance office, reported that the deficit ballooned when football attendance in 1996 dropped to a season average of 25,196, the lowest attendance figure since 1991 and the worst in the Pac-10. Hiring Mike Riley, moreover, added to the debt load. McCambridge agreed with Schroeder that the deficit could be fixed without affecting the rest of the university, a dubious claim given that tuition had already been increased.[33]

Lee Schroeder faced a daunting task in the fall of 1997, overseeing the search for a new athletic director and resolving the department's burgeoning debt of $5.3 million. The athletic department, he told the faculty senate, had consistently reported large expenditures in the face of declining revenue. By cutting operating expenses, the department expected to be debt free by 2003. Schroeder reported that for the first time the Beaver Club had contributed to women's athletics to help meet gender equity requirements. When senators asked if there were reprimands when the athletic department exceeded its earlier debt limit, Schroeder indicated there were no penalties.[34]

The faculty senate's dance with the athletic department deficit continued into 1998, when President Risser met with faculty representatives in February. Senator Mike Oriard pointed out that most of the deficit had occurred recently and wanted to know why the athletics department was allowed to go further into debt. The problems were long-standing, the president replied, and would continue for another year before they would reverse. Risser believed it would take six to seven years before the department would be debt free. To move forward, the department adopted accounting procedures similar to other units on campus and the athletic director would approve all charges over $100. The department would also make monthly accounting reports to the faculty senate to assure that it was lowering its debt.[35]

When new Athletic Director Mitch Barnhart came aboard in the spring of 1998, he posted five departmental objectives: foster good relations with the public, follow the rules, see that athletes leave the university with degrees, be fiscally responsible, and put competitive teams in play. He told the faculty senate that he would reorganize the department, add members to the Athletics Advisory Committee, and forbid coaches from leading teams in prayer. After an additional loan from the university of $1.75 million, Barnhart learned late in the spring that his department's accumulated deficit at the end of the fiscal year was expected to be $8.6 million. He met with the senate again in March 1999, reporting that the deficit would be reduced to $6 million by the end of June. With the lowest athletic budget in the Pac-10, Barnhart told senators that the athletic department had reduced its spending by $2 million during the last year.[36]

When the athletic department's fiscal crisis worsened in the spring of 1999, President Risser, Rob Spector (the new head of finance and administration), and Mitch Barnhart brought their case to the State Board of Higher Education in May. Because the athletic department was unable to pay the promised $2 million to the university, the board ordered OSU to reduce the department's debt to $6 million by June 30. Spector, who later met with the faculty senate, told senators that the athletic deficit was impossible to resolve without access to additional institutional funds, including an increase in student fees. Although a variety of sources supported athletics, under the present formula, athletics would never be sustainable. Spector pointed to other schools in the Pac-10 where universities had to write off athletic debts. Displeased with Spector's remarks, physics professor Robin Landau responded that "Athletics matter and academics don't." Robert Robson from mathematics thought raising student fees was a disturbing option, sending a negative message to students. Spector replied that student fees at the University of Oregon and Portland State were already higher than those at OSU.[37]

To keep faith with the chancellor's office and the state board, President Risser sent an e-mail circular to the faculty in June 1999 explaining his decision to invest additional institutional funds in the athletic program. In addition to conventional problems with the department's debt, he added another, "lapses in past management." He repeated the state board's mandate that the university reduce its debt to $6 million by the end of the month. While donors had made significant contributions, the remainder of the money would come from the university's regular budget. "The additional funding to Athletics," Risser indicated, "will reduce the funds available for other campus programs." Although no one delighted in the decision to take money from the limited resources available for academic programs, the state board's directive left no other choice.[38]

The university's decision to tap institutional funds and increase student fees to bail out the athletic department struck a responsive chord with the *Oregonian*. Using an advertisement from the Oregon Lottery—"You can't win if you don't play"—the newspaper endorsed OSU's decision to increase general fund support for its beleaguered athletic program. Although it deplored raising student fees, the editorial argued that athletic and academic programs at major universities were "joined at the hip." If Oregon State was to participate in top-level sports competition, it would need to field competitive teams equal to other Pac-10 schools. To do so would require improved funding strategies, and if teams made postseason play, it might lessen the university's contribution to athletics. With student admissions increasing and the football and basketball teams winning, the *Oregonian* believed OSU's athletics were moving in the right direction.[39]

To fully comply with the state board's decree, the university drafted long-term procedures to stabilize and sustain its athletic programs. Except for a few elite Division 1 institutions, Risser indicated, most universities were subsidizing athletics. Looking to the future, the administration would increase its investment in athletics by about $2 million a year, bringing the annual total to $4.4 million. The additional funds would come from increases in student fees, accelerated fund-raising, and greater success in Pac-10 competition. The president instituted another procedural change to deter athletics from accumulating more debt—funding for athletics would be determined on an annual basis.[40] When the president released his message to the faculty, the football program was already turning around—Mike Riley's 1997 team finished three and nine, and the 1998 squad was five and six, the last win coming when running back Ken Simonton scored in double overtime over rival University of Oregon—the Beavers best record since 1971. When Riley left to coach the San Diego Chargers in 1998, the university hired celebrated college coach Dennis Erickson, who guided the Beavers to a seven and five record in 1999 and their first bowl game since

1965. The Beavers went eleven and one in 1999 and trounced Notre Dame in the Fiesta Bowl at the end of the season.[41]

The governor's office took notice of Oregon's higher education system when John Kitzhaber, campaigning for a second term in 1996, appointed a task force "to develop a strategy to better connect higher education with the economy." The governor commissioned the group to think "outside the box," and draft an educational blueprint to enable the state to prosper in the next century. In its December 1997 report, the higher education and the economy task force recommended restructuring the state system of higher education to give greater attention to students and to encourage collaboration and competition among institutions—community colleges, public universities, and private schools. The task force's signal argument was to decentralize the public schools, "shifting more policy, authority, responsibility, and account-ability to each institution."[42]

Kitzhaber praised the task force for establishing a framework to bring higher education "in line with today's economic and technological realities." He cautioned, however, that Oregon's institutions must never "lose sight of the intrinsic value of a liberal arts education." The governor enthusiastically ap-proved the recommendation that institutions be given greater autonomy in de-termining curricular programs and that budgetary structures be decentralized "to better target scarce resources."[43] This was the opening salvo in decisions that would culminate in the demise of the centralized system adopted in 1932.

Under the old budget allocation system, tuition from all public univer-sities was pooled and distributed among schools to maintain an equitable balance. President Risser saw great potential for OSU when the Oregon State System of Higher Education recommended a new funding model that would grant greater fiscal autonomy to state institutions. The new approach, he believed, would leave tuition revenue with the institution enrolling the students and transform the way schools did business. Decentralized fund-ing and decision-making were changes "for which Oregon State University is ready." With enrollment at 16,091 in the fall of 1999, a 10 percent in-crease over the previous year, OSU was well-positioned for the next decade, because the university offered a greater diversity of programs than other state institutions. Those policy changes are reminders of Risser's prescient remarks in his first University Day address in 1996: "If we don't change, we won't be in business." That bold statement was borne out when the univer-sity offered some eighty distance education courses through OSU Statewide in the spring of 1999.[44]

OSU reaped an 8.8 percent increase in revenue in 1999 under the new budget formula, with state appropriations accounting for a substantial part of that amount. The darker side to this seemingly bright revenue story were student tuition and fee increases from 11.4 percent to 18.3 percent of the university's budget over the previous decade. Administrators attempted to offset those costs through an accelerated commitment to student scholarships. Significant increases in enrollment, however, made the task difficult, with a 7.4 percent uptick in the fall of 2001, 8.1 percent in 2009, and 8.2 percent in 2010.[45] While the university managed the upward-spiraling numbers with crowded classrooms and new hires—many of them part-time faculty—the housing and parking crunch in surrounding neighborhoods contributed to irate residents and protests to the Corvallis City Council.

Other problems, especially labor issues, were beyond the institution's control. Strikes and union organizing involving classified staff confronted the Byrne administration on occasion. In his last year as president, Byrne was involved in a dispute with classified employees, who were members of the Oregon Public Employees Union (OPEU). Under confusing circumstances, the union and the Oregon State System of Higher Education dueled over protocols and whether union leaders could communicate via e-mail. Another problem for unions was lapsed contracts. Deadlines would pass while both parties were still negotiating, raising questions about whether the next agreement would stipulate back wages since the end of the previous contract.[46]

Those issues surfaced during a threatened strike in the spring of 1995, when OPEU filed notice to strike over wages and benefits since the lapsed contract. President Byrne alerted non-union faculty and staff of their responsibility to provide services to students and urged all employees to maintain mutual respect for one another. A seven-day strike ensued before state negotiators and the union reached an agreement after a bargaining session lasting twenty-six hours. The state awarded classified employees a 5 percent increase in wages beginning July 1, 1995, and another 2 percent in May 1997. Of the state's seventeen thousand classified employees, approximately twelve thousand took part in the walkout. While OSU was able to fulfill most of its instructional tasks, the strike disrupted motor vehicle services and welfare offices across the state.[47]

With another contract about to expire four years later, history repeated itself, with the State Board of Higher Education engaging in prolonged negotiations over wages, selective pay adjustments, and benefits. OPEU declared an impasse and announced that it would schedule a strike vote if there was no agreement by September 8, 1999. In a message to university presidents, Chancellor Joseph Cox explained the state board's mediation efforts and the union's "unfortunate decision" to declare an impasse. Citing the needs of the university system, he said he thought the contract offer to classified staff was fair. On the Corvallis campus, Jacqueline Rudolph, director of human resources, prepared for a strike. In a "CONFIDENTIAL" letter to senior administrators, she enclosed "Strike Planning Information" from previous years and asked that copies be provided to strike coordinators for each unit. "*This person must be an unclassified employee*," she emphasized.[48]

Tim Spencer, a facilities services carpenter at OSU, took exception to the chancellor's circular, pointing out that "the gap between higher paid executives, like yourself, and the average working person grows"; therefore, the state's offer was unfair. He sent a copy of the letter to President Risser, emphasizing that his coworkers cared about the university's facilities and the people they served and hoped to avoid a strike. With classes only weeks away, OPEU was readying for a strike vote when the union came to an agreement with the state for across-the-board pay increases of 5 percent for the duration of the four-year contract.[49]

Paralleling OPEU's negotiations with the state, OSU's graduate assistants entered labor-management negotiations in the mid-1990s, claiming they were employees of the university and should have collective bargaining rights. Graduate assistants at the University of Oregon had initiated efforts to organize in 1975 and 1976, but failed to make significant headway until they aligned themselves with the American Federation of Teachers (AFT). Even then it took another year before they were able to conduct a successful election to form a union and enter into a bargaining agreement with the university. Among issues of concern to graduate students at Oregon State was the institution's refusal to provide health coverage, a privilege enjoyed by their colleagues at the UO. Informally organized as graduate student employees, the students wanted health coverage comparable to their graduate counterparts at other institutions. After three years of attempting to convince the university to provide them with health care, they formed the Coalition of Graduate Employees in April 1998 and affiliated with the American Federation of Teachers.[50]

Despite legal obstacles the university used to thwart the unionization effort, matters moved quickly in 1998. The AFT, a valuable ally, provided financial support for staff and operating costs, knowledgeable organizers to assist in dealing with the administration, and lobbyists to present their case to the Oregon legislature. In the fall of 1998, OSU's student senate voted to support the coalition's push for union recognition. In the next few months graduate student organizers completed a successful "card drive," gathering signatures of more than 30 percent of graduate student employees to qualify for a vote on unionization. With the election scheduled in the fall of 1999, Provost Roy Arnold sent a memorandum to deans and unit administrators cautioning everyone to consider the effects a union would have on collegial relations between professor and student. It was important, he believed, for every student to understand "how representation by a union and governance by that relationship by the collective bargaining process will impact them and their educational experience."[51]

Although the provost cautioned that a union would disrupt relations between student and professor, graduate student employees voted overwhelmingly in the fall of 1999 to approve the Coalition of Graduate Employees as their bargaining agent. With the assistance of AFT, the coalition negotiated its first contract in the spring of 2001, providing grievance procedures, stipulations about working conditions (limits on hours per term), minimum salary, and $110 per term support for health coverage. The union's second contract, in 2004, included health coverage for graduate student employees and a requirement that the university provide contact information for all graduate students working at the university, a request denied in the past. Two years later the contract was renegotiated to eliminate the requirement for graduate assistants to pay student fees. In succeeding years, contracts increased the university's contribution to health insurance and improved the salaries of the lowest paid graduate employees.[52]

Paul Risser struggled with other troublesome questions during his brief but busy seven-year tenure. The College of Veterinary Medicine created a mini-crisis of its own in 1995 when Dean Loren Kohler resigned and Norman Hutton replaced him as interim dean. At the end of a year of turmoil, Dean Hutton requested the Cooperative State Research, Education and Extension Service to conduct a review of the college to assist in developing research guidelines for the still-to-be-identified new dean. Describing the college's operations "as a committee of the whole without departments," the Cooperative State Research team characterized the college's teaching and research as reasonable given its limited enrollment and small faculty. The college's research committee, however, was dysfunctional, unable to agree on proposals involving scientific critiques. Because of those limitations, the research team advised the college to seek external professionals, such as faculty at Washington State University, to review its research proposals. Pursuing such a review would assure the scientific merits of proposals.[53]

Rancor in the College of Veterinary Medicine intensified in early 1996 in the midst of searches for a new dean and several junior faculty positions. In an e-mail to President Risser and Provost Arnold, Hutton reported that the college was receiving a flood of mail related to personnel decisions, with most of the letters from people "financially connected" to a local veterinary clinic. In another letter to Risser and Arnold, Al Smith, a veterinary medicine colleague, wrote that three members of the department, including Aaron Horowitz, told an Oregon legislator from Roseburg that the college had decided to defer the selection of new faculty hires until after the new dean was aboard. Smith claimed that Horowitz's story was "totally at variance with the truth." When a faculty member made a motion to delay hiring, Horowitz immediately offered a second and then spent ten minutes deriding the interim dean. Several faculty walked out in disgust, with one person commenting that the college's behavior was embarrassing. Smith worried that Horowitz had written to the president and provost claiming to speak for the entire faculty, when that was untrue. Former Dean Kohler, Smith believed, was orchestrating the chaos because he had been forced to resign.[54]

Horowitz, in fact, had written Arnold the same day, with a copy to Risser, explaining that interim dean Hutton had been high-handed in dismissing three fixed-term faculty. They would be employed through September 30, 1996, after which they would be free to apply, with other candidates, for the positions they were currently holding. Hinting at hidden agendas and the interim dean's "shadow cabinet," Horowitz asked the provost to overrule Hutton's decision and to maintain the status quo until the new dean was hired. From that point the controversy broadened, including the intervention of State Representative Bill Fisher of Roseburg, who wrote Chancellor Joseph Cox that the OSU veterinary college was suffering through "strife and turmoil," and a "storm of protest," with "no trust in leadership." The faculty discord "was a no-win task for Dr. Hutton," who had done his best under very trying circumstances. Whoever was hired as dean, Fisher warned, should "know from 'Day One' what lies ahead."[55]

When the college's search committee forwarded three finalists for the dean's position to the president's office, Risser appointed Robert C. "Bob" Wilson to be the next dean beginning June 1, 1996. Head of the Department of Physiology and Pharmacology in the College of Veterinary Medicine at Auburn University, Wilson also edited the *Journal of Veterinary Medicine Education*. Because of the verbal combat in the college, a three-member committee from the Association of American Veterinary Medicine Colleges joined Wilson in his first few days on the job. Their subsequent report confirmed that the faculty was divided among warring factions, an alienated staff, and students disconnected from the college. Although the college had talented faculty, there was "little sense of unity or common purpose," realities that required special attention. "Faculty comity and polity are the most serious problems at the College," the report contended.[56]

The external veterinary committee recommended new operating procedures, an off-campus retreat, a reduction in administrative personnel, streamlining responsibilities, and revising the college's relationship with its cooperating veterinary unit at Washington State University. The reviewers closed their report with "good luck and Godspeed." According to provost emeritus Roy Arnold, Bob Wilson succeeded in quieting the waters and bringing the college's behavior to an even keel. During his three years as dean, Wilson's leadership began the "healing process," and when he left in 1999 for a veterinary position in the Southeast—"not because of any internal pressure for him to leave OSU"—Arnold indicates that his successor, L. J. Koong, continued moving the college away from its earlier factionalism.[57]

Beyond the occasional internal discord among college faculties, the university struggled with less savory matters related to race and other adverse social issues. An ugly incident occurred in February 1996, when two white students shouted racial epithets from a dormitory balcony and spit at and attempted to urinate on a black student. When word spread of the verbal and physical abuse, some 1,500 black and white students staged a protest rally just as campus police moved in to arrest one student, Eric Hutchinson. The other suspect, Christopher John Curry, turned himself in the next day. When the two pleaded guilty to misdemeanor charges of attempting intimidation, Judge Robert Gardner sentenced them to two weeks in jail, fines of $450 (plus court costs), eighty hours of community service, and two years' probation. The judge ordered both men to read a book on racism and to write a report for the court.[58]

In the wake of the dormitory incident, President Risser directed an inquiry into the racial climate at the university, declaring that the institution should be more active in combating racism. He challenged colleagues "to place diversity at the core of OSU's institutional identity." In an important series of proposals to the president's cabinet in September 1999, a multicultural task force outlined four major recommendations "to create and sustain a diverse campus community that is welcoming, supportive and inclusive of its students, faculty and staff." Despite the university's efforts, the report contended, students, faculty, and staff of color continued to face offensive interactions on a daily basis. The task force proposed sensitivity training for all lead administrators and campus vendors, an "action team" to respond to incidents, and better use of data on minorities.[59]

Despite the efforts of campus administrators to stay abreast of untoward behavior, the new millennium witnessed the reoccurrence of boorish and crude episodes that drew media attention to the university. Cultural differences came into play in February 2006 when the *Barometer* published a column, "The Islamic Double Standard," accusing Muslims of overreacting to a Danish newspaper's cartoons of the prophet Muhammed. Nathaniel Blake's article was filled with vile references about Islam, and the prophet himself, and likened Muslims to savages, "Bluntly put, we expect Muslims to behave barbarously." The sizable number of Muslim students on campus gathered the next day to protest Blake's column and the Danish cartoons, passing out flyers that acknowledged the importance of free speech but reminding the campus community to respect the values of others.[60]

An especially troubling incident took place in October of 2006, when a nineteen-year-old fraternity student with a .22 rifle shot a homeless man who was rummaging through a trash container. Following a court trial, Joshua Grimes was sentenced to 150 days in jail. The jury also found Grimes and his fraternity, Alpha Gamma Rho, responsible for $41,000 in medical expenses and noneconomic damages to the victim, Dennis Sanderson. Benton County district attorney John Haroldson had accused Grimes of shooting Sanderson for sport. Subsequent investigation indicated that fraternity brothers had earlier shot BB guns at homeless people outside their house. Sanderson asked after the trial, "Where does a 19-year-old kid learn that much hate?"[61]

In addition to social discord on campus, university administrators continued to face hot-button environmental issues. Because of their unique missions, land-grant institutions were often at the center of disputes involving land, water, and atmospheric problems. Because OSU's undergraduate and graduate programs specialized in training students for employment with public agencies, the private sector, and nonprofit environmental organizations, its research and curricular agendas often touched on sensitive topics. University graduates in fisheries and wildlife, forestry, water resources, aquatic environments, ecosystem and atmospheric sciences, and engineering fields possessed expertise related to the crosscurrents and margins of our troubled relations with the planet. By the 1980s and 1990s, environmental scientists were at the center of policy questions such as the spotted owl/old-growth forest conundrum and the relationship between declining anadromous fish runs and the health of Northwest waterways. Presidents MacVicar, Byrne, and Risser, and his successor, Ed Ray, regularly fielded appeals for redress from constituencies on both sides of those debates.

When ecologists and fishery biologists began stressing the importance of riparian vegetation to sustain healthy streams, cattle grazing across the vast arid stretches of central and eastern Oregon caught the attention of the news media. Because of the intersection between grazing and streamside protection, the controversy ultimately involved Oregon State University scientists. The issue culminated when the Oregon Natural Desert Association and other environmentalists succeeded in placing the Clean Streams Initiative, Measure 38, before voters in November 1996—"the waters of the State of Oregon shall be protected from water pollution caused by livestock." The heated campaign for and against the measure invited exaggerations from both sides, with rural opponents suggesting that passage of Measure 38 threatened public access to state and federal lands for fishing, hunting, and camping. The "Vote No on Measure 38: Don't Fence Oregon" campaign easily prevailed, defeating the initiative 64 percent opposed to 36 percent in favor.[62]

OSU's College of Agricultural Sciences and its Departments of Rangeland Resources and Fisheries and Wildlife were usually at the center of such debates. Founded in the late 1980s, the thousand-member Oregon Natural Desert Association was the foremost proponent of Measure 38 and a watchdog over OSU's scientific work. One significant incident arose in 1996, when rangeland resources' Larry Larson (and son Shane Larson) published an article in *Rangelands* challenging conventional research that removing riparian vegetation caused the warming of streams. In "Riparian Shade and Stream Temperatures: A Perspective," the Larsons argued that shade from riparian vegetation "does not control stream temperature."[63]

After voters defeated Measure 38, the Oregon Natural Desert Association's Bill Marlett and Joy Belsky—respectively, executive director and staff ecologist of the Oregon Natural Desert Association—argued that Larson's article was specious, inaccurate, and "inappropriate for a representative of a major university." In a January 1997 letter to College of Agriculture dean Thayne Dutson, they charged Larson with trivializing Oregon's Department of Environmental Quality's new stream temperature standards and the effects of grazing on water quality. Because livestock browsing along streams contributed to rising water temperatures on public lands in the West, Belsky (the scientist) argued that Larson's findings conflicted with the research of hydrologists, range scientists, and fisheries biologists.[64]

In a follow-up letter to President Risser, Belsky introduced herself as a grasslands ecologist with the Oregon Natural Desert Association (and congratulated Risser's appointment as OSU president). Then she cut to the quick, characterizing the university's Department of Rangeland Resources as very traditional, the standard for many land-grant schools. Some of the faculty, however, went "overboard with their advocacy, bending science to favor ranchers" in maintaining grazing at unsustainable levels. In the long run such practices were not in the best interests of ranchers. Risser responded quickly, praising Belsky for her "well-reasoned letter" to Thayne Dutson. The president explained that he was out of the loop on the issue, and that he would speak to Dutson about the matter. He indicated, however, that it was "difficult for us to 'control' positions taken by faculty members," but agreed that the university could insist upon reasonable science-based approaches to such research problems.[65]

Belsky wrote again a few months later, praising the president and the College of Agriculture for its "excellent one-day workshop . . . on riparian use, ecology and management" and the impressive quality of the speakers and their scholarship. She was pleased, too, that presenters did not support the research of OSU professors who argued that cattle did not damage streams and that riparian vegetation did not affect water temperature. Eastern Oregon ranchers faced serious problems, she admitted, but providing them with misinformation only worsened the situation. Belsky was an informed critic, aware that cattle prices and beef consumption were down, that cheap Mexican beef was flooding the market, and that production costs and distance to markets hurt western ranchers. Their greatest difficulty, however, was age, with the average Oregon rancher sixty years old. Belsky urged the university to use its considerable talents and experience to address the real problems facing eastern Oregon ranchers. Belsky closed with the observation that "range management in Oregon is more of a religion than a science. Religion doesn't restore lands and human livelihoods. Good science and creativity can."[66]

An even more explosive issue followed in the wake of the five-hundred-thousand-acre Biscuit Fire in southwestern Oregon, when forestry graduate student Donald Donato published research findings in *Science* in January 2006 demonstrating that salvage logging hampered forest recovery following fire. Donato's publication, which came in the midst of a congressional bill to accelerate logging on public lands following fire, attracted the ire of several College of Forestry faculty, who asked the editor of *Science* to withhold publication of the print edition because the research was flawed. The critics were responding to the online account that appeared on January 5. *Science* general editor Donald Kennedy told the press he had no intention of suppressing the article, because it had been through an in-depth independent review. "They're trying to rewind history," he charged. Adding fuel to the controversy was Donato's significant achievement—a graduate student publishing in the nation's most prestigious scientific journal.[67]

The university's forestry dean, Hal Salwasser, joined his colleagues in questioning Donato's research, adding to the chorus of people charging the university with censoring an individual's research findings. Kathleen Dean Moore, who taught environmental ethics at OSU, told the *Oregonian*: "The university isn't about secrecy, it's about discussion. It's about hearing all the voices so we can learn from them." University of Washington's James Karr thought the incident would have a chilling effect on other OSU researchers. Richard Waring, a retired professor of forest sciences in Corvallis, feared the incident would intimidate graduate students and hurt the college's ability to attract top graduate students.[68] The college, in effect, was struggling with its long tradition of serving the region's powerful timber industry against the emergence, since the 1970s, of ecosystems approaches to studying landscapes.

Because of the torrent of criticisms centered on the College of Forestry, Dean Salwasser reversed direction and, in a note to the faculty, "profoundly regret[ed] the negative debate that recent events have generated." In retrospect, he should have congratulated Donato for having his research published in *Science*: "Few faculty, let alone graduate students get their work published in this prestigious journal." The dean's apology aside, the intense media attention led the Bureau of Land Management (BLM) to withhold its grant to the university for studying landscapes following fire. When *Science*'s editor Kennedy clarified his error—involving two sentences that Donato insisted be deleted in the online version—the BLM quickly restored the grant.[69]

Donato's travail, however, continued when he was called to testify in Medford before congressional hearings on the bill to expand logging on public lands following fire. In the wake of Washington representative Brian Baird's withering and abusive attacks, Donato calmly responded that his statistical approach was sound. As it turns out, Donato's research in *Science* represented work on his master's degree. He went on to complete his PhD in 2008, continuing his research and publishing additional studies on the same project. After traveling the country and the world on a couple of postdoctoral appointments, he accepted a position with the State of Washington's Department of Natural Resources as a forest ecologist.[70]

Jane Lubchenco's presidential address in 1997 to the prestigious American Association for the Advancement of Science was a signal achievement for the environmental sciences at Oregon State University. Her presentation,

Other than Linus Pauling, who was an alumnus, Jane Lubchenco may be the most renowned scientist ever to be associated with Oregon State University. A marine ecologist and environmental scientist who came to the university in 1977, Lubchenco established herself as one of the most widely cited ecologists in the world by the time she left Corvallis to head the National Oceanographic and Atmospheric Administration (2009–2013). Among her many awards were MacArthur and Pew fellowships and the Niernenberg Prize for Science in the Public Interest. She also served as president of the American Association for the Advancement of Science in 1997. Courtesy of the OSU Special Collections and Archives Research Center.

"Entering the Century of the Environment: A New Social Contract," challenged the scientific community to reexamine its social contract to effectively confront environmental and social crises around the globe. Lubchenco's address was a tour de force, citing the present moment as one of great challenges and responsibilities for scientists. Despite the splendid achievements of the scientific enterprise, scientists had not been "fully prepared to face the formidable challenges ahead." Scientists, Lubchenco believed, should reconsider their work in light of new realities rooted "in the natural and social worlds."[71]

Investments in science since the 1960s, "an unwritten social contract with scientists," had been predicated on the belief that funding scientific research would win the Cold War and the space race and deliver humankind from disease. Although that enterprise had been immensely successful, Lubchenco argued, it did little to prepare nations for challenges such as the explosive growth in the human population, with the majority of it occurring in the developing world. Because conventional responses offered little redress, it was important to move quickly to develop a population policy that "empowers women through education, family planning choices, political equity, and better health care." The formula for achieving that objective was simple—women who are educated have fewer children.[72]

Lubchenco compared the exponential growth in human numbers with another startling trend—a similar *per capita* growth in energy use. The unsustainable exploitation of land and oceanic resources powered those tendencies, with the developed world (less than 25 percent of the earth's population) consuming more than 75 percent of the world's resources and producing about 75 percent of its pollution. Lubchenco's message posited a sharp social critique, pointing to class inequities between rich and poor nations of the world and within nations. It was important to acknowledge that while "*rates* of poverty, illiteracy, and malnutrition were declining, the *number* of people affected by each was increasing." The evidence revealed the appalling ignorance and unwillingness of policymakers to take action on such matters.[73]

In an interview with *The Christian Science Monitor* in the summer of 1997, Lubchenco returned again to the pace at which humans were altering the physical world about them: "We're changing things faster than we understand them. We're changing the world in ways that it's never been changed before, at faster rates and over larger scales. And we don't know the consequences." She urged caution, because the results were "not likely to be in our favor."[74] Eleven years later, Lubchenco, Oregon State University's internationally renowned marine ecologist and environmental scientist, would be the first woman to head the National and Oceanic and Atmospheric Administration (NOAA), a position she held until 2014 when she returned to Corvallis as Distinguished Professor and Advisor in Marine Studies.

Jane Lubchenco set the standard for the increasing sophistication and advances in scholarship that characterized Oregon State University in the twenty-first century. While the built environment of the campus was undergoing a dramatic transformation, equally important changes were occurring among the faculty, where scientific breakthroughs, patenting new inventions, cutting-edge engineering and forest science research, and award-winning writers were becoming the norm. Through the presidencies of John Byrne and Paul Risser, the university joined the ranks of the nation's leading land-grant institutions. Ed Ray, who became president in July 2003 and who benefitted from an infrastructure of stunning new buildings and great advances in research and scholarship, would further burnish the university's reputation.

Epilogue

A Twenty-First-Century University

Frank Bruni's column in the *New York Times* on February 15, 2015—"College's Priceless Value"—took issue with the belief that the purpose of attending college was simply to improve the prospects of landing a good job. Bruni emphasized the importance of critical thinking and the ability to write and speak clearly, insisting that a college education should not be equated with trade school. Taking courses, especially in the humanities, increased cultural literacy and the ability to think outside the box. One year earlier, Oregon State University president Ed Ray offered a similar suggestion, that the most appropriate education for students was training "in the arts and sciences, because the core skills that they're developing—critical thinking, the . . . appreciation of other sociopolitical views and cultures, the ability to write effectively— those are adaptable to almost any career."[1]

The president thought the vocational argument—at the center of the university's land-grant tradition—carried weight in the sciences, technology, engineering, and mathematics. But, he asked, what about the prospects for humanities graduates? Because of the rapid pace of global change, anticipating employment possibilities for tomorrow's graduates was difficult to predict. The ability to adapt would be at a premium, and liberal arts graduates would "be the most adaptable to change." With OSU's academic strength in its professional colleges, it was important for students to weigh quality of life and the richness of the educational experience. Ray acknowledged the power of his supply and demand training as an economist—"If you want to do abstract art, you've got to figure out how you're going to get somebody to pay you to do that." Attending a university provided students the opportunity to learn what they enjoy doing. If they "chase the money" and find no joy, they were squandering the opportunity to "keep body and soul together."[2]

Beyond their academic majors, OSU's twenty-first-century students have been exposed to troublesome economic and political forces shaping higher education in the United States. Rising costs to attend universities and colleges, reflecting in part the yawning gap in the nation's distribution of wealth, has limited access to higher education for countless young people. Moreover, many students who graduate are burdened with loan payments extending well into the future. In the last thirty years, state legislators have placed a premium on building prisons and incarcerating people with nonviolent drug offenses, expenses that limit appropriations for education at all levels. As Oregon State University celebrates its sesquicentennial, there is nothing equivalent to the GI Bill following the Second World War, when veterans made up 50 percent of students at many institutions. With independent governing boards guiding each of Oregon's public universities, there is little indication that schools are reducing tuition and student fees. The Oregon University System, disbanded in July 2015, lacked the leverage to lower tuition charges, even if it had the will to do so. As *Oregonian* columnist David Sarasohn argues, Oregon has always been more parsimonious in supporting higher education than neighboring Washington.[3]

Sarasohn's column prefaced an Urban Institute report of November 2015, "Financing Public Higher Education," that provides striking data on enrollment and state support for universities and colleges. The detailed analysis, comparing increases in tuition among public universities and colleges amid declining state appropriations, reveals varying degrees of access and affordability for different states. Although funding has increased in a few states, it has plummeted in others. The Urban Institute study, covering the years from 2000 to 2014, shows a surge in enrollment during the Great Recession (2007–2010), when Oregon ranked first in the nation, with an increase of 29 percent in student admissions. "Unusually large increases in enrollment," the report noted, "contributed to the per-student funding decline of close to 50 percent in Arizona and Oregon." For the fourteen-year period between 2000 and 2014, Oregon ranked eighth from the bottom in inflation-adjusted appropriations for higher education.[4]

For hard-pressed students, the hope of financing a college education in the United States has become daunting. Tuition increases over the last three decades have surpassed inflation, while state support has declined. Oregon fits this pattern. While health-care spending increased 600 percent between 1978 and 2013, tuition increased twice that much. President Ray acknowledged those trends when OSU joined ten other public research universities in forming the University Innovation Alliance, whose purpose was to improve opportunities for low-income, first-generation students to attend college. The president asked the *Oregonian*'s editorial board, "How do we close that gap between the richer and poorer students?"—a question relevant to Oregon State because 30 percent of its 2012 freshman class was eligible for Pell grants.

Members of the alliance, he told the board, had on hand $11.4 million—half of it from the Ford Foundation, the Bill and Melinda Gates Foundation, and other donors—and the other half from member institutions. The *Oregonian* believed the initiative was promising, but it would work only if "the alliance does more than just generate ideas."[5]

The president raised the inequality issue again in his state of the university address in January 2015. America was becoming a nation "of 'haves' and 'have nots,'" Ray warned, a development that "tears at the fabric of our society and undermines our democracy."[6] In the face of such inequities, he intended to make OSU "a showcase of access to higher education," high-quality degrees, and improved retention and graduation rates. In the midst of new buildings infilling the campus, Ray emphasized that OSU must be more than its built environment. In a presentation to the faculty senate that fall, the president repeated the troubling issue of affordability, reminding senators of the yawning gulf between the haves and have-nots in earning college degrees. He believed, however, that the university was making progress in improving opportunities for lower-income students to succeed through the "bridge to success program," enabling Pell grant recipients to work toward degrees without the burden of paying tuition and fees. The celebrated Campaign for OSU, the president indicated, had raised $189 million for needy students.[7]

There was more to President Ray's meeting with the faculty senate when he mentioned the university's proud tradition as one of the nation's "peoples colleges." Through 147 years and counting, the institution's reach across the state had served Oregon's students and citizens in many capacities. According to ECO Northwest, a regional consulting firm, OSU's annual global economic reach was $2.371 billion, with the school supporting 31,660 jobs in Oregon. Beyond its responsibility for employment, the president estimated that OSU's public programs generated $2.5 for every dollar it received in state funding. Ray concluded with the observation that the next ten years would see the university building upon the expansion of its virtual classroom and construction projects and focusing on "renewing, renovating and repurposing our physical facilities." The future would be "about the quality of space rather than the quantity."[8]

In the midst of the university's feverish growth, it is important to review Ed Ray's tenure as president. Meeting with the faculty senate in October 2009, he presented an ambitious blueprint to elevate Oregon State into the top ranks of the nation's land-grant universities. To achieve that objective, Ray listed several targets OSU should reach by 2025: (1) an enrollment of thirty thousand to thirty-five thousand students; (2) a tenured and tenure-track faculty of about 1,500; (3) increasing retention and graduation rates and attracting more diverse faculty and students; (4) collapsing departmental and college financial and personnel positions into seven business hubs; (5) terminating low-enrollment courses and merging departments and colleges; and (6) augmenting revenue from private donors and research grants to replace declining state funds. Writing for the *Gazette-Times*, Bennett Hall described Ray's presentation as a roadmap to raise OSU's academic profile.[9]

President Ray's proposals to the faculty senate had been taking shape since 2004, when the senate agreed to policies that would reorganize, merge, or eliminate programs. The purpose of the agreement was to reposition the university to become a top-flight land-grant institution. It reaffirmed the university's "commitment to tenure, academic freedom, affirmative action, and accountability," and assured the faculty that its input would be "incorporated to the extent possible." The reorganization would be implemented through "shared governance," with consultations involving Provost Sabah Randhawa and a faculty senate standing committee. Final decisions would rest with the president.[10] This was the seminal document that would lead to the most significant restructuring of the institution since the creation of the Oregon State System of Higher Education in the early 1930s.

The discussions that followed in the next several months included a potential merger between the College of Liberal Arts and the College of Science. By the fall of 2009, restructuring had progressed to the point that the faculty senate expected to spend the entire academic year focusing on the reorganization, with anticipated cost savings to be realized in the future. In a lengthy interview in the *Oregon Stater*, Provost Randhawa thought the university's present structure created "a reactionary situation," and that the institution had a strategic and fiscal imperative to change—to reduce courses and programs, to cut administrative costs, and to vest power in people to make their own decisions. Because the university was always slow to change, the big challenge would be moving away from "college-centric and program centric" strategies. College deans would be giving up personal power to divisional structures requiring fewer administrators. The university's research arm should be strengthened with "corporate-to-corporate relationship[s]," although it would be important "to protect the integrity of our research."[11]

Completed in 2014, OSU's administrative structure differed dramatically from that shown in the organizational chart of 2007. The new arrangement reveals a streamlined, abbreviated profile, with fewer administrators reporting directly to the president. College deans and their respective units are shunted to one side under the provost and executive vice president. If,

An economist who served as provost at Ohio State University, Edward J. Ray was appointed the fourteenth president of Oregon State University in the summer of 2003. During his tenure as president, Ray has overseen the construction of a dizzying array of new buildings, the most the campus has experienced since the presidency of William Jasper Kerr (1907–1932). Enrollment has topped more than 30,000 students, and OSU-Cascades, the university's branch campus in Bend, opened its own campus in the fall of 2016. Under President Ray's leadership, the institution completed The Campaign for OSU, a capital drive that raised $1.14 billion from some 106,000 donors. Courtesy of the OSU Special Collections and Archives Research Center.

as Provost Randhawa argued in 2009, the university was too college-centric, the new administrative structure indicated that colleges were no longer at the center of institutional operations. The eleven colleges survived, however, with a few departments moving to other colleges. Restructuring within individual colleges followed no particular pattern. While the fourteen departments in the College of Liberal Arts were folded into six schools, the College of Science emerged with a School of Life Sciences and several of its traditional departments. The College of Forestry rearranged its undergraduate programs into three broad areas—Forest Engineering and Management, Forest Ecosystems and Society, and Renewable Materials. In a complex graphic, the College of Business had twelve discipline directors, a research faculty and a teaching faculty, with all faculty listed under disciplinary specialties.[12]

In the midst of the university's reorganization meetings, enrollment was literally in liftoff, with 20,250 students registered for the fall of 2009. Those numbers increased to 30,451 students in the fall of 2015. While enrollment was building toward the president's goal, other objectives were falling into place: research funding doubled, the university hired 180 new tenured/tenure-track faculty, administrative offices were consolidated, academic units were reduced from sixty-three to forty-two, and building continued apace, including the expansion of Reser Stadium. Most significant, the university's fund-raising enterprise, Campaign for OSU, had boosted its total from $650 million in 2009 to one billion dollars in 2013.[13]

The legendary Yankee catcher Yogi Berra may have phrased Oregon State University's looming growth dilemma best when he remarked, "The future ain't what it used to be." The university's rapid expansion in the twenty-first century, with student numbers climbing from 16,788 in the fall of 2000 to 23,761 in 2010 and 30,451 in 2015, exacerbated tensions between the university and near-campus neighborhoods. While conflicts between "town and gown" date from the institution's founding, districts adjacent to the university became increasingly troubled with traffic problems, parking, loud parties, trash, public drunkenness, and the general belief that livability was being compromised.

Those stresses led to the creation of Citizens for a Livable Corvallis, a group whose goal was to preserve established neighborhoods. The coalition's objectives included remodeling older buildings, requiring new structures to be compatible with existing architecture, solving parking problems, and addressing differences between students and longtime residents. The coalition wanted to rein in developers, who were replacing single-family dwellings with apartment buildings and destroying neighborhoods. Charlyn Ellis, a Livable Corvallis spokesperson, remarked, "We're in the path of the wrecking ball." Acknowledging the need for more housing, Livable Corvallis wanted reasonable and thoughtful attention to parking, excessive traffic, and the erosion of neighborhoods. The university should be a good neighbor and work with the neighborhood associations.[14]

More significant and far-reaching was the formation of Collaboration Corvallis, a fifteen member board appointed for three years by OSU's president and the Corvallis mayor. The board included police officers, neighborhood representatives, student government members, sorority and fraternity leaders, a city councilor, a member of OSU's faculty senate, a Corvallis rental property agent, a Monroe Street business representative, OSU's Student Health Services, and Jonathan Stoll of OSU's Office of Corvallis Community Relations. Reports of the three-year run of Collaboration Corvallis—its successes and failures—largely hinge on whom one consults.[15]

University spokespersons highlighted several initiatives: requiring freshmen to live on campus, publishing a guide outlining community standards, handing out notices to those violating municipal codes, and hiring staff to monitor student behavior and to act as a liaison with neighborhoods and law enforcement. The Corvallis City Council increased fines related to alcohol and placed a measure on the ballot to hire three additional police officers. The city also joined the International Town & Gown Association and sent representatives to its 2013 annual meeting. The cochairs of Collaboration

Corvallis, city councilor Roen Hogg and OSU's Jonathan Stoll, deemed the first year a success: the university built a new residence hall, the city expanded residential parking districts and extended bus services. With unfinished items on the menu, the cochairs would continue working toward creating "a more unified and prosperous community.[16]

One resident compared relations between the city and the university to a high school football team playing a Pac-12 school, in which one side was subjecting itself to abuse by merely taking the field. The writer charged that Collaboration Corvallis committees ignored the need to build on-campus parking structures that would not "take core campus real estate." As the university's spatial expansion spread beyond campus, "Corvallis will slowly become a glorified company town." When the Corvallis City Council unanimously passed a measure in the summer of 2014 to expand the city's parking districts to five blocks from campus, resident Paul Cauthorn organized a petition drive to refer the issue to voters. To the surprise of many, including *Gazette-Times* reporter James Day, nearly 60 percent of voters turned down the expanded parking-district plan.[17] The key to the measure's defeat was a fee homeowners would pay to park in their own neighborhoods.

Although relations between the university and neighborhoods were still tense, the *Gazette-Times* defended the university in the spring of 2015. An interim agreement between the city and OSU would guarantee "no further degradation in parking in the neighborhoods surrounding OSU." The arrangement provided the city with time to repurpose its relationship with "its most important institution." When the university opened Tebeau Hall in 2014, Don Larson, director of housing and dining services, observed that the school had substantially increased on campus living. Requiring freshman to live on campus and plans to provide housing for upper-division and graduate students and those with families would mitigate off-campus tensions.[18]

When Collaboration Corvallis wrapped up its deliberations in the spring of 2015, the university and city appointed a new board, the Community Relations Advisory Group, to oversee near-campus parking and congestion, and the old bugaboos of alcohol, partying, and trash. OSU's Jonathan Stoll and city councilor Roen Hogg continued as cochairs. Parking continued to be the most vexing issue. Residents in the Central Park area, squeezed between downtown and the university, complained that parking problems affected livability in the neighborhood. Barbara Corden put the case simply: "All we are asking for is a chance to park in our neighborhood." The once-quiet area was now filled with parked vehicles and still others speeding down streets looking for a place to park. Newly elected mayor Biff Traber thought Corvallis was moving prudently, seeking data to protect neighborhoods from students and faculty using off-campus streets for free parking.[19]

By the fall of 2015, evidence suggested that new city ordinances, increased university staffing, and cooperating property managers were paying off. Voters approved a tax levy providing a "livability patrol" of three police officers that resulted in declining campus violations for noise, fights, loud music, and parties. OSU officials, responsible for holding off-campus students accountable for their behavior, reported a 45 percent drop in their caseload over a two-year period. "No one is declaring victory," James Day wrote for the *Gazette-Times*, "but there is a sense that things ARE getting better." Carl Yeh of the student conduct office pointed to decreases in "livability crime" as evidence that cooperation between the city and OSU was succeeding. Charlyn Ellis of the Chintimini neighborhood admitted that student behavior had improved, and President Ray thought students understood that the university was serious about encouraging acceptable behavior.[20]

Missing from the narrative about student behavior were their voluntary services to the community. OSU's Center for Civic Engagement provided freshman with community service opportunities. The information included volunteer services for the homeless and how to assist people in transitioning to homes and employment. The center partnered with other campus units, sponsoring Hunger and Homelessness Awareness Week before Thanksgiving in 2015, events that involved educational forums and raising funds. Mid-valley nonprofits also provided several volunteer venues for Corvallis Parks and Recreation programs, Boys and Girls Clubs activities, and other work-related tasks.[21]

The Center for Civic Engagement's special mission, "experiential learning," provided students with information about service opportunities appropriate to their interests. The fall 2015 list included Last Thursday Packing Parties (Linn-Benton Food Share); Willamette River Restoration; Albany Habitat Restoration; Garden Work Parties; Fresh Grown Cooking for Kids; and Spaghetti Sundays for Jackson Street Youth Services. Because student community volunteers had increased dramatically, Mike Beilstein, Ward 5 city councilor, argued that despite the troubles of recent years, Oregon State was a tremendous asset to Corvallis. As the community adjusts to more students, Beilstein believed citizens will "return to a state of semi-contentment and peace in the relation of campus and neighbors."[22]

While state support for tuition has been declining for several decades, reductions in public funds for higher education also extend to federal research dollars that have been flat for several years. Because of the university's need for research support, the private sector has increased research sponsorship from $25 million in 2010 to $45 million in 2015. OSU's Research Office viewed this turn of events, flatline federal funding and increased private support, as a positive, noting that research funding during the fiscal year 2015 reached $308.9 million, up from the previous high, $288 million. Vice president for research Cynthia Sagers called those figures "phenomenal" for an institution "of our size in this funding environment."[23]

The question—and danger—for universities that increasingly rely on corporate funds for teaching and research is the influence of money in redirecting an institution's conventional responsibilities. As authors James Cote and Anton Allahar indicate, when a school accepts corporate money for building projects and endowing chairs, it "cannot bite the hand that feeds it and so must mute criticisms of specific corporations or of the entire process of corporatization itself." Despite those words of caution, there is copious evidence that university and college research offices are aggressively pursuing private-sector funding. Building relationships, the University of California, Santa Barbara Office of Research, website declares, "is the cornerstone to securing extramural funding from private foundations." UC Santa Barbara represents the norm in its quest for recent research funding. Although the federal government funded more than 65 percent of university research in 1965, those figures reversed in 2006 when private interests funded 65 percent. Those changes prompted the *New York Times* to declare in 2014 that "American science, long a source of national power and pride, is increasingly becoming a private enterprise."[24]

Two communities beyond Corvallis—Newport's Hatfield Marine Science Center and the OSU-Cascades campus in Bend—have long-standing teaching and research links to Oregon State University. The Hatfield Center cooperates with eight state and federal agencies and the nearby NOAA Marine Operations Center to conduct marine and coastal scientific investigations. OSU launched an ambitious new research and teaching model in 2015—the Marine Studies Initiative—to advance understanding of near coast and oceanic waters and to promote sustainability in the face of increasing ocean pollution, climate change, and natural hazards. Based on learning through experience, the initiative will establish a new interdisciplinary undergraduate degree in marine studies, with enrollees studying in Corvallis and then in a new building at the Marine Science Center. The curriculum and research will involve natural and social sciences and anticipates five hundred resident students in Newport by 2025.[25]

The Hatfield Center also houses a first of its kind in the nation, the Coastal Oregon Marine Experiment Station, established in 1989. The brainstorm of local fisherman Barry Fisher, the unit followed the pattern of OSU's eleven agricultural experiment stations around the state. Celebrating its twenty-fifth anniversary in 2014, the station carries out research on coastal ecosystems and their marine resources, with its objective the sustainable use of aquatic life. Gil Sylvia, the director of the station in 2014, reported that its work paralleled the agricultural experiment stations—"research that will help provide economic benefits, social support, and resource conservation to coastal communities." The station's research has been interdisciplinary, cooperating with the Coastal Zone Management Association and the seafood industry in promoting the marketing of whiting, developing the albacore fishery, and studying salmon genetics and shellfish propagation at the Astoria Food Laboratory.[26]

OSU's Cascades campus, long in gestation, triggered local opposition, appeals, and threatened lawsuits when the university announced plans to purchase 10.44 acres of undeveloped land on the city's west side in proximity to newer homes. Organized opposition—Truth in Site—and letters to the *Bend Bulletin* objected to the location, accusing Corvallis administrators of "shortsighted vision" in placing the campus in the midst of a thriving neighborhood. Becky Johnson, vice president of OSU-Cascades, defended the westside location as the result of some eighty committee members deliberating issues such as transportation, neighborhood suitability, and housing. Those opposing the westside campus, she feared, would "deny Central Oregon a university for many years."[27]

The City of Bend and OSU-Cascades signed a memorandum of understanding in January 2014 to establish a campus ready for use by the fall of 2015. OSU-Cascades agreed to build a four-year school in Bend that would minimize "any adverse impacts to existing neighborhoods and public infrastructure." The city would assist with land use laws and work with OSU on community involvement and mediating disputes. OSU-Cascades promised to purchase 10.44 acres on the west side and to appoint a project manager to coordinate planning—the city agreeing to expedite planning and construction hurdles to achieve the anticipated completion date, with the understanding that it could not control delays, "including land-use appeals."[28] The following months underscored the city's wisdom in its proviso regarding appeals.

As soon as OSU-Cascades purchased the 10.44 acres, Truth in Site opponents appealed the application to build on the land to the city's hearings officer, who upheld OSU's application. What ensued were successive appeals to the Bend City Council, the Land Use Board of Appeals (LUBA), and eventually to the Oregon Court of Appeals in September 2015—all of them affirming the

OSU-Cascades, a branch of Oregon State University established in 2001, opened its own campus in the fall of 2016, culminating a thirty-year effort to establish a four-year university in central Oregon. OSU-Cascades enrolled 1,250 students in the fall of 2016, with 93 students attending nearby Central Oregon Community College (COCC). Among the enrollees in 2016, 70 percent were from central Oregon, 35 percent of them the first in their family to attend college. The branch campus plans to expand beyond its present ten acres. Courtesy of OSU News and Research Communications.

hearings officer's decision. Immediately following LUBA's decision in June 2015, OSU-Cascades broke ground at the site, revising expectations to have buildings ready for occupation in the fall of 2016. Oregon Public Broadcasting aired its popular Think Out Loud program in Bend shortly after LUBA's decision and declared that most people in central Oregon supported the campus, despite the objections of those who worried about housing, traffic, and livability.[29]

OSU officials were confident following LUBA's decision, with Becky Johnson announcing that OSU would move ahead with planning and building "instead of waiting for these legal battles to work their way through the system." Bend's city attorney, Mary Winters, was delighted that the courts agreed with the city council's interpretation of its codes. Truth in Site, however, did not go quietly, objecting to plans for parking, access to campus, sidewalk requirements, and questioning whether the city had violated its own land use guidelines. In the interim, OSU moved forward with options to purchase an adjacent forty-six acres, much of it a former pumice mine, and another property, once a demolition landfill. If geological, environmental, and engineering investigations proved the area suitable for development, OSU-Cascades would be able to enroll between three thousand and five thousand students.[30]

While construction moved ahead on the Cascades campus, university administrators faced the reoccurrence of troubling matters related to sexual assault and student attitudes on race. An endemic problem on college campuses—sexual assaults—gained national notoriety in 2015 with the publication of Corvallis-born John Krakauer's *Missoula: Rape and the Justice System in a College Town*, an account of sexual assault involving athletes at the University of Montana. Well before the publication of Krakauer's book, statistical evidence indicated that women students nationwide were experiencing rape in alarming numbers. Closer to home, a brave Portland woman came forward in 2014 with details about being gang raped by four OSU football players when she visited Corvallis in 1998. While Brenda Tracy remained anonymous in the aftermath of the assault, her story gained traction when John Canzano, an *Oregonian* sports columnist and radio talk host, interviewed Tracy in the fall of 2014 and concluded, after a careful review of the case, "that the university community failed the woman." When she first reported the assault, local law enforcement officials made "hasty and questionable decisions," in part because she refused to testify in court. To make matters worse, evidence was destroyed well before the statute of limitations expired. Tracy subsequently earned a nursing degree at Oregon Health and Sciences University and a master of business administration—and, most important, a sense of self-worth—after the harrowing experiences of 1998.[31]

With the *Oregonian* and OregonLive.com publishing three segments of the case in November 2014, OSU President Ed Ray sought police reports to see if the university's code of student conduct would have any effect on the sixteen-year-old case. He praised Tracy's efforts "to reclaim her sense of self-worth" and personally apologized "for any failure on our part" in providing assistance. The president's open-ended apology bore fruit the following year, when the university hired Brenda Tracy as a consultant to assist in efforts to prevent sexual violence. Her story continued when President Ray presented to Pac-12 presidents a measure that would ban athletes accused of serious misconduct from transferring to member schools. Ray was building on Tracy's petition to Pac-12 presidents, asking them to reexamine their transfer policies: "We need to stop transferring around student-athletes with serious criminal issues. . . . If you're recruiting an athlete, why aren't you looking at criminal histories?" Tracy was undoubtedly responding to a widely reported incident of a basketball player who transferred to the University of Oregon and was involved in sexual assault charges—after he had been dismissed at another institution for similar accusations. The Eugene school subsequently dismissed him.[32]

OSU had already banned admittance to student transfers who were barred from enrolling at their previous institutions when it demanded full disclosure from transfers regarding their status at the former school. The university was "committed to combating sexual violence in society," Ray announced, thereby enhancing safety for OSU students. The revised policy extended beyond sexual assault to all forms of unacceptable student behavior. Steve Clark, vice president for university relations, indicated that transfers would be denied admission if they were ineligible to enroll elsewhere because of serious violations of student conduct codes. The Portland *Oregonian* praised Oregon State "for addressing a problem that has received growing national attention" and crediting Brenda Tracy for helping develop the new policy.[33]

In an age of instant media, African Americans protesting inequitable race relations can have an immediate effect on campuses across the nation. This was true in the case of the University of Missouri in November 2015, when student and faculty protests forced the resignation of the president of the university system (Timothy Wolfe) and the chancellor of the Columbia campus, R. Bowen Loftin, who would relinquish his office at the end of the year. The turmoil in Columbia had been building for months, with African American students repeatedly bringing attention to racist incidents that the president seemed to ignore. The protestors were buoyed when a graduate student launched a hunger strike, promising not to eat until Wolfe resigned. Nine of the university's deans called for the removal of the chancellor, and then the ultimate blow—Missouri football players refused to play their next game if Wolfe remained in office.[34]

The University of Missouri's troubles spread to college campuses across the nation—from the prestigious Ivy League to Claremont McKenna College and UCLA campuses in southern California. To indicate the immediacy with which the protests spread—three days after the Missouri resignations, a group of OSU students met with President Ray and asked him to call a forum to discuss issues of inclusivity and the need for greater attention to racial awareness at the university. In contrast to the Missouri executives, Ray acted promptly, arranging a meeting in Gill Coliseum on Monday, November 16, and cancelling his participation in a board meeting of the Association of Public and Land-grant Universities. His memorandum announcing the assembly was unequivocal: Oregon State was committed to "a fully inclusive, caring and safe community." The purpose of the gathering in Gill was "listening and learning from . . . students, faculty and staff of color . . . who may feel marginalized."[35]

The Monday evening event was quiet and respectful, with some twenty students, most of them women, addressing the five hundred or more people in the audience. Asked to speak at the end of the event, President Ray said he would meet with the meeting's organizers on strategies to make OSU a more inclusive campus: "You will be hearing from me soon with specific actions to take." If the persistence of racism on campus was the issue, a live feed of the event proved the point, with an online anonymous chat hosting a torrent of vile, racist, and sexist cant targeting specific speakers and people of color. People claiming to have attended OSU authored many of the posts. A few of those in Gill who followed the chat on their smartphones read them aloud to the audience. President Ray responded to the live-chat vulgarities the next day in a broadcast e-mail, describing such behavior as "racist, negative and hateful" and contrary to OSU's values.[36]

Despite public incidents of racial bigotry and the lack of tolerance for cultural difference, Oregon State University has become significantly more diverse with the passing decades. In concert with statistics predicting that nonwhite minorities will become the majority in the nation by 2050, OSU's enrollment is moving—if incrementally—in the same direction. With a fall term head count of 8.1 percent minorities in 1983, the university's resident minorities had grown to 22.6 percent of the student population in 2015, with the most significant increase occurring since 1990, as epilogue table 1 indicates.

Table 14.1. Total Enrollment and Percent US Minorities

Year	Fall Term Enrollment	Percent US Minorities
1983	16,065	8.1%
1990	16,362	9.9%
2000	16,777	13.4%
2010	24,370	17.3%
2015	30,451	22.6%

That trend will continue as the State of Oregon's population becomes more diverse. One projection shows states with predominantly white demographics—Utah, Kansas, South Carolina, Pennsylvania, Michigan, and Oregon—having 40 percent minority populations by 2060.[37]

During his tenure at Oregon State University, Ed Ray has overseen the construction of a dizzying array of new buildings, the most extensive the campus has experienced since the presidency of William Jasper Kerr (1907–1932). New buildings, large and small, number nearly thirty structures between 2000 and 2015, ranging from the Merritt Truax Indoor Practice Facility, completed shortly before Ray arrived in Corvallis, to the ninety-thousand-square-foot Student Experience Center, opened in April 2014. Two new dormitories

Except for the quadrangles in front of Valley Library and the Memorial Union, new buildings constructed in the twenty-first century now occupy many of the former green spaces on campus. Among the more notable structures visible in this aerial photo are the Student Experience Center, International Living-Learning Center, Beth Ray Center for Academic Support, Kelley Engineering Center, Austin Hall, Linus Pauling Science Center, and the Hallie Ford Center for Healthy Children and Families. Courtesy of OSU News and Research Communications.

opened, Halsell Hall in 2002 and Tebeau Hall in 2014, named after the first African American woman and man to attend the university. The International Living-Learning Center, which opened in 2011, combines residency and education to honor cultural diversity. The center houses approximately three hundred residents and provides access to twenty-six classrooms, an auditorium, and a resident faculty. American students living in the double rooms are required to have an international roommate.[38]

Two new buildings especially noteworthy are the Beth Ray Center for Academic Support and the Student Experience Center. The Beth Ray Center, named in honor of the president's wife, who died in 2014, opened in 2012. Located across Twenty-Sixth Street from Reser Stadium and Gill Coliseum, the three-story building provides academic support and counseling to athletes and all other students needing assistance. At the groundbreaking, President Ray indicated that no one would be excluded from the building's services. The Ray Center includes classrooms, a computer laboratory, and tutorial rooms. The much larger Student Experience Center houses student programs and activities formerly located in the Memorial Union and Snell Hall. While serving more than seventy programs, the building's environment emphasizes and focuses on welcoming diverse populations. A large atrium extends from the center across the paved courtyard to the Memorial Union, providing shelter from winter rain and summer sun.[39]

Two major college buildings opened during Ray's tenure—the Kelley Engineering Center (2005) and Austin Hall, serving the College of Business (2014). The huge 153,000-square-foot Kelley building is strikingly innovative, with an abundance of natural light, sky bridges, glass-walled conference rooms, and an e-café. The building houses the School of Electrical Engineering and Computer Science and collaborative research programs. The Kelley Center provides a first-floor coffee/lunch venue with comfortable tables for work and conversation. At four floors and one hundred thousand square feet, Austin Hall houses ten classrooms and twenty-three big-screen project rooms, the latter popular with students. The building offers a marketplace, with chairs and sofas for relaxing. The building's Reser Student Success Center (for advising) comes with event space and a café.[40]

Although this survey leaves unmentioned significant structures, two recent buildings deserve mention—the Linus Pauling Science Center and the Hallie Ford Center for Healthy Children and Families. The Pauling Center, named in honor of the only two-time winner of the Nobel Prize, is a four-story, 105,000-square-foot building that houses the Linus Pauling Institute, a leading center for scientific research. The structure is unique, its third floor embracing a large contiguous laboratory and noisy equipment, with research areas in small hallways. The open laboratory environment is a marked departure from the four-walled labs of old. The Hallie Ford enterprise provides four research areas: Healthy Development in Early Childhood; Healthy Development for Youth and Young Adults; Parenting and Family Life; and Healthy Lifestyles and Obesity Prevention in Children and Families. Hallie Ford, the widow of Roseburg lumberman Kenneth Ford, provided the generous bequest for the building. Speaking at the grand opening, President Ray predicted the Hallie Ford Center would "make a profound difference in the health of our communities."[41]

The person at the center of most of the frenzied construction projects—President Ed Ray—has guided the ship of state through perilous waters, none more significant than the legislature's decision to allow the state's public universities to form their own governing boards. The origins of this dramatic change in the governing structures begins with the restive president of the University of Oregon, Richard Lariviere, who began pushing for greater autonomy for the Eugene school in the 2011 legislative session. At the same time, Oregon University System lobbyists were seeking to give public institutions greater independence. Lariviere was in a hurry, and through the summer and fall of that year he ignored Governor John Kitzhaber's order to keep pay increases below 6 percent, angering other university presidents, the OUS board, and Kitzhaber. When the OUS board met in early December, it voted not to renew the UO president's contract. Lariviere's successor, Michael Gottfredson, then placed establishing an independent governing board at the top of his agenda.[42]

Lariviere was obviously impatient, because the 2011 legislative session had already passed Senate Bill 242, giving public universities more independence and control over their budgets. The president of the OUS board called the reform measure "a sea change in higher education, . . . almost a new beginning." Portland State University president Wim Wiewel praised the new policy for allowing universities to solve their own problems. Most important, the board now had the authority to permit institutions to create their own governing boards, an initiative the University of Oregon and Portland State University desired. With the vantage of hindsight, it is difficult to understand the sense of pique that drove the popular Lariviere to ignore the governor's guidelines on pay raises in the face of tight budgetary times. In the wake of Lariviere's dismissal, Chancellor George Pernsteiner told the *Oregonian* that the president "was convinced he knew what was best for the University of Oregon, and it had to be done right now."[43]

The legislature's Special Committee on University Governance moved the ball farther downfield in October 2012, proposing a bill that would enable the UO and PSU to establish their own governing boards, including the hiring and firing of presidents. The draft measure also gave the independent boards the freedom to establish their own budgets and tuition rates irrespective of what happened at other institutions. Ed Ray argued that several provisions in the bill should be extended to schools without boards. The OSU president initially feared that independent boards would erode the coordinated management of the state's seven universities. He worried, too, that such an approach would unleash a "competitive advocacy process," with institutions competing against each other in the legislature.[44]

Although President Ray initially opposed the move toward autonomous boards, when the University of Oregon and Portland State declared in favor of the new approach, their decisions forced the OSU president's hand. The 2013 legislative session passed Senate Bill 270, "Establishment and Independence of Governing Boards," a measure offering transparency, accountability, and support for all the universities. OSU moved quickly, with the Oregon Senate confirming its fourteen-member board of trustees in November 2013. The new board, with Ed Ray as ex officio, represented a mix of talented education, civic, and business leaders who would guide the university's mission "in teaching, discovery and service as an internationally recognized public research university." President emeritus John Byrne praised Ray's decision for the university to have its own governing board. Because the university's land-grant reach was statewide, faculty and staff worked with all Oregonians. Although problems loomed ahead, Byrne thought the independent board would help the university move "into closer harmony with the people it serves." There may be risks, but "that's a risk worth taking."[45]

In the second decade of the twenty-first century, Oregon State University functions in a decentralized state system of higher education under its own board of trustees and as the only institution with a statewide presence. With leadership talents in education, civic, and business life, board members provide oversight, guiding the institution's traditional mission of serving Oregon citizens. Senate Bill 80, signed by Governor Kate Brown in the summer of 2015, formally abolished the Oregon University System and replaced it with the Higher Education Coordinating Commission with limited powers. To be sure, OSU's trustees have avoided embarrassment such as the University of Oregon's in having a president, Michael Gottfredson, abruptly resign one month after its board was empowered to hire and fire presidents. As he exited, Gottfredson offered the conventional announcement that he wanted to spend more time with his family. Those close to the UO indicated that the president was forced out, angering influential boosters when he failed to properly handle sexual assault charges against three basketball players. A Corvallis *Gazette-Times* editorial commented that the University of Oregon board was "setting a poor example for its counterparts."[46]

As Oregon State approaches its sesquicentennial, students arriving on campus will be entering academic and social environments that depart sharply from those of previous generations. In addition to a student body whose ethnic diversity has increased significantly, class sizes are larger, with some survey courses enrolling three hundred or more students. OSU's ratio of twenty-three students per teacher compares with the national average of fifteen to one. Although adjuncts (temporary hires), who teach courses, have grown in number, the university still has a greater percentage of full-time faculty teaching courses than most institutions. According to OSU's director of institutional research, Salvador Castillo, rough data indicate that 71 percent of OSU's teachers were full time in 2013, compared with the national average of 51 percent.[47]

Today's students have access to a truly revolutionary technology that dwarfs anything comparable prior to 1990. Students entering Oregon Agricultural College in 1910 and those enrolling at OSU in 1990 still shared much in common—in both decades professors lectured and students took notes and wrote examinations in Blue Books. Beginning in 1910 and continuing for most of the decade, several developments took place that would become hallmarks of the institution as it evolved from an agricultural school to a state college and, in 1960, to a university. Athletic teams were first referred to as Beavers in 1910, the same year that the school had its first student council, and the Armory (now McAlexander Fieldhouse) was completed. During the decade, the title for the annual yearbook changed from the *Orange* to the *Beaver*, and the college's Student Store (to become the OSU Bookstore) opened. Before 1920, the institution was home to other standards of the modern university—student health services, the Reserve Officers Training Corps (formerly the Cadet Corps), and the Panhellenic and Interfraternity councils.[48]

Eighty years later, Beaver athletes were everywhere on campus, the student council was functioning with greater autonomy, and McAlexander Fieldhouse was home to ROTC (although now, all branches of the military services are present). The *Beaver* yearbook still celebrated campus events, musicals and plays, football and basketball games, with women's sports becoming increasingly prominent with the enactment of Title IX in the 1970s. Around campus in 1990, most faculty and staff offices were still equipped with rotary-dial telephones and typewriters. Although there were a few automobiles around the college in 1910, they multiplied with the passing years and were omnipresent by 1990, with students, faculty, and staff vehicles filling parking lots. Bicycles, becoming a popular mode of exercise and transportation early in the century, were ubiquitous following the Second World War—by the 1980s they ranged from sleek road bikes to rugged trail models. Despite a dramatically transformed technology—electric in place of manual typewriters, enhanced radios and television, and, for students, an abundance of stereos—certain traditional routines still prevailed in the early 1990s.[49]

As the university approaches its sesquicentennial, all facets of the educational system have been transformed—course materials are online, classroom instruction is incredibly varied (using Skype to access specialists beyond Corvallis), students create blogs or web pages for presentations, and, for the professor, a wealth of information sits literally at one's fingertips. Social media has revolutionized student life, enhancing communication with professors and classmates. Most students have laptops and handheld mobile devices, and communicate via Facebook, Twitter, and other media. Few students possessed such technologies as recent as 1995. For unthinking students today, a world absent these technologies would be unfathomable. In the present media environment, students write much more through informal communication, but likely with less attention to grammatical propriety. Their worlds buzz with cyber-speed, but with little time to ponder a way forward. Andrew Delbanco, director of American studies at Columbia University, recently observed that faculty still live by the fifty-minute lecture, while students "are accustomed to dealing with multiple information streams in short bursts." The downside to this new environment is the absence, for many, of substantive *personal* associations with their peers and teachers.[50]

Beyond the world of cyberspace, student living quarters and dining arrangements have changed, with conventional dormitories of an earlier age giving way to buildings such as Halsell and Tebeau Halls. Carrie Halsell Residence Hall, named after the first African American woman graduate, opened in 2002 with double- and single-bedroom suites sharing a commons area and a bathroom. Halsell offers more independence for older students, and its fourth floor is reserved for the university Honors College. William Tebeau Hall, opened in 2014, offers three-bedroom suites and a shared bathroom. Each floor has additional community bathrooms, a kitchen, study area, and a laundry room. On-campus dining services have changed as well, with the old single-cafeteria arrangements—take what's put before you—giving way to a variety of food courts with healthier options, including locally sourced food, nutritional items unavailable twenty years earlier. McNary and Arnold dining centers feature multiple options, emphasizing nutrition and providing varieties of food, including global fare.[51]

As Oregon State University enters the bright sunlight of its sesquicentennial year, the institution stands proudly with other schools in the land-grant tradition—exemplars in rendering services to citizens of the state as well as providing comprehensive educational programs to students. With its two satellite campuses—OSU-Cascades in Bend and the marine science program in Newport—the school is the largest institution of higher learning in the state, with its presence in every one of Oregon's thirty-six counties, five forest research laboratories around the state, and six agricultural experiment stations. The school remains at the center of cultural life in the City of Corvallis, a position it has held for at least a century. Corvallis mayor Biff Traber calls OSU "a critical element of the city's character," reflecting, perhaps, that 58 percent of the community's adults hold bachelor's degrees.[52] With comprehensive programs in land and water stewardship and training for scientists in myriad venues to handle problems related to climate change, today's university looks to the future, well-prepared to meet the challenges of tomorrow.

Appendix 1
Presidents of Oregon State (1868–2017)

William Asa Finley (1868–1872)
Joseph Emery (1872, acting)
Benjamin Lee Arnold (1872–1892)
John Davidson Letcher (1892)
John McKnight Bloss (1892–1896)
Henry B. Miller (1896–1897)
Thomas Milton Gatch (1897–1907)
William Jasper Kerr (1907–1932)
George Wilcox Peavy (1932–1934, acting; 1934–1940)
Frank Llewellyn Ballard (1940–1941)
Francois Archibald Gilfillan (1941–1942, acting)
August LeRoy Strand (1942–1961)
James Herbert Jensen (1961–1969)
Roy Alton Young (1969–1970, acting)
Robert William MacVicar (1970–1984)
John Vincent Byrne (1984–1995)
Paul G. Risser (1996–2002)
Timothy P. White (2002–2003, acting)
Edward John Ray (2003–present)

Appendix 2
Administrative Structure of Oregon State, 2017

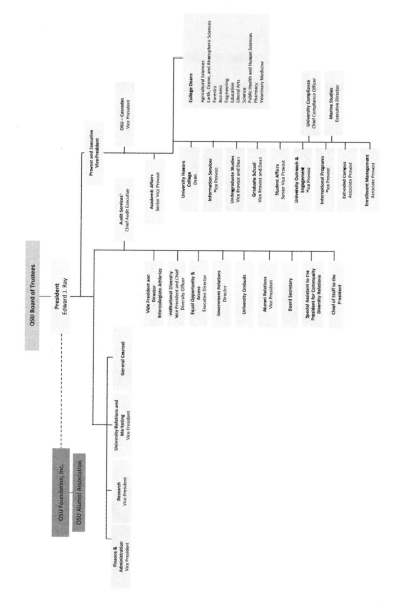

Notes

PROLOGUE

1 Linda P. B. Katehi, "Innovation and the Mission of the Land Grant University," n.p., *The People's Vanguard of Davis*, March 2, 2015, http://www.davisvanguard.org/author/ vanguard-administrator/; John R. Campbell, *Reclaiming a Lost Heritage: Land Grant and Other Higher Education Initiatives for the Twenty-First Century* (East Lansing: Michigan State University Press, 1998), 17; Robert Rydell, Jeffrey Safford, and Pierce Mullen, *In the People's Interest: A Centennial History of Montana State University* (Bozeman: Montana State University Foundation, 1992), 1; and "U of M Celebrates 150 Years of Land-Grant Mission," University of Minnesota Extension, Spring 2012, http://landgrant150.umn.edu/.

2 Clyde A. Milner II, Carol A. O'Connor, and Martha A. Sandweiss, eds., *The Oxford History of the American West* (New York: Oxford University Press, 1994), 607, 215; Paul S. Boyer, ed., *The Oxford Companion to United States History* (New York: Oxford University Press, 2001), 34; *Oregonian*, August 12, 1862; and Roger L. Williams, *The Origins of Federal Support for Higher Education: George W. Atherton and the Land-Grant College Movement* (University Park: Pennsylvania State University Press, 1991), 34–41.

3 Katehi, "Innovation and the Mission of the Land Grant University," n.p.

4 Roger L. Geiger, *The History of American Higher Education: Learning and Culture from the Founding to World War II* (Princeton: Princeton University Press, 2015), 297; and Earle D. Ross, *The Land-Grant Idea at Iowa State College: A Centennial Trial Balance, 1858–1958* (Ames: Iowa State College Press, 1958), 49.

5 Madison Kuhn, *Michigan State: The First Hundred Years* (East Lansing: Michigan State University Press, 1955), 14–15; and Eldon L. Johnson, "Misconceptions about the Early Land-Grant Colleges, *Journal of Higher Education* 52 (July-August, 1981), 333–336.

6 Ibid., 340–345; and *The Land-Grant Tradition* (Washington, DC: Association of Public Land-Grant Universities, 2012), 27.

7 Johnson, "Misconceptions about the Early Land-Grant Colleges," 345–350.

8 United States Census Bureau, Quick Facts, Oregon, http://quickfacts.census.gov/qfd/ states/41000.html; and William G. Robbins and Katrine Barber, *Nature's Northwest: The North Pacific Slope in the Twentieth Century* (Tucson: University of Arizona Press, 2010), 228–231. To indicate the significance of Oregon's rapidly changing cultural environment, the 1960 census lists the state's white population at 97.9 percent.

9 Pirsig is quoted in Rydell, Safford, and Mullen, *In the People's Interest*, ix.

10 E. David Cronon and John W. Jenkins, *The University of Wisconsin: A History* (Madison: University of Wisconsin Press, 1994), xiii.

11 See Paul M. Buhle and Edward Rice-Maxim, *William Appleman Williams: The Tragedy of Empire* (New York: Routledge, 1995), 196–197.

CHAPTER ONE: BEGINNINGS

1 Michael David Cohen, *Reconstructing the Campus: Higher Education and the American Civil War* (Charlottesville: University of Virginia Press, 2012), 57; Clyde A. Milner II, Carol A. O'Connor, and Martha A. Sandweiss, eds., *The Oxford History of the American*

West (New York: Oxford University Press, 1994), 607, 215; and Paul S. Boyer, ed., *The Oxford Companion to United States History* (New York: Oxford University Press, 2001), 34.

2 Historical Note, Columbia Conference of the Methodist Episcopal Church, South, 1866–1893, archival note to the finding aid, Oregon State University Special Collections and Archives (hereafter SCARC), Corvallis, Oregon; and untitled handwritten document in the Benton County Historical Society (hereafter BCHS), Philomath, Oregon, August 28, 1860.

3 General Commission on Archives and History: The United Methodist Church, http:// www.gcah.org/cite/c.ghKJIOPHIoE/b3522575/.

4 Historical Note, Columbia Conference of the Methodist Episcopal Church, South, 1866–1893, archival note to the finding aid, SCARC, Corvallis, Oregon; John R. Thelin, *A History of Higher Education, Second Edition* (Baltimore: Johns Hopkins University Press, 2011), 76–77; and "Yale: Traditions and History," http://www.yale.edu/traditions. history. The land-grant origin of present-day Kansas State University was linked to a defunct Methodist college when it opened as Kansas State Agricultural College in 1863. See Roger L. Geiger, *The History of American Higher Education: Learning and Culture from the Founding to World War II* (Princeton, NJ: Princeton University Press, 2015), 302.

5 Inaugural address of Governor L. F. Grover to the Legislative Assembly, September 14, 1870, Salem, Oregon, copy in Record Group (hereafter RG) 013, subgroup (hereafter sub.) 6, reel 15 (SCARC); Jerry A. O'Callaghan, *The Disposition of the Public Domain in Oregon*, Committee Print, 86th Cong., 2nd Sess. (Washington, DC, 1960), 63; and William G. Robbins, *Oregon, This Storied Land* (Portland: Oregon Historical Society Press, 2005), 46–55.

6 Roger L. Williams, *The Origins of Federal Support for Higher Education: George W. Atherton and the Land-Grant College Movement* (University Park: Pennsylvania State University Press, 1991), 34–41; and Morris Bishop, *A History of Cornell* (Ithaca: Cornell University Press, 1962), 57–59.

7 *Oregonian*, March 7 and April 23, 1863; "An Act to accept the proposal of the Congress of the United States granting lands to the state of Oregon for agricultural colleges," *General Statutes of Oregon* (1862), 60–61; and Geiger, *The History of American Higher Education*, 284–285.

8 Earle D. Ross, *The Land-Grant Idea at Iowa State College* (Ames: Iowa State College Press, 1958), 34–36; *General Laws of the State of Oregon* (1868), 40–41 and 430–431; and *Oregonian*, April 9, 1864, and October 3 and December 28, 1868.

9 John E. Smith, *Corvallis College* (Corvallis: Self-published, 1953), 5–9; and *Oregonian*, April 21, 1893. For a brief account of Bellinger's career, see Oliver Tatom, "Charles Bellinger (1839–1905)," *Oregon Encyclopedia of History and Culture,* http://oregonency-clopedia.org/entry/view/bellinger_charles_1839_1905_/.

10 John B. Horner, "History of Oregon State College, 1865–1907," *Oregon Historical Quarterly* 31 (March 1930), 42–43; J. G. Flook, handwritten note, "Resolved that a select committee of three be appointed . . . ," September 30, 1868, BCHS doc.; and David Peterson del Mar, "Fourteenth Amendment," *Oregon Encyclopedia of History and Culture*, http://oregonen-cyclopedia.org/articles/14th_amendment/#.VkDsu9jlvA4.

11 Columbia Conference of the Methodist Episcopal Church, South (hereafter Columbia Conference), October 26, 1866, August 25, 1867, and September 1, 1869; and Corvallis College, Articles of Incorporation; all in SCARC.

12 Columbia Conference, Fourth Session, September 1, 1869; and Board of Trustees Records, 1871–1889, RG 033, in SCARC, August 22 and October 31, 1868.

13 The title "agricultural college" is a misnomer, because Corvallis College officials commonly used the term "department" when referring to the courses it taught. President Benjamin Arnold used "Corvallis State Agricultural College" on the title page of the annual catalogue. By the late 1870s, however, "Corvallis College" returned to the title page of the catalogue and appeared on college diplomas. Before the state assumed control of the school in 1885, some version of "State Agricultural College" was used in various reports.

Beginning in 1889, the Corvallis *Gazette* referred to "Oregon Agricultural College," and in the next decade it served as the regular reference for the institution. See Smith, *Corvallis College,* 43.

14 Board of Trustees Records, September 1 and December 13, 1869; and *Fourth Annual Catalogue of Corvallis College, 1868–1869* (Salem, 1869), 16.

15 Columbia Conference, September 9, 1870.

16 *Acts and Resolutions of the Legislature of the State of Oregon* (1870), 17–20; Board of Trustees Records, October 29 and November 12, 1870; and *Messages and Documents: Report on Agricultural College Lands* (1870), 21–26.

17 Board of Trustees Records, Circular of State Agricultural College, March 1, 1873.

18 Frederick G. Young, "Financial History of the State of Oregon—IV, Part III, Public Expenditures," *Oregon Historical Quarterly* 11 (1910), 296–297; Thelin, *A History of American Higher Education,* 72.

19 *Oregonian,* October 14, 1871. The *Oregonian* quoted at length a recent article appearing in the *Farmer.* For a brief biography of Minto, see William L. Lang, "John Minto (1822–1915)," *The Oregon Encyclopedia,* http://www.oregonencyclopedia.org/articles/minto_john_1822_1915_/#.VRWpvNjwuic.

20 National Trust for Preservation, Willamette Falls Navigation Canal and Locks, https://savingplaces.org/places/willamette-falls-navigation-canal-and-locks#.VjfMu9jluOU; Chronological History of Oregon State University, OSU Libraries-University Archives (hereafter Chronological History), http://archives.library.oregonstate.edu/chronology/chron_1860.html; Benton County Historical Society Timeline, http://www.bentoncountymuseum.org/timeline/decade.cfm?decade=1870; *Oregonian,* April 8, 1867; and *Willamette Farmer,* April 26, 1873.

21 *Corvallis Gazette,* December 14, 1872, and January 4, 1873.

22 Biographical Note, Guide to the Benjamin Lea Arnold Collection, SCARC.

23 Biennial Report of the Agricultural College, August 12, 1872, sub. 12, box 9, RG 013; and *Catalogue of Corvallis College, 1871–1872* (Salem, 1872), 20.

24 Board of Trustees Records, October 18, 1873, and June 15, 1874.

25 Chronological History; Board of Trustees Records, September 24, 1874; and Columbia Conference, Ninth Session, September 14, 1874 (emphasis original).

26 Biennial Report of the Agricultural College, 1874, sub. 12, box 9, RG 013. The faculty's teaching responsibilities are stunning, with Professor B. J. Hawthorne responsible for six classes every day: Latin (twenty-two students); Latin (nineteen students); German (ten students); Greek (three students); French (seven students); and English Grammar (seventeen students).

27 *Oregonian,* December 15, 1873.

28 *General Laws of the State of Oregon* (1876), 52–63.

29 *Oregonian,* March 14, 1876.

30 Ibid., May 24, 1876; and *Eleventh Annual Catalogue of Corvallis Agricultural College, 1875–1876* (Salem, 1876), 8–13.

31 *Oregonian,* March 6, 1878.

32 These figures are from several issues of the *General Catalogue,* but especially from the *Annual Catalogue of the State Agricultural College of the State of Oregon for 1889–1890,* Oregon State Agricultural College (1890), 30–32.

33 *Biennial Reports of the State Agricultural College,* 1876 and 1880.

34 *Biennial Message of Governor W. W. Thayer* (1882), 19–20 and 23–29.

35 *Biennial Report of the State Agricultural College,* 1882; and *The Laws of Oregon* (1882), 26. Minto's appearance was related to his interest in the Corvallis enterprise as a secular school of agriculture and mechanical arts. Moreover, the M.E. Church, South, was struggling mightily to support Corvallis College by 1882, and Minto was well aware of the weaknesses of the agricultural department.

36 *Biennial Report of the State Agricultural College,* 1884.

37 Columbia Conference, September 18, 1875, September 15, 1876, and ca. 1878.

38 Ibid., 1881, and Appendix to the 18th Session, ca. 1882 (emphasis original).

39 Board of Trustees Records, August 18, 1882.

40 Ibid.

41 Ibid., Book 1, Minutes, February 3, 1882, box 3, RG 32.

42 Columbia Conference, September 3, 1884; and ca. 1884–1885. The conference minutes sometimes refer to the "Board of Trustees" and the "Regents." The board of trustees initially thought the conference's decision "would be improper at this time." On the motion of Reverend J. R. N. Bell, however, the board agreed to follow the mandate of the conference. See Board of Trustees Records, January 29, 1885.

43 *The Laws of Oregon and the Resolutions and Memorials of the Thirteenth Regular Session of the Legislative Assembly* (1885), 10–19. The House vote on the Senate bill to situate the agricultural college in Corvallis was fifty-six to four. See *Journal of the House* (1885), 286–287.

44 Columbia Conference, September 1, 1885, and September 18, 1886.

45 Board of Trustees Records, March 24, 1887.

46 *Oregonian*, March 28, 1887. An *Oregonian* editorial the next day supported the argument that the legislature lacked "authority to bestow the State Agricultural endowment upon a sectarian school in perpetuity."

47 *Oregonian*, September 10, 1884.

48 Ibid., December 22, 1887.

49 Ibid., January 30 and December 7, 1888.

50 Biennial Message of Governor Sylvester Pennoyer to the Legislative, *Journal of the House of the Oregon Legislative Assembly*, Fifteenth Regular Session, 1889 (Salem: Frank C. Baker, State Printer, 1889), Appendix A.

51 *Report of Special Committee on Corvallis College. Fifteenth Regular Session of the Oregon Legislature* (Salem: Frank C. Baker, State Printer, 1889), copy in Pubs, 1-10d, SCARC.

52 *Oregonian,* February 12, 1889.

53 Oregon Supreme Court, October 3, 1892, Joseph Liggett et al., v. W. S. Ladd et al., no. 4473, box 148; and Corvallis *Gazette*, October 7, 1892.

54 *Biennial Report of the Oregon State Agricultural College* (1889), 5–7, and (1893), 14–15; and Geiger, *The History of American Higher Education*, 297.

55 *Biennial Report of the Oregon State Agricultural College* (1889), 5–7, and (1893), 14–15; Geiger, *The History of American Higher Education*, 297; and Cohen, *Reconstructing the Campus*, 130.

CHAPTER TWO: COMING OF AGE

1 William G. Robbins, *Landscapes of Promise: The Oregon Story, 1800–1940* (Seattle: University of Washington Press, 1997), 189; and Dorothy O. Johansen, *Empire of the Columbia: A History of the Pacific Northwest* (New York: Harper and Row, 1967), 282.

2 *Biennial Report of the Oregon State Agricultural College* (1889), 5–7, in Presidents Office Records, RG 013, sub. 12, box 9 (hereafter *Biennial Report*).

3 Ibid., 6–9

4 Ibid. (1891), 3; (1893), 14–15; and Minute Book 2, May 2, 1893, box 3, Administrative Council Records, RG 32.

5 Ibid. (1893), 3–5 and 15. For a brief biography of William Ladd, see Friends of the Ladd Carriage House, http://www.laddcarriagehouse.org/WSLadd.htm.

6 *Oregonian*, June 12 and October 1, 1888. For a profile of Wallis Nash, see George Edmonston, Jr., "Wallis Nash . . . A 'Gift' to Corvallis College from Victorian England," www.osualum.com/s/359/index.aspx?pgid=542.

7 A Chronological History of OSU, http://scarc.library.oregonstate.edu/university-history. html (hereafter Chronological History); Wallis Nash, memo regarding the appointment

of the president, July 18, 1888; handwritten note, "Official designation is The State Agricultural College of the State of Oregon," May 5, 1889; and Wallis Nash to President Arnold, October 16, 1889; all in Presidents Office Records, 1870–2002, RG 013, sub. 6, reel 1.

8   Nash to Arnold, November 19, 1888; and Nash to Arnold, ca. 1889, RG 013, sub. 1, box 1.

9   Ibid., April 18 and June 19, 1890.

10 Nash to Arnold, October 29, 1889, RG 013, sub. 6, reel 1.

11 Ibid., 1885, 14–15; and 1887, 56.

12 Alan I. Marcus, *Agricultural Science and the Quest for Legitimacy: Farmers, Agricultural Colleges, and Experiment Stations, 1870–1890* (Ames: Iowa State University Press, 1985), 171–172, 185–186, 198–201, 217–221; and *100 Years of Progress: The Oregon Agricultural Experiment Station, Oregon State University, 1888–1889* (Corvallis: Oregon State University, 1990), 11.

13 *Biennial Report* (1889), 7–10.

14 Board of Regents Records, April 1888, box 6, and October 3, 1889, box 5, both in Board of Regents Records, RG 008; *100 Years of Progress*, 11; and Regulations Governing Oregon Agricultural Experiment Station, box 1, RG 008.

15 Board of Regents Records, box 5, October 3, 1889; and ca. early 1891.

16 *Biennial Report* (1889), 5; and Arnold to P. H. Irish, RG 013, sub. 6, reel 1.

17 *Biennial Report* (1891), 5.

18 Chronological History (1888); Nash to Arnold, April 28, 1890; and George Coote to Arnold, January 2, 1891; both in sub. 6, reel 1.

19 *100 Years of Progress*, 12–15.

20 Earle D. Ross, *The Land-Grant Idea and Iowa State College: A Centennial Trial Balance, 1858–1958* (Ames: Iowa State College Press, 1958), 83; Madison Kuhn, *1855, Michigan State: The First Hundred Years* (East Lansing: Michigan State University Press, 1955), 137–141; and Marcus, *Agricultural Science*, 38–40.

21 John Bloss, Notes on Farmers' Institutes, July 7, 1895, box 1, sub. 3; and W. M. Hilleary, December 16, 1896, reel 1, sub. 6; both in RG 013.

22 USDA, National Institute of Food and Agriculture, http://www.crees.esda.gov/about/offices/legis/secondmorrill.html.

23 Ralph D. Christy and Lionel Williamson, eds., *A Century of Service: Land-Grant Colleges and Universities, 1890–1990* (New Brunswick, NJ: Transaction Publishers, 1992), vii–ix, xiii–xxi; and The Secretary of the Interior from Governor Sylvester Pennoyer, September 24, 1890, box 1, RG 008.

24 *Biennial Report* (1891), 6–9.

25 Minute Book 2, October 5, 1891, box 3, RG 32.

26 Biographical Note, John McKnight Bloss Collection, 1870–1968, http://scarc.library.oregonstate.edu/coll/bloss/; and Chronological History, 1892–1896.

27 Bloss to Gentlemen, June 6, 1995, sub. 6, reel 1.

28 George Coote to Wallis Nash, June 30, 1892; G. A. Covell to Nash, July 16, 1892; and Moses Craig to Nash, July 1, 1892; all in box 1, RG 008.

29 G. W. Shaw to Nash, January 10 and March 23, 1893; and W. E. Yates to H. B. Miller, August 5, 1886; all in box 1, RG 008 (emphasis original).

30 Margaret Snell to Respected Board of Regents, March 14, 1891, box 1, RG 008.

31 Roger L. Williams, *The Origins of Federal Support for Higher Education: George W. Atherton and the Land-Grant College Movement* (University Park: Pennsylvania State University Press, 1991), 6–8, 209, and 216; H. T. French to George Atherton, March 4, 1892; and Henry Alvord to Dear Sir, February 28, 1893; both in box 1, sub. 2, RG 013.

32 Circular, Association of American Agricultural Colleges and Experiment Stations; Report of the Zoologist at the College Station to J. M. Bloss, June 12, 1892; both in box 1, sub. 2, RG 013; and *Oregonian*, March 11 and May 14, 1893. The *Chicago Tribune* is quoted in the Corvallis *Gazette*, June 16, 1893.

33 Morris Bishop, *A History of Cornell* (Ithaca: Cornell University Press, 1962), 125–126.

34 Chronological History, 1873; and J. C. Kelton, Adjutant General to President of the State Agricultural College, November 15 and December 6, 1888; both in reel 1, sub. 6, RG 013. The first cadet uniforms and caps were Confederate gray. For the reference to blue uniforms, see *Oregonian*, June 10, 1900.

35 The reference to using troops to enforce public laws reflects a turbulent period in American history in which violent class conflicts threatened the very fiber of the nation, and state and local officials called out the National Guard to restore order. For a big picture of this period, see J. Anthony Lukas, *Big Trouble: A Murder in a Small Western Town Sets Off a Struggle for the Soul of America* (New York: Touchstone Books, 1997).

36 *Biennial Report* (1894), 6, 12; and (1896), 10; both in box 9, sub. 12, RG 013; and C. E. Dentler to the President of the Agricultural College, June 4, 1895, box 1, sub. 3, RG 013. The faculty also endorsed the call for construction of an armory or gymnasium. See Minute Book 2, October 23, 1896, box 3, RG 32.

37 Wallis Nash to H. B. Miller, August 7, 1896, box 2, sub. 4, RG 013.

38 Report of the President to the Secretary of Agriculture and Secretary of the Interior, June 30, 1897, box 2, sub. 4, RG 013.

39 Casualties during the Spanish-American War, http://www.spanamwar.com/casualties.htm; and *Oregonian*, June 3, 1893.

40 *Oregonian*, August 30, 1894; and Corvallis *Gazette*, July 16 and August 4, 1893.

41 *Annual Report of the Oregon Agricultural College and Experiment Station* (hereafter *Annual Report*) (1897), box 9, sub. 12, RG 013, 4–6.

42 John Bloss to Bureau of Education and Department of Interior, June 30, 1893, box 1, sub. 4, RG 013; Corvallis *Gazette*, June 30, 1893; and *Annual Report* (1897), 3

43 For biographical sketches of Bloss, see http://scarc.library.oregonstate.edu/omeka/exhibits/show/presidents/bloss/bloss/; and Gatch, http://scarc.library.oregonstate.edu/omeka/exhibits/show/presidents/gatch/gatch/.

44 *Annual Report* (1897), box 9, sub. 12, RG 013, 3–11. The faculty found fault with advanced students who were still struggling with their command of good English. See Minute Book 2, January 25, 1897, box 3, RG 32.

45 Minute Book 2, March 22, 1897, box 3, RG 32.

46 Ibid., 10–11; and "Historical Note," College of Pharmacy Records, RG 105, SCARC.

47 For a concise but very brief account of the Spanish-American War, see the entry in *The Oxford Companion to United States History*, ed. Paul S. Boyer (New York: Oxford University Press, 2001), 736–737.

48 *Oregonian*, June 23, 1898; and Boyer, ed., *The Oxford Companion to United States History*, 736–737.

49 *Oregonian*, September 15, 1989.

50 Ibid., August 15 and October 31, 1899; and Proceedings of the Faculty, ca. fall 1899, Minute Book 3; both in box 3, RG 32.

51 Chronological History, 1898; and *Annual Report* (1900), 8–9.

52 *Annual Report* (1901), 3–5, box 9, sub. 12, RG 013.

53 *Annual Report* (1902), 13–17, box 9, sub. 12, RG 013.

54 *Oregonian*, June 27, 1903.

55 *Annual Report* (1901), 5, box 9, sub. 12, RG 013; and *100 Years of Progress*, 24–25.

56 *Oregonian*, March 3, 1902.

57 Ibid., July 18, 1902.

58 *Annual Report* (1903), 4–5, box 9, sub. 12, RG 013.

59 These figures are gleaned from the following sources: *Annual Reports* (1904, 1905, 1906, 1907, and 1908), box 9, sub. 12, RG 013.

60 Ibid. (1905), 8.

61 For a summary of Gatch's career, see J. F. Santee, "Thomas Milton Gatch, Educator," *Oregon Historical Quarterly* 32 (June 1931), 114–122; *Oregonian*, July 20, 1906; and Gatch, http://scarc.library.oregonstate.edu/omeka/exhibits/show/presidents/gatch/gatch/.

62 I am indebted to Don McIlvenna and Darold Wax of OSU's History Department for this summary paragraph on Kerr. Interested readers should see Don E. McIlvenna and Darold D. Wax, "W. J. Kerr, Land-Grant President in Utah and Oregon, 1900–1908," *Oregon Historical Quarterly* 85 (1984), 387–405; and McIlvenna and Wax, "W. J. Kerr, Land-Grant President in Utah and Oregon, 1900–1908, Part 2," *Oregon Historical Quarterly* 86 (1985), 4–22.

63 Board of Regents to W. J. Kerr, May 4, 1907; L. A. Ostien to E. E. Wilson, May 10, 1907; Newton E. Clemenson to Gatch, June 14, 1907, box 2, sub. 5, RG 013; and McIlvenna and Wax, "W. J. Kerr, Land-Grant President in Utah and Oregon, 1900–1908, Part 2," 14–16, 20.

64 *Annual Report* (1908), 13–16, box 9, sub. 12, RG 013.

65 Kuhn, *Michigan State*, 215; Nelson Amendment, Agricultural Appropriation Act, Approved by the President March 4, 1907, copy in box 2, sub. 5, RG 013; *Biennial Report of the President* (1909), 34, box 9, sub. 12, RG 013; and *Oregonian*, August 16, 1907.

66 The Corvallis institution shifted from biennial reports to annual reports in 1897 and then reverted back to biennial reports ten years later.

67 *Biennial Report* (1909) v, 35–39, in box 9, sub. 12, RG 013. The *Oregonian* (July 2, 1908) called for more "equitable funding" for the agricultural college because of "its growing importance and the unquestioned value and merit of its work." The *Grants Pass Outlook* (January 23, 1909) thought the state was "doing very little" to aid students who were studying disciplines vital to the state's economy.

68 *Biennial Report* (1910) 11–12.

69 Ibid., xiv–xv.

CHAPTER THREE: IN WAR AND PEACE

1 Benton County Historical Timeline, 1910s, http://www.bentoncountymuseum.org/timeline/decade.cfm?decade+1910.

2 Portland, Oregon, Population History, 1890–2012, http://www.biggestuscities.com/city/portland-oregon; and Benton County Historical Timeline, 1910s.

3 *Oregonian*, September 11, 1910.

4 Ralph D. Christy and Lionel Williamson, eds., *A Century of Service: Land-Grant Colleges and Universities, 1890–1990* (New Brunswick, NJ: Transaction Publishers, 1992), 59–60.

5 *Capital Journal*, February 4, 1911, photocopy in box 5, sub. 7, RG 013.

6 *Biennial Report* (1912), xxxiii, xlii–xliii, box 9, sub. 12, RG 013.

7 *Oregonian*, January 29, 1911.

8 Christy and Williamson, eds., *A Century of Service: Land-Grant Colleges and Universities, 1890–1990*, 59–60; and Kerr to H. D. Hetzel, October 3, 1911, box 5, sub. 7, RG 013.

9 Kerr to Hetzel, October 3, 1911; and Kerr to James Withycombe, April 14, and Withycombe to Kerr, April 24, 1913; all in box 5, sub. 7, RG 013.

10 Photocopy, 68th Cong., 2nd Sess., H.R. 7951, "An Act to provide for cooperative agricultural work between the agricultural colleges in the several states," box 5, sub. 7, RG 013; and *Biennial Report* (1914), 2, box 9, sub. 12, RG 013. For land-grant institutions that operated extension programs before passage of the Smith-Lever Act in 1913, see Julius Willard Turrass, *History of the Kansas State College of Agriculture and Applied Science* (Manhattan: Kansas State University Press, 1940), 165, https://archive.org/details/HistoryOfTheKansasStateCollegeOfAgricultureAndAppliedScience; Morris Bishop, *A History of Cornell* (Ithaca: Cornell University Press, 1962), 283 and 313–314; Madison Kuhn, *Michigan State: The First Hundred Years* (East Lansing: Michigan State University Press, 1955), 169 and 203–204; Earle Dudley Ross, *The Land-Grant Idea at Iowa State*

    College: A Centennial Trial Balance, 1858–1958 (Ames: Iowa State College Press, 1958),
    129; and Robert W. Topping, *A Century Beyond: The History of Purdue University* (West
    Lafayette, IN: Purdue University Press, 1988), 169.

11 See John R. Campbell, *Reclaiming A Lost Heritage: Land-Grant and Other Higher Education
    Initiatives for the Twenty-First Century* (East Lansing: Michigan State University Press,
    1998), 137.

12 Ira Katznelson, *Fear Itself: The New Deal and the Origins of Our Time* (New York: Liveright
    Publishing Corporation, 2013), 146–147.

13 *Biennial Report* (1916), 4; and *Biennial Report* (1916), xiv–xiv and 31–33; both in box 9,
    sub. 12, RG 013.

14 *Biennial Report* (1920), 38–41.

15 Withycombe to Kerr, n.d., box 5, sub. 7, RG 013.

16 *Biennial Report* (1914), v–xxvi, box 9, sub. 12, RG 013.

17 See chapters 3 and 5 in this volume for the State Board of Higher Curricula.

18 *Oregonian*, February 13, 17, and 22, 1913.

19 Ibid., April 5, 12, and 25, 1913.

20 Ibid., June 10, 1913. The *Medford Sun* is quoted in this issue.

21 *Oregonian*, November 2 and 6, 1913; and *Oregon Blue Book, 1999–2000* (Salem: Office of
    the Secretary of State, 1999), 292.

22 *Biennial Report* (1916), viii–ix; and *Biennial Report* (1918), xvii; both in box 9, sub. 12, RG
    013.

23 For miscellaneous documents pertaining to the millage increase, see Percy A. Cupper to
    President W. J. Kerr, March 20, 1920; W. J. Kerr to Alumni and Former Students, March
    23, 1920; Facts Concerning the Crisis at the State University, Agricultural College and
    Normal School, as copied from the *Official Voters' Pamphlet of the State of Oregon* (1920);
    Address by W. J. Kerr, Lincoln High School Auditorium (Portland), May 10, 1920; all in
    reel 15, sub. 6, RG 013; *Oregonian*, May 16, 1920; *Oregon Blue Book*, 294; and Corvallis
    Daily Gazette-Times, May 23, 1920.

24 W. J. Kerr to P. F. Claxton, September 2, 1920, reel 15, sub. 6, RG 013.

25 *Oregonian*, April 23, 1922, and November 11, 1923; and *Oregon Blue Book, 1999–2000*,
    294.

26 *OSU Historic Guidelines Workbook* (ca. 2012); and Olmsted Brothers to W. J. Kerr,
    October 1, 1909, http://ir.library.oregonstate.edu/xmlui/bitstream/handle/1957/7930/
    Rep_on_Org_Agr_1909.pdf?sequence=1, pp. 1–3.

27 Olmsted Brothers to W. J. Kerr, October 1, 1909, 4–60.

28 *OSU Historic Guidelines Workbook*; and Larry Landis to the author, January 14, 2004.

29 Oregon State University Archives, Corvallis, Oregon (hereafter Admin. Records), October
    4, 1917, box 2, RG 32.

30 *Oregonian*, November 29, 1917.

31 Ibid., December 1, 3, 9, and 13, 1917.

32 Boyer, ed., *The Oxford Companion to United States History*, 843–844.

33 *Oregon State Agricultural College Bulletin*, No. 470 (September 1930), 34, box 5, sub. 7, RG
    013 (emphasis original).

34 Ibid.; and William G. Robbins, *Oregon, This Storied Land* (Portland: Oregon Historical
    Society, 2005), 108.

35 *Oregon State Agricultural College Bulletin*, no. 470 (September 1930), 34, box 5, sub. 7, RG
    013; *Biennial Report* (1920), 7; Oregon State Defense Council Records, Publications and
    Ephemera, box 8, folders 1 and 3, Oregon State Archives, Salem (hereafter State Archives);
    and Admin. Records, April 18 and 20, 1917, box 2, RG 32.

36 Admin. Records, April 18 and 28, 1917, box 2, RG 32.

37 Ibid., February 27 and March 12, 1918. For an early and important account of the War
    Garden Movement, see Charles Lathrop Pack, *The War Garden Victorious* (Philadelphia:
    J. B. Lippincott, 1919).

38 Oregon Agricultural College, President's Biennial Report, 1920–1922, RG 013, sub. 12, box 9, p. 11; Educational Activities in War Work (Oregon), State Archives, http://www.arcweb.sos.state.or.us/pages/records/governors/.../biography.html; and W. Stull Holt, *The Federal Board for Vocational Education: Its History, Activities, and Organization* (New York: D. Appleton, 1922).

39 Educational Activities in War Work (Oregon); and Oregon Agricultural College Training Detachment, August 9, 1918, box 135, Memorabilia Collection (hereafter MC).

40 David Noble, *America by Design: Science, Technology, and the Rise of Corporate Capitalism* (New York: Oxford University Press, 1977), 216–219.

41 *The S.A.T.C.* (typescript); Report of the Student Army Training Corps (typescript); and Adolph Zielfe to The Pharmaceutical Profession, September 14, 1918; all in box 135, MC.

42 Guide to the Records of the Student Army Training Corps, 1916–1921, New York University Archives, Historical Note, http://dlib.nyu.edu/findingaids/html/archives/satc_content.htmy; Student Army Training Corps, Dartmouth College ROTC, http://www.dartmouth.edu/~rotc/satc.html; and "The Corps Comes to Oregon," On the Home Front, College Campuses Mobilize for the War, http://arcweb.sos.state.or.us/pages/exhibits/war/ww1/satc.html.

43 *The S.A.T.C.*, box 135, MC; *Oregonian*, July 26, August 9, and August 18, 1918; and "The Corps Comes to Oregon," On the Home Front, Oregon State Archives.

44 Admin. Records, September 11, 1918, box 2, RG 32; *The S.A.T.C.*; and Zielfe to The Pharmaceutical Profession, September 14, 1918, box 135, MC.

45 Admin. Records, October 12, 1918, box 2, RG 32; *The S.A.T.C.*; Report of the Student Army Training Corps; both in box 135, MC; and *Oregonian*, October 24, 1918.

46 Ross, *The Land-Grant Idea at Iowa State College*, 165–167.

47 Bishop, *A History of Cornell*, 430–432; and Robert W. Topping, *A Century and Beyond: The History of Purdue University* (West Lafayette, IN: Purdue University Press, 1988), 176–177. A similar situation prevailed on the Michigan State College campus in East Lansing, where six hundred men were inducted into the SATC. Like the experiences on other campuses, influenza disrupted the Michigan State program, and SATC barracks were turned into quarantined hospitals. Ironically, the quarantine was lifted on November 7, four days before the signing of the Armistice. See Kuhn, *Michigan State*, 270–272.

48 Admin. Records, October 1 and 4 and December 6, 1917, and October 12, 1918; all in box 2, RG 32.

49 "The Great Pandemic: The United States, 1918–1919—Oregon," http://www.flu.gov/pandemic/history/1918/; Cain Allen, "Spanish Flu in Astoria," The Oregon History Project, http://www.ohs.org/education/oregonhistory/historical_records/dspDocument.cfm?doc_ID=46A2006A-ADD6-25C8-E3210AE3EB77F83C; Ivan M. Woolcy, "The 1918 'Spanish Influenza' Epidemic in Oregon," *Oregon Historical Quarterly* 64 (1963), 246–258; and *Oregonian*, October 11, 14, and 19, 1918. For an important study of the global effects of the epidemic, see John M. Barry, *The Great Influenza Epidemic: The Epic Story of the Deadliest Plague in History* (New York: Viking, 2004).

50 Woolcy, "The 1918 'Spanish Influenza' Epidemic," 255; and *Oregonian*, November 1 and 10 and December 12, 1918.

51 *Oregonian*, November 12 and 24, 1918; and *Barometer*, November 13, 1918.

52 "After the War: Easing the Shift to Civilian Life," Oregon At War, http://arcweb.sos.state.or.us/pages/exhibits/war/ww1/satc.html.

53 Grant Covell to Edwin Reed, January 9, 1919, MC 135.

54 Noble, *America by Design*, 45–46; and Covell to Reed, January 9, 1919, MC 135.

55 *Oregonian*, January 8 and February 9, 1919; and William Jasper Kerr, "Education and the World War," address to the annual meeting of the National Education Association, ca. summer 1918, reel 82, sub. 7, RG 013.

56 On the Home Front, Oregon's New Police Force, http://arcweb.sos.state.or.us/pages/exhibits/war/ww1/satc.html. For Withycombe's obituary and President Kerr's tribute, see the *Oregonian*, March 5, 1919.

57 *Oregonian*, February 9, 1919; and Admin. Records, December 30, 1918, box 2, RG 32.

58 For Warren Harding's use of the word "normalcy" see Boyer, ed., *The Oxford Companion to United States History*, 327.

59 *Biennial Report* (1922), 5.

60 *Biennial Report* (1920), 23.

61 Ibid. (1920), 24; and (1922), 15.

62 Admin. Records, February 12, 1921, box 2, RG 32; and *Biennial Report* (1922), 13–14, box 9, sub. 12, RG 013.

63 Admin. Records, September 14, 1922, box 2, RG 32.

64 Ibid., October 10, 1923, and September 18, 1924.

65 Ibid., January 15, 1925; and *Oregonian*, March 15,1920, November 14, 1921, and March 12, 1922.

66 *Biennial Report* (1924), 1–6, box 9, sub. 12, RG 013.

67 Oregon State Agricultural College to the University of Illinois, March 5, 1924, box 5, sub. 7, RG 013.

68 *Biennial Report* (1926), v–viii, box 9, sub. 12, RG 013.

69 Ibid., viii–ix.

70 Ibid., ix–xi.

71 Ibid., xxi–xxviii.

CHAPTER FOUR: STUDENT LIFE, 1868–1940

1 Admin. Records, September 10, 1873, June 15, 1874, and February 12, 1875; all in box 3, RG 32.

2 Board of Trustees Records, RG 33, September 1 and December 13, 1869.

3 Ibid., June 17, 1873, April 21, 1876.

4 Chronological History of Oregon State University, 1880–1889, http://archives.library.oregonstate.edu/chronology/chron_head.html; and Benton County Timeline, Benton County Historical Society and Museum, http://www.bentoncountymuseum.org/timeline/index.cfm.

5 Admin. Records, September 13, 1888, box 3, RG 32.

6 Ibid., October 23, 1888; and February 24, 1890; and February 15, 1892.

7 Chronological History of OSU, 1870–1879; and Admin. Records, April 27, 1889, January 27, 1890, and December 7, 1891, box 3, RG 32. While the Alumni Association dates its origins to 1873, its earliest records begin in 1888. See Alumni Association Records, http://scarc.library.oregonstate.edu/coll/rg035/index.html.

8 Admin. Records, February 10, 1890, and ca. 1900, box 3, RG 32.

9 Ibid., ca. 1890 and 1891, box 3, RG 32.

10 Earle D. Ross, *The Land-Grant Idea at Iowa State College* (Ames: Iowa State University Press, 1958), 42; Morris Bishop, *A History of Cornell* (Ithaca: Cornell University Press, 129–132 and 246–250; Madison Kuhn, *Michigan State University: The First Hundred Years* (East Lansing: Michigan State University Press, 1955), 92–94 and 208–209.

11 Admin. Records, January 13 and February 15, 1892, box 3, RG 32.

12 Ibid., September 10, 1892.

13 Chronological History, 1892; John Letcher, G. Shaw, and F. L. Washburn to Executive Committee of the Board, November 18, 1891, box 1, RG 008; Wallis Nash to John Letcher, February 27, 1892, box 1, sub. 2, RG 013; and Admin. Records, Minute Book 2, February 10, 1889, and January 13 and September 10, 1892; all in box 3, RG 32.

14 Admin. Records, April 19 and May 2, 1893, box 3, RG 32; Football Photograph Collection, 1894–2000, SCARC, http://scarc.library.oregonstate.edu/coll/p004/biographicalnote.

html; 1907 Beaver Baseball Team, http://scarc.library.oregonstate.edu/omeka/items/show/8956; and *Barometer* (1900 Souvenir Edition).

15 Admin. Records, March 27, 1897, box 3, RG 32. The faculty subsequently agreed to tax themselves thirty cents for every $100 of salary as a contribution to football.

16 Ibid., April 3, 9, 10, and June 13, 1900.

17 The *Hayseed* (1894), 50–51. The *Hayseed* was the name of the college's first yearbook, which can be accessed online through the Valley Library at Oregon State University, ScholarsArchive@OSU.

18 Admin. Records, April 18, 1899, box 3, RG 32; and Larry Landis to the author, February 21, 2014.

19 Admin. Records, January 1903 and February 15, 1906, box 3, RG 32.

20 C. E. Wilson, compiler, *Benton County, Oregon Illustrated* (Corvallis: Benton County Citizens' League, 1904), 3, 7, 11, and 15.

21 *Catalogue of the Agricultural College of the State of Oregon 1905–1906* (Corvallis: Agricultural College Press, 1906), 14 (emphasis original).

22 Ibid., 15–19.

23 Ibid., 19–24.

24 Ibid., ca. fall 1900 and ca. fall 1901. What began as all-faculty weekly meetings evolved first into the faculty council and, by 1900, into the administrative council.

25 Admin. Records, late May 1901 and June 5, 1901, box 3, RG 32.

26 Ibid., May 21 and June 4, 1902.

27 Ibid., ca. January 1903; *Biennial Report* (1912), viii–xv, box 12, RG 013; and Historical Note, Associated Students of Oregon State University Records, 1917–2006, http://scarc.library.oregonstate.edu/coll/rg011/biographicalnote.html.

28 Ross, *The Land-Grant Idea at Iowa State College*, 86; Kuhn, *Michigan State*, 35 and 186. This brief review of the early Adelphian Society on campus is based on a brief article in the *Gem* (April 1883, vol. 1, no. 3: 7), one of the society's two surviving copies. See the *Gem*, Publications Group, Pub 10-21b, SCARC, http://ir.library.oregonstate.edu/xmlui/handle/1957/8098. Also see the Historical Note, Adelphian Literary Society Records, 1882–1891, SCARC, http://scarc.library.oregonstate.edu/coll/rg048/index.html.

29 The *Gem*, vol. 1, no. 1 (February 1883); vol. 1, no. 3 (April 1883).

30 The *Hayseed* (1894), 4–5.

31 Charles J. McIntosh, "Story of the Oregon State College Barometer, 1947–1948," unpublished manuscript, SCARC, http://scarc.library.oregonstate.edu/coll/barometer/index.html.

32 The Morrill Act quotation is in Bishop, *A History of Cornell*, 68. See *Barometer* (Souvenir Edition, 1900); "Historical Note," Oregon State Military Photographs, 1875–1975, SCARC, http://scarc.library.oregonstate.edu/coll/p002/biographicalnote.html; and Admin. Records, box 3, RG 32, which regularly dealt with issues related to military drill.

33 The building was renamed McAlexander Fieldhouse in 1971 in honor of Major General Ulysses S. Grant McAlexander, who served two stints as commandant of cadets—1907 to 1911 and 1915 to 1916.

34 "Historical Note," Reserve Officer Training Corps Records, 1890–1965, SCARC, http://scarc.library.oregonstate.edu/coll/rg058/biographicalnote.html; and Oregon State University Military Photographs Collection, SCARC, http://scarc.library.oregonstate.edu/coll/p002/catalogue/p002III.html.

35 OSU Chronological History, SCARC, http://archives.library.oregonstate.edu/chronology/chron_head.html; and *Daily Barometer*, November 18, 1908.

36 *Oregon Blue Book, 1999–2000* (Salem: Oregon Secretary of State, 1999), 288 and 292; "Liquor Control, Temperance, and the Call for Prohibition," State Archives, http://arcweb.sos.state.or.us/pages/exhibits/50th/prohibition1temperance; and *Oregonian*, June 17, 1928.

37 "Liquor Control, Temperance, and the Call for Prohibition," and "The Prohibition Years: Bootleggers and Imagination," both in State Archives, http://arcweb.sos.state.or.us/pages/exhibits/50th/prohibition1temperance; and Admin. Records, April 25, 1929, box 2, RG 32. Also see Normal Clark, *The Dry Years: Prohibition and Social Change in Washington* (Seattle: University of Washington Press, 1988).

38 *Oregonian*, November 12 and 13, 1910; and Admin. Records, box 2, November 15, 1910.

39 *Oregonian*, November 14, 15, and 16, 1910.

40 Ibid., November 22, 1910; *Oregon Journal*, February 13, 1912; the *Daily Emerald*, February 17, 1912; and Portland *People's Press*, December 23, 1912; all news clippings in box 5, sub. 7, RG 013.

41 Admin. Records, October 29, 1913, and October 1914; and George Edmonston, Jr., "Chapt. 22: Student Life and Government (1915–1940)," http://www.osualum.com/s/359/index.aspx?sid=359?gid=1&pgid=529.

42 Admin. Records, November 2, 1909, box 2, RG 32.

43 Ibid., ca. spring 1913.

44 Ibid., February 9, 1909, and September 9, 1910.

45 Ibid., December 7, 8, and 18, 1911; February 17 and 18, 1913; and May 26, 1914.

46 *Oregonian*, April 5 and 7, 1917; and February 10, 1918.

47 Ibid., April 7 and 9, 1917.

48 Ibid., July 22, November 3, and November 18, 1917.

49 Ibid., February 3 and March 24, 1918.

50 Ibid., April 4, November 10, and December 4, 1917; and June 8 and September 29, 1918.

51 Paula Fass, *The Damned and the Beautiful: American Youth in the 1920s* (New York: Oxford University Press, 1977), 7, 350–353, and 374–376.

52 *Barometer*, February 7, 1923.

53 Ibid., February 10, 1923.

54 Fass, *The Damned and the Beautiful*, 144–146.

55 Admin. Records, February 28 and March 1 and 8, box 2, RG 32.

56 Ibid., March 1 and 8; and *Barometer*, March 10, 1923.

57 *Oregonian*, March 2, 1923; and Admin. Records, September 12, 1923, box 2, RG 32.

58 Admin. Records, November 1, 1926, box 2, RG 32; and Fass, *The Damned and the Beautiful*, 24–25 and 291–306.

59 E. C. Allworth to President W. J. Kerr, December 30, 1926; Frank Ward to Allworth, December 31, 1926; and F. A. Gilfillan to Allworth, January 22, 1927; all in reel 15, sub. 6, RG 013.

60 "Is the Title 'Agricultural College' a Misnomer," reel 15, sub. 6, RG. 013.

61 William Jasper Kerr to George Peavy, January 31, 1934; Peavy to Kerr, February 8, 1934; Peavy to Frederick Hunter, April 1, 1937; Charles Byrne to Peavy, April 17, 1937; and Peavy to E. B. Lemon, April 20, 1937; all in reel 15, sub. 6, RG 013.

62 The 1931 *Beaver*, http://oregondigital.org/sets/osu-yearbooks. No pagination visible.

63 Ibid.

64 Ibid., illegible signature to Charles Mak, April 23, 1931 (image in yearbook).

65 *General Catalogue, 1931–1932*, Oregon State Agricultural College (Corvallis: College Press, 1931), 2–3, 5–6, 42–64.

66 Ibid., 81–82.

67 The 1931 *Beaver*.

68 Jayne Walters Scrapbook, 1934–1940, MSS Walters.

CHAPTER FIVE: THE "REAL" CIVIL WAR—CURRICULUM

1 W. J. Kerr, "The Relations of the Land-Grant Colleges to the State Universities," synopsis of a paper read at the 19th Annual Convention of the American Association of Agricultural

Colleges and Experiment Stations, held at Washington, DC, November 14–16, 1905, 1–3, reel 82, sub. 7, RG 013.

2 Ibid., 6.

3 Ibid., 6–8.

4 Chronological History of Oregon State University, 1909, in http://archives.library.oregon-state.edu/chronology/chron_head.html; and *Oregonian*, February 3 and 7, 1909.

5 *Oregonian*, February 3, 7, and 25, 1909.

6 Ibid., March 11, 1909.

7 Ibid., April 30, 1910; April 4, 1911; and January 1, 1912.

8 Ibid., January 1, 1912.

9 *Biennial Report* (1912–1914), viii–ix, box 9, sub. 12, RG 013.

10 *Oregonian*, June 14, August 26 and 27, 1913.

11 Ibid., December 3 and 21, 2013; and January 7 and 20, 1914.

12 Ibid., January 24 and 25 and February 3 and 4, 1914.

13 Ibid., February 6, 1914.

14 Ibid., February 10, 1914.

15 *Biennial Report* (1918–1920), 7–10.

16 *Biennial Report* (1920–1922), 11–12.

17 Ibid., 12.

18 *Oregonian*, May 14, 1925; and Brief: Oregon State Agricultural College to the Oregon State Board of Higher Curricula, May 18, 1925, reel 82, sub. 7, RG 013, 1–2.

19 *Oregonian*, May 15, 1925.

20 Brief: Oregon State Agricultural College, May 18, 1925, 1, 2–4.

21 Ibid., 1, 5–7, and 16–18.

22 Oregon State Agricultural College to the Oregon State Board of Higher Curricula, Outline of a Suggested Division of Work between the University of Oregon and the Oregon State Agricultural College, June 5, 1925, reel 82, sub. 7, RG 013.

23 *Oregonian*, July 15, 1925.

24 *Biennial Report* (1924–1926), 9–10, box 9, sub. 12, RG 013.

25 Earle D. Ross, *The Land-Grant Idea at Iowa State College* (Ames: Iowa State College Press, 1958), 156, 176–181.

26 Robert Rydell, Jeffrey Safford, and Pierce Mullen, *In the People's Interest: A Centennial History of Montana State University* (Bozeman: Montana State University Foundation, 1992), 3–4, 23, 25, 66, 133, 136–138, and 283–285.

27 Madison Kuhn, *Michigan State: The First Hundred Years* (East Lansing: Michigan State University Press, 1955), 6–9, 76–82, 188–189, 196, and 266–267.

28 Morris Bishop, *A History of Cornell* (Ithaca: Cornell University Press, 1962), 310–316 and 366–367.

29 Ibid., 563, 567; and "Executive Summary," 2007 Impact Report, in History: Advancing Cornell as New York State's Land Grant University, http://landgrant.cornell.edu/history.cfm.

30 *Oregonian*, May 4 and June 8, 1927.

31 Ibid., January 1, 1928.

32 Statement of Oregon State Agricultural College to the State Board of Higher Curricula, May 2, 1928, reel 82, sub. 7, RG 013, 2. This document quotes the university's brief submitted to the board (emphasis original).

33 Ibid., 3–8; and Admin. Records, September 17, 1929, box 2, RG 32.

34 Statement of Oregon State Agricultural College to the State Board of Higher Curricula, May 2, 1928, reel 82, sub. 7, RG 013, 9–11.

35 *Oregonian*, February 9 and 10, 1929.

36 Ibid., February 22, 1929.

37 Ibid., February 27 and 28, 1929.

38 *Biennial Report of the Oregon State Board of Higher Education, 1929–1930* (Salem: State Board of Higher Education, 1930), 1–4.

39 *Oregonian*, March 3, 1929.

40 Ibid., January 14 and 28; and May 2, 1930; and Admin. Records, April 9, 1929, box 2, RG 32.

41 *Oregonian*, April 4, 1931.

42 *Survey of Oregon State Institutions of Higher Learning*, US Department of Interior, Office of Education, Bulletin No. 8 (1931), box 7, sub. 7, RG 013, 1–4.

43 Ibid., 4–6, 92, and 95.

44 Ibid., 97–98, 123–124, 129.

45 Ibid., 577–579, 593, and 603.

46 For the early Depression in Oregon and the Northwest, see Carlos Arnaldo Schwantes, *The Pacific Northwest: An Interpretive History* (Lincoln: University of Nebraska Press, 1996), 381–385; Dorothy O. Johansen, *Empire of the Columbia: A History of the Pacific Northwest* (New York: Harper and Row, 1967), 501–512; and William G. Robbins, *Oregon, This Storied Land* (Portland: Oregon Historical Society Press, 2005), 115–123.

47 *Oregonian*, March 12, 1931.

48 Ibid., April 4, 1931.

49 Ibid., April 2 and June 8, 1931.

50 Oregon State Agricultural College, Revised Budget Estimates for Eighteen-Month Period, July 1, 1931, to December 31, 1932, June 18, 1931, reel 82, sub. 7, RG 013, 1–4; and Admin. Records, box 2, RG 32, June 8, 1931.

51 *Oregonian*, June 23–24, 1931.

52 Ibid., November 10, 1931; and Admin. Records, November 12, 1931, box 2, RG 32.

53 *Biennial Report* (1931–1932), 7–8. There is a voluminous collection of documents in the President's Office Records of William Jasper Kerr, reel 83, sub. 7, RG 013, in SCARC.

54 *Oregonian*, March 8, 1932.

55 *Report of the Curricula Committee to the State Board of Higher Education* (Salem: State Board of Higher Education, 1932), 1–13; and *Oregonian*, March 8, 1932.

56 This summary of the state's newspaper commentaries is in the *Oregonian*, March 3, 1932.

57 *Oregonian*, March 9, 1932.

58 *Biennial Report* (1931–1932), 9, 13–17.

59 Paraphrased and quoted from James Roland McBride, "Science at a Land-Grant College: The Science Controversy in Oregon, 1931–1932, and the Early Development of the College of Science at Oregon State University" (Master of Science thesis, Oregon State University, 1976), 141–142.

CHAPTER SIX: THE ACADEMY IN THE GREAT DEPRESSION

1 William G. Robbins and Katrine Barber, *Nature's Northwest: The North Pacific Slope in the Twentieth Century* (Tucson: University of Arizona Press, 2011), 103–105; E. Kimbark McColl, *The Growth of a City: Power and Politics in Portland, Oregon, 1915–1950* (Portland: Georgian Press, 1979), 453–455; and Mary Gallagher, Benton County Historical Museum, e-mail to the author, n.d.

2 Richard White, *"It's Your Misfortune and None of My Own": A New History of the American West* (Norman: University of Oklahoma Press, 1991), 472.

3 Admin. Records, June 8, October 26, and November 12, 1931; all in box 2, RG 32.

4 Admin. Records, January 23, May 4, and October 8, 1932, box 2, RG 32.

5 *Oregonian*, May 10, 11, 12, 15, and June 5, 1932.

6 Ibid., June 30, July 22, September 5 and 7, 1932.

7 Although the institution's official name listed in college catalogues did not change until 1937, the school was commonly referred to as Oregon State College by 1932. See "Chronological History of OSU," SCARC.

8   *Oregonian*, September 8, 1932; and *Oregon Blue Book, 1999–2000* (Salem: Office of the Secretary of State, 1999), 296.

9   Oregon State System of Higher Education, *Biennial Report* (1931–1932), 24–25, box 10, sub. 12, RG 013.

10 *Biennial Report* (1933–1934), 112, box 10, sub. 12, RG 013; and Bruce Tabb, Special Collections Librarian, University of Oregon Libraries, to the author, May 1, 2015.

11 *Biennial Report* (1933 1934), 112, box 10, sub. 12, RG 013.

12 Ibid., 112–113.

13 Ibid., 113.

14 Herman Frank Swartz, "The Superfluous Generation," commencement address, June 4, 1934, reel 14, sub. 6, RG 013.

15 Ibid., and Corvallis *Gazette-Times*, June 6, 1934.

16 W. H. Patterson to The President, June 6, 1934, reel 14, sub. 6, RG 013. Patterson sent copies of the letter to Chancellor Kerr and his superior at the Presidio in San Francisco.

17 Ibid., Patterson to The President. Patterson had earlier made similar charges about the League for Industrial Democracy in a letter to the *Barometer*, May 16, 1934. For a biography of Sweetland, see the author's *A Man for All Seasons: Monroe Sweetland and the Liberal Paradox* (Corvallis: Oregon State University Press, 2015). The Portland waterfront strike of 1934 was one component of a coast-wide walkout of longshore workers, an event that captured national headlines. For the Portland action, see MacColl, *The Growth of a City*, 467–480.

18 Peavy to Patterson; Peavy to General Malin Craig, June 8, 1934; and news clipping, Eugene *News*, June 9, 1934; all in reel 14, sub. 6, RG 013. The Eugene *News* quoted from both the *Gazette-Times* and *Democrat-Herald*.

19 Confidential Memorandum Relative to Colonel Patterson, June 14, 1934, reel 14, sub. 6, RG 013.

20 Ibid.; interview with Colonel Patterson, June 25, 1934.

21 "Enrollment—Fall End-of-Term, 1912 through 2000," *2001 Fact Book* (Corvallis: Oregon State University, 2001), 46; Oregon State System of Higher Education, *Biennial Report* (1933–1934), 112, box 10, sub. 12, RG 013.

22 *Biennial Report* (1935–1936), 108.

23 Admin. Records, May 28, 1936, box 2, RG 32.

24 Oregon State System of Higher Education, *Biennial Report* (1935–1936), 2, sub. 12, RG 013.

25 Ibid., 9–10.

26 University Faculty Meeting, untitled document, November 6, 1933; and "Controversy in Higher Education—Who Started It?" both in reel 10, sub. 6, RG 013.

27 J. Leo Fairbanks to M. Ellwood Smith, October 25; Smith to Peavy, October 26; Peavy to Boyer, October 29, 1934; and Peavy to Charles Byrne, September 4, 1935; all in reel 10, sub. 6, RG 013.

28 Byrne to E. P. Jackson, September 8; Peavy to Byrne, September 10; Byrne to Peavy, September 11; and Peavy to Byrne, September 12, 1935; all in reel 10, sub. 6, RG 013.

29 W. A. Jensen to E. M. Smith, February 10 and March 19, 1937; Jensen to Smith, February 10, 1938; Manager, Business Office, to John V. Bennes, March 9, 1938; Jensen To Those Concerned, November 8, 1939, in Buildings—Gilbert Hall; Glenna K. Carter, History of Oregon State University Student Health Service (1969), in Buildings—Student Health Services; all in MC 37; and Larry Landis e-mail to the author, April 22, 2014.

30 Jensen To Those Concerned, May 2, 1940; Jensen, *WPA Project 1940*, May 8, 1940; and Sponsor's Proposal No. 26; all in MC 37.

31 For an account of Dawson's and Gorham's projects and the McDonald quote, see Sarah Baker Munro, *Timberline Lodge: The History, Art, and Craft of an American Icon* (Portland: Timber Press, 2009), 73, 91, 204–205.

32 Jensen, Conference with WPA officials, November 11, 1935; Jensen, Conference with Burt Brown Barker and Mr. Dieck, February 3, 1936; and R. G. Dieck to Jensen, August 1, 1936; all in MC 37; and Munro, *Timberline Lodge*, 80.

33 Jensen, Conference with Mr. Dieck—Art Projects, July 28, 1936, MC 37; and Peavy to Dieck August 6, and Dieck to Peavy, August 10, 1936; both in MC 167.

34 Jensen, Memo, November 16, 1936, MC 167.

35 Ibid.

36 Jensen to Burt Brown Barker, December 30, 1936, MC 167.

37 Untitled, undated four-page summary of Dawson's work, MC 166.

38 Wood Mosaic Murals, n.d., in MC 167.

39 Royal Jackson, "McDonald-Dunn Forests: Human Use and Occupation," School of Forestry, Oregon State University, 1980, 135–139, in Royal Jackson Papers, SCARC. For an overview of the national work of the CCC, see William G. Robbins, *American Forestry: A History of National, State, and Private Cooperation* (Lincoln: University of Nebraska Press, 1985), 140–149.

40 Jackson, "McDonald-Dunn Forests," 140–146.

41 Ibid., 146–147.

42 Ibid., 148–150.

43 Ibid., 150–151.

44 Stephen J. Pyne, *Fire in America: A Cultural History of Wildland and Rural Fire* (Princeton, NJ: Princeton University Press, 1982), 365–367.

45 Jackson, "McDonald-Dunn Forests," 154–158. Today's McDonald Forest had its beginnings in the early 1920s with the small property that makes up Peavy Arboretum. Dean of Forestry George Peavy then began raising money to expand the perimeters of the forest for research purposes.

46 Admin. Records, May 28, 1937, box 2, RG 32.

47 Ibid., December 11, 1937.

48 Ibid. (emphasis original).

49 Peavy to Chancellor Frederick Hunter, March 3, 1938; and Degrees for Work Done at the University of Oregon Medical School, March 2, 1938; both in Admin. Records, box 2, RG 32.

50 Admin. Records, March 31, 1938.

51 Ibid., January 16, 1940.

52 *Biennial Report of the Chancellor, 1937–1938*, 9–12 and 23–24.

53 Excerpt from "University of Oregon, President's Biennial Report to the Chancellor, 1939–1940," 7–8, reel 10, sub. 6, RG 013.

54 *Oregon Statesman*, June 15, 1941; and F. A. Gilfillan to Hunter, July 17, 1941, reel 10, sub. 6, RG 013.

55 Gilfillan Memorandum, September 25, 1941, reel 10, sub. 6, RG 013.

56 Roseburg *News-Review*, October 9, 1941; and G. F. Chambers to Hunter, October 14, 1941, reel 10, sub. 6, RG 013.

57 *Oregonian*, October 29, 1941.

58 Ibid.

59 James Roland McBride, "Science at a Land-Grant College: The Science Controversy in Oregon, 1931–1932, and the Early Development of the College of Science at Oregon State University" (Master of Science thesis, Oregon State University, 1976), 161–165.

60 Admin. Records, November 10 and December 11, 1941, box 2, RG 32; Statements by Representatives of Oregon State College before Curricula Committee of State Board of Higher Education, December 8, 1941, reel 82, sub. 7, RG 013; and *Oregonian*, November 9, 24; December 7, 1941; and April 29, 1942.

61 David M. Kennedy, *Freedom from Fear: The American People in Depression and War, 1929–1945* (New York: Oxford University Press, 1999), 384–405.

62 Ibid., 417–425.

63 George Peavy to Carl E. Ladd, July 26, 1940, reel 4, sub. 6, RG 013; and *Biennial Report of Oregon State College, 1939–1940*, 108–109, box 10, sub. 10, RG 013.

64 *Biennial Report of the Chancellor, 1939–1940*, 8–9, box 10, sub. 12, RG 013.

65 Howard A. Starret to George Peavy, March 5, 1941; William A Schoenfeld to F. A. Gilfillan, April 7, 1941; and Earl Mason to Gilfillan, April 12, 1941; all in reel 12, sub. 6, RG 013.

66 Starret to Gilfillan, March 31 and April 19, 1941; and Engineering Experiment Station to Gilfillan, April 7, 1941; all in reel 12, sub. 6, RG 013.

67 Irvin Stewart to Gilfillan, June 28, 1941; Gilfillan to R. H. Dearborn, July 2, 1941; Delmar Goode to G. U. Copson, October 15, 1941; M. Ellwood Smith to Goode, October 16, 1941; Earl Mason to Goode, October 20, 1941, Carl Salser to Goode, October 21, 1941; and E. C. Gilbert to Goode, October 21, 1941; all in reel 12, sub. 6, RG 013

68 Kennedy, *Freedom from Fear*, 433–471; and Ira Katznelson, *Fear Itself: The New Deal and the Origins of Our Time* (New York: Liveright Publishing, 2013), 306–312.

CHAPTER SEVEN: WARTIME: 1938–1950

1 George Edmonston Jr., chapter 24: WW II, http://www.osualum.com/s/359/index.aspx?s id–359&gid=1&pgid=527&sparam=Yoshihara&scontid=0; and *Oregonian*, December 5, 1941.

2 Ibid., December 8, 1941.

3 Rebecca Landis, "Freedom Lost," *The Oregon Stater* 79 (October 1995), 14–17; and Glenn Bakkum to Gilfillan, December 14, 1941, reel 20, sub. 6, RG 013.

4 *Oregonian*, January 2, 6, 15, and 18, 1942.

5 Admin. Records, January 6 and ca. February 1942, box 2, RG 32.

6 Ibid., ca. February and May 28, 1942; and *Oregonian*, March 11, 1942.

7 Tom Arai and thirty-five signatories to F. A. Gilfillan, December 11, 1941; and Gilfillan to each of the thirty-six signers of the letter, December 18, 1941; both in reel 20, sub. 6, RG 013.

8 David M. Kennedy, *Freedom from Fear: The American People in Depression and War* (New York: Oxford University Press, 1999), 752–753; and Admin. Records, T. P. Cramer to John L. Dewitt, March 27, 1942; and R. P. Bronson to Cramer, March 30, 1942; both in box 2, RG 32.

9 Robert Sproul to Representative John Tolan, April 7, 1942, reel 20, sub. 6, RG 013.

10 University of California Proposal for the Continued Collegiate Training of Citizens of Japanese Ancestry forced by Evacuation orders to Interrupt Studies, ca. spring 1942, reel 20, sub. 6, RG 013. For additional information about Sproul's initiative, see United States Commission on Wartime Relocation and Internment of Civilians, *Personal Justice Denied: Report of the Commission on Wartime Relocation and Internment of Civilians* (Washington, DC: Civil Liberties Public Education Fund, 1983), 181–182.

11 Gilfillan to Hunter, April 24, 1942; T. P. Cramer to Col. Magill, Jr., April 20 and 25, 1942; and Herman Goebel, Jr. to Cramer, April 29, 1942; all in reel 20, sub. 6, RG 013.

12 *Personal Justice Denied*, 180–181.

13 Teiko Ishida to F. L. Ballard, April 27, 1942; Robert O'Brien to Buena Maris, May 5, 1942; both in *Personal Justice Denied*; and *Oregonian*, May 6 and 7, 1942.

14 *Oregonian*, May 23 and June 12 and 28, 1942.

15 T. P Cramer to Wartime Civil Control Administration, May 20, 1942; and Ernest Leonetti to Cramer, May 21, 1942; both in reel 20, sub. 6, RG 013.

16 T. Holcomb to The President, September 10, 1940; President Ballard to Deans of the Schools Concerned, September 24, 1940; Carl Larson to Ballard, March 1, 1941; and Holcomb to Ballard, May 27, 1941; all in reel 14, sub. 6, RG 013.

17 C. W. Nimitz to Dr. Colbe, January 10, 1941; and Eric Barr, The Navy Wants Engineering Students, n.d.; both in reel 14, sub. 6, RG 013.

18 Selective Service System, Memorandum to State Directors, September 21, 1941; National Roster of Scientific and Specialized Personnel to F. A. Gilfillan, n.d.; both in reel 14, sub. 6, RG 013; Navy Department to Commandants of all Naval Districts, December 18, 1941; and National Resource Planning Board, January 2, 1942; both in reel 12, sub. 6, RG 013.

19 Leonard Carmichael to Mr. President, January 27, 1942; C. S. Marsh to Mr. President, January 29, 1942; Gilfillan to Carmichael, April 20, 1942; and Carmichael to Gilfillan, May 5, 1942; all in reel 12, sub. 6, RG 013.

20 Clifford Grabstein and six others to Gilfillan, April 18, 1942; Frederick Hunter to Gilfillan, April 24, 1942; and Stuart Henderson Britt to Gilfillan, May 7, 1942; all in reel 14, sub. 6, RG 013.

21 Admin. Records, "A Plan for Wartime," March 10, 1942, box 2, RG 32.

22 Ibid., May 28, 1942; *Oregonian*, June 10, 1942.

23 For more on Strand, see "August Leroy Strand (1942–1961)," Presidents of Oregon State University, SCARC, http://scarc.library.oregonstate.edu/omeka/exhibits/show/presidents/ strand/strand; Robert Rydell, Jeffrey Safford, and Pierce Mullen, *In The People's Interest: A Centennial History of Montana State University* (Bozeman: Montana State University Press, 1992), 56–57, 77; *Oregonian*, September 6, 1942; and A. L. Strand to the Students of Oregon State College, September 2, 1942, *Preview: Oregon State College*, vol. 5 (1943), n.p.

24 Leonard Carmichael to the President, June 15, 1942; A. L. Strand to Gilfillan, December 30, 1942; and Alexander Corey to Gilfillan, January 29, 1943; all in Admin. Records, box 2, RG 32.

25 Melissa Hunter to T. P Cramer, January 8, 1942; C. C. Cochran to Cramer, January 10, 1942; Gilfillan to Randall Jacobs, January 15 and February 5, 1942; and Jacobs to Gilfillan, January 26, 1942; all in reel 12, sub. 6, RG 013.

26 Delmer Goode to Gilfillan, January 31, 1942; George Peavy to Gilfillan, February 2, 1942; L. E. Heifeld to Ballard, February 26, 1942; Melissa Hunter to A. L. Strand, November 23, 1942; Strand to John C. Webb, November 24, 1942; and Webb to Strand, December 5, 1942; all in reel 12, sub. 6, RG 013.

27 *Biennial Report of Oregon State College, 1941–1942*, 113–114, 138, box 10, sub. 12, RG 013.

28 Ibid., 116–117, 139.

29 Ibid., 144–145.

30 Admin. Records, July 16, 1942, box 2, RG 32.

31 F. A. Gilfillan and T. P. Cramer to President Strand, October 7, 1942; and Gilfillan and Cramer to Frederick Hunter, October 7, 1942; both in Admin. Records, box 2, RG 32.

32 Ibid., Gilfillan and Cramer to Hunter, October 7, 1942.

33 Admin. Records, September 20 and October 14, 1942, box 2, RG 32.

34 Robert B. Palmer, Bell I. Wiley, and William R. Keast, Historical Division, Department of the Army, Washington, DC, 1948, The Army Specialized Training Program and the Army Ground Forces, http://www.astpww2.org/.

35 Housing Space, December 10, 1942; Available Classroom Space, December 18, 1942; and Recreation Facilities, December 18, 1942; all in reel 14, sub. 6, RG 013.

36 *Biennial Report of Oregon State College, 1943–1944*, n.p., box 10, sub. 12, RG 013.

37 Ibid.; Military Department (OSC), Biennial Report, May 18, 1944, box 11, sub. 12, RG 013; and Palmer, Wiley, and Keast, The Army Specialized Training Program and the Army Ground Forces, http://www.astpww2.org/.

38 *Biennial Report of Oregon State College, 1943–1944*, n.p., box 10, sub. 12, RG 013; and Curtis F. Jones, "The Army Specialized Training Program: Gateway to the Foreign Service," http://www.unc.edu/depts/diplomat/AD_Issues/amdipl_6/jones_astp.html.

39 Robert W. Topping, *A Century and Beyond: The History of Purdue University* (West Lafayette, IN: Purdue University Press, 1988), 239–240; Morris Bishop, *A History of Cornell* (Ithaca: Cornell University Press, 1962), 540–544; Earle D. Ross, *The Land-Grant Idea at Iowa State College: A Centennial Trial Balance, 1858–1958* (Ames: Iowa State

College Press, 1958), 214–215; and Madison Kuhn, *Michigan State: The First Hundred Years* (East Lansing: Michigan State University Press, 1955), 410–411.

40 U.S. War Department Chooses a Site, in Benton County Historical Society Collections, Philomath, Oregon; T. P. Cramer to F. A. Cuthbert, February 11, 1942; and Cramer memorandum, February 28, 1942; both in reel 12, sub. 6, RG 013.

41 U.S. War Department Chooses a Site, in Benton County Historical Society Collections; "Camp Adair: Oregon's Second Largest City," http://www.offbeatoregon.com/H1004d_CampAdair.html; and John H. Baker, *Camp Adair: The Story of a World War II Cantonment* (Newport, OR: John H. Baker, 2003).

42 S. H. Graf. War Activities Report, Department of Mechanical Engineering, December 23, 1945, box 2, OSC History of WWII Project Records (MSS OSC WW2).

43 U.S. War Department Chooses a Site, in Benton County Historical Society Collections; *Oregonian*, September 11, 1943; and Oregon State University Special Collections and Archives, http://scarc.library.oregonstate.edu/col/rg193/catalogue/full.html. The author's father-in-law, James Brewer, from Winfield, Louisiana, trained at Camp Adair and met his future wife, Patricia Skaling (from Salem) at a United Services Organization dance at the Adair field house.

44 U.S. War Department Chooses a Site, in Benton County Historical Society Collections; "Camp Adair: Oregon's Second Largest City," http://www.offbeatoregon.com/H1004d_CampAdair.html; Baker, *Camp Adair*; Richard Engeman, "Adair Village," Oregon Encyclopedia, http://www.oregonencyclopedia.org/; and Larry Landis to the author, May 13, 2015.

45 Oregon State University, *2001 Fact Book*, 46; *Oregonian*, June 16, 1943; *Oregonian*, July 19, 1942; and *Biennial Report, 1943–1944*, n.p.

46 M. Ellwood Smith to Strand, May 17, 1944, box 11, sub. 12, RG 013; *Biennial Report, 1943–1944*, n.p.; and *Oregonian*, July 3, 5, and 27, 1943.

47 Ava B. Milam, Foreward [sic]—Report of the Oregon Nutrition Committee, n.d., OSC History of WWII Project Records (MSS OSC WW2).

48 War-time Services: Lorna C. Jessup, Mabel Winston, and Maud Wilson, OSC History of WWII Project Records (MSS OSC WW2).

49 War-time Services: William Carlson to D. M. Goode, November 20, 1945, ibid.

50 *Oregonian*, June 17, 1943; and *Biennial Report, 1943–1944*, n.p.

51 *Biennial Report, 1943–1944*, n.p.; and *Oregonian*, June 19 and 20, 1943.

52 *Oregonian*, October 24, 27, and 28, 1943.

53 *Biennial Report, 1943–1944*, n.p.: and *Oregonian*, August 8, 1943.

54 Admin. Records, August 13, 1943, box 2, RG 32.

55 *Oregonian*, May 15 and 16 and July 26, 1944.

56 Ibid., December 21, 1944.

57 Ibid., August 16, 1944; and William G. Robbins, *Oregon, This Storied Land* (Portland: Oregon Historical Society, 2005), 125–127.

58 *Oregonian*, October 15, 1944; and January 6, 1945.

59 Association of Land-Grant Colleges and Universities to Presidents of ALGCAU, November 8, 1943, reel 4, sub. 6, RG 013 (emphasis original).

60 Special Committee on Senate Bill-1946, Association of Land-Grant Colleges and Universities to Presidents of Land-Grant Colleges and Universities, July 25, 1941; and Strand to Congressman James Mott, August 21, 1944; both in reel 4, sub. 6, RG 013.

61 Kennedy, *Freedom from Fear*, 784–787; and Ira Katznelson, *Fear Itself: The New Deal and the Origins of Our Time* (New York: Liveright Publishing, 2013), 368–369.

62 Kennedy, *Freedom from Fear*, 787; Katznelson, *Fear Itself*, 368–369; Hilary Herbold, "Never A Level Playing Field: Blacks and the G.I. Bill," *Journal of Blacks in Higher Education* (Winter, 1994–1995), 104–105, 107, 108; Mark Boulton, "How the G.I. Bill Failed African-American Vietnam War Veterans," *Journal of Blacks in Higher Education* 58 (Winter 2007/08), 57–61; and Nick Klotz, "'When Affirmative Action Was White': Uncivil

Rights," *New York Times*, August 28, 2005. Klotz makes use of Katznelson's earlier book, *When Affirmative Action Was White: The Untold Story of Racial Inequality in Twentieth-Century America* (New York: W. W. Norton, 2005).

63 Strand to E. O. Holland, September 20, 1944, reel 4, sub. 6, RG 013; and *Biennial Report, 1945–1946*, box 10, sub. 12, RG 013.

64 *Biennial Report, 1945–1946*, 7–8, and 45–46; Larry Landis to the author, June 4, 2014; and US Cadet Nurse Corps, http://www.rochestergeneral.org/about-us/rochester-general-hospital/about-us/rochester-medical-museum-and-archives/online-exhibits/united-states-cadet-nurse-corps-1943-1948/.

65 *Biennial Report of Oregon State College, 1945–1946*, 2, box 11, sub. 12, RG 013.

66 Ibid., 1–2.

67 Ibid., 3–4.

68 Ibid., 4–5.

69 Ibid., 5–6.

70 *State Board of Higher Education Biennial Report, 1945–1946*, 15–18; Enrollment—Fall End-of-Term 1912 through 2000; and *Oregonian*, September 17 and 26, 1946.

71 *Oregonian*, September 27, 1946.

72 John R. Thelin, Jason R. Edwards, and Eric Mogen, "Higher Education in the United States, Historical Development," http://education.stateuniversity.com/pages/2044/Higher-Education-in-United-States.html.

CHAPTER EIGHT: CAMPUS AND COMMUNITY IN THE COLD WAR

1 David Halberstam, *The Fifties* (New York: Villard Books, 1993), ix–xi.

2 David M. Kennedy, *Freedom from Fear: The American People in Depression and War, 1929–1945* (New York: Oxford University Press, 1999), 854–855.

3 William G. Robbins, *Oregon, This Storied Land* (Portland: Oregon Historical Society Press, 2005), 135–136; Chronological History of Oregon State University, SCARC; and Oregon, Resident Population, US Census Bureau, http://www.census.gov/dmd/www/resapport/states/oregon.pdf.

4 Salem *Statesman Journal*, July 14, 2013; Dorothy Johansen, *Empire of the Columbia* (New York: Harper and Row, 1967), 608–609; and William G. Robbins and Katrine Barber, *Nature's Northwest: The North Pacific Slope in the Twentieth Century* (Tucson: University of Arizona Press, 2011), 228–229.

5 *Biennial Report of Oregon State College, 1947–1948*, 117; and *Biennial Report of Oregon State College, 1949–1950*, 68; both in box 10, sub. 12, RG 013.

6 A. Ellwood Smith Papers, 1913–1961, Biographical Note, http://scarc.library.oregonstate.edu/coll/smithme/biographicalnote.html, SCARC; and Oregon State College, Lower Division, Report for the Biennium, 1948–1950, box 11, sub. 12, RG 013.

7 *Oregon State College Catalogue, 1948–49*, 6–7, SCARC; and *Biennial Report of Oregon State College, 1949–1950*, 63. The chancellor's office had to approve all printed material made available to the public.

8 *Oregon State College Catalogue, 1948–49*, 108–109. For Paul Packer's views on liberal education, see the *Oregonian*, June 15, 1947.

9 *Oregonian*, June 15, 1947; and *Biennial Report of the Chancellor, 1951–1952*, 9.

10 This brief summary of the onset of the Cold War is from James T. Patterson, *Grand Expectations: The United States, 1945–1974* (New York: Oxford University Press, 1996), 126–136.

11 Ellen W. Schrecker, *No Ivory Tower: McCarthyism and the Universities* (New York: Oxford University Press, 1986), 94–102.

12 For a full account of the Spitzer case, see William G. Robbins, "The Academy and Cold War Politics: Oregon State College and the Ralph Spitzer Case," *Pacific Northwest Quarterly* 104 (Fall 2013), 159–175. For the legislative measure, see Michael Munk, "Oregon Tests

Academic Freedom in (Cold) Wartime: The Reed College Trustees versus Stanley Moore," *Oregon Historical Quarterly* 97 (Fall 1996), 262–264.

13 Schrecker, *No Ivory Tower*, 102–104. See Allen Reed to Linus Pauling, March 5, 1949, folder 34.2, box 2.034, Political Issues, Biographical, Ava Helen and Linus Pauling Papers, SCARC (hereafter LP Biographical). Reed was editor of the *Barometer* and suspicious of Terry Spitzer's politics. For her letters to the editor, see the *Barometer* issues of January 20 and 30, February 5 and 12, May 7 and 28, and October 27, 1948.

14 Ralph Spitzer to Linus Pauling, April 6 and August 22, 1945; Spitzer to Ed Yunker, Appeals Committee, Faculty Council, February 14, 1949; and Faculty Committee on Reviews and Appeals Findings, March 15, 1949; all in LP Biographical, 1. Correspondence, in SCARC.

15 Russell I. Thackrey to A. L. Strand, February 25, 1949, reel 84, sub. 11, RG 013.

16 Clark G. Kuebler to Strand, May 2, 1953; and Strand to Kuebler to May 27, 1953; all in Ralph Spitzer, Personnel File, SCARC. Ralph and Terry Spitzer eventually settled in Vancouver, British Columbia, where Ralph pursued a successful career as a pathologist and Terry earned a PhD in childhood psychology.

17 Patterson, *Grand Expectations*, 169–170 and 207–212; *College Now* (1951), Pubs 10–24j, SCARC.

18 David Arm to Members of the Engineering Division, Association of Land-Grant Colleges and Universities, November 13, 1950; Association of Land-Grant Colleges and Universities, Report of the Executive Secretary to the Senate of the Association, November 14, 1950; The National Emergency (National Defense Committee), November 1950; Recommendations of the Committee on National Defense, Association of Land-Grant Colleges and Universities, November 15, 1950; and Resolutions, R. O. T. C. Legislation, n.d.; all in reel 3, sub. 11, RG 013. The last document supported congressional measures to strengthen the nation's ROTC programs and the secretary of defense's request to Congress for funding to build armories, storage and class rooms, and other drill facilities for ROTC instruction.

19 *Biennial Report of the Chancellor, 1951–1952*, 9 10, box 10, sub. 12, RG 013; http://archives.library.illinois.edu/alaarchon/?p=collections/controlcard&id=7502; and War Mobilization Committee, Memorandum, November 8, 1950; and Extracts from mobilization reports, February 14, 1951; both in reel 122, sub. 11, RG 013. For a study of mobilization and civil defense, see Steven Casey, *Selling the Korean War: Propaganda, Politics, and Public Opinion* (New York: Oxford University Press, 2008), especially the chapter, "Mobilizing for a Police Action," 67–94.

20 Extracts from mobilization reports, February 14, 1951, reel 122, sub. 11, RG 013.

21 Public Law 875, "To authorize Federal assistance to States and local governments . . . in providing disaster assistance; and Executive Order 10186 creating the Federal Civil Defense Administration, Civil Defense Museum; both in http://www.civildefensemuseum.com/; *Civil Defense Plan, Benton County, Oregon* (1951); and *What You Should Know about Biological Warfare*, n.d.; both in reel 122, sub. 11, RG 013.

22 H. A. Bork to J. E. McNealy, February 14 and 26, 1951, reel 122, sub. 11, RG 013; Jack Carmichael to The President, March 5, 1951; and E. B. Lemon to Carmichael, March 10, 1951, both in reel 122, sub. 11, RG 013.

23 William A. McClenaghan, "The Case of *Magruder's American Government*," *Saturday Review*, April 9, 1952, 17–18; Camp Magruder, A Methodist Youth Camp, https://www.google.com/#q=camp+magruder; and "McCarthyism in the Classrooms," *Atlanta Constitution*, October 30, 1952, copy in reel 2, sub. 11, RG 013.

24 McClenaghan, "The Case of *Magruder's American Government*"; and Henry Ruppel to Strand, May 26, 1951; both in reel 2, sub. 11, RG 013.

25 Strand to Ruppel, May 28, 1951; and Strand to Aili Valuton, August 1951; both in reel 2, sub. 11, RG 013.

26 Strand to the *Montana Standard*, September 28, 1951; and George McVey to Strand, October 18, 1951; both in reel 2, sub. 11, RG 013.

27 Typescript of the *Atlanta Constitution*, October 30, 1951; and McClenaghan to Strand; both in reel 2, sub. 11, RG 013.

28 *Oregonian*, December 12 and 24, 1951, and February 3, 1952; and P. A. Wright to Social Studies Department at OSC, December 3, 1951, reel 2, sub. 11, RG 013.

29 W. A. McClenaghan, "The Case of Magruder's American Government," *Saturday Review* (April 9, 1952), 17–18.

30 Ibid., 18.

31 Enrollment—Fall End-of-Term, 1912 through 2000, *2001 Fact Book*, 46; and *Biennial Report of Oregon State College, 1951–1952*, 62–63, box 10, sub. 12, RG 013.

32 *Biennial Report of Oregon State College, 1951–1952*, 72–73, box 10, sub. 12, RG 013.

33 Ibid., 1955–1956, 49–50.

34 Ibid., 50–51, 56.

35 Ibid., 79; and ibid., 1953–1954, 1.

36 *Biennial Report of Oregon State College, 1957–1958*, 61–62, box 10, sub. 12, RG 013.

37 Typescript, Oregon State College, President's Biennial Report, 1953–1954, 2–4, box 11, sub. 12, RG 013; and Admin. Records, box 2, RG 32.

38 Typescript, Oregon State College, President's Biennial Report, 1953–1954, 2–4, box 11, sub. 12, RG 013, 4–7.

39 *Oregonian*, January 6, 1953.

40 Ibid., February 20 and March 11, 1953.

41 Typescript, Source Material from Deans and Division and Department Heads for the Biennial Report, 1955–1956, 9–12, box 11, sub. 12, RG 013; and *Biennial Report of Oregon State College, 1955–1956*, 56, box 10, sub. 12, RG 013.

42 Colby Typescript, 12–13; and *Biennial Report of Oregon State College, 1955–1956*, 56, box 10, sub. 12, RG 013.

43 Lower Division Policy Committee, Tentative Curricula in General Studies, April 10, 1956; Colby to Strand, May 18, 1956; Strand to Colby, June 1, 1956; Walter Foreman to Strand, October 30, 1956; and Colby to Strand, November 7, 1956; all in reel 134, sub. 11, RG 013; and Lower Division, Extension of Degrees, box 12, sub. 12, RG 013.

44 *Oregonian*, February 17, April 2, June 12, and Sept 27, 1957; College of Liberal Arts, Historical Note, http://scarc.library.oregonstate.edu/coll/rg143/biographicalnote.html; and A Chronological History of OSU, http://scarc.library.oregonstate.edu/chronology/chron_head.html.

45 Curriculum Committee Minutes, February 6, April 3 and 12, May 3, October 2, 1957; and President Strand to John R. Richards, November 30, 1957; all in Curriculum Coordination Records, 1924–1981, SCARC.

46 *Oregonian*, September 16, 1959.

47 Ibid., September 17, 1959.

48 Ibid., October 27 and 28, 1959.

49 President Strand, School of Humanities and Social Sciences, Report for the Biennium, July 1958 to June 1960, box 12, sub. 12, RG 013; and O. Meredith Wilson to Chancellor John R. Richards, December 23, 1959, Digital Collections, University of Oregon Libraries, http://oregondigital.org/cdm4/document.php?CISOROOT=/uopres&CISOPTR=1538&REC=1.

50 Robert Rydell, Jeffrey Safford, and Pierce Mullen, *In The People's Interest: A Centennial History of Montana State University* (Bozeman: Montana State University Foundation, 1992), 267–270; Madison Kuhn, *Michigan State: The First Hundred Years* (East Lansing: Michigan State University Press, 1955), 286–288, 418–424, and 471; and Keith R. Widder, *Michigan Agricultural College: The Evolution of a Land-Grant Philosophy, 1855–1925* (East Lansing: Michigan State University Press, 2005), 169–170.

51 Earle Dudley Ross, *The Land-Grant Idea at Iowa State College* (Ames: Iowa State University Press, 1958), 158–159 and 290–291; Tanya Zanish-Belcher, "History of Iowa State," http://www.add.lib.iastate.edu/spcl/exhibits/150/index.html; and History of the College of Arts and Sciences, http://www.las.iastate.edu/about-the-college/#points-of-pride; Robert W.

Topping, *A Century Beyond: The History of Purdue University* (West Lafayette, IN: Purdue University Press, 1988), 314, 320–321, and 324; and Purdue University History, http://www.purdue.edu/purdue/about/history.html.

52 Charles B. Gale, Charles E. Keegan III, et al., *Oregon's Forest Products Industry and Timber Harvest, 2008: Industry Trends and Impacts of the Great Recession through 2010*, USDA, Forest Service, Pacific Northwest Research Station, General Technical Report, PNW-GTR-868 (September 2012), 3; William G. Robbins, "The Western Lumber Industry: A Twentieth-Century Perspective," in *The Twentieth-Century West: Historical Interpretations*, Gerald D. Nash and Richard W. Etulain, eds. (Albuquerque: University of New Mexico Press, 1989), 247; and Walter McCulloch, Biennial Report, 1957–1958, p. 3, box 12, sub. 12, RG 013.

53 Walter McCulloch, Biennial Report, 1957–1958, 3, box 12, sub. 12, RG 013.

54 Ibid., 4–5; and College of Forestry Records, 1911–1997, SCARC.

55 Gilfillan to Strand, May 10, 1958, 1–2 and 15, box 12, sub. 12, RG 013; Halberstam, *The Fifties*, 623–625; and "Sputnik and The Dawn of the Space Age," http://history.nasa.gov/sputnik/.

56 Gilfillan to Strand, June 15, 1960, 52–53, box 12, sub. 12, RG 013.

57 The author is grateful to former graduate student Craig Biegel, whose excellent research paper, "A Visionary at Work: Wayne V. Burt and the Early Years of Oceanography at Oregon State University," was a valuable contribution to my 2008 seminar, Science in the OSU Archives.

58 Wayne Burt to Gilfillan, June 3, 1960, box 12, sub. 12, RG 013.

59 Admin. Records, May 23, 1951, box 2, RG 32.

60 "Linus Pauling and the International Peace Movement," http://scarc.library.oregonstate.edu/coll/pauling/peace/narrative/page10.html; and "U.S. Supreme Court Strikes Down Loyalty Oaths for Washington State Employees," HistoryLink.Org, http://www.historylink.org/index.cfm?DisplayPage=output.cfm&File_Id=5200.

61 Admin. Records, May 13 and June 10, 1953.

62 Ibid., September 11, 1952, and May 27 and June 10, 1953.

63 Ibid., April 27, 1955.

64 Ibid.

65 James Herbert Jensen, http://scarc.library.oregonstate.edu/omeka/exhibits/show/presidents/jensen/jensen/; and Chronological History of Oregon State University, http://scarc.library.oregonstate.edu/chronology/chron_head.html.

CHAPTER NINE: CIVIL RIGHTS, CAMPUS DISORDER, AND CHANGE

1 For a summary of this cursory discussion of the 1960s, see James T. Patterson, *Grand Expectations: The United States, 1945–1974* (New York: Oxford University Press, 1996), 442–449.

2 For an extended commentary on these issues, see William G. Robbins, "Town and Country in Oregon: A Conflicted Legacy," in *Toward One Oregon: Rural-Urban Interdependence and the Evolution of a State*, Michael Hibbard, Ethan Seltzer, Bruce Weber, and Beth Emshoff, eds. (Corvallis: Oregon State University Press, 2011), 71–76.

3 James Herbert Jensen, President of Oregon State University, SCARC; and *Oregonian*, September 15, 1961.

4 "Historical Note," Western Water Resources Research Institute, SCARC.

5 J. Kenneth Munford Papers, 1866–1996; and Admin. Records, January 11, 1961, RG 32; both in SCARC.

6 Oregon State University Press, History, http://osupress.oregonstate.edu/; and Biographical Note, Helen M. Gilkey Papers, 1907–1974, SCARC.

7 Admin. Records, April 26, 1961, box 2, RG 32; and William H. Carlson, "The Library of Oregon State University: A Centennial History," Corvallis, Oregon, 1966, 81, William H. Carlson Papers, 1924–1981, SCARC.

8 Admin. Records, April 26, 1961, box 2, RG 32; and Carlson, "The Library of Oregon State University," 81–82.

9 Plan of Organization, 1965, box 2, RG 32.

10 *Oregonian*, April 16, May 4, December 24, 1962; November 22, 1963; and April 20 and May 9, 1964.

11 Biegel, "A Visionary at Work: Wayne V. Burt and the Early Years of Oceanography at Oregon State University," 8–12, copy in the author's possession.

12 Ibid., 13–14.

13 Ibid., 14–15.

14 Admin. Records, May 24 and October 25, 1961, box 2, RG 32.

15 Ibid., May 23, 1962.

16 Ibid.

17 Ibid., August 21, 1961.

18 Ibid., November 1, 1967.

19 James T. Patterson, *Grand Expectations: The United States, 1945–1974* (New York: Oxford University Press, 1996), 543–547, and 726–729.

20 Ibid., 538–541; "Economic Opportunity Act of 1964," http://wps.prenhall.com/wps/media/objects/751/769950/Documents_Library/eoa1964.htm; and typescript, presidential report for 1964–1965, 14, reel 134, sub. 11, RG 013.

21 Admin. Records, February 3 and November 3, 1965, box 2, RG 32; and *Report of the President* (1963–1964), 5–6, box 10, sub. 12, RG013.

22 *Report of the President* (1963–1964), 6–7, box 10, sub. 12, RG 013; Assumptions, Objectives, and Principles for the Long Range Development Plan of Oregon State University, typescript, 1–3, reel 134, sub. 11, RG 013; and L. A. Demonte and A. R. Wagner, Oregon State University, Long Range Development Plan, June 1964 (hereafter Demonte-Wagner Plan), 2–3, Memorabilia Collection, box 101.

23 Demonte-Wagner Plan, 13.

24 Long Range Development Plan, typescript, 2; and Demonte-Wagner Plan, 6–7.

25 Demonte-Wagner Plan, 16–17.

26 Ibid., 6.

27 Biennial Report of the Chancellor (1965–1966), 1–2, box 10, sub. 12, RG 013.

28 Ibid., 6–7. It should be noted that while the board expanded undergraduate liberal arts programs at Oregon State, the same board authorized master's degree programs at Portland State College in English, economics, history, psychology, sociology, speech, anthropology, and political science. See the *Oregonian*, July 27, 1966.

29 Untitled typescript, president's biennial report, 1965–1966, 2–4, reel 134, sub. 11, RG 013.

30 Biennial Report of the Chancellor (1965–1966), 8–9.

31 *Oregonian*, March 13, 1966.

32 Ibid., July 27, 1966.

33 Ibid., October 26, 1966.

34 Rodney Waldron, Biennial Report, 1967–1968, William Jasper Kerr Library, 1–2, box 13, sub. 12, RG 013.

35 Ibid., 3–4.

36 Ibid., 4.

37 Ibid., 18–20.

38 Untitled typescript, president's biennial report, 1965–1966, 8–9, reel 134, sub. 11, RG 013; and Council of Deans Meeting, July 30, 1965, box 13, sub. 11, RG 013.

39 Untitled typescript, president's biennial report, 1965–1966, 10–11, reel 134, sub. 11, RG 013. Monroe Sweetland was the Oregon legislature's chief sponsor of Oregon community

colleges. See the author's *A Man for All Seasons: Monroe Sweetland and the Liberal Paradox* (Corvallis: Oregon State University Press, 2015), 157–158.

40 Untitled typescript, president's biennial report, 1965–1966, 10–11, reel 134, sub. 11, RG 013, 11–12. Paul Risser made those remarks when he delivered a campus-wide address in the fall of 1996. The author was in the audience.

41 Chronological History of Oregon State University, 1950–1959, in SCARC. For the association between foreign aid assistance and American foreign policy, see James T. Patterson, *Grand Expectations: The United States, 1945–1974* (New York: Oxford University Press, 1996), 496–497; and "Agency for International Development," in Paul S. Boyer, ed., *The Oxford Companion to United States History* (New York: Oxford University Press, 2001), 15.

42 "A New Century Begins," Report of the President, 1968, 5–6, box 10, sub. 12, RG 013.

43 *Biennial Report of the President* (1965–1966), 11, box 10, sub. 12, RG 013.

44 Minutes of the Council of Deans Meeting, October 13, 1965, box 13, sub. 11, RG 013.

45 J. Kenneth Munford to Jensen, March 11 and April 13, 1963, ibid.

46 George Carson to Jensen, December 2, 1964, ibid.

47 Jensen to Schools and Departments, November 17, 1966; and conversations on August 11, 2014, with Mike Dicianna (archival staff) and Larry Landis, director, Special Collections and Archives.

48 Rodney Waldron to Jensen, August 27, 1965, box 13, sub. 11, RG 013.

49 Waldron to Jensen, June 30, 1967.

50 Based on the author's conversations with archivist Larry Landis.

51 *Oregonian*, August 30, 1967, and May 23, 1968.

52 *Oregonian*, October 27, 1968.

53 *Charter Day Convocation: Commemorating the One Hundredth Anniversary of the Founding of Oregon State University* (Sunday, October 27, 1968), MC 36.

54 Fred Harvey Harrington, "A Look at the Next 100 Years," Centennial Lectures, http://ir.library.oregonstate.edu/xmlui/handle/1957/23790.

55 Jensen to Academic and Executive Deans, 10-12, box 16, sub. 13, RG 013.

56 Ibid., 10.

57 Ibid.

58 Jensen to Academic and Executive Deans, July 12, 1968, 6–7, box 16, sub. 13, RG 013.

59 The "Berkeley incident" refers to the Free Speech Movement on the University of California campus in 1964. "Columbia Fiasco" refers to the student strike and takeover of buildings on the Columbia University campus and their forcible removal by the New York City Police Department.

60 Roy Lieuallen, "Colleges, Universities Strive to Develop Human Resources," *Biennial Report* (1967–1968), 10, box 10, sub. 12, RG 013.

61 Standard Operating Procedure of University Police in Certain Emergencies, May 15, 1968, box 13, sub. 11, RG 013.

62 C. H. Blumenfeld, Procedures for Control of Campus Disorders, September 17, 1968, box 13, sub. 11, RG 013; and *Daily Barometer*, November 8, 1968.

63 James Jensen, Faculty Day Talk, September 19, 1968, box 13, sub. 11, RG 013.

64 *Barometer*, July 16, 1968. The quotations refer to Olsen's articles.

65 Ibid., November 8 and 21, 1968.

66 Ibid., January 14 and 16, 1969; and Black Student Union Proposal, January 14, 1969, box 13, sub. 11, RG 013.

67 *Barometer*, January 16, 1969.

68 Ibid.

69 Ibid., February 20 and 25, 1969; and Michael Oriard, *Bowled Over: Big-Time College Football from the Sixties to the BCS ERA* (Chapel Hill: University of North Carolina Press, 2009), 92. Contrary to the contemporary story that the initial encounter was between Andros and Milton, retrospective interviews, according to Oriard, indicate that Boghosian was the first member of the football staff to see Milton with facial hair.

70   *Barometer*, February 25 and 26, 1969.

71   *Oregonian*, February 25, 1969.

72   Ibid., March 7, 1969.

73   Ibid., March 9, 1969.

74   Oriard, *Bowled Over*, 94–95.

75   *Barometer*, August 5, 1969. The author was involved "on the ground floor" with others in teaching such a class, when History Department chair Thomas McClintock asked me in the summer of 1972 if I were interested in teaching a course in History of the American Indian. I agreed and taught the class in Milam Auditorium in the spring of 1973 to some 260 students.

CHAPTER TEN: FEDERAL POLICIES BECOME PREEMINENT

1   Address by Oregon Governor Tom McCall to the Annual State Lions Convention (hereafter Governor McCall Address), May 22, 1970, box 22, sub. 14, RG 013. McCall's reference to "unwanted nerve gas" involved a Department of Defense plan to ship thirteen thousand tons of nerve and mustard agents for storage at the Umatilla Army Depot. With pressure from Washington's senator Henry Jackson and Oregon's Mark Hatfield, the army subsequently decided on a site on Kodiak Island, Alaska. See *Oregonian*, May 24 and October 18 and 24, 1970.

2   Governor McCall Address. The governor's fears about citizen backlash were confirmed when voters easily defeated "GO-19" on May 27, 1970, a ballot measure that would have lowered the voting franchise to age nineteen. See *Barometer*, May 28, 1970.

3   Governor McCall Address.

4   *Barometer*, May 2, 5, and 8, 1970.

5   Ibid., May 26, 1970

6   Ibid., May 8, 1970.

7   Ibid., May 9, 1970.

8   Ibid., May 14, 1970.

9   Ibid., May 20 and 22, 1970.

10   James T. Patterson, *Grand Expectations: The United States, 1945–1974* (New York: Oxford University Press, 1996), 543–547, 642, 723, and 730; and Title IX, Education Amendments of 1972, Office of the Assistant Secretary for Administration and Management, U. S. Department of Labor, http://www.dol.gov/oasam/regs/statutes/titleix.htm.

11   Patterson, *Great Expectations*, 726–730.

12   *Barometer*, April 24, 1970.

13   HJ Andrews Experimental Forest, Long Term Ecological Research, http://andrewsforest. oregonstate.edu/lter/about.cfm?topnav=2; and Max G. Geier, *Necessary Work: Discovering Old Forests, New Outlooks, and Community on the H.J. Andrews Experimental Forest, 1948–2000*, USDA, Forest Service, Pacific Northwest Research Station, General Technical Report PNW-GTR-687 (March 2007), 1–5 and 135–137.

14   Jean Anderson, "Mapping OSU's Future," *Oregon Stater* (1971), 13–15; and The Commission on University Goals, *Report to the President of Oregon State University* (August 1970), xxxxi.

15   The Commission on University Goals, *Report to the President*, xxvii.

16   Ibid., xxxiii–xxxviii.

17   Ibid., xxxvi–xxxviii.

18   Emery N. Castle, *Reflections of a Pragmatic Economist: My Intellectual Journey* (Corvallis: Oregon State University Press, 2010), 167–169.

19   Biographical Sketch of Robert MacVicar; and MacVicar Vita; both in box 23, sub. 14, RG 013.

20   Jean Anderson, "Mapping OSU's Future," *Oregon Stater* (1970), 18–19, box 13, sub. 11, RG 013.

21 Katie Laux (Senior Paper), "From Bancroft Way to Woody Hall: Student Demands and University Failures at the University of California at Berkeley and Southern Illinois University at Carbondale," http://www.illinoishistory.com/katielaux-protestpaper.htm.

22 As a new member of the faculty in the fall of 1971, the author recalls rumors that MacVicar was brought in to "bust heads" if students misbehaved.

23 Robert MacVicar to Roy Lieuallen, July 12, 1970, box 18, sub. 14, RG 013.

24 MacVicar to James A. Sullivan, September 16, 1970, box 18, sub. 14, RG 013. It should be noted that MacVicar was also chagrined at the state board for allowing the Oregon Student Public Interest Group (OSPIRG) to participate on campuses through the customary student fee mechanism. He wrote one alumnus that his personal freedom was limited in the matter because of the board's decision. While this was "an unfortunate intrusion into higher education," he assured the alum if OSPIRG's actions were harmful to the interests of the university, he would "deal with them promptly." See MacVicar to Harold Pasley, April 12, 1971, box 18, sub. 14, RG 013.

25 MacVicar to Jason Boe, September 28, 1970, box 18, sub. 14, RG 013; and National Association of State Universities and Land-Grant Colleges, Circular, September 24 and 25, 1970; both in box 22, sub. 14, RG 013.

26 MacVicar to James Jensen, November 30, 1971, box 18, sub. 14, RG 013.

27 MacVicar to Lee Kolmer, March 12, 1971, box 18, sub. 14, RG 013; and Equal Opportunity, Oregon State University, June 23, 1971, 1, box 22, sub. 14, RG 013.

28 Equal Opportunity, Oregon State University, June 23, 1971, 1–3, box 22, sub. 14, RG 013.

29 Marlaina Kiner to MacVicar, January 3, 1972, box 2, RG 172, Affirmative Action Office Records.

30 Ibid.

31 Anthony Burch, Acting Director, Affirmative Action/Equal Opportunity Program, to Deans, Directors, and Department Heads, March 15, 1972, box 2, RG 172.

32 MacVicar to Marlaina Kiner, September 18, 1972, box 18, sub. 4, RG 013. The salary adjustments for women were a consequence of the findings of the president's ad hoc committee to review the faculty status of women. See MacVicar to Members of the OSU Faculty, March 27 and 29, 1972; both in box 22, sub. 14, RG 013.

33 Anti-Discrimination Board, n.d., box 22, sub. 14, RG 013; and Oregonian, March 24, 1972. The initial board members were appointed in January.

34 Juan Mendoza to Robert MacVicar, February 2, 1972, box 22, sub. 14, RG 013; and Barometer, February 2, 1972.

35 Higher Education Guidelines, Executive Order 11246, HEW Office of Civil Rights, October 1, 1972; and Karla Brown to MacVicar, M. Popovich, and A.D. Burch, November 28, 1972; both in box 21, sub. 4, RG 013 (emphasis original).

36 Marlaina Kiner to MacVicar, November 1972, box 21, sub. 14, RG 013.

37 Cheryl M. Fields, "Colleges Told: Hire the Best Qualified," Chronicle of Higher Education (December 23, 1974), box 21, sub. 14, RG 013.

38 MacVicar to Kiner, February 5, 1973, ibid.

39 The schools of humanities and social science and science became the College of Liberal Arts and College of Science in 1973. MacVicar to Kiner, May 25, 1973, box 18, sub. 14, RG 013; and Oregon State University Affirmative Action Plan, Approved by OCR/HEW, December 1975, box 21, sub. 14, RG 013.

40 MacVicar to Kiner, August 29, 1977; MacVicar to Allen Momohara, September 28, 1978; and Conciliation Agreement, signed by R. MacVicar and Virginia Balderma, acting director Office of Civil Rights, HEW Region X, September 28, 1978; all in box 2, RG 172.

41 Susan Ware, Title IX: A Brief History with Documents (Boston: Bedford/St. Martin's, 2007), 1–3; and Iram Valentin, "Title IX: A Brief History," Women's Equity Act Resource Center, 1–4, http://www.google.com/url?sa=t&rct=j&q=&esrc=s&source=web&cd=1&ved=0CCAQFjAA&url=http%3A%2F%2Fwww2.edc.org%2FWomensEquity%2Fpdffiles

%2Ft9digest.pdf&ei=hahGVIPJL9WjyASM6oH4Bw&usg=AFQjCNFjZ4HdhTdXk79io
AA0nk1F2rM8gg.

42 Title IX Compliance, 1975–2000, Intercollegiate Athletics Records, 1908–2013, http://
scarc.library.oregonstate.edu/coll/rg007/catalogue/rg007IX.html.

43 MacVicar to Pat Ingram, September 25, 1973, box 18, sub. 14, RG 013; and Tom McCall to
Dan Evans, April 2, 1974, box 21, sub. 14, RG 013.

44 MacVicar to John Fuzak, June 11, 1975, box 18, sub. 14, RG 013; and John Davis to
MacVicar, July 30, 1975, box 21, sub. 14, RG 013.

45 Charlotte Lambert to Faculty, Department of Education, November 17, 1975; and Lambert
to James Long, November 17, 1975; both in box 21, sub. 14, RG 013.

46 Jack Rainey to Pearl Spears Gray, February 9, 1977, box 21, sub. 14, RG 013.

47 Annual Report, 1974–75, Women's Intercollegiate Athletics Board, box 22, sub. 14, RG
013.

48 MacVicar to Robert Aiken, May 25, 1976, box 19, sub. 14, RG 013.

49 MacVicar to Kiner, August 10, 1977, ibid. The Pac-8 became the Pac-10 in 1978 when the
University of Arizona and Arizona State University joined the conference.

50 Michael Oriard, *Bowled Over: Big-Time College Football from the Sixties to the BCS Era*
(Chapel Hill: University of North Carolina Press, 2009), 225–226; and Dee Andros to
Athletic Board Members, December 13, 1977, box 21, sub. 14, RG 013.

51 Sylvia Moore to Dee Andros, December 14, 1978; and Judy Loosley and Wilbur Cooney
to MacVicar, February 28, 1978; both in box 21, sub. 14, RG 013.

52 William Kirkpatrick to MacVicar, February 27, 1978; Ruth Stiehl to Wilbur Cooney,
February 28, 1978; and Craig Fletcher to MacVicar, February 27, 1978; all in box 21, sub.
14, RG 013.

53 Sylvia Moore to MacVicar, April 27 and June 21, 1978; both in box 21, sub. 14, RG 013.

54 MacVicar to Office of Civil Rights, February 12, 1979; MacVicar to Joseph Califano, July
16, 1979; both in box 19, sub. 14, RG 013: and Nancy Gerou to Clifford Smith, December
10, 1979, box 19, sub. 14, RG 013.

55 Valentin, "Title IX: A Brief History," 5–7; and Oriard, *Bowled Over*, 225–227. More recently, Andrew Zimbalist pointed to the "counting chicanery" that major universities use
to exaggerate the number of female athletes—women's rowing teams sometimes list one
hundred crew members, "a preposterously high number" to offset football squads of 120
players on NCAA Division I teams. See *New York Times*, March 26, 2016.

56 MacVicar to C. Dean Smith, August 20, 1973, box 18, sub. 14, RG 013.

57 MacVicar to Helen Hoyer, June 28, 1976; and MacVicar to Oregon Liquor Control
Commission; both in box 19, sub. 14, RG 013.

58 MacVicar to Oregon Liquor Control Commission, November 1, 1978 and February 27,
1979; both in box 19, sub. 14, RG 013.

59 MacVicar to Alan Berg, April 3, 1979; MacVicar to H. H. "Bob" Harper, March 17, 1981;
MacVicar to Cheryl J. Gettis, April 22, 1982; and MacVicar to Kenneth Thompson, July 28,
1982; all in box 19, sub. 14, RG 013.

60 MacVicar to Hattie W. Williams, Sept 25, 1979, box 19, sub. 14, RG 013.

61 Peter G. Boag, "The World Fire Created: Field Burning in the Willamette Valley,"
Columbia 5 (Summer 1991), 7–9; and Frank S. Conklin et al., *Burning Grass Seed Fields in
the Willamette Valley: The Search for Solutions*, Extension Miscellaneous Publication 8397,
February 1989, Oregon State University Extension Service, 10–12.

62 Oregon Seed Council, *Grass Seed: The Tiny Giant* (Salem: c. 1975), n.p.; Conklin et al.,
Burning Grass Seed Fields, 14–15, 25; and Boag, "The World Fire Created," 11.

63 Oregon Seed Council, "Oregon Grown Grass Seed," n.d., n.p.; and "Open Field Burning in
the Willamette Valley, www.deq.state.or.us/aq/factsheets/07aq019_field.pdf.

64 Arthur W. Galston, "Herbicides: A Mixed Blessing," *Bioscience* (February 1979), 85; and
Thomas Whiteside, "The Pendulum and the Toxic Cloud," *New Yorker* (July 1977), 30–32.
For an earlier symposium at OSU led by Michael Newton, see *Symposium Proceedings:*

Herbicides and Vegetation Management in Forests, Ranges, and Noncrop Lands (Corvallis: Oregon State University, 1967).

65 Carol Van Strum, "Back to the Future: EPA Reinvents the Wheel on Reproductive Effects of Dioxin," *Synthesis/Regeneration* (Summer 1995), 2; and *Oregonian*, January 12, 1977.

66 *Oregonian*, June 6, 1973.

67 Phil Keisling, "OSU's Herbicide Connection," *Willamette Week* 6 (December 17, 1979), 1–6; and John D. Walstad and Frank N. Dost, *The Health Risks of Herbicides in Forestry: A Review of the Scientific Literature*, Special Publication 10, April 1984, Forest Research Lab, College of Forestry, Oregon State University, 3, 28.

68 MacVicar to Lawrence E. Langdon, February 25 and May 9, 1983; both in box 20, sub. 14, RG 013.

69 MacVicar to James Jensen, July 21, 1971, box 18, sub. 14, RG 013.

70 MacVicar to David King, October 25, 1978, box 19, sub. 14, RG 013.

71 MacVicar to Cleora Adams, December 3, 1975, box 18, sub. 14, RG 013.

72 MacVicar to Dean Gordon Gilkey, February 16, 1976; and MacVicar to E. E. Easton, February 19, 1976; both in box 19, sub. 14, RG 013.

73 MacVicar to Miles Romney, August 12, 1976, box 19, sub. 14, RG 013.

74 MacVicar form letter, September 24, 1976; and MacVicar to Mansel Keene, September 24, 1976; both in box 19, sub. 14, RG 013.

75 MacVicar to Emery Castle, January 5, 1977; and MacVicar to Evlon Niederfrank, May 24, 1979; both in box 19, sub. 14, RG 013.

76 MacVicar to Paul Foreman, August 23, 1970; and MacVicar to Kenneth Myers, March 23, 1972; both in box 18, sub. 14, RG 013.

77 MacVicar to Polanski, November 20, 1973, box 18, sub. 14, RG 013; and MacVicar to Einar Nordahl, March 19, 1981, box 19, sub. 14, RG 013.

78 MacVicar to Mitch Gitman, July 13, 1983, box 20, sub. 14, RG 013.

CHAPTER ELEVEN: BECOMING A MODERN UNIVERSITY

1 William G. Robbins, *Oregon, This Storied Land* (Portland: Oregon Historical Society Press, 2005), 179–181.

2 William G. Robbins, "Town and Country in Oregon: A Conflicted Legacy," in *Toward One Oregon: Rural-Urban Interdependence and the Evolution of a State*, ed. Michael Hibbard, Ethan Seltzer, Bruce Weber, and Beth Emshoff (Corvallis: Oregon State University Press, 2011), 73–76.

3 "John Vincent Byrne (1984–1995)," Presidents of Oregon State University, in http://scarc.library.oregonstate.edu/omeka/exhibits/show/presidents/byrne/byrne/; and Robert MacVicar to Edward D. McDowell et al., June 11, 1984, box 20, sub. 14, RG 013; and *Oregonian*, November 18, 1984.

4 John V. Byrne, *Undercurrents: From Oceanographer to University President* (Oregon State University Press, forthcoming, spring 2018) (emphasis original). All references will refer to "Part 3: President of a Land-Grant University, 1984–1995."

5 *Oregonian*, November 18, 1984; Andros to John Byrne, November 5, 1984, box 40, sub. 15, RG 013; and Byrne, *Undercurrents*, Part 3, 352.

6 *Oregonian*, November 22 and 24, 1984; and Statement by President John V. Byrne Concerning OSU Football Coaching, November 23, 1984, box 40, sub. 15, RG013.

7 *Oregonian*, November 27 and December 1, 6, and 12, 1984.

8 Byrne, *Undercurrents*, Part 3.

9 *Oregonian*, December 15 and 17, 1984; and Peter E. Pifer to Byrne, n.d., box 40, sub. 15, RG 013.

10 Byrne to Andros (two documents), box 25, sub. 15, RG 013.

11 Barnes D. Rogers to MacVicar, October 8, 1979; Kathy Douglas to MacVicar, October 9, 1979; Harold J. Peterson to MacVicar, October 10, 1979; N. B. Guistina to MacVicar,

October 10, 1979; Harold Hewitt to MacVicar, October 11, 1979; illegible signature to MacVicar, October 11, 1979; Bonnie Graham and Leal W. Graham to MacVicar, October 15, 1979, and Dick Farnes to MacVicar, October 19, 1979; all in box 21, sub. 14, RG 013.

12 *Oregonian*, December 29, 1984, and January 3, 1985; and Byrne to Personnel, Department of Intercollegiate Athletics, box 25, sub. 15, RG 013.

13 Athletic Director Andros Moves to New OSU Post February 1, Oregon State University, Department of Information, January 2, 1985, box 41, sub. 15, RG 013.

14 Byrne to John Carey, March 25, 1985, box 25, sub. 15, RG 013.

15 Byrne to Harold Enarson, Charles Sturtz, and Robert Clodius, February 8, 1985, box 25, sub. 15, RG 013.

16 Harold Enarson to Byrne, March 22, 1985, box 25, sub. 15, RG 013 (emphasis original).

17 Ibid.

18 Charles Sturtz to Byrne, March 27, 1985; and Robert Clodius to Byrne, March 28, 1985; both in box 25, sub. 15, RG 013.

19 Byrne to President's Office Staff et al., April 19, 1985, box 25, sub. 16, RG 013; and *Oregonian*, April 24, 1985.

20 Byrne to Jonathan D. Istok, May 14, 1985, box 25, sub. 15, RG 013.

21 Byrne to William E. Davis, Chancellor, June 10, 1985; and Byrne to University Community, June 21, 1985; both in box 25, sub. 15, 1985.

22 Byrne, *Undercurrents*, Part 3; and "Statement of Principles for Guiding the Long-Range Planning at Oregon State University," Faculty Forum Papers, February 20, 1986, Faculty Senate Records, 1944–2012, Born-Digital Materials, SCARC.

23 Byrne, *Undercurrents*, Part 3; "Statement of Principles for Guiding the Long-Range Planning at Oregon State University"; Byrne to Dear Colleagues, March 20, 1987; and "Preparing for the Future: Strategic Planning at Oregon State University," all in box 25, sub. 15, RG 013.

24 Byrne to Dear Colleagues, March 20, 1987, box 25, sub. 15, RG 013; and Byrne, *Undercurrents*, Part 3, 304.

25 *2001 Fact Book* (Oregon State University), 46; and Fourth-Week Fall Term Enrollment, University of Oregon, courtesy UO Office of Institutional Research.

26 "Higher Education and Economic Issues in Oregon, *City Club of Portland Bulletin* (City Club of Portland, April 1994), 213–214.

27 Byrne to Chancellor William E. Davis, October 6, 1987, box 32, sub. 15, RG 013; and Byrne, *Undercurrents*, Part 3.

28 *Oregonian*, January 13 and 17 and June 24, 1987; and Byrne to Davis, June 13, 1988, box 32, sub. 4, RG 013 (emphasis original).

29 Byrne, *Undercurrents*, Part 3.

30 Byrne to Dennis Connell, March 9, 1987; Byrne to William E. Davis, February 9, 1988; Byrne to Academic Deans, December 10, 1988; and Byrne to Dear Faculty, December 10, 1988; all in box 32, sub. 15, RG 013 (emphasis original).

31 Northwest Association of Schools and Colleges, Commission on Colleges, Evaluation Committee Report, Oregon State University (February 27–28 and March 1–2, 1990), 1–4.

32 Ibid., 5–7, 15, 29–37, and 42–45.

33 Byrne to Davis, April 2, 1987; Byrne to Norman H. Martinson, May 19, 1988; and Byrne to George Pasero, July 18, 1988; all in box 32, sub. 15, RG 013.

34 Byrne to Jud Blakely, July 19 and September 15, 1988; both in box 32, sub. 15, RG 013.

35 Summary meeting of the Athletic Advisory Board, February 23, 1988; and Bob Frank to Lynn Snyder, March 7, 1988; both in box 1, Intercollegiate Athletic Records, RG 007.

36 Lynn Snyder to Byrne, August 7, 1989; Eugene *Register-Guard* (photocopy), October 20, 1990; both in box 1, RG 007; and "Sports (Action) Lottery Funding, OUS /chancellor's Office Budget Brief," www.ous.edu.../budget/.../Sports_Lottery_budget.

37 "Governor Barbara Roberts," Oregon Historical Society, http://www.ohs.org/education/focus/governor-barbara-roberts.cfm; and "Ballot Measure 5 Turns 20," *Think Out Loud*,

Oregon Public Broadcasting, November 8, 2010, http://www.opb.org/radio/programs/thinkoutloud/ballotmeasure5.

38 Byrne, Crossing the Divide to New Realities: An Oregon State University Annual Report for 1990–1991, box 33, sub. 15, RG 013. The author chaired the Department of History in 1990–1991 and recalls the use of the word "discontinuing" in announcing department closures.

39 Brent S. Steel and William Lunch, "Educational Policy," in *Oregon Politics and Government versus Conservative Populists*, ed. Richard Clucas, Mark Henkels, and Brent Steel (Lincoln: University of Nebraska Press, 2005), 282.

40 Clucas et al., *Oregon Politics and Government*, 282.

41 Byrne to Jud Blakely, January 17 and February 11, 1991, box 33, sub. 15, RG 013.

42 David Schacht to Byrne, November 8, 1991, box 41, sub. 15, RG 013.

43 Ray Leidich to Byrne, October 15, 1991; Janet Meranda to Chancellor's Office, October 18, 1991; and Arnold Appleby to Thomas Bartlett, October 21, 1991; all in box 41, sub. 15, RG 013.

44 Weldon Ihrig to Byrne, October 31, 1990, box 41, sub. 15, RG 013; Dutch Baughman to Beaver Club Board, May 29, 1991; and Baughman to Beaver Believers, October 11, 1991; both in box 2, RG 007.

45 Craig Hosterman to Byrne, November 8, 1991, and Zoe Ann Holmes to Byrne, November 8, 1991; both in box 41, sub. 15, RG 013; Glenn Klein to State Board of Higher Education, October 22, 1991, box 41, sub. 15, RG 013; and Athletics Advisory Committee minutes, October 21, 1991, box 2, RG 007.

46 Sally Maleug to Byrne, May 20, 1992, box 2, RG 007.

47 Ibid.

48 Byrne, *Undercurrents*, Part 3.

49 Chronological History of Oregon State University, 1981, SCARC; and MacVicar, no title, n.d., box 20, sub. 14, RG 103.

50 Robert Lundeen to Byrne, November 29, 1984; Byrne to Lundeen, December 31, 1984; both in box 33; and Byrne to Lundeen, June 23 and October 29, 1986, box 25; both in sub. 15, RG 013.

51 Byrne to Lundeen, May 3 and June 19, 1986; and Byrne to Development Office, June 15, 1990; all in box 32, sub. 15, RG 013.

52 George Edmonston Jr., "F. Wayne Valley: A Tribute," *Oregon Stater* 20, no. 7 (November 1986), 9.

53 Byrne to OSU Foundation Staff, October 7 and December 12, 1985; and January 28, 1986; all in box 25, sub. 15, RG 013.

54 Byrne to Valley, June 26, 1986; Byrne to OSU Foundation, July 16, 1986; and Byrne to Valley, September 2, 1986; all in box 25, sub. 15, RG 013. Byrne first met Wayne Valley in December 1985, while attending a meeting of the Pac-10 presidents and athletic directors in San Francisco. That the two liked each other is clear from Byrne's remembering of some of their conversations. See Byrne, *Undercurrents*, Part 3.

55 Byrne, *Undercurrents*, Part 3.

56 Byrne to Officers of the OSU Foundation, September 3 and October 1, 1987; and Byrne to Members of the Academic Council, October 9, 1987; all in box 32, sub. 15, RG 013.

57 Byrne, visit with Paul O'Connor, October 5, 1988; Byrne to Gladys Valley, August 7, 1989, and August 3, 1990; all in box 32, sub. 15, RG 013.

58 Byrne to OSU Foundation, July 31 and November 3, 1986; both in box 25, sub. 15, RG 013; Byrne to Tom Autzen, August 28, 1986, and January 5, 1990; and Byrne to Vivienne B. Snow, January 5, 1990; all in box 32, sub. 15, RG 013; and Byrne to Autzen, December 12, 1990, box 33, sub. 15, RG 013.

59 Byrne to Development Office, January 8 and May 27, 1988; and Byrne to L. L. "Stub" Stewart and Faye Stewart, September 12, 1988; all in box 32, sub. 15, RG 013.

60 Byrne to Roger W. Heyns, November 14, 1986, box 25, sub. 15, RG 013; Byrne to Joseph W. Cox, November 7, 1995, box 33, RG 013; and Byrne, *Undercurrents*, Part 3.

61 Byrne, *Undercurrents*, Part 3; and Faculty Senate Library Committee to Faculty Senate Executive Committee, March 17, 1989, box 3, Faculty Senate Records, 1944–2012, RG 044.

62 Byrne, *Undercurrents*, Part 3; and Melvin George to Byrne, September 22, 1988, box 38, sub. 15, RG 013. An anonymous person told the author that the president's transfer of unrestricted gifts from colleges to the library upset some deans.

63 Byrne to George, November 23, 1993, box 38, sub. 15, RG 013; and Oregon State University Libraries, *Messenger*, vol. 10, no. 2 (Fall 1995), 4–7.

64 Byrne, *Undercurrents*, Part 3; "The New Valley Library: A Gathering Place for Learning," http://oregonstate.edu/admin/President/2000Report/Valley_Library.html; and archivist Larry Landis to the author, December 11, 2014.

65 Emery N. Castle, *Reflections of a Pragmatic Economist*, 67–68; Byrne, *Undercurrents*, Part 3, 335.

66 Author's discussion with John Byrne, March 4, 2015.

67 Center for the Humanities Records, 1975–2000, Record Group 221, http://scarc.library.oregonstate.edu/coll/rg221/index.html.

68 Ibid.; and Byrne, *Undercurrents*, Part 3.

69 For a seminal critique of the production model, see Paul W. Hirt, *A Conspiracy of Optimism: Management of the National Forests since World War Two* (Lincoln: University of Nebraska Press, 1994).

70 Chris Frissell and Richard Nawa to Ronald J. McCormick, May 8, 1988; and Nawa and Frissell to Robert J. Devlin, May 10, 1988; both in box 35, sub. 15, RG 013.

71 Byrne to Troy Reinhart, June 22, 1988, box 32, sub. 15, RG 013; Reinhart to Byrne, June 27, 1988; Carl Stoltenberg to Byrne, July 11, 1988; and Byrne to Richard Tubb, July 12, 1988; all in box 35, sub. 15, RG 013.

72 Frissell to Ben Worthington, January 12, 1989, box 35, sub. 15, RG 013.

73 Ibid., Dennis Hayward to Byrne, February 22, 1989.

74 Ibid., Bill Liss and Frissell to Byrne, March 1, 1989.

75 Richard Tubb to Byrne, March 10, 1989; Rocky McVay and David Werschel to Frissell, March 10, 1989; and Carl Stoltenberg to Byrne, March 22, 1989; all in box 35, sub. 15, RG 013.

76 Byrne to Liss and Frissell, April 3, 1989; and Byrne to Peter Bahls, April 10, 1989; both in box 32, sub. 15, RG 013.

77 Byrne to Philip D. Whanger, September 20, 1991; Byrne to Faculty and Staff, May 5, 1992; both in box 33, sub. 15, RG 013; and Byrne, *Undercurrents*, Part 3, 307–308.

78 KPMG Peat Marwick/ARC, Administrative Cost Structure Assessment, Final Report, July 1992, box 29, sub. 15, RG 013.

79 Ibid.; Byrne to P. M. deLaubenfels, July 14, 1992, box 33, sub. 15, RG 013; and Byrne, *Undercurrents*, Part 3.

80 Byrne to Dear Colleagues, August 11, 1992; and Byrne to Jud Blakely, August 24, 1992; both in box 33, sub. 15, RG 013.

81 Faculty Senate Minutes, February 4, June 3, October 7, and November 4, 1993, http://senate.oregonstate.edu/archives.

CHAPTER TWELVE: STUDENT LIFE, 1940–2010

1 "Biography," Andy Landforce Oral History Interviews, May–December, 2013, SCARC.

2 Ibid.; the *Beaver*, 1939, 302; and the *Beaver*, 1941, 87.

3 The *Beaver*, 1942; *Oregonian*, October 4 and December 14, 1941.

4 *Oregonian*, January 15 and December 27, 1942.

5   Ibid., October 24, 1942. The loosely structured war savings staff was under the auspices of the federal government's War Manpower Commission, with an explicit mission to urge citizens to purchase war bonds. See Federal Reserve Bank of San Francisco, https://fraser. stlouisfed.org/docs/publications/.../rev_frbsf_19430401.pdf.

6   *Oregonian*, January 17 and October 24, 1943.

7   The *Beaver*, 1943.

8   Ibid., and *Oregonian*, November 26, 1944.

9   *Oregonian*, September 5, 9, 16, 17, 21, 24, and 26.

10 Ibid., September 24, 1944, April 8 and May 20, 1945. As an entering freshman at Danbury State College in 1958 (after a four-year stint in the US Navy), the author refused to wear the traditional blue and white beanie during Freshman Week.

11 The *Beaver*, 1945 and 1946.

12 "A State of Change: Oregon after World War II," http://arcweb.sos.state.or.us/pages/exhib-its/ww2/after/oregon.htm; and the *Beaver*, 1951.

13 *Barometer*, May 20, 1947; May 21, 1948; September 28, 1949; June 4, 1952, May 6, 1960; and Benjamin D. Forgard, "The Evolution of School Spirit and Tradition at Oregon State University," March 2012, MC, box 157.

14 Lynn Bell, "Homecoming Traditions Evolve with the Changing Times," *Oregon Stater* (October 1995).

15 Gleaned from the *Beaver* yearbooks from the 1950s.

16 *Barometer*, October 13, 1949; and Admin. Records, October 16, 1930; March 3, 1933; and April 26, 1934, all in box 2, RG 32.

17 George Peavy to Those Addressed, March 7, 1939, reel 14, sub. 6, RG 013.

18 *Oregon State College Bulletin, Catalogue Issue* (1951–1952), 71.

19 Ibid., 72–110 and 476.

20 Ibid., 1961–1962, 13–14, 18, 28–30, 37, and 411–412.

21 *Oregon State University Bulletin* (Catalogue Issue, 1971–72), 30–31; Jack Van de Water e-mail to the author, January 20, 2015; Corvallis *Gazette-Times*, October 17, 1970; and *Barometer*, October 20, 1970.

22 *Oregon State University Bulletin* (Catalogue Issue, 1971–72), 30; *Barometer*, October 29, November 24, and December 9, 1970; and Corvallis *Gazette-Times*, November 30, 1970.

23 "The Oregon/Baden-Wurttemberg Exchange Program, Celebrating over 45 Years of Cooperation in Higher Education," copy courtesy of the Office of Global Opportunities, Division of International Programs, Oregon State University.

24 *Staff Newsletter*, January 29, 1971; *Barometer*, March 2, 1971; Corvallis *Gazette Times*, May 1, 1971; and "History," document provided to the author from the Office of Global Opportunities, Division of International Programs, Oregon State University.

25 *Oregonian*, January 29, May 1, and July 19, 1950.

26 Ibid., September 26, 1950, and April 15, 1951.

27 Ibid., April 18 and 20, 1954.

28 Ibid., May 1, 1960.

29 Ibid., December 18, 1967.

30 Ibid., August 26, 1970; November 24, 1971; September 29, 1974; and September 19, 1975.

31 Ibid., June 23 and November 13, 1983; February 21, 1984; and March 12, 1985.

32 Delta Kappa/Delta Chi, Local History, http://osudeltachi.org/localhistory.php; *Oregonian*, September 23, 1982; and Delta Chi, http://studentlife.oregonstate.edu/chapter-profile/delta-chi.

33 "New fraternity Is More than an Animal House," http://www.kval.com/news/local/130937448.html; and http://studentlife.oregonstate.edu/chapter-profile/phi-kappa-psi.

34 Albany *Democrat-Herald*, October 28, 2012.

35 Fraternities and Sororities (Greek Life), http://studentlife.oregonstate.edu/feature-story/greek-community.

36 Corvallis *Gazette-Times*, August 25, 1969; *Barometer*, June 24 and July 3 and 29, 1969.

37 Flyer, "The Draft: Hassle it to Death"; Dear Mr. Senator, May 7, 1970; Your Decision, May 11, 1970; Mass Political Action Day, May 16, 1970; and March on Safeway and ROTC; all in MC 152.

38 Larry Landis, "Alternative and Underground Newspapers at OSU," *Oregon Stater* (June 1996).

39 The *Scab Sheet*, vol. 1, no. 1 (March 4, 1969). All underground newspaper issues are in Oregon State University, Valley Library, ScholarsArchive@OSU, http://www.ir.library. oregonstate.edu/xmlui/. The background information about the *Scab Sheet* is in vol. 1, no. 8 (May 3, 1969).

40 The *Scab Sheet*, vol. 1, no. 3 (March 6, 1969); no. 4 (March 7, 1969); and no. 5 (March 11, 1969).

41 Ibid., vol. 1, no. 8 (May 3, 1969); and no. 10 (n.d.).

42 The *Daily Planet*, vol. 1, no. 1 (November 2–15, 1970); and no. 2 (November 16–29, 1970); all in MC 152.

43 Ibid., no. 2 (November 16–29, 1970).

44 Brian Plinski, "Murder Comes to Oregon State," research paper for History 310, box 2, College of Liberal Arts Records, 1945–2008, RG 143. Plinski's paper provides a well-documented and accurate summary of the Wyckoff murder and trial from February 8 to May 23, 1972. Nancy Wyckoff earned an "A" grade in the first term of the author's United States History course. She was also enrolled in the winter term for the same course.

45 Corvallis *Gazette-Times*, March 1, 1972; and *Oregonian*, February 19, 1972.

46 *Oregonian*, May 16, 17, and 23.

47 *Oregon State University General Catalogue* (1981–1982), 2.

48 Ibid., 16–20.

49 The *Beaver*, 1981, 26 and 67; and *Oregonian*, February 13 and 17, 1980.

50 The *Beaver*, 1981, 24–32.

51 Ibid., 38–39, 42, and 46.

52 The *Beaver*, 1990, 2, 5, 8, 11, and 30–33.

53 The *Beaver*, 1991, 11, 28–29, and 33.

54 *General Catalogue* (1990–1991), 1–4, 17, and 32.

55 *General Catalogue* (1990–1991), 1–2.

56 Ibid., 21–22.

57 The *Beaver*, 2000, 6, 8, 13–14, and 22.

58 The *Beaver*, 2002, 10–15; and news release, Corvallis, Oregon, September 13, 2011, http:// www.osubeavers.com/ViewArticle.dbml?DB_OEM_ID=30800&ATCLID=207825307.

59 Dexter Filkins, *The Forever War* (New York: Alfred A. Knopf, 2008). On the morning of 9/11, the author was a visiting professor at the University of Idaho and recalls listening to NPR's Jacki Lyden, who was at her home in Brooklyn looking across the water toward lower Manhattan, telling the NPR desk in Washington, DC, that her skyline had disappeared.

60 The *Beaver*, 2002, 25–26, and 44.

61 Ibid. 2005, 14–16.

62 Ibid., 20–21.

63 Ibid., 36.

64 Ibid., 61; and Kelly Sullivan to the author, October 5, 2014.

65 Student Life's Annual Report, 2013–2014, http://studentlife.oregonstate.edu/ AnnualReport2014.

66 Ibid., 3–9.

67 The *Beaver*, 2010, 28, 38, and 47.

CHAPTER THIRTEEN: INTO THE FUTURE

1 This data is from the following sources: *Chronological History of Oregon State University*, http://scarc.library.oregonstate.edu/chronology/chron_head.html; *Oregon University System 2013 Fact Book*, 12–13; University of Oregon, Fall Term Enrollment (Fourth Week), courtesy of UO Office of Institutional Research; *2001 Fact Book*, Oregon State University, 46; Population of Oregon: 1950–2020, Oregon's Demographic Trends, Office of Economic Analysis, Department of Administrative Services, State of Oregon; and Vernon Mayfield to the author, December 12, 2014.

2 *2001 Fact Book*, Oregon State University; Oregon University System *Fact Book* (2001); and Chronological History of Oregon State University.

3 *Oregon Stater* (1996), 7.

4 Chronological History of Oregon State University; and Larry Pribyl to the author, February 27, 2015. The author was also one of the first three faculty offering televised classes to Bend.

5 For thoughtful reflections on these issues, see Scott Jaschik, "Loan Scandal Escalates," *Inside Higher Ed*, https://insidehighered.com; Derek Bok, *Universities in the Marketplace: The Commercialization of Higher Education* (Princeton, NJ: Princeton University Press, 2003), 1–11, 37–39; and James L. Schulman and William G. Bowen, *The Game of Life: College Sports and Educational Values* (Princeton, NJ: Princeton University Press, 2001), 257.

6 Chronological History of Oregon State University; and Paul Risser Obituary, http://www.oregonlive.com/education/index.ssf/2014/07/paul_risser_who_led_oregon_sta.html.

7 Byrne to Officers of the OSU Foundation, September 3 and October 1, 1987; Byrne to Members of the Academic Council, October 9, 1987; all in box 32, sub. 15, RG 013; and John Evey to Paul Risser, February 11 and 12, 1996, box 58, sub. 17, RG 013.

8 John Evey to Paul Risser, February 11 and 12, 1996, box 58, sub. 17, RG 013.

9 Evey to Risser, February 22, 1996, box 58, sub. 17, RG 013; and Risser to Robert Bruce, February 6, 1996, box 53, sub. 17, RG 013.

10 Cliff Dalton to Risser, n.d., box 58, sub. 17, RG 013.

11 Paul G. Risser, University Development—*Oregon State University*, April 15, 1996.

12 Gene Kersey, Phase I Work Plan, May 6, 1996, box 58, sub. 17, RG 013; and John Evey, Transition Plan, June 1, 1996, box 58, sub. 17, RG 013.

13 Risser to OSU Advancement Community, June 5, 1998; Roy Arnold to Jill Wooten, June 5, 1998; and President Risser, Provost Arnold, and Vice President Zuniga Forbes to OSU Advancement Community; all in box 58, sub. 17, RG 013.

14 OSU Learning Option in Bend, 1996; David Stauth, Advisers Available for Distance Degree Program, August 13, 1996; Joseph Cox to Neil Bryant, March 13, 1997; all in box 59, sub. 17, RG 013; and *Bend Bulletin*, December 29, 1996.

15 Central Oregon University Center II: Meeting the Higher Education Needs of Central Oregon, June 6, 1997; and Dick Markwood to Joe Cox and Paul Risser, July 21, 1997; both in box 59, sub. 17, RG 013.

16 Forrest Rogers to Paul Risser, Roy Arnold, et al. July 18, 1997; Rogers to Risser and Arnold, October 23, 1997; Memorandum of Agreement, January 1, 1998; and *Bend Bulletin*, July 19, 1998; all in box 59, sub. 17, RG 013.

17 *Bend Bulletin*, July 21 and October 28, 1998; and Joseph Cox, "'Central Oregon University,' The 'Compelling 20 Year Vision,'" September 1, 1998; both in box 59, sub. 17, RG 013

18 *Bend Bulletin*, December 10, 1998; Central Oregon: Marketing and Communication Plan, January 25, 1999; Oregon University System, Central Oregon Regional Advisory Board Appointed, March 4, 1998; OSU Expands Commitment to Central Oregon, May 3, 1999; all in box 59, sub. 17, RG 013; Risser to OSU Community, June 26, 2000; and Risser to OSU Campus Community, February 7, 2001; both in box 53, sub. 17, RG 013.

19 Arthur Golden to Risser, April 21, 2001; and Risser to Golden, May 10, 2001; both in box 59, sub. 17, RG 013.

20 The University Extension Education Transition Committee, Organizing, Planning, and Implementing Extended Education: A Report to the Provost and Executive Vice President, Oregon State University, April 1994, box 56, sub. 17, RG 013.

21 Report Submitted to the Associate Provost for Information Services, June 1995, box 56, sub. 17, RG 013.

22 Oregon State University Distance Education Plan, Executive Summary, Jan 28, 1997; and Oregon State University Distance Education Business Plan, January 28, 1997; both in box 56, sub. 17, RG 013.

23 News release, Oregon State University to Offer Statewide Degrees, March 4, 1997, box 54, sub. 17, RG 013. The author was in the audience when Risser made this statement in his candidate's address. There was nothing particularly new about his remarks, because administrators at land-grant institutions had been making variants of that theme for several decades. For one striking example, see the University of Wisconsin publication, Robert Foss, ed., A Story of Public Service: The Boundaries of the Campus are the Boundaries of the State, Bulletin of the University of Wisconsin, Serial No. 2281 (January 1938).

24 Roy Arnold to Bonnie Dasenko et al., November 4, 1997, box 56, sub. 17, RG 013.

25 Ibid.; Bok, Universities in the Marketplace, 9–10. As associate dean of the College of Liberal Arts, the author attended a meeting in the fall of 1997 with Provost Arnold and other college administrators where questions arose about the integrity of distance education courses. Arnold assured everyone that academic responsibility would rest with campus academic units.

26 "Good News Talking Points," Some of the Things Happening at Oregon State University in 1997–98, March 17, 1998, box 54, sub. 17, RG 013.

27 Jonathan D. Weaver to Risser, two letters; both November 20, 1996, box 53, sub. 17, RG 013; and Oregonian, October 15, 1996.

28 Faculty Senate Minutes, Faculty Senate, Oregon State University, February 1, 1996, http://senate.oregonstate.edu/archives.

29 New York Times, October 6, 1996; and Oregonian, October 15, 1996, news clippings in box 53, sub. 17, RG 013.

30 Gazette-Times, November 15, 1996; Stewart Laney and Mark Shepard to Risser, November 16, 1996; John Fagan, Gazette-Times news clipping, n.d; Holly Dunning to Risser, n.d; Hezekiah Bishop and Lavella Bishop to Risser, November 20, 1996; Mike McGuire to Risser, November 13, 1996; Brad Ils to Risser, November 21, 1996; Earl Fleming to Risser, November 23, 1996; and Jonathan Weaver to Risser, November 20, 1996 (and many more); all in box 53, sub. 17, RG 013. The athletes cited favorably in Fagan's column, A. C. Green, Jeff Hart, and Steve Largent, were professional athletes who openly avowed their Christian faith.

31 Melvin Adams to Risser, n.d.; Oregonian, n.d. photocopy; both in box 53, sub. 17, RG 013; Spokesman-Review, August 5, 1997, http://m.spokesman.com/stories/1997/aug/02/paper-reports-osu-ad-will-be-fired-all-news-to-me/; and Associated Press, August 5, 1997, http://news.google.com/newspapers?nid=894&dat=19970806&id=w7oKAAAAIB AJ&sjid=gU0DAAAAIBAJ&pg=3177,860271.

32 Oregon State University Department of Athletics, ca. late 1997, box 56, sub. 17, RG 013.

33 Ibid.; Gazette-Times, November 8, 1997; and Barometer, November 10, 1997.

34 Faculty Senate Minutes, Faculty Senate, Oregon State University, December 4, 1997.

35 Ibid.

36 Faculty Senate Minutes, April 2, 1998, and March 4, 1999; and Mark McCambridge to Mike Green, May 6, 1998, box 55, sub. 17, RG 013.

37 Special Report to Members of the Oregon State Board of Higher Education on Oregon State University Intercollegiate Athletics, May 21, 1999, box 56, sub. 17, RG 013; and Faculty Senate Minutes, June 3, 1999.

38 Risser e-mail to Oregon State University Faculty, June 15, 1999, box 53, sub. 17, RG 013.

39 Oregonian, June 9, 1999.

40 Risser e-mail to Oregon State University Faculty, June 15, 1999, box 53, sub. 17, RG 013.

41 *Oregonian,* November 6, 1999.

42 Report of the Governor's Task Force on Higher Education and the Economy, December 15, 1997, box 56, sub. 17, RG 013.

43 John Kitzhaber, Response to Task Force Reports on Higher Education and the Economy and College Access, December 19, 1997, box 54, sub. 17, RG 013.

44 OSU Momentum into the 21st century, ca. 1998, http://sites.oregonstate.edu/presidents-report/2000Report/Momentum2.html.

45 Ibid.; and Enrollment Summary Fall Term 2010, Oregon State University, 19, http://oregonstate.edu/admin/aa/ir/enrollmentdemographic-reports#enroll-sum.

46 *Spokesman-Review,* May 21, 1995, http://m.spokesman.com/stories/1995/may/21/oregon-makes-tentative-deal-with-workers-contract/.

47 John Byrne to Dear Colleagues, May 1, 1995, box 58, sub. 17, RG 013; and *Spokesman-Review,* May 21, 1995, http://www.spokesman.com/stories/1995/may/09/state-workers-strike-puts-pinch-on-services-to/.

48 Joseph Cox to University Presidents, August 6, 1999; and Jacqueline Rudolph to President, Provost, and Senior Administrators, August 23, 1999; both in box 58, sub. 17, RG 013.

49 Joseph Cox to University Presidents, August 6, 1999; Tim Spencer to Cox, August 16, 1999; Spencer to Risser, August 18, 1999; David Shaw to President, Provost, and Senior Administrators, October 29, 1999; all in box 58, sub. 17, RG 013; and *Medford Mail Tribune,* September 8, 1999, http://www.mailtribune.com/article/19970614/News/30614 9993?template=printart.

50 The Coalition of Graduate Employees, Oregon State University, History, http://cge6069.org/about/history/; and Graduate Teaching Fellows, University of Oregon, History of GTTF, http://gttf3544.net/about/history-of-gtff/.

51 Summary of Graduate Student Issues, n.d.; The Coalition of Graduate Employees, Oregon State University, November 7, 1998; news clipping in *Gazette-Times,* November 7, 1998; and Roy Arnold to Deans, Directors, and Department Heads, September 22, 1999; all in box 56, sub. 17, RG 013.

52 Coalition of Graduate Employees: History, http://cge6069.org/about/history/.

53 Cooperative State Research, Education and Extension Service, United States Department of Agriculture Review, College of Veterinary Medicine, Oregon State University, January 9–11, 1996, box 56, sub. 17, RG 013.

54 Al Smith to Arnold and Cc. to Risser, January 26, 1996, box 56, sub. 17, RG 013.

55 Aaron Horowitz to Risser, January 26, 1996; Horowitz to Arnold and Cc. to Risser, January 29, 1996; and Bill Fisher to Joseph Cox, January 30, 1996; all in box 56, sub. 17, RG 013.

56 "Wilson Named New Dean of Veterinary Medicine," news release, February 26, 1996, http://oregonstate.edu/ua/ncs/archives/1996/feb/wilson-named-new-dean-veterinary-medicine; and Lester M. Crawford, John R. Shadduck, and Robert D. Phemister to Robert Wilson, July 2, 1996, box 56, sub. 17, RG 013.

57 Crawford, Shadduck, and Phemister to Wilson, July 2, 1996, box 56, sub. 17, RG 013; and Roy Arnold to the author, March 17, 2015.

58 *Seattle Times,* March 14 and April 2, 2006.

59 Paul G. Risser, "Diversity Report," http://leadership.oregonstate.edu/president/reports-and-initiatives/diversity-report; and "Recommendations to the President's Cabinet," September 27, 1999, http://leadership.oregonstate.edu/president/diversity/recommendations.

60 *Barometer,* February 8, 2006.

61 *Gazette-Times,* April 17, 2007, and November 3, 2009.

62 *Oregon Blue Book,* Initiative, Referendum, and Recall, 1996–1999, http://bluebook.state.or.us/state/elections/elections22.htm; and Nancy Langston, *Where Land and Water Meet: A Western Landscape Transformed* (Seattle: University of Washington Press, 2003), 143–144.

63 See L. L. Larson and S. L. Larson, "Riparian Shade and Stream Temperature: A Perspective," *Rangelands* 18 (1996), 149–152.

64 Bill Marlett and Joy Belsky to Thayne Dutson, with Ccs. to Governor Kitzhaber, Paul Risser, et al., January 17, 1997, box 55, sub. 17, RG 013.

65 Belsky to Risser, January 21, 1997; and Risser to Belsky, February 3, 1997; both in box 55, sub. 17, RG 013.

66 Belsky to Risser, June 11, 1997, box 53, sub. 17, RG 013.

67 Lee Sherman, The Biscuit Fire 10 Years Later, http://fes.forestry.oregonstate.edu/biscuit-fire-10-years-later; and *Oregonian*, January 20, 2006.

68 *Oregonian*, January 20 and 22, 2006.

69 Ibid., January 29, 2006.

70 Ibid., February 12, 2006; and Daniel Donato to the author, December 14, 2015.

71 Jane Lubchenco to Risser, March 3, 1997; and Lubchenco, Presidential Address to the American Association for the Advancement of Science, February 15, 1997; both in box 55, sub. 17, RG 013.

72 Lubchenco, Presidential Address to the American Association for the Advancement of Science.

73 Ibid. (emphasis original).

74 Brad Knickerbocker, "Conversations with Outstanding Americans: Jane Lubchenco," *Christian Science Monitor*, August 15, 1997, photocopy, box 55, sub. 17, RG 013.

EPILOGUE: A TWENTY-FIRST-CENTURY UNIVERSITY

1 Frank Bruni, "College's Priceless Value," *New York Times*, February 11, 2015; and Ed Said, "Is College for Getting a Job or Finding One's Passion?" *Oregon Stater* (Winter 2014), 14.

2 Ed Said, "Is College for Getting a Job or Finding One's Passion?"

3 Susan Mettler, *Degrees of Inequality: How the Politics of Higher Education Sabotaged the American Dream* (New York: Basic Books, 2014), 7, 112–113. For a sampling of Sarasohn's writings on the issue, see "The higher-ed Mississippi of the West Coast," May 20, 2015, http://www.oregonlive.com/opinion/index.ssf/2015/08/david_sarasohn_oregons_dismal.html; and "Oregon's dismal college rankings," August 28, 2015, http://www.oregonlive.com/opinion/index.ssf/2015/08/david_sarasohn_oregons_dismal.html.

4 Sandy Baum and Martha Johnson, "Financing Public Higher Education: Variation across States," Urban Institute (November 2015), 3–4, 10–11, and 15, www.urban.org/.../2000501-Financing-Public-Higher-Education-Variations.

5 *Oregonian*, September 15, 2014.

6 Text of President Ed Ray's state of the university address, January 30, 2015, http://oregonstate.edu/dept/ncs/lifeatosu/2015/osu-president-ed-ray-challenges-state-to-improve-access-to-higher-education/. Also see Corvallis *Gazette-Times*, January 31, 2015.

7 *Gazette-Times*, January 31, 2015; and "The Journey Continues," President Ray's address to the Faculty Senate, October 8, 2015, http://leadership.oregonstate.edu/president/journey-continues.

8 "The Journey Continues."

9 Bennett Hall, "Agent of Change," *Gazette-Times*, August 4, 2013. For the full version of the president's address, see Ed Ray, "Setting Our Course," Life at OSU, http://oregonstate.edu/dept/ncs/lifeatosu/2009/setting-our-course/.

10 Faculty Senate, Institutional Policy and Procedures for Program Reorganization or Elimination, approved by President Edward Ray, March 9, 2005, http://oregonstate.edu/senate/reorg/.

11 Dialog with the Provost, October 11, 2007, Faculty Senate Minutes, Faculty Senate, Oregon State University, http://oregonstate.edu/senate/min/2007/20071011.html; and, Minutes, Budget and Fiscal Planning Committee, Faculty Senate, October 6, 2009, http://oregonstate.edu/senate/committees/bfpmin/20091006.html; and "OSU Begins Historic

Realignment," and interview with Provost Sabah Randhawa, *Oregon Stater* (October 9, 2009), http://www.osualum.com/s/359/index.aspx?sid=359&gid=1001&pgid=1209.

12 OSU Administrative Structure, September 2014, http://search.oregonstate.edu/?q=Administrative+Structure%2C+2014&client=default_frontend, and OSU Administrative Structure, September 2007, http://oregonstate.edu/admin/aa/ir/org-charts#06-07. See also Appendix 2 for OSU's Administrative Structure in 2017, http://oregonstate.edu/admin/aa/ir/sites/default/files/orgchart-university-feb-2017.pdf.

13 Enrollment and Demographic Reports, Office of Institutional Research, http://oregonstate.edu/admin/aa/ir/enrollmentdemographic-reports#enroll-sum; Growth in Licensing and Industry Funding Spurs Research at Oregon State University, http://oregonstate.edu/ua/ncs/archives/2013/sep/growth-licensing-and-industry-funding-spurs-research-oregon-state-university; and Monthly Campaign Update—Campaign for OSU, http://search.oregonstate.edu/?q=2013%2C+Campaign+for+OSU&client=default_frontend$!.

14 Citizens for a Livable Corvallis, http://hardingneighborhood.org/node/37; and *Gazette-Times*, April 22, 2012.

15 Enrollment Summary Fall Term 2010, History of Student Enrollment, Office of Institutional Research, Oregon State University, 19, http://oregonstate.edu/admin/aa/ir/enrollmentdemographic-reports; Corvallis *Gazette-Times*, April 22, 1913; and Collaboration Corvallis, http://blogs.oregonstate.edu/collaboration/.

16 "As I See It: Collaboration Corvallis Producing Results," Corvallis *Gazette-Times*, September 13, 2013.

17 Tom Jensen, "Letters," Corvallis *Gazette-Times*, August 15, 2013; and *Gazette-Times*, August 26 and November 5, 2014.

18 Corvallis *Gazette-Times*, April 6 and 7, 2015.

19 Ibid., May 12, July 5, and September 8, 2015.

20 Ibid., October 24, 2015.

21 Center for Civic Engagement, Oregon State University, http://sli.oregonstate.edu/cce.

22 Ibid.; and *Gazette-Times*, September 14, 2015.

23 Corvallis *Gazette-Times*, May 21, 2015; and *Bend Bulletin*, September 9, 2015.

24 Scott Jaschik, "Lowering Higher Education," February 23, 2011, interview with James Cote and Anton Allahar, https://www.insidehighered.com/news/2011/02/23/interview; UC Santa Barbara, Office of Research, http://www.research.ucsb.edu/toolbox/funding-agency-links/private-funding-agencies/; Jennifer Washburn, "Science's Worst Enemy: Corporate Funding," *Discover Magazine* (October 2007), http://discovermagazine.com/2007/oct/sciences-worst-enemy-private-funding; and William Broad, "Billionaires with Big Ideas Are Privatizing American Science," *New York Times*, March 15, 2014, http://www.nytimes.com/2014/03/16/science/billionaires-with-big-ideas-are-privatizing-american-science.html?_r=0.

25 Marine Studies Initiative, Hatfield Marine Science Center, http://marinestudies.oregonstate.edu.

26 Newport *News-Times*, April 4, 2014.

27 Tracy Farrell, Letter to the Editor, and Becky Johnson, op-ed column; both in *Bend Bulletin*, June 7, 2014.

28 City of Bend/Oregon State University-Cascades, Memorandum of Understanding, January 16, 2014. See the *Bend Bulletin*, January 30, 2014.

29 For a summary of the appeals process, see City of Bend, OSU-Cascades Planning, http://www.bend.or.us/index.aspx?page=1086.

30 Oregon Public Broadcasting News, November 1, 2015, www.opb.org/news; and "OSU Cascades Nears Deal on Pumice Mine," *Bend Bulletin*, November 16, 2015.

31 John Krakauer, *Missoula: Rape and the Justice System in a College Town* (New York: Doubleday, 2015); and John Canzano, "Official Regrets, Little More in Brenda Tracy Case," *Oregonian*, December 31, 2014.

32 *Oregonian*, November 17, 2014, and July 11 and September 26, 2015.

33 News and Research Communications, Oregon State University, OSU Adopts Stricter Student Transfer Admissions Policy to Address Sexual Violence, Campus Safety, http://oregonstate.edu/ua/ncs/archives/2015/nov/osu-adopts-stricter-student-transfer-admissions-policy-address-sexual-violence-cam; *Gazette-Times*, December 1, 2015; and *Oregonian*, December 2, 2015.

34 *New York Times*, November 9 and 10, 2015.

35 Ed Ray to The OSU Community, November 12, 2015, inform-c13-bounces@lists.oregonstate.edu_on_behalf_of_President's_Office.

36 Corvallis *Gazette-Times*, November 16 and 18, 2015.

37 The enrollment figures represent student numbers on the main campus, including those taking courses through Ecampus. Although the data does not include enrollment on the Cascades campus, those students taking Ecampus classes are counted in the main campus total. Salvador Castillo, director of institutional research, to the author, December 10 and 29, 2015. For the future projections of Oregon's population ratios, see Jeff Mapes, "A Graphic Look at Oregon's More Diverse Future as Minority Population and Electorate Grows," April 14, 2015, www.oregonlive.com.

38 *Gazette-Times*, April 26, 2015; Halsell Hall, http://oregonstate.edu/uhds/halsell; Tebeau Hall, http://oregonstate.edu/uhds/tebeau; and International Living-Learning Center, http://oregonstate.edu/uhds/illc. The author is grateful to student archival worker Geoff Somnitz for assembling the list of new buildings.

39 Beth Ray Center for Academic Support, http://success.oregonstate.edu/beth-ray-center-academic-support; and Memorial Union Student Experience Center, SEC History, http://mu.oregonstate.edu/sec/sec-history.

40 About the Kelley Engineering Center, http://eecs.oregonstate.edu/about-eecs/our-building; and College of Business, Austin Hall, http://business.oregonstate.edu/austin-hall.

41 Linus Pauling Institute, Oregon State University, http://lpi.oregonstate.edu/; and Hallie E. Ford Center for Healthy Children and Families, http://health.oregonstate.edu/hallie-ford.

42 *Oregonian*, December 3, 2011; and Eugene *Weekly*, July 9, 2015.

43 *Oregonian*, June 27 and December 3, 2011.

44 Government Relations Update, no. 46, November 9, 2012; and Comments by Ed Ray for the Oregon Education Investment Board, October 25, 2012, http://oregonstate.edu/government/update-archive.

45 Seventy-Seventh Oregon Legislative Assembly—2013 Regular Session, and Board of Trustees of Oregon State University, http://leadership.oregonstate.edu/trustees; Government Relations Update, no. 54, July 17, 2013, http://oregonstate.edu/government/update-archive; and John V. Byrne to the Editor, Corvallis *Gazette-Times*, August 1, 2013.

46 Oregon State University, Board of Trustees, http://leadership.oregonstate.edu/trustees; Eugene *Weekly*, July 9, 2015; *Oregonian*, August 13, 2014; and *Gazette-Times*, September 18, 2015.

47 Oregon State University, Faculty Statistics, 2013, http://www.collegefactual.com/colleges/oregon-state-university/academic-life/faculty-co; and Salvadore Castillo to the author, December 11, 2015.

48 A Chronological History of Oregon State University, SCARC.

49 The first yearbook issue, the *Orange*, ran local sporting goods advertisements for outdoor equipment, including bicycles.

50 Andrew Delbanco, *College: What It Was, Is, and Should Be* (Princeton, NJ: Princeton University Press, 2011), 21. My thanks to Bill Husband, Larry Landis, and Ben Mutschler for their assistance in framing this argument.

51 University Housing and Dining Services, Residence Halls, http://uhds.oregonstate.edu/halls; and http://uhds.oregonstate.edu/dining.

52 *Gazette-Times*, November 8, 2016; and Hannah O'Leary, "Corvallis: The City Where We Live, Study, Work and Play," *Oregon Stater* (Fall 2016), 20–21.

Index

Note: Photographs and documents are indicated with an italic page number or span. Tables are indicated an italic "*t*" next to the page number. Material from the Notes section are indicated by an italic "*n*" and note number next to the page number.